A Solution for Transnational Labour Regulation?

Axel Hauser-Ditz/Markus Hertwig/
Ludger Pries/Luitpold Rampeltshammer

A Solution for Transnational Labour Regulation?

Company Internationalization and European Works Councils in the Automotive Sector

Translated by Pete Burgess

PL ACADEMIC RESEARCH

Bibliographic Information published by the Deutsche Nationalbibliothek
The Deutsche Nationalbibliothek lists this publication in the Deutsche Nationalbibliografie; detailed bibliographic data is available in the internet at http://dnb.d-nb.de.

The publication of this English edition has been made possible through a grant by the Hans Böckler Foundation, Düsseldorf.

Library of Congress Cataloging-in-Publication Data
Names: Hauser-Ditz, Axel, author. | Hertwig, Markus, author. | Pries, Ludger, author.
Title: A solution for transnational labour regulation? : company internationalization and European works councils in the automotive sector / Axel Hauser-Ditz, Markus Hertwig, Ludger Pries, Luitpold Rampeltshammer.
Description: 1 Edition. | New York : Peter Lang, 2015. | Includes bibliographical references.
Identifiers: LCCN 2015038777 | ISBN 9783631670576
Subjects: LCSH: Automobile industry and trade–European Union countries. | Works councils–European Union countries. | Trade regulation–European Union countries.
Classification: LCC HD9710.E852 H38 2015 | DDC 338.7/629222094–dc23 LC record available at http://lccn.loc.gov/2015038777

ISBN 978-3-631-67057-6 (Print)
E-ISBN 978-3-653-06272-4 (E-Book)
DOI 10.3726/978-3-653-06272-4

PL Academic Research is an Imprint of Peter Lang GmbH.

Peter Lang – Frankfurt am Main · Bern · Bruxelles · New York · Oxford · Warszawa · Wien

This publication has been peer reviewed.

www.peterlang.com

Contents

List of Tables

List of Figures

Introduction to the English edition[1]

Between 2007 and 2010, the authors conducted a research project on European Works Councils (EWCs) in eight large automotive manufactures headquartered in four countries: Germany, France, Japan and the United States. The project was financed by the German Research Foundation ("Der Europäische Betriebsrat als transnationale Organisation") and carried out at the Ruhr-Universität Bochum. This volume is the – enlarged – English edition of the final report originally published in German in 2010. The intervening period has been marked by a number of significant developments first and foremost the financial and economic crisis, which had a major impact on the businesses and strategies of the companies we studied as well as their bodies for cross-border employee representation.

The aim of this introduction is to provide an update on the major developments in this period that affected both the companies and the EWCs. The main concern is how EWCs were affected by the crisis, and in what ways changes in companies' structures and strategies triggered changes in the structures and activities of the EWCs. The findings included in this update are interpreted using the same theoretical framework already developed for the German edition. As a consequence, the results also indicate whether this theoretical model has retained its validity in view of the fact that although it expressly included scope for change and development, it did not originally address the issue of the possible structural shifts induced by economic crisis.

1.1 Daimler-Benz and Volkswagen – driving through the crisis and onwards

Compared to the other international car producers, the two companies with their headquarters in Germany, Daimler-Benz and Volkswagen, were quite successful in driving through the 2007/2008 financial and economic crisis. By 2013 they had managed to stabilize their worldwide structure, increase production and undertake substantial innovations to their product portfolio. At the same time, employee representative bodies at (national) company and European level were able to consolidate or even extend further their influence as strong players and negotiators. During the period considered here the European Group Works Council of Volkswagen in particular was party to substantial and innovative initiatives to strengthen workers' rights in the group as a whole globally.

1 In particular, we want to thank Pete Burgess for his translation. With his expertise, patience and commitment he has not only made the English publication possible but also gave very valuable impulses and suggestions regarding the content. We deeply appreciate the research assistance of Valentin Gube for updating information and thank him sincerely for his support and commitment. Furthermore, we thank the Hans Böckler Foundation for their generous grant, which allowed us to publish this English edition in the first place.

Daimer-Benz recovering after the crisis and Chrysler adventure

For Daimler, the year 2007 not only marked the beginning of the financial and economic crisis, but also the end of its cooperation with Chrysler that had begun in 1998. In terms of labour relations, the decade during which Daimler-Chrysler had existed as a single corporate entity had always represented a highly complex enterprise. The European and the World Works Council, had been dominated from the outset by the German Daimler-Benz culture of 'conflictual partnership'. Following the merger of Daimler and Chrysler the US-American United Automobile Workers Union UAW and its then President Steve Jokisch had been invited to join the employee side of the Supervisory Board (Aufsichtsrat) of the new consortium. However, according to the German side, they did not take this opportunity seriously: for example, they did not attend all the meetings of the Supervisory Board. Just as the two companies never truly adopted a joint strategy and structure for products and production, neither did the two different cultures of employee relations and employment regulation in the German and the US-American parts of the business combine or pursue a common approach. For Daimler, the period after 2007 could be characterized as successfully exiting a very bumpy road.

Between 2008 and 2013, the equity share of the company owned by institutional investors decreased from 73 to 58 per cent, with the proportion held by private investors rising from 17 to 22 per cent. The share owned by the Kuwait Investment Authority remained at 7 per cent, whereas Renault-Nissan bought an equity stake of just 3 per, and a new Abu Dhabi located investor (Aabar Investments) entered with a stake of 9 per cent. During the period 2008 to 2013, the number of cars produced by Daimler rose from almost 2.1 to 2.4 million units, and the corresponding share of cars produced in Germany as a share of the company's global car production increased slightly from 57 to 58 per cent. Related to the EU, the share produced in Germany increased from 83 to 84 per cent. The share of employment in Germany as a share of worldwide employment in Daimler remained stable at 61 per cent.

One important activity of the World Employee Committee (WEC) concerns defining and monitoring the principles of social responsibility for the company's operations throughout the world. Management must inform the WEC about any serious problems that might arise in connection with these standards, which also encompass cooperation between management and workers' representatives at all the group's plants. In 2008 the procedure for dealing with grievances related to corporate social responsibility was redefined and clarified. It now also requires suppliers to respect minimum social standards.[2] At the European level, resisting the worsening of working and employment conditions was a regular issue on the EWC's agenda. Two developments observable in all EU countries were those of expanding precarious employment and raising the retirement age. Although these challenges

---

2 See http://nachhaltigkeit.daimler.com/daimler/annual/2012/nb/German/pdf/09_DAI_NB-2011_Mitarbeiter_online.pdf.

did not directly originate from Daimler management, they had an impact on the environment in which Daimler operated and, therefore, employment conditions at the company, despite raising new and innovative demands, ensured that the work of the EWC was dominated by defending existing rights and standards. [3]

The World Employee Committee (WEC) and the European Works Council were re-elected in spring 2014. While the number of official representatives in the WEC was stable at 13, the number of EWC representatives increased from 28 to 31 (from Belgium, Czech Republic, Denmark, France, Germany, Hungary, Italy, Luxembourg, Netherlands, Portugal, Spain, Sweden and United Kingdom). Three of the five members of the EWC's presidency came from Germany, one from Spain and one from Italy. All in all, during the period under consideration, the EWC and the WEC consolidated their activities and were mainly concerned with defending established levels of pay and conditions, employment levels, and standards for employee participation.

Volkswagen's way to world leadership

Between 2008 and 2013, worldwide production by the Volkswagen consortium increased from 6.4 million to 9.7 million units (Volkswagen 2013: 1; Volkswagen 2008: 117), almost enabling Volkswagen to reach its goal of overtaking Toyota as the world's biggest car producer (the Japanese company produced just short of 10 million cars in 2013). It has often been alleged that the highly developed system of codetermination at VW has deterred investors; nonetheless, and despite these arrangements and the strong employee rights they include, shareholders all over the world appear to continue to trust in the German company. This is reflected in the development of the shareholder structure between 2008 and 2013. While Porsche reduced its stake in Volkswagen from 37.4 to 32.2 per cent, international institutional investors increased theirs from 17.7 to 24.3 per cent, with Qatar Holding LLC entering the ranks of institutional shareholders and buying 15.6 per cent and the regional government of Lower Saxony maintaining stable its share of 12.7 per cent. By contrast, private shareholders nearly halved their stake from 24.2 to 12.5 per cent, with domestic institutional investors in Germany reducing theirs from 5.9 to 2.7 per cent (Volkswagen 2013: 87; Volkswagen 2008: 120).

The fact that Volkswagen was not badly affected by the 2007/2008 financial and economic crisis meant that the company was able to continue and even strengthen its worldwide expansion, mainly in China and other Asian countries. And while VW had 61 production plants in 21 countries in 2008, by 2013 this had risen to 107 sites in 26 countries (Volkswagen 2013: 124; Volkswagen 2008: 1). The company grew so fast, in particular in China, that in 2012, and in the following year, a new production plant was opened almost every month. For Volkswagen, this short period after the global financial crisis proved to be decisive in the globalization of its production structures. Whereas in 2008 half of worldwide production (53 per cent)

3 See http://www.daimler.igm.de/wir/presse/meldung.html?id=45322.

was still carried out in Germany, by 2013 this share had fallen to just a quarter (25.3 per cent) (Volkswagen 2008: 122; Volkswagen 2013: 83). In the same time period, the German share of European production remained stable at almost 57 per cent. This reflects the rapid growth of the company outside Europe, mainly in Asia. Total employment increased from 337,789 in 2008 to 545,696 in 2013, and the share of overall employment in the group in Germany fell from 53 to 45 per cent (Volkswagen 2008: 122; Volkswagen 2013: 83).

All these data reflect the very robust growth and accelerated pace of globalization in the group's production and employment structure The pace of expansion, as reflected in vigorous growth rates in sales, production, production sites and employment, is very noteworthy when compared with developments at the other global carmakers during this period. At the same time, the forums for employee representation at company level, especially the EWC, increased their activities and negotiating power. A number of unique and innovative initiatives were pushed forward by the company-level works council, the EWC, the World Works Council and, at national level, the German metalworkers' union IG Metall as well as internationally by IndustriAll Global Union. In 2008, for example, at the height of the crisis, the EWC was extended to the company's sales and financial service subsidiaries in Europe.[4]

In October 2009 the EWC (Volkswagen European Group Works Council), the VW Management Board and the International Metalworkers' Federation signed the 'Charter on Labour Relations within the Volkswagen Group'. This Charter is unique when compared with other International Framework Agreements (IFAs) or other kinds of agreements concluded at company level in any global group. Recognizing that labour regulation varies in all the countries in which Volkswagen operates, the Charter defines minimum employee participation rights for all subsidiaries in those countries represented on the Global and the European Group Works Council. The Charter shall apply for all companies and sites represented on the Volkswagen Group's European Group Works Council and Group Global Works Council. (...) The Charter defines in-house participation rights in the said area of application.'[5] It provides for a representative employee body to be established, which should have rights of information, consultation and co-determination. An annex to the Charter specifies which form of participation (information, consultation or co-determination) should apply to which issue. According to the Charter, the rights and structures for participation should be negotiated and signed by management and the employee side in a plant-level agreement. As an update of this Charter, in May 2012 the Volkswagen EWC together with the Human Resource CEOs of all VW's European companies organized a two-day-conference with representatives

4 See http://www.euro-br.eu/fileadmin/downloads/agreements/volkswagen-de.pdf.

5 http://www.audi.com/content/dam/com/EN/corporate-responsibility/operations/vw_charter_on_labour_relations.pdf.

of all plants covered by the Charter to evaluate the implementation of and practical experience with the Charter.[6]

In 2010, celebrations were organized to celebrate the fiftieth anniversary of the 'Volkswagen Law' and the twentieth anniversary of the establishment of the Volkswagen EWC, attended by both top management and senior politicians – including the then Federal Employment Minister, Dr. Ursula von der Leyen. The Volkswagen Law, which gives the State of Lower Saxony and employee representatives enhanced rights on the company's Supervisory Board (Aufsichtsrat), had been put under pressure by the European Commission, which had questioned the law's compatibility with the EU's principles of free competition. The Volkswagen Law was resolutely defended by the works councils, the VW EWC, IG Metall and many politicians. However, the European Commission brought repeated proceedings at the European Court of Justice against both the German government and Volkswagen for infringement of EU law. Finally, in October 2013 the European Court of Justice dismissed the Commission's action and upheld the essential provisions of the Volkswagen Law.[7]

Following the signature of the 'Charter on Labour Relations' in 2009, the EWC undertook many other initiatives and activities to improve employees' rights and conditions of employment. For instance, in 2011 a health checkup programme, previously introduced in Germany (at Audi in 2006 and at Volkswagen in 2010), was extended to the international level.[8] In 2012, the EWC was also active when management intensified cooperation between the MAN, the Volkswagen commercial vehicle brand, and Scania. Given that such forms of cooperation always aim at achieving synergies – possibly leading to cuts in production and/or employment at some operations – the EWC was strongly involved in these negotiations from the outset.[9] But the most important and publicly recognized activity was the joint signature of the 'Charter on Temporary Work for the Volkswagen Group' on 30th November 2012.[10]

This Charter was signed by the Group Management Board, the European Group Works Council, the Volkswagen World Works Council and IndustriALL. It defines the principles governing practice on temporary work contracts for the Volkswagen group globally and aims at guaranteeing minimum employment standards for such employees. The agreement stipulates that temporary work should be used only for

6 https://www.volkswagen-media-services.com/detailpage/-/detail/Volkswagen-Konzern-setzt-Charta-der-Arbeitsbeziehungen-an-internationalen-Standorten-erfolgreich-um/view/257025/4bfe15cfbe84821583ab35d545a06faa?p_p_auth=CIwH9mIS.

7 http://curia.europa.eu/jcms/upload/docs/application/pdf/2013-10/cp130138en.pdf.

8 http://autogramm.volkswagen.de/06_11/aktuell/aktuell_12.html.

9 https://www.volkswagen-media-services.com/en/detailpage/-/detail/Cooperation-among-Volkswagen-Groups-commercial-vehicles-brands-making-headway--Projects-well-on-their-way/view/654827/7da646559962098bdc3db4602fcc762a?p_p_auth=zVtA2YgH.

10 http://www.volkswagenag.com/content/vwcorp/info_center/de/news/2012/11/charta.html, http://www.industriall-union.org/volkswagen-limits-precarious-work-globally and http://autogramm.volkswagen.de/12_12/aktuell/aktuell_02.html.

result of drop in sales at both companies, the degree of capacity utilization of French plants decreased from 77 per cent in 2007 to 62 per cent in 2013 (Statista.com 2015).

The reactions of management in both companies were similar: both asked the French state for support, both cut costs, especially by reducing employment, both shifted production to low cost countries, and both aimed to save money by cooperating with other companies. The overarching aim of these measures was directed at cutting costs in order to stay competitive.

In 2009, the French government granted a €3 billion low-interest loan to the PSA bank as well as to the Renault bank. Moreover, in 2014, the French state bought a 14 per cent stake in PSA shares, worth €800 million to stabilize the company.[13]

The management of Renault negotiated with the French trade unions to tackle costs. Management and unions (with the exception of the CGT) signed an agreement in which 7,500 jobs would be cut by the end of 2016 (no compulsory redundancies but early retirement schemes and severance compensation offers), working time increased by 6.5 per cent and wages frozen in 2013, with only slight increases in subsequent years in return for the promise that no plant would be closed in France. In addition, there was an increase in the number of contract workers. Altogether, Renault aimed to cut costs by €400 million by 2016.

Similarly, in 2012, PSA management negotiated an agreement with French unions to secure competitiveness. The trade unions (with the exception of the CGT) accepted the closure of the assembly plant in Aulnay-sous-Bois and the loss of 3,000 jobs there, as well as the reduction of 11,200 jobs by 2015. In addition, wages were frozen for one year and overtime supplements reduced. In return, the company offered guarantees for new investments and the development of new models as well as promising not to close another factory in France over the following three years. Between 2008 and 2013, Renault cut its workforce by 5.6 per cent and PSA by 5.2 per cent (Renault and PSA company reports, various years).

In 2000, 53 per cent of all vehicles produced by the Renault Group (including contract producers) were manufactured in France; by 2008, this figure had dropped to 29.6 per cent and by 2013 to 18.7 per cent. Conversely, the share of production in Latin America increased from 5.9 per cent in 2000 to 10.2 per cent in 2008 and to 17.9 per cent in 2013; and the share of vehicles produced in Morocco rose from 0.26 per cent in 2000 to 1.4 per cent in 2008 and to 6.2 per cent in 2013. The share produced in Romania rose from 10 per cent in 2000 to 12.7 per cent in 2013. While the increase in production in Latin America mirrored the demand in these regions, the increase in Morocco and Romania was mainly aimed at cutting labour costs.

PSA also reduced production in French plants from 59.7 per cent of the total in 2000 to 40.6 per cent in 2008. By the end of 2013, this figure had dropped to 33.14 per cent. By contrast, production in China rose from 5.1 per cent in 2008 to 19.6

13 The Chinese car producer Dongfeng also invested 800 million Euros in order to buy a 14% share of the company. The share of the Peugeot family decreased due to this increase of capital stock from 25% to 14%.

per cent in 2013; in Iran from 1.8 per cent in 2000 to 9.0 per cent in 2011; and in Latin America from 2.7 per cent in 2000 to 8 per cent in 2008 and then 9.3 per cent in 2013[14]. In 2011, PSA opened a plant in Tamil Nadu, India.

In order to reduce costs further and enter new markets, both companies engaged in cooperation with other car producers. In 2008, Renault signed a strategic partnership agreement with AVTOVAZ, a Russian car producer. This produces cars in four plants in Russia, mainly for the Russian market. In addition, in September 2013, a pooled purchasing structure for Renault, Nissan and AVTOVAZ was introduced. Daimler and Renault agreed to develop joint vehicle platforms and powertrains in April 2010 and defined ten common projects. In addition, in 2014, both jointly developed three vehicles (Renault Twingo, Smart fortwo and Smart forfour) and they started a new joint venture in Mexico where they share a new production facility.

EWCs at Renault and PSA: 'keep on doing it the French way'

Despite the difficult economic situation facing the French car producers and their attempts to regain competitiveness in contested markets, the mode of cooperation between these group's managements and their European Works Councils remained firmly anchored in the French tradition.

At Renault, negotiations on reducing employment were conducted solely at national level. Agreements on competitiveness were negotiated at national level in France, Brazil, Romania and Spain between management and the trade unions. Since the biggest burden of employment reduction took place in France, French unions negotiated with group management about terms and conditions.

Similarly, at PSA, negotiations on the closure of the Aulnay plant, reducing employment in France and other countries in Europe remained exclusively at national level. The EWC was informed about the measures, but management refused to discuss them at European level. Instead, it stated that the measures were purely national issues and therefore had to be dealt with nationally. Agreements on competitiveness were negotiated in France and in other countries: in most instances, the EWC was not informed by management.

Accordingly, the EWCs at both companies did not play a coordinating role in negotiations. Nevertheless, the EWC at Renault supported national subsidiaries by informing them that national negotiations were taking place in different countries. As such, the main functions of both EWCs have not changed over the course of the crisis: these were, firstly, to receive and disseminate information obtained from management; and secondly, to discuss issues of concern with the CEO or the head of the Human Resource Department. While information and consultation took place at both the national and European levels, negotiations were restricted to the national or local levels.

---

14 All figures in this section are taken from the OICA website (http://www.oica.net/category/production-statistics/2000-statistics/).

Internal cooperation within both EWCs remained consensus-oriented. At both EWCs, the only contested issue was the election of EWC secretaries, who were elected in secret ballots; the EWC secretary at Renault is a member of the CFDT and the PSA EWC secretary of the FO.

Despite this continuity, some changes took place at the Renault EWC. These altered not only how cooperation functioned between the EWC and group management but also among EWC members. In terms of structural changes, the Renault EWC was affiliated to the French HR department while the Steering Committee was connected to the group's executive management. Especially the latter resulted in a change in the mode of operation of the EWC. This raised the profile of the Steering Committee as information flowed to it directly from group management. This was forwarded earlier and was held to be more comprehensive, in turn strengthening the position of the EWC in relation to local employee representation bodies given the detail and comprehensiveness of the information the EWC provides. In addition, the Renault EWC secretary, who was elected in 2011 and re-elected in 2013, also realigned the structure of the discussion between EWC members and management representatives at meetings of the full body. National employee representations are now supposed to submit detailed questions before the meetings, which the EWC secretary passes to management. In their presentations, the members of the management can directly address these issues. Meetings of the Steering Committee are no longer solely in Paris, but rotate between different locations, strengthening the connection between the EWC and the local employee representatives. Furthermore, the role of the EWC secretary as a moderator within the nationally and ideologically divided body and between local or national employee representatives and group management became more important. Due to these structural changes, communication between the Steering Committee and the members of the EWC increased in terms of both substance and timing. Altogether, the significance and the status of the EWC within the architecture of employee representation at the company are now higher than before the crisis. This has also been the case for the significance of the EWC from group management's perspective. The EWC functions as a channel of information for management over changes and developments at local level. Moreover, the EWC serves as a corrective for and a supplement to internal managerial information procedures.

In 2011, the Renault EWC and group management renewed the agreement on the functioning of the EWC, with some minor changes on facilities, equipment and finance. The agreement also defined the number of members of and visitors to the EWC as well as how the French members were to be selected. Compared to the distribution of seats in 2008, the agreement now provides for 17 French members (18 in 2008), three from Spain (four in 2008), and three from Romania (one in 2008). The seats for Belgium and Hungary were removed. In 2008, five guests were invited to participate as visitors from non-EU countries; in 2011 an additional visitor from Morocco was added. In total, the full body now consists of 34 full members and 6 visitors (2008: 34 members and 5 visitors). Therefore, the increased internationalization of the company has also resulted in a redistribution of seats within the EWC. Although visitors do not have voting rights, the main function of information and consultation has been extended to non-EU countries. The *Comité de Group* can, therefore, be classified as a combination of an EWC and a World Works Council.

The most significant event for the Renault EWC in recent years was the signing of a transnational framework agreement ('Committing Together for Sustainable Growth and Development') with Group management, the Group Works' Council and IndustriALL Global Union. The main aim is to foster social dialogue at international level. The five key areas of action are respect for fundamental social rights at work (elimination of child and forced labour and discrimination as well as freedom of association and recognition of the right to collective bargaining); social responsibility towards employees (encouraging social dialogue, health and safety at work and social protection); societal responsibility (supporting educational projects and road safety projects); and relationships with sub-contractors and suppliers. (Renault communicates this agreement to its suppliers and sub-contractors and asks them to commit to fundamental social rights but does not take responsibility for the actions of the suppliers and sub-contractors). If suppliers or sub-contractors breach these rights, Renault may take corrective measures, including termination of the contract. The effective implementation of the agreement will be overseen jointly by the EWC, management and IndustriALL, with a global review every three years.

In addition to the main body and the steering committee, the PSA EWC introduced a 'Committee Liaison' in which representatives of countries with large numbers of employees (France, Spain, UK and Germany) meet once a month in Paris. During these meetings, management informs representatives about new developments within the company (such as which models are produced at which facilities, and which platforms will be replaced). This information is helpful especially for EWC members outside of France. However, critical comments or questions regarding the consequences are addressed by management often only months after the meetings. The procedure for plenary EWC meetings has been changed inasmuch as once the PSA CEO, Carlos Tavares, has finished his speech on the main developments of the past year, a consultant mandated by the EWC makes a presentation on their audit of the company's finances. The EWC and PSA management also revised the Social Charter to address environmental concerns and strengthen PSA's reputation as an environmentally-friendly company. The section on employment was left unchanged.

At both PSA and Renault, the turbulence whipped up by the crisis did not culminate in a significantly different mode of interaction between management and EWC. Yet at Renault, the crisis, combined with the election of a new EWC secretary, seems to have triggered coordinating activity within the EWC. However, the essential nature of the relationship to the central management was not significantly altered.

1.3 Honda and Toyota: The Japanese model of EWCs under pressure

For the EWCs of Honda and Toyota, the financial and economic crisis had a tangible impact as it was the first incident that threatened jobs and plants across Europe, and thus created considerable pressures for employees to use their EWC as a means to become involved. The European businesses of both Japanese companies had been an impeccable success story for decades (Luethge/Byosière 2009): production, sales, net profits and employment figures had been (almost) constantly rising. Eventually, even these companies were caught up in the economic and financial crisis. After 2009, demand began to drop with dramatic falls in sales and profits, and eventually too in jobs.

Since their founding and up until the eve of the crisis, the EWCs at Honda and Toyota, HECCG and TEF, were characterized by a generally *low level of activity*, matched by an organizational structure that gave authority to the company but left little scope for independent employee representation. Despite a high frequency of formal meetings and information and consultation procedures, both EWCs were more or less management driven bodies, designed to serve the companies' desire for legitimacy as well as meet a number of specific HR requirements (Timming, 2007). Neither of the two EWCs was able to represent employees' interests effectively.

After 2008/9, representatives' overall involvement in cross-border issues rose. Triggered by the consequences of crisis-driven restructuring, meetings of both HECCG and TEF became engaged in receiving information and, as far as management allowed, in discussing the effects of the crisis. Since 2009, both EWCs encountered a number of changes that can be traced back to the effects of the crisis on these companies' (European) business operations. While most changes concern the pattern of coordination, there is also evidence that some structural adjustments have taken place.

Honda and the HECCG: stagnation despite activation

At Honda, the number of units sold worldwide climbed from 2,184 to 3,391 million between 1997 and 2006, and the number of employees rose by nearly 50,000 (from 101,000 in 1997 to 145,000 in 2006) (Honda Annual Reports; Luethge/Byosière 2009: 126). During the financial and economic crisis, net sales and the number of units sold within Honda's automobile business (the largest division within Honda Europe) declined after 2008, falling by more than 20 per cent between 2010 and 2011. Over the same period, net income slumped by 23 per cent (Honda Review of Operations Automobile Business 2011: 1).

In response to the crisis, management opted for a number of strategies to minimize costs and deal with the drop in demand. First, as sales fell, management decided to cut production at the *British Swindon plant* (Honda UK Manufacturing, HUM) by 50%. As a consequence, approximately 1,000 employees (out of 4,000) left Honda, beginning in 2009. The company offered a voluntary severance programme that was accepted by a large number of employees, avoiding compulsory redundancies. In 2011, HUM still employed 3,000 people. Second, the *motorcycle business* in Spain was restructured, with some production transferred to Italy. Of the former 360 employees, 180 left the company in 2009. Third, as a response to decreasing sales,

Honda aimed to streamline its *sales activities*. In 2010, about 100 people were made redundant at various European distribution locations. Finally, a reform of Honda's European *administration* affected all locations in Europe. Most of the accountancy function was removed from local operations and concentrated in Krakow, Poland. This affected about 10 employees at each operation (80 throughout Europe). In sum, the number of employees declined by 1,300 from 7,200 in 2009 to 5,900 by 2011 (Honda manager, Belgium).

The strategy that served to activate the HECCG appears to be the restructuring of Honda's administration. As this strategy concerned all European locations, employees had the feeling that a new 'mode' of restructuring had begun: the reform of administration 'was for many locations. This was the first time that everybody was affected' (HECCG employee representative, Belgium). As a result, employee representatives' interest in HECCG meetings increased significantly, raising both the quality of questions that employee representatives submitted for management to answer during the meeting as well their quantity, with the number increasing from 100 to 200.

The most noteworthy sign of activation has been the establishment of a new routine for HECCG meetings. This amended routine appears to have acquired greater relevance as it was subsequently enshrined in the 2010 revision of the EWC agreement and hence has represented a shift in the structural characteristics of the body. Following the marked upswing in the number of questions raised at the HECCG in the autumn of 2009, HECCG officials recognized that it was no longer possible to run the questions and answer session effectively. One suggested solution was that employee representatives would discuss, select and prioritize questions and discard any duplicates. This significance of this event lies in the fact that, firstly, for the first time HECCG employee representatives met separately without being accompanied by managers. And secondly, the new procedure altered the responsibilities for coordination and planning within the HECCG. As the HECCG management coordinator was not supposed to moderate the 'employee pre-meeting', an 'employee coordinator' had to be chosen. The new procedure has now been institutionalized as a regular item on each HECCG agenda, supplemented by a distinct time frame and corresponding facilities (such as a separate meeting room).

The new routine triggered further changes. Even though the establishment of an employee coordinator was rather an unintended side-effect of a step primarily intended to enable the HECCG to continue to function, especially before the HECCG meetings, communication was increased as the employee coordinator would now contact other employee representatives to gather issues and questions.

In one case, the HECCG even exhibited some collective action. In the face of the large number of redundancies that had happened since 2009, employee representatives presented a statement to management, expressing their concern about the situation and the loss of jobs. Again, this suggestion produced a side effect: as some representatives objected to this form of activity, this triggered the first discussions between employee representatives. Finally, a joint statement was passed and read out to the management at a regular HECCG meeting in 2010.

Toyota and the TEF: employee representatives taking over?

For Toyota, the years preceding 2007 had seen a steady expansion in its European activities. Between 2005 and 2008, car production rose by 180,000 units, from 638,000 to more than 814,000, with increases in both sales and net profits. The crisis that hit Toyota in 2008 led to a dramatic drop in output of 220,000 units. Sales fell by some 30 per cent after 2009, reaching a low point of 808,311 in 2010. For the first time, TME registered losses totalling nearly €1 billion in 2008.

Toyota management responded with a number of different strategies (TEF members, Germany/Belgium). Firstly, production was stopped for four weeks (at the beginning of 2009) at the Burnaston plant (UK), which was severely affected by the decline in demand. In August 2009, management finally decided to shut down one shift completely. However, this announcement did not provoke reaction from employees as the company had announced one month before that the Burnaston plant been assigned the production of the new hybrid model *Auris*: this was interpreted as a commitment to the plant that management subsequently delivered on. Secondly, a so-called *cost saving programme* was rolled out in every location and department throughout Europe. This comprised a range of measures, including cutting travel costs and lowering bonuses. Overall, each location was required to reduce costs by 10 per cent. Thirdly, on 4 November 2009, management announced Toyota's withdrawal from its Formula 1 racing activities shortly after it became obvious that TME was about to report huge losses. As a consequence, Toyota Motor Sport GmbH in Cologne/Germany was dissolved with a loss of 650 jobs. Finally, management announced redundancies in some of the National Marketing and Sales Companies (NMSCs) throughout Europe. In sum, nearly 8,500 jobs went between 2008 and 2010. In the headquarters administration, NMSCs, and logistics, half the employees lost their jobs over a three-year period (from 8,496 in 2008 to 4,175 in 2010). A further 4,300 jobs were cut at the company's production facilities. All these steps also marked a breach with Toyota's basic corporate principle of offering lifelong employment.

As with the HECCG, the activation of the TEF was triggered when incidents happened that affected a large number of locations. Most of the strategies pursued by management were dealt with during regular TEF or steering committee meetings. Extraordinary meetings of the full EWC and the steering committee were scheduled following the introduction of the cost savings programme and the closure of the Formula 1 plant in Cologne.

As a reaction to these developments, there was an increase in coordination between employee representatives leading to new forms of cooperation that ultimately challenged the existing (power) structure in the body and generated conflicts between different groups of actors within the TEF. First and foremost, differences emerged between the new 'activists' and the existing coordinator, who was committed to 'slower pace' TEF. In relation to the roll-out of the cost saving programme, representatives agreed on a two-fold strategy. Firstly, they decided to spread information about the measures each local management would demand in order to achieve the 10 per cent cost reduction target. Secondly, each location agreed not to sign any agreement until information about local demands in all subsidiaries had been gathered and discussed. A further meeting was then planned in the near future for this discussion.

Conflicts arose between the TEF coordinator and advisor and some TEF members, as the coordinator had not embarked on the information gathering exercise that had been agreed. This sort of conflict was not entirely new. Ever since the German works council members had been elected to the TEF and steering committee in 2007[15] they had been critical of and challenged the inactivity of the TEF secretary. Given the seriousness of the situation, German members decided to take the initiative and began to collect information from the other representatives and ask about how negotiations were proceeding, and what the outcomes were. This course of action was noteworthy as it ran counter to the official TEF routine, which requires communication to be facilitated centrally by the secretary. In a second special meeting, the results of the survey on the cost saving programme were presented by the German members. Although the results were frustrating for the more active representatives, as some locations had already reached agreements and hence had failed to comply with the agreed arrangements, the process was a demonstration of the fact that some representatives were no longer willing to accept a mere symbolic TEF, but demanded greater involvement.

Toyota management's strategies triggered two types of collective action on the part of the TEF. Firstly, the strategy of treating issues solely as national, and consequently denying the TEF any role in them, provoked a reaction from TEF members. Again, it was mainly the German works councils who were most irritated by this line of argument, which was also extended to the redundancy plans for the NMSCs. However, given that these proposals relied on systematically benchmarking the NMSCs, employee representatives commissioned an expert opinion together with the EMF on the question of what was a transnational issue. This was discussed at a full TEF meeting in 2010 and based on it, employee representatives drafted a statement directed at management in which they demanded more involvement.

Secondly, the TEF increased its activity through a symbolic action in response to the way the company had behaved in the case of the Formula 1 closure. Management had not only failed to inform the TEF, even the German employees in Cologne had only found out through the media. Although the withdrawal was not a transnational issue, it was still a major restructuring affecting 650 employees. Employee representatives chose two strategies to demonstrate their dissatisfaction with management. Firstly, they refused to participate in the group photograph of management and employee representatives customarily taken at full TEF meetings and later published in the annual Toyota European Sustainability Report. Secondly, employees refused to take part in the 'tree planting', which is a traditional Toyota ceremony held on the occasion of the signing of a new agreement. Despite the

15 Previous members of the German works council were more reluctant and, as a consequence, replaced by the current German representatives in 2007.

cultural differences within the TEF about the forum's goals and procedures and the harmonistic Toyota culture, it was remarkable that all employee representatives participated in this collective action.

Eventually, the changes in the patterns of coordination patterns within the TEF also altered its *structural characteristics* in terms of the distribution of knowledge and power. The activity of some TEF members – mainly the German works councils – improved the level of information for the whole TEF. In addition to the survey on the cost savings programme, a German member started to write and distribute minutes to all TEF members. As the secretary had repeatedly refused to send minutes, the flow of information was improved to all representatives.

The influence of those representatives calling for a more active TEF clearly began to grow from around 2009. Although collective strategies were only partly effective, they clearly demonstrated the will of these active members to improve employee representation in the TEF. This has led to an increase in interchange between the secretary and the German representatives. For example, the secretary has travelled to Cologne on a couple of occasions to meet local works council members and provide information normally only accessible to members of the Belgian economic council.

However, despite the changes and improvements in independent employee representation, it appears that both the HECCG and TEF have *resisted* deeper changes, as their basic characteristics have remained essentially stable. According to Hertwig (2015), neither the HECCG nor TEF were able to influence management decisions in a significant way. For instance, neither body was engaged in negotiations over redundancy packages, social plans or relocation decisions. Both Honda and Toyota continued to deal with these issues locally and then only when legal requirements forced them to. There was only a marginal shift in the unequal distribution of power between management and employees.

Secondly, neither the TEF nor HECCG witnessed any changes in their cultural-institutional patterns. Their internal (cultural) heterogeneity remained, with only slight glimpses of a common vision when representatives engaged in collective action. However, these were outliers, and did not lead to the emergence of a common identity. Despite the challenges affecting all employees, there was little convergence between the views and approaches of individual representatives.

The relative stability of TEF and HEEC stems largely from those factors that explained the specific patterns exhibited by these bodies from the outset. Both EWCs reflect the strong influence of the cultures of employment relations that characterize these *companies* and their *country-of-origin* (Marginson et al. 2004). As with other employees, most EWC members tend to conform to these. Those aspects are accompanied by management strategies that aim at maintaining tight control over these bodies.

1.4 Ford and GM: Decay of the best-practice EWCs

Up until the crisis, the EWCs at GME and Ford were both widely recognized as 'best practice models' of cross-border employee representation, clearly exceeding the scope envisaged in the EWC Directive. Based on a high level of European solidarity, a decentralized organization and strong coordination of EWC activities, both bodies had achieved a considerable output in terms of substantive agreements negotiated between EWC and management. However, the companies as well as their EWCs suffered severely during the crisis. For quite a while, even the existence of GME was imperilled and at Ford a number of interlinked changes damaged not only relationships within the EWC but also the cooperative culture that had prevailed between EWC and management. Whereas both companies ultimately managed to survive, cross-border employee representation reverted to national egoism, rendering the future of what had been pacemakers an uncertain one.

GM: the crisis as centrifugal force for company and EWC

GME's economic situation deteriorated during the financial and economic crisis, with a drastic drop in its market share in Western Europe. Global production reached a low of 6,459,000 units in 2009 – a decline of some 180,000 units in one year (from 8,282,803 in 2008). 2010 brought some signs of recovery, and in 2013, GM managed to produce 9,628,912 units worldwide. In Europe, however, production plummeted from 1,643,717 units in 2008 to roughly 876,271 in 2013, reflecting the specific problems of GM's European plants.

Following its strategic path, GME pursued a strategy of rigid cost reductions. In order to reduce overcapacity the plants in Antwerp (2010) and Bochum (at the end of 2014) were shut down. Saab was then sold in 2010, so that by 2013 GM comprised just 11 brands globally. In spring 2013, after lengthy negotiations, GM sold its French plants to the supplier ZF. Additional strategies were the cancellation of shifts and job losses at almost all plants. Between 2008 and 2013, global employment sank from 239,000 to 219,000. In the EU, more than 24,000 jobs were lost (GME facts and figures, various years).

In stark contrast to the other OEMs in our sample, the crisis put the very survival of GME in doubt. In late 2008, after a sharp decrease in sales in both North America and Europe, GM asked several governments for state loans.[16] With the insolvency of General Motors on June 1st 2009, and several attempts to sell the European plants (for instance, to the Austrian-Canadian supplier Magna), the unity of GME as a group was at risk.

At least partly as a consequence of the crisis, the GME EEF passed through a phase of drastic change between 2008 and 2013. In essence, what was formerly the 'best practice EWC' was no longer able to cope with the complexity and multiplicity of threats that endangered the company's survival – and with this the foundations of the EWC itself. As uncertainty about the future mounted, employee representatives reverted to national solutions, abandoning their previous European strategy.

16 For instance the German government granted a € 1.5 billion short-term loan in order to secure employment at all four German production plants.

Most significant for this shift was the reintroduction of local and national negotiations, with individual operations resorting to plant-egoism. According to interviewees, the reversion to national solutions was triggered by national negotiations in the UK. In May 2012, employee representatives at Ellesmere Port and national union officials *secretly* negotiated with GME management to secure production of the new Astra, accepting far-reaching concessions such as a wage freeze and further flexibilization of working time. The conditions of the agreement were accepted by 94 per cent of the UK workforce. Similar negotiations took place in Germany, Spain and Poland. The EEF was informed about the course of local negotiations and their content and timing, but in stark contrast to previous periods of restructuring its role changed completely: the EEF's function was no longer that of 'focal actor' but rather became restricted to an 'information hub'. As with the sale of the French plants, the EEF played no role in bargaining and was simply informed about national level developments.

Yet, despite these signs of disintegration, communication among the members of the EEF continued to be intense with many meetings of both the EEF and its working groups. The EEF undoubtedly remained active in respect to coordination and activities. However, in view of the fact that this coordination was no longer the precursor for collective strategies or bargaining with management, the EEF lost its former influence over management decisions. 'Unfortunately, we went away from [European] framework agreements and back to mere information about the outcome of national negotiations', as one informant put it.

The disintegration of the EEF was clearly a product of the restructuring of the company. The closure and sale of plants as well as the reduction of employment in several plants had direct consequences for the structure and the culture of the EEF: a plant, once it is closed, was no longer eligible to send representatives to the EWC, and hence, the changes in the structures of the company had a direct impact on the EWC. The body's composition changed as French and Saab-delegates left and new members from Austria or Hungary joined. The fact that some individuals who had embodied the culture of solidarity ceased to be members of the EWC meant that personal networks and relationships based on trust, which had sustained the EWC and reinforced its culture and principles, vanished. This erosion was exacerbated when the longstanding and committed chairman Klaus Franz retired in 2012.

Another consequence affected what had previously been a fairly equal distribution of power: as the distribution of seats within the EWC changed, the EWC office in Rüsselsheim, Germany, became a kind of EWC 'centre'. Thus, the weight the German plants already possessed – through the influence flowing from German codetermination rights and the fact that the EWC chair had been occupied by the German works council chair – increased even more. The newly achieved dominance of the German plants is also reflected in the production figures: in 2013, 41.5 per cent of car production was located in Germany against just 37 per cent in 2008 (GM 2013).

Even though the EEF, over a period of nearly ten years, had learned to cope with crises, the post-2007 financial and economic crisis evidently added a new quality to the challenges facing cross-border employee representation, stretching the capacities of the body almost beyond what could deal with. While previous crises had put pressure on a small number of locations (for instance, the Delta platform sites), the more recent crisis affected nearly all operations. Uncertainty about the future of GME spurred national egoisms. The insolvency of GM, the subsequent announcements of and then withdrawal of the decision to sell GME, the closure of Antwerp – an open breach of the guarantees by the GME management in a European Framework Agreement – the announcement of the closure of the Bochum plant, the sale of Saab, and the constant rumours of further plant closures set in motion a centrifugal process in which the strategy of solidarity collapsed. In this situation, the state loans opened a new option for employee representatives to achieve their goals: they looked to their *governments* for assistance to secure employment at their home plants (Bernaciak 2013).

However, EWC representatives report that important changes have begun at GME since 2012 that might improve the basis for European representation. In terms of business structures, the German CEO is also now the CEO of GME as well as a member of the GM board in Detroit, holding out the prospect of better connections to the global HQ. GME management, according to EWC representatives, now apparently favours more cooperative employment relations and the corporate culture has become more transparent. Information has also improved in the European economic committee. On production, there is a closer connection between the Opel and Buick brands, which might improve the situation for the European plants. Whether the foundations of trust and solidarity have remained intact (Pernicka et al. 2014) or might be reestablished in the near future remains an open question, however.

Ford of Europe: Disintegration of the FEWC – and a shift to the global level?

Ford of Europe entered into a deep recession from around 2010 that was only temporarily buffered by the scrappage schemes introduced by some EU governments. In 2012, Ford made a pre-tax loss of $1,753 million. Employment in Europe fell from 67,000 in 2007[17] to 46,000 in 2012,[18] a drop of nearly a third over five years. However, since 2012 there have been some indicators of recovery. While the number of global facilities sank from 88 to 65 between 2008 and 2013, the number of units produced rose from 5,407,00 in 2008 to 6,077,126 in 2013 (OICA), and total employment changed only slightly, edging up to 181,000 in 2013 from 179,000 in 2008. Between 2008 and 2013, management pursued a range of measures to cut costs and shrink employment at various levels within the company, with serious repercussions for employees throughout

17 Fourth Quarter and Full Year 2007 Earnings Review & 2008 Outlook (24.01.2008), Appendix 8 of 20, http://media.ford.com/pdf/4Q2007_Slides.pdf (24.02.2011).

18 2012 Fourth Quarter and Full Year Earnings Review and 2013 Outlook (29.01.2013), Appendix 4 of 11, http://media.ford.com/images/10031/4Q2012_Financial_Slides.pdf (12.05.2013).

Europe. First and foremost, the decision – announced at the end of 2012 – to close two plants in the UK and one in Belgium came as a surprise for many observers, as Ford had up until then not opted for such drastic measures in its European business. Management strategies also included cost-reductions in production, reducing shifts, and appeals for early retirements and the dismissal of temporary workers.

The expected fall in demand, coupled with overcapacity in Europe, prompted great anxieties among the EWC members. Concerning the cost-reduction plans, most representatives would have preferred to bargain nationally or locally, skipping the European level: 'Each country inevitably does its own thing. And it's very hard to expect people to do anything different. You know, it's about protection' (EWC member, UK). Company-level agreements to maintain employment locally were almost simultaneously negotiated in Germany, Spain and Belgium by local workplace employee representative bodies or trade unions. As with the GM EEF, the FEWC secretariat only served as a communication channel between the European and the national levels and as a discussion forum for the employee side, but ceased to take the initiative on Europe-wide solutions.

Ford management further promoted such national egoisms. In stark contrast to the previous decade, European HR management abandoned its cooperative approach towards the FEWC and began trying to play locations off against each other in local bargaining. For instance, management only informed the EWC after final decisions about plant closures had been taken, removing any scope to bargain.

In this situation, mistrust between the EWC members emerged. To gain a relative advantage in comparison to others, some EWC members withheld details of ongoing negotiations or chose to present selected details only. Other EWC members interpreted the fact that some members failed to attend EWC meetings as a 'confrontation avoidance strategy', thus adding to frictions within the FEWC. As the details of national collective bargaining agreements were not an issue during the meetings with the company, management was able to impose concession bargaining on national employee representatives.

Another factor causing frictions concerned the dominant role of the German employee representatives. Some EWC members accused the Germans of not sharing details of specific measures, such as the amount of cost cuts that had been imposed by management. While being secretly criticized for not using their strength to support their European colleagues, for their part the Germans expressed annoyance at the lack of initiative and 'victim mentality' of some EWC members. In particular, EWC members from outside Germany were vehement in their demands for more fairness in how production volumes were allocated: 'So that not one country gets 90 per cent of the work, while a small country next to it only 10 per cent' (EWC member). In fact, German production as a share of overall Ford output in Europe increased between 2008 and 2013 from 37 per cent to 59.7 per cent.

The fading of co-operative practice within FEWC and the erosion of trust and solidarity can be traced back to a number of intertwined factors. Firstly, the crisis posed a new quality of threat to both employees and operations as a whole. The acuteness of the situation was heightened by the fact that many EWC members were aware of the economic need to close one plant due to overcapacity in Europe (Jürgens/Krzywdzinski 2010). As a consequence, the decision to close *three* plants (UK and Belgium) came as a particular shock in November 2012. Because of the difficult European market and decreasing profits in Europe, EWC members had anticipated some radical measures in *one* country but closures in two countries, and of more than one plant at once, had not been expected.

Since the FEWC had never been confronted with complete plant closures of this kind, in contrast to the GM EEF, national employee representatives did not trust their EWC to work out an acceptable solution. They were also unwilling to transfer any of their local or national power to the European level for the purpose of European bargaining. Despite appreciating the need to mobilize at European level, EWC members still strongly believed that the instruments available at national level were better suited to deal with the problems.

A catalyst for the erosion of trust was a change in the composition of the FEWC. Between 2007 and 2013, the FEWC experienced a number of important changes. In 2010, the former EWC chair retired; at around the same time, a number of long-standing EWC members from other countries also left the body due to retirement. As with the GME EEF, those changes in personnel clearly marked a break as it led to a weakening of trust within the forum that had been based, on the personal relationships between representatives. Under the pressure of the crisis, the pessimistic attitudes that many members held towards the prospects of a common future within and through the FEWC made it hard to sustain cooperation. Some newly elected representatives appeared to question the 'traditional' FEWC culture. Overall, the motivation among EWC members to intensify their efforts for the common good varied significantly. In particular, the newer and younger EWC members were very skeptical about exercising employee representation at the European level, with their main expectation being that of gaining access to central management. Under these conditions, there was little room to think and act in terms of European solidarity.

While cross-border advocacy among the European plants have suffered, new representational institutions have emerged at global level. In 2012, Ford signed a global framework agreement under which the company committed itself to establish a 'Ford Global Information Sharing Forum'. Resembling 'world works councils', such as the one at VW, the forum is supposed to hold annual meetings and deal with global issues. However, it remains an open question whether the shift of representational capacity to the world level will be to revitalize cooperation among European representatives.

1.5 A transnational solution? The theoretical concept revisited

In the original German edition, we elaborated a theoretical framework for analyzing and explaining EWCs (outlined in more detail in Chapter 3 of this volume). The trajectories of the eight EWCs since 2008 seem to reconfirm the usefulness of this explanatory framework. In a nutshell, the framework suggests two 'adjustments' to EWC research that are intended to provide a more precise systematization and rigorous understanding of EWC developments. These are, firstly, an approach to developing a typology of EWCs structures and activities (organizational type); and secondly, an explanatory framework with explanatory factors and assumptions about causal relations to help researchers understand and explain how EWCs' structures and activities operate.

The first suggestion was to view EWCs as non-profit organizations that exist and act inside a for-profit organization (Pries 2008; Hertwig et al. 2009). It is a common insight in international management research that firms exhibit certain spatially-dispersed structures that reflect the fact that they cover a plurality of nations and locations. Our study was prompted by the idea that this is true not only for international companies, but also for EWCs – which may be regarded as a specific type of international organization, an international *interest organization*. Consequently, we chose to characterize firms and EWCs, drawing on dimensions developed for research on international firms (Perlmutter 1969; Bartlett/Ghoshal 1989; Doz et al. 2001). We assumed that both firms *and* EWCs are characterized by a specific distribution of resources (facilities, production volumes or EWC seats), power (decision taking and influence on decisions), culture (expectations, beliefs or world views), and knowledge (R & D or strategic information).

Furthermore, we argued that different organizational elements are integrated and *coordinated* in a way that may conform to a particular pattern. As far as firms are concerned, the question arose as to how management 'governs' spatially diffused production processes; for EWCs, we asked how representatives communicate and interact, how strategies are developed, and how EWC structures impact on coordination. The constellation of structures (centralized vs. decentralized) and coordination patterns (strong vs. weak) allowed us to build an ex ante matrix of four internationalization types — focal, global, multinational and transnational — that were used as a summary characterization of both international firms as well as EWCs. Characterizing EWCs not only according to their relationship with management and unions (conflictual or cooperative), which was the classic approach of the first generation of EWC studies, but rather primarily in line with the spatial configuration of their resources and patterns of communication and cooperation offered new insights into the structural challenges, power distribution and action dynamics in EWCs as organizations.

The second suggestion was to build categories of factors deemed likely to influence EWC structures and behaviour. Here, we drew on existing EWC research, which had already identified a large number of conditions that bear on EWCs. However, only a few studies had attempted to 'cluster' these effects systematically with the aim of a broader theorization of EWC research (Müller/Hoffmann 2001; Marginson et al. 2004). Furthermore, viewing EWC as specific forms of organization allows the wider theoretical repertoire of organizational research to be applied to EWCs, providing further fresh insights and explanations. As a consequence, our study uses a broad theoretical approach that refrains from the actor-centered models that have tended to dominate EWC research from its origins and mid-2000s (Lecher et al. 2001). By contrast, it argues for an equal significance for actors *and* structures as the foundation for understanding an EWC's structures, operations and outcomes.

A central concern of this study is the question of how the structures and activities of the company (the company type) and the structures and activities of the EWC (the EWC type) are related. We have argued that, in some instances, there may be an 'organizational fit', meaning that the structures and activities of EWCs, to some extent, can be predicted once the characteristics of the company have been ascertained. In broad terms, the 'organizational fit' hypothesis asserts that EWCs are influenced by the structures and strategies of their company; as the company is both environment for and counterpart of the EWC, it is likely that employee representatives will take their company's structures and strategies into account. This notion marks a conceptual innovation as it adds to previous concepts that have, variously, stressed the importance of the antagonism between capital and labour, national egoisms, or local idiosyncrasies.

The findings of the original study as well as our update illustrate the importance of this argument. At GM, the decentralized structure of the company's European facilities, at least until 2007, built the basis for a decentralized EWC; at the same time, management's insistent whip-sawing activities ('strong coordination') generated a high demand for cooperation and joint strategy building ('strong coordination') on part of employee representatives. Our findings on developments during the crisis support the argument that the structure and operation of the firm have a strong impact on an EWC's patterns and activities. In all our cases, the strategies adopted by companies to respond to the crisis were the pivotal object of EWC reactions. At GME, the *re*-structuring of the company – the closure and sale of facilities – had a direct impact on the composition of the EWC. Basically, beyond the notion of 'fit', we believe it is important to depict the *mechanisms* that lead to *fit* or *non-fit* as these might provide a deeper understanding of the way in which companies affect EWCs' structures and practices (Hauser-Ditz et al. 2013).

Although the study placed special emphasis on the 'fit' hypothesis, which was seen as a previously underrated element in EWC research, this was not the sole theoretical approach. In fact, we proposed a broad theoretical model comprising *four* theoretical rationales in all - of which the company type was only *one* element. In the original report, based on our review of previous research, we argued that besides company type (1), historical paths, trajectories, or critical incidents (2), national and organizational cultures (3) and individual persons, actors and actor strategies (4) could also serve to explain why a EWC reveals certain structures, engages in certain practices, and achieves an (empirically observed) pattern of employee representation. The relevance of each of those four factors, as we have argued, is an empirical question and depends on the concrete case under investigation. Hence, it is no surprise – and no contradiction to the model – that in our own empirical data, the 'fit' between company and EWC type is only strong in five of the eight case studies.

In the updated reports, our finding is that Volkswagen, Daimler, PSA and Renault mainly reflect the trajectory and country-of-origin argument. Daimler and

Volkswagen clearly differ from the other firms in the sample in that they continued to grow despite the crisis, which did not exert a collective threat on employees and sites. Representational arrangements have not only been stabilized but extended to other areas (global facilities) of these companies. This is consistent with the general trend of a strengthened regime of works councils in German economy in general. The strength of corporate culture, which is also intertwined with path developments, can be observed at Toyota and Honda. Here business culture exercises a strong influence on employees', and with this on EWC members', understanding of cross-border representation. As a result, most employees largely comply with company values, norms, and expectations. In these cases, issues of power and management strategies to fragment representatives to forestall effective representation also play a role.

A growing number of empirical studies have now used the four-factor-model to analyze EWCs (Gold/Rees 2013; Hauser-Ditz et al. 2013; Hertwig 2015; Hauser-Ditz et al. 2015). However, in some studies this approach has been reduced to the 'fit-hypothesis', in so doing losing the holistic notion underpinning the original model. For instance, it has been argued that the organizational fit-hypothesis culminates in 'determinism', as the type of corporate internationalization is supposed to lead to a specific type of EWC (Kotthoff/Whittall 2014). In fact, given that our approach comprises four categories of factors, it suggests rather multi-causality, with virtually no room for a single determinant. Moreover, our own case study research has demonstrated that not one factor alone accounts for the variance in EWC structures and patterns of coordination. And because the proposed approach builds on the accumulation of knowledge gathered from a large number of studies on EWCs, it is unlikely to remain static and is open to the inclusion of insights derived from the growing volume of empirical research.

In this respect, the findings of the 'update' on developments at both the companies' and EWCs between 2008 and 2013 support the arguments of our original study. Our initial conclusion was that the 'transnational' form or a close fit between company type and EWC type was not automatically the 'best way' and certainly not a definitive solution to the challenges and hurdles of cross-border labour advocacy. As in the cases of GME and Ford, the EWC type and its relationship to the company type is only one element in any explanation of an EWC's specific form and effectiveness. However, developments at GME and Ford illustrate the effects of structural changes and the shifts from a transnational to a more focal or global form of internationalization. Nonetheless, it appears that the transnational type of EWC at GME and Ford in combination with strong and committed actors (chairperson), national institutions of labour relations and a common identity (national and EWC culture) provided a good basis for representational effectiveness. The more recent developments that we have outlined here demonstrate that the erosion of the EWCs' transnational character, the departure of long-standing and committed members together with the weakening of the original culture led to a decline in representational capability.

Conversely, the strong headquarters bias of company structures and EWC activities at Daimler-Benz and Volkswagen underline that in these cases organizational fit between a global company and a global EWC (in the sense of centralized resource structures and strong coordination of activities) was helpful to employee representative bodies, which were even able to grow in strength and influence after the crisis. In these cases, however, it was not only organizational fit that contributed to their resilience but also a prior trajectory of decades of strong workers' involvement at all levels of these companies, based on the German dual system of labour regulation with strong industrial unions and strong work councils. Accordingly, the organizational form of an EWC – be it global, multinational, focal or transnational – is only one factor in the representational outcome of cross-border employee representation.

1.6 References

Bartlett, C., Ghoshal, S. (1989). Managing across borders: the transnational solution, London: Century Business.

Bernaciak, M. (2013). Cross-border competition and trade union responses in the enlarged EU: Evidence from the automotive industry in Germany and Poland, in: European Journal of Industrial Relations 16 (2), S. 119–135.

Doz, A., Santos, J., Williamson, P. (2001). From global to metanational. How companies win in the knowledge economy., Boston: Harvard Business School Press.

Gold, M., Rees, C. (2013). What makes an effective European works council? Considerations based on three case studies., in: Transfer. European Review of Labour and Research 19 (4), S. 539–551.

Hauser-Ditz, A., Hertwig, M., Mählmeyer, V., Rampeltshammer, L. (2013). Transnationalisierung der Automobilindustrie als Herausforderung für Europäische Betriebsräte., in: Maletzky, M./Seeliger, M./Wannöffel, M. (Hrsg.): Arbeit, Organisation und Mobilität. Festschrift für Ludger Pries zum 60. Geburtstag, Frankfurt, M.: Campus, S. 192–230.

Hauser-Ditz, A., Mählmeyer, V., Pries, L. (2015). Überfordert im Managen von Vielfalt? Euro-Betriebsräte im Strukturwandel der Automobilzulieferindustrie., Frankfurt/M.: Campus.

Hertwig, M. (2015). European works councils and the crisis. Change and resistance in cross-border employee representation at Honda and Toyota, in: British Journal of Industrial Relations 53 (2), S. 326–349.

Hertwig, M., Pries, L., Rampeltshammer, L. (2009). European Works Councils as international non-profit-organisations: an organisational research approach to a crucial element of Europeanisation, in: Hertwig, M./Pries, L./Rampeltshammer, L. (Hrsg.): European Works Councils in Complementary Perspectives, Brüssel, S. 13–46.

Jürgens, U., Krzywdzinski, M. (2010). Die neue Ost-West-Arbeitsteilung. Arbeitsmodelle und industrielle Beziehungen in der europäischen Automobilindustrie Frankfurt/M.; New York: Campus.

Kotthoff, H., Whittall, M. (2014). Paths to transnational solidarity, Bern: Peter Lang.

Lecher, W., Platzer, H.-W., Rüb, S., Weiner, K.-P. (2001). European Works Councils: Developments, Types and Networking., Aldershot: Ashgate Publishing, Ltd.

Luethge, D. J., Byosière, P. (2009). Honda: Serendipity or Strategy from 1997–2007?, in: Freyssenet, M. (Hrsg.): The Second Automobile Revolution. Trajectories of the World Carmakers in the 21st Century, New York: Palgrave McMillan, S. 112–128.

Marginson, P., Hall, M., Hoffmann, A., Müller, T. (2004). The Impact of European Works Councils on Management Decision-Making in UK and US-based Multinationals: A Case Study Multinationals, in: British Journal of Industrial Relations 42 (2), S. 209–233.

Müller, T., Hoffmann, A. (2001). EWC Research: A Review of the Literature, Warwick: Industrial Relations research Unit University of Warwick.

Perlmutter, H. V. (1969). The Tortuous Evolution of the Multinational Corporation, in: Columbia Journal of World Business (1–2), S. 9–18.

Pernicka, S., Glassner, V., Dittmar, N. (2014). When does solidarity end? Transnational solidarity during and after the crisis – the GM/Opel case revisited. Paper for the IREC 2014 Conference: Dublin.

Pries, L. (2008). European Works Councils as Transnational Interest Organisations?, in: Pries, L. (Hrsg.): Rethinking Transnationalism: the Meso-link of Organisations Milton Park, N.Y: Routledge, S. .

Volkswagen 2013, Volkswagen Annual Report. Wolfsburg: Volkswagen.

Preface and acknowledgements

This study sets out the results of a research project on the developmental dynamics and effectiveness of European Works Councils (EWC) in the automotive industry that was undertaken by the Department of Sociology and Organisation, Migration and Codetermination at the Ruhr University, Bochum, between 2007 and 2010 and financially supported by the German Research Foundation (Deutsche Forschungsgemeinschaft – DFG). The immediate project team consisted of Axel Hauser-Ditz, Markus Hertwig, Ludger Pries and Luitpold Rampeltshammer. Jessica Buchholz, Valentina Mählmeyer, Martin Seeliger and Katharina Westerholt were the research assistants on the project and made a contribution that went considerably beyond the normal call of duty. The project team are grateful to Susanne Axt-Sokolowski for her work in the practical organisation of the research. We were greatly helped by Veronika Dehnen in preparing and undertaking a number of interviews in France.

Holm-Detlev Köhler (Spain), Hiroshi Kumon (Japan), Miguel Martínez Lucio (UK), Udo Rehfeldt and Elsie Charraon (France), and Stanislaw Rudolph (Poland) contributed to the successful completion of the research through their expert knowledge, advice and critical comments as well as establishing contacts for field research. In addition, we are grateful for the comments on individual sections of this book by Thomas Haipeter, Ulrich Jürgens, Günter Koch, Georg Leutert, Thomas Metz, Tommaso Pardi, Frederic Speidel, Manfred Wannöffel and Georg Wolter.

Finally, we would like to express our gratitude to all the institutions and individuals involved in the project, and in particular to our interviewees for the time they made available and their interest in our research.

Bochum, July 2015

Axel Hauser-Ditz, Markus Hertwig,
Ludger Pries, Luitpold Rampeltshammer

List of abbreviations

AG	Aktiengesellschaft (stock corporation = German public liability company)
CC.OO	Comisiones Obreras
CFCT	Confédération française des travailleurs chrétiens
CFDT	Confédération française démocratique du travail
CGC	Confédération générale des cadres
CGIL	Confederazione Generale Italiana del Lavoro (Italian Confederation of Labour – trade union confederation)
CGT	Confédération générale du travail (General Confederation of Labour – France)
CKD	Complete Knock-Down
EEF	European Employee Forum (GM EWC)
EMF	European Metalworkers' Federation
EMU	Economic and Monetary Union
ETUC	European Trade Union Confederation
ETUF	European Trade Union Federation
ETUF-TCL	European Trade Union Federation of Textiles, Clothing and Leather
ETUI-REHS	European Trade Union Institute – Research, Education, Health and Safety
EU	European Union
Eucob@n	European Collective Bargaining Network
EWC	European Works Council
FIM-CISL	Federazione Italiana Metalmeccanici – Confederazione Italiana Sindacati Lavoratori (CISL affiliated trade union for metalworkers)
FIOM-CGIL	Federazione Impiegati Operai Metallurgici – Confederazione Generale Italiana del Lavoro (CGIL-affiliate for metworking)
FO	Force Ouvrière
FPC	Fair-Practices-Committee
GM	General Motors
GME	General Motors Europe

GMTUCG	General Motors Trade Union Coordination Group
HECCG	Honda European Communication and Consultation Group (Honda EWC)
HPS	Honda Production System
ICCP	Information, Computer and Communications Policy Committee
ILO	International Labour Organization
IMF	International Metalworkers' Federation
NMSC	National Marketing and Sales Company
OEM	Original Equipment Manufacturer (refers here to vehicle brand)
SE	Societas Europaea (European Company)
SNB	Special Negotiating Body
TEF	Toyota European Forum (Toyota EWC)
UAW	United Automobile, Aerospace and Agricultural Implement Workers of America
UGT	Unión General de Trabajadores (General Union of Workers: Spanish trade union centre, historically affiliated with the Spanish Socialist Workers' Party, PSOE)
WEC	World Employment Committee (Daimler World Company Council)
WCC	World Company Council

Chapter 1: Introduction

The period since the 1990s has seen the emergence of an extensive body of social science research into the movement towards greater European unity. In particular, the issue of Europeanisation, understood as a multi-dimensional and multi-level process of cross-border sociation (*Vergesellschaftung*), has been the object of a large number of studies from both a political-science and sociological perspective.[19] One important element in this process has been the establishment of European Works Councils (EWC), and one of the intentions behind the 1994 EWC Directive was to support the social and political dimension of European unity. The final form of the Directive was the outcome of three decades of difficult negotiations and the examination of a wide range of proposed models. In its final form, it created a new institutional order for employee participation and the regulation of interests in 'Community-scale' enterprises with at least 1,000 employees overall in a minimum of two EU Member States, and with at least 150 employees in each.

This new institution was developed and became established through a complex process that entailed, firstly, the adoption of supranational (EU-) Directives and corresponding transposing legislation at national level; and, secondly, the emergence of a practice of cross-border interest regulation by the immediate actors concerned (companies, trade unions, workplace employee representatives) that preceded, ran parallel to and followed the introduction of these legal instruments (Keller, 2001; Lecher et al., 2001; Pardi, 2006; Pries, 2010). By 2010 some 950 EWCs had been established in such enterprises, corresponding to more than a third of all companies within the Directive's scope (see Chapter 2.1 below). In total, these companies employed some 17 million employees. In view of the growth in corporate cross-border activity, EWCs could emerge as a significant mechanism through which economic Europeanisation is complemented by a social process in which patterns of interest representation and collective bargaining arrangements are also Europeanised.

However, such conjecture about the longer-term prospects for EWCs also raises the issue of their present-day role in the Europeanisation and internationalisation of companies, both in general and also in the specific area of the regulation of terms and conditions of employment within European-scale companies? Are EWCs successful in exercising significant information and consultation functions within processes through which management and employees regulate their interests? Or are they merely a clearing-house for contacts between employee representatives from different countries and operations? From the perspective of management, do EWCs represent a burdensome bureaucratic, and possibly costly, additional institution that has to be dealt with? Or are they an important means for communication and

19 „Vergesellschaftung" here refers to processes of social interaction that increasingly span national borders.

possibly even a serious negotiating partner? Do trade unions see EWCs as helpful forums within the Europeanisation of interest representation, or are they viewed sceptically, possibly mistrustfully, as bodies that might act as competing ('syndicalist') institutions or, at most, a place at which divergent local interests encounter each other? And finally, are they little more than bodies that exist in name only, and whose work and activities pass unnoticed by the employees they aim to represent?

Research into EWCs since the mid-1990s has delivered a number of interesting findings about the conditions under which EWCs have been constituted, their formal legal bases, their practice, and their effectiveness as a means of interest regulation. In the course of this work, some answers have emerged in response to the questions posed immediately above (see also Chapter 2 for an overview). However, although there is no lack of rich empirical work on EWCs, covering a broad spectrum of branches and national settings, a number of researchers have lamented the field's theoretical shortcomings (see, for example, Müller and Hoffmann, 2002: 108, 111). In terms of the object of research, this concern has an internal and an external aspect. The external aspects of this 'conceptual deficit' relate to the fact that there is little mutual exchange between EWC research and other social science research dealing with Europeanisation. For example, Münch (2001) has engaged with the diverse dimensions of the social unification of Europe in a complex and nuanced way:[20] however, there is no explicit consideration of the role that EWCs might play in this process. The multi-level approach to Europeanisation that characterises a good deal of political science research has also remained focused on political parties and interest associations, with little consideration of EWCs (and Social Dialogue) as a distinct object of research. And for its part, EWC research has devoted little attention to these studies.

The internal aspect of the 'conceptual deficit' in EWC research is mainly a product of the lack of a theoretical foundation able to anchor empirical research. Those theoretical models that have been formulated usually draw on industrial relations perspectives, which remain strongly oriented to national structures of interest representation and focus on EWCs as an actor in the relationship between capital and labour. Such studies often centre on assigning EWCs to distinctive types, structured in accordance with the nature of exchange and power relations between EWCs and management, national arrangements for employee representation, and trade unions. Correspondingly less attention is paid to the multi-dimensional and multi-level nature of EWCs. Since EWCs are composed of elements that are distributed socially and spatially across different countries, the individual and collective actors brought together within them act (and where appropriate, negotiate) on the basis of diverse national-cultural systems of institutions and traditions. However, in order to be able to act externally in a collective and purposive way they must organise forms of internal coordination. A simple borrowing from traditional industrial relations research, largely developed for nation-state frames of reference, is, therefore,

20 Münch (2004) refers expressly to the implementation of national employment and social policies within the context of Europeanisation.

insufficient. Equally, EWCs cannot be studied through the simple application of theoretical and analytical instruments developed for and in the context of research into German works councils as the outstanding paradigm of workplace employee representation.

A further critical point, and in part one promoted by the lack of appropriate theoretical penetration of the field, turns on the methodology adopted by many EWC studies. In empirical studies, the dynamics and practice of EWCs are often ascertained through an analysis of interest-driven behaviour and the perceptions of a small number of actors that are held to be significant – frequently representatives of management and employees at corporate headquarters and in some cases in one additional selected country. This methodological restriction ultimately leads to the exclusion of the interests, strategies, perceptions and interpretations of the bulk of the actors involved – namely EWC members drawn from a wider range of countries, trade union traditions and represented social groups (either just employees or also management) – or their indirect reflection in the statements collected from senior EWC members or their advisers.

Against this background, we set three main objectives for our research. Firstly, to develop a theoretical-analytical framework for the study of EWCs and their contextual factors that responds, at least to some degree, to the 'conceptual deficit' noted above. To this end, we undertook a systematic review of the industrial relations research that has typified previous EWC studies and complemented this with concepts drawn from transnationalisation and organisational research, and in particular from research into cross-border corporate organisation (Chapter 2.2).[21] We also propose a conceptual innovation that is intended to offer a specific analytical perspective on EWCs: this is that from the standpoint of transnational organisational sociology, an EWC may be viewed as a pluri-local non-profit organisation that exists as a platform for interaction within an internationally-operating company and which acts in relation to this company. Our characterisation of EWCs (and also of EU-scale companies) is based on an *ex ante* typology of international organisations that draws on the schema of global, international, multinational and transnational companies originally proposed by Bartlett and Ghoshal (1989).

21 A number of terms are used in the literature to characterise companies that operate across national borders (international, multinational, transnational etc.): there is no single agreed nomenclature. In some studies the various designations are used to make a substantive characterisation of different types of internationally-operating companies (see, for example, Perlmutter, 1969; or Bartlett and Ghoshal, 1989 [2008]). In this study, the concepts 'cross border' and 'international' are used synonymously and in a very broad sense to denote all organisations that operate in more than one country on an enduring basis and with their own resource base and structures. The term 'international organisation' is therefore deliberately used as broader and more encompassing term. By contrast, the concepts 'focal', 'global', 'multinational', and 'transnational' are used to denote the substantive characteristics of international organisations: see Chapter 2.1 for a more precise definition of these terms.

Our second aim, based on this theoretical approach, was to assign the EWCs of selected companies in the vehicle manufacturing industry to a category within this typology and, in addition, to offer a causal explanation for this allocation. This rests on a theoretical model that makes use of four dimensions of influence (Chapter 3.1 and 3.2). The model encompasses both explanatory factors already conceptualised in previous EWC studies, and which have been shown empirically to have explanatory relevance, as well as considerations drawn from concepts in the field of organisational studies that aim to explicate organisational structures and practices. The four explanatory dimensions are:

a) The *home-country effect* or the influence of national institutional-cultural contexts.
b) The *path dependency* or historical evolution of the corresponding (corporate and EWC) organisations.
c) The orientations, strategies and other specific features of the *relevant actors.*
d) The structures or *international type* of the company – subsequently referred to as the *'organisational fit'* between the type of company and the corresponding type of EWC.

The systematic application of these four dimensions is intended to facilitate a combination of theoretical perspectives that aims to integrate considerations of both structure and agency. The institutional, historical, actor-related and situational contextual conditions of EWCs are, as a consequence, seen, as it were, as 'crystallisations' of preceding developments and events as well as constituting filters and limitations that structure the scope for future action. This approach is intended to avoid the twin traps of voluntarism and determinism when examining the scope of EWCs.

Finally, the third aim of the study consists in offering a reflection on the effectiveness of EWCs as bodies for the regulation of interests. 'Effectiveness' is not equated here with the publicly visible activities of EWCs, including their manifestation in forms of conflict. *Rather, the central field for assessing EWC effectiveness is their capacity to secure guarantees from companies to retain employment and operations in Europe.* To this end, we have developed an approach that embraces a number of dimensions of the 'outputs' of interest representation to enable EWCs to be compared (Chapter 3.3).

From a methodological standpoint, applying concepts from transnationalisation research requires a particular approach to survey design. The notion that EWCs represent non-profit organisations, whose spatially distributed actors or groups of actors are embedded in distinctive national-cultural and institutional contexts, and who therefore dispose over specific patterns of interests, perceptions and values, calls for appropriate account to be taken of *sub-groups.* In order to avoid a centre-periphery bias, we extended our research, firstly, beyond the home country to other countries in which companies in the study have operations; and, secondly, to representatives of employees and management at other European locations as well as the EWC leadership and members from the home country.

The empirical section of the study applies these approaches to eight internationally operating vehicle manufacturers of European significance: Daimler, Volkswagen, PSA, Renault, Honda, Toyota, Ford, and General Motors. As well as looking at previous studies and analysing secondary documentary data, primary data collection principally entailed expert interviews at the facilities of these companies in five countries (provided they were represented there): Germany, France, United Kingdom, Poland, and Spain as well as, where appropriate, the country in which the company had its EU headquarters. In addition, expert interviews were also carried out in interest organisations and amongst researchers (see Chapter 3.3). Chapters 4–11 present the results of the eight case studies structured by type of company and EWC. Chapter 12 sets out a cross-sectional evaluation based on the main areas of interest by EWC type, by regulatory effectiveness, and in terms of an explanation of these findings using the four dimensions of influence noted above. This chapter also draws together and synthesises the key findings of the study and raises issues for future research.

Chapter 2: The current state of research

Space forbids a fully comprehensive treatment of the range of current EWC studies and a number of systematic overviews of the literature have been compiled by other researchers (see Hertwig et al., 2009; Müller and Hoffmann, 2001; Waddington and Kerckhofs, 2003; Whittall et al., 2007). Rather, our intention here is to highlight some of the key features of previous research and reflect on what we consider to be some of the limitations of this work, which, in some respects, have constituted a springboard for our own work (Chapter 2.1). In order to explain our theoretical framework, we then consider the issue of internationally operating for-profit and non-profit organisations (Chapter 2.2).

2.1 Research on European Works Councils

2.1.1 Phases of EWC development

Interest in researching EWCs as the first cross-border institution for company-level employee representation pre-dates the 1994 adoption of the EWC Directive, but was given a substantial boost following its transposition into national law. EWC research has drawn on a number of disciplinary approaches and perspectives. Historical analyses customarily distinguish three phases of EWC development (see Rivest, 1996; Platzer and Weiner, 1998: 393ff. ; Keller, 2001). During the first phase, prior to the adoption of the Directive, the research focus was on analyses of the strategies deployed by actors in their engagement with the Directive (Hall, 1992; Danis and Hoffmann, 1995) and the establishment of forums for employee information and consultation on a voluntaristic basis. During this phase, forty-nine 'pioneer' EWCs were established in forty-six companies (Kerckhofs, 2003: 15). Despite the voluntaristic nature of these agreements, these pioneer cases played an important role as models of practice, allowing trade unions to pressure political actors to move ahead with the adoption of a Directive (Nagel, 1999: 325f.).

The second phase encompassed the period between the adoption of the Directive in 1994 and its transposition into national law in September 1996. According to Kerckhofs, some 400 voluntary EWC agreements (so-called 'Article 13 agreements') were concluded during this period. The notable feature of Article 13 agreement was that companies were not obliged to comply with the stipulations of the Directive. Rather, 'company-specific' arrangements could be agreed between companies and employee representatives, with the guarantee that they could continue in force and be deemed to be compliant even after the transposition date (Hoffmann, 1997; Lecher et al., 2002: 148–9). This scope for negotiation 'in the shadow of the law' (Bercusson, 1992) came to an end once the date for the transposition of the Directive into national law was reached in September 1996.

The third phase began with the introduction of the standard 'statutory procedure' (Lecher et al., 2002: 5) under Article 6 of the Directive. Research in this period was principally concerned with the implementation of the Directive (Jäger, 1996; Buschak, 1997), the successful establishment of EWCs (Whittall, 200b on BMW; Eller-Braatz and Klebe, 1998; Haipeter, 2006; and Kotthoff, 2006b on GM) and the activities of EWCs (see, for example, Bartmann, 2005; Dehnen and Rampeltshammer, 2010; Klemm and Siebens, 2004).

EWC studies from a legal perspective have analysed, for example, the specific modalities of national transposition of the Directive, either in a single country (Bercusson and Dickens, 1996 for the UK; Blanke, 1999, for Germany) or as a comparison of several countries (Buschak, 1997; Bueggel, 2002). Studies have also considered the effectiveness with which the Directive has been transposed (with country studies on France, Germany, Belgium, and the Netherlands in Rigaux and Dorssemont, 1999).

A number of economic studies have adopted a quantitative perspective, examining, for example, the relationship between the establishment of EWCs and salient company characteristics, such as branch or company size. An econometric analysis of voluntary EWC agreements by Addison and Belfield (2002) did not establish any significant correlation between productivity/company performance and the existence of an EWC. A more recent study by Vitols (2009: 7) looked at the social welfare impact of EWCs for shareholders, creditors, managers and employees. It concludes that EWCs have no negative impacts on creditors and shareholders, and 'clear positive benefits' (ibid.) for managers and employees.

In contrast, political science research has concentrated on factors such as power, interests, institutions and dynamic processes, such as the conditions under which EWCs emerge and develop within a European multi-level system (Jachtenfuchs and Kohler-Koch, 1996), with EWCs seen as actors in power and exchange relationships. In their analysis of the economic and political factors explaining the existence or non-existence of an EWC, Streeck and Vitols saw political factors (strength of home-country employee representatives, influence of the French Socialist Party) as having greater explanatory power than socio-economic variables (concentration of production or internationalisation of employment), and, as a consequence, concluded that 'voluntary supranational works councils are rooted in diverse national political and institutional conditions, especially the power and access to political and legal resources of national unions and employers' (Streeck and Vitols, 1995: 268).

Research from the perspective of industrial relations theory has focused on the nexus constituted by the triangle of labour (workplace employee representatives and trade unions), capital (company managements and employer associations) and the state (Müller-Jentsch, 1997). Within this tradition, the prime research objects have been EWCs' functions and operational characteristics. In relation to the functions of EWCs, research has looked at the extent to which EWCs promote the democratisation of work (Ramsay, 1997), their contribution to the development of industrial citizenship rights in the form of 'social citizenship' (Streeck, 1999), or the development of a European identity (Whittall et al., 2007).

One strand of research has focused on the question as to whether the establishment of EWCs might add impetus to a newly-emerging system of employment regulation at European level. The EWC Directive is seen by several researchers as a major step in this direction (Martin and Ross, 1999; Hoffmann et al., 2002; Müller and Platzer, 2003; Weiss, 2006; Platzer, 2009; Lecher and Platzer, 2003). For Müller and Platzer, the novel quality of the EWC as an institution lies in three aspects: regulation, subsidiarity, and the priority of negotiation. From this perspective, the European system of industrial relations constitutes one element of a multi-level system characterised by the linking of the national and supra-national levels (see in particular, Schulten, 1998).

Transnationalism research has, as yet, had little engagement with the issue of EWCs. Within this approach, EWCs are conceptualised as internationally-operating organisations (Pries, 2008a; Pries, 2010; see too Hertwig et al., 2009), the operation of which can serve as one element in an emerging network structure of the transnational regulation of employment that emerges from the synthesis and integration of a number of different levels (national and supranational) of regulatory mechanism. This approach also emphasises the *variety* of developmental paths and patterns of processes of internationalisation. In addition to the strategies adopted by the actors, structural and institutional contextual conditions also play a determining role, and empirical research has focused on their mutual interaction (Pries, 2008a: 330).

As far as assessment of the regulatory potential of EWCs is concerned, Germany has witnessed a particularly controversial debate, typically characterised as a confrontation between a 'pessimistic-sceptical' view and an 'optimistic' standpoint. The 'Euro-sceptical' position has highlighted the lack of codetermination rights, in the German sense, of EWCs: as a consequence, EWCs have been seen as having little effective purchase on the central problems and tasks of cross-border interest representation (Keller, 2001: 100). Streeck summarised the pessimistic position very vividly: since EWCs did not have codetermination rights and were simply an extension of national interests in European forums, they were 'neither European nor works councils' (Streeck, 1997: 325).

By contrast, the optimistic position argues that despite their limited powers, EWCs possess the potential to develop into effective cross-border interest representation bodies. Lecher et al., for example, argued that there were clear signs that EWCs could develop into supportive pillars of a system of European industrial relations (Lecher et al., 1999: 256ff.). This stance was bolstered by the findings of Müller and Hoffman, who discerned a process of EWC development evidenced in the fact that 'the actual practice usually exceeds the formal content of EWC agreement' (Müller and Hoffmann, 2002: 229). The position was supported by Telljohann (2005), who, based on a sample of fifty EWCs, noted that EWCs could assume roles that went beyond their formal legal provisions. Blanke also noted that the introduction of

EWCs represented a noteworthy step towards supra-national interest representation (Blanke, 1999: 522; see too Müller-Jentsch, 2007: 140; Müller and Platzer, 2003: 79).[22]

As far as the theoretical perspectives applied to EWCs are concerned, these have been dominated by an actor-centrered view. Only more recently have some contributions begun to note the significance of structural factors – and in particular the influences of national structures of employee representation, sector, company-specific factors and the standpoint of management – as explanatory elements of the functions and operation of EWCs (Marginson et al., 2004: 212; Telljohann, 2005; Kotthoff, 2006a: 174; Pries, 2008b; Hertwig et al., 2008; Hertwig et al., 2009). Two studies by Marginson (1992; 1998) indicated that a uni-dimensional approach is unable to explain the differing operational features of EWCs and that company structures had a significant impact on whether an EWC was likely to be established in a firm. For Marginson, these structural factors included the existence of a European level of management, an integrated production structure, and single ownership. Subsequent research, building on this work, has looked at the influence of EWCs on the process and outcomes of management decision-making processes in British and US companies (Marginson et al., 2004). The results of this study suggest that in addition to actor-related factors (management's attitude towards the EWC, interaction within the EWC) structural factors (business focus, European management structure) also play an important role in explaining variance in the influence of EWCs on management decisions.

2.1.2 Coverage rate and characteristics of EWCs

According to the European Trade Union Institute (ETUI) EWC databank, by early-2010 a total of 1,154 EWCs had been established, of which 952 were still active. Of the 2,358 companies within the scope of the Directive and which were in a position to have an EWC, 898 had done so by early-2010, equivalent to a coverage rate of 37.6 per cent. The ETUI data also indicates that the coverage rate for larger firms is higher than for smaller. In companies with fewer than 5,000 employees, the coverage rate is 27.9 per cent; in companies with more 10,000 employees it is 63.9 per cent.

In addition to studies on the spread and coverage rate of EWCs, another strand of research has focused on analysing EWC 'installation' agreements, under which EWCs were initially established. The evidence indicates that such agreements played an in important role in determining EWCs' areas of activity and shaping their forms of action (Carley and Hall, 1996; Gilman and Marginson, 2002). Based on an analysis of 344 EWC agreements, Gilman and Marginson identified four key influencing factors that explained variations in their provisions: 1) a sector effect, 2) country-of-origin effect, 3) statutory model effect (that is, the effect of the EWC Directive or the subsidiary

22 One further central concern of EWC research has been the question of the feedback effects of EWCs on national systems of employment regulation.

requirements on the constitution of EWCs), 4) a learning effect (that is, imitation and adoption of good practice) (Gilman and Marginson, 2002: 46ff.).

A third line of research has looked at the functions and operational features of EWCs, with a focus on two main aspects: the conditions that influence the structure of EWCs, and the significance of EWCs for interest representation. As far as the structure and effectiveness of EWCs is concerned, several early studies proposed EWC typologies. In their study of (a total of) twenty-three EWCs, Lecher et al. (Lecher et al., 1999; Müller and Platzer, 2003) looked at EWCs' activities in terms of four fields of interaction: between EWC members, between management and the EWC, between trade unions and the EWC, and between national employee representatives and the EWC. This material was then used to compile an initial typology of EWCs that consisted of four types: symbolic, service, project-oriented, and participative. These terms essentially denote differences in the effectiveness of EWCs. According to Lecher and Platzer, only a small minority of EWCs had advanced sufficiently to constitute effective actors (Lecher et al., 2002: 179 footnote 3), and nor was there any automatic evolution from a symbolic to a participative EWC (Lecher and Platzer, 2003: 599; see too Platzer, 2009).

Based on a study of twelve cases, Kotthoff suggests a similar typology, using five categories and with EWCs allocated along seven dimensions (Kotthoff, 2006a): structure and organisation of the EWC, structure and organisation of the company, internal EWC relationships, 'everyday Europeanisation',[23] EWC and union EWC support activities, and the relationship between EWCs and individuals. Drawing on Perlmutter (1969), Bicknell's EWC ty pology rests on the distinction between ethnocentric, polycentric and Eurocentric patterns of internationalisation. The basis of the typology is the 'strategic disposition towards international development' (Bicknell, 2007: 117), operationalised using nine variables. In applying these factors to EWCs with a marked German influence, Bicknell notes that these are either predominantly ethnocentric or polycentric, but not Eurocentric.

In regard to the significance of EWCs for the representation of employee interests, Waddington, using a survey of 473 EWC members, concluded that the quality of participation in EWCs varied considerably in relation to the information and consultation provisions in the Directive. Many EWCs were not informed or only insufficiently informed about important matters, and still fewer consulted. Set against the requirements of the Directive, participation by many EWCs was seen as inadequate.

2.1.3 Research on EWCs in the automotive industry

A number of studies of EWCs have looked at the activities and strategies of individual EWCs in crisis situations, such as plant closures. One focus of these case

23 Kotthoff defined 'everyday Europeanisation' in terms of the impact of EWCs on national and workplace works councils in Germany, posed as the questions: 'Does the fact that an EWC exists and is active in the company mean that the thoughts and actions of the national works councils become more European?' .... 'Is Europe a dimension of everyday activity at local operations' (Kotthoff,, 2006a: 159).

studies has been the car industry. In part, this is due to the fact that some of the larger vehicle manufacturers were pioneers in establishing EWCs. By 1996, for example, before the expiry of the 'Article 13' phase, all the European car manufacturers had established European information and consultation bodies (Hancké, 2000). Moreover, the very active dynamics of automotive companies in the fields of internationalisation, restructuring, technological change, and market development, would suggest a need on their part to develop processes for cross-border interest regulation.

During the early phase, some researchers were extremely sceptical about the role of EWCs in the European automotive industry. It was argued, for example, that they were used by management or trade unions, in the latter case primarily to defend or advance local interests, with the overall impact being a further twist to downward spirals in pay and employment conditions at company-level (Hancké, 2000). Zagelmeyer (2001), for example, referred critically to 'brothers in arms in the European car wars' when analysing such local 'alliances for jobs' – the German term for micro-corporatist agreements – intended to secure the continued existence of specific plants through raising their competitiveness.

This critical assessment contrasts with the large number of publications that have viewed the development of EWCs in the European car industry as an authentically European – and effective – means of interest representation able to transcend national or plant-level interests. Eller-Braatz and Klebe (1998), for example, showed how the EWC at General Motors was able to build a cross-national common position amongst employee representatives on a proposed benchmarking exercise in the teeth of determined management resistance. The EWC was able both to control and mitigate competition between employee representatives from different plants based on an 'imaginative and timely combination of national information and codetermination rights' (Eller-Braatz and Klebe, 1998: 449). Resolving this conflict within the EWC not only strengthened the position of national employee representatives, but also, and notably, that of the EWC itself in terms of its internal cohesion, which proved to be a stabilising factor in subsequent developments. In later conflicts, prompted by large-scale restructuring affecting a number of plants, the EWC was in a position to attain a degree of participation that went far beyond the provisions of the EWC Directive (Martmann and Blum-Geenen, 2007; Rott, 2008; Dehnen and Rampeltshammer, 2010).[24] In his analysis of the General Motors EWC, Fetzer (2008) uses the term 'risk community' to describe a process in which employee representatives form themselves into an effective unit to reduce the risk of inter-plant competition, and consequent transfers of production, under two conditions: firstly,

---

24 Haipeter (2008) cites five critical factors that explain the development of the EWC at General Motors: the emergence of an integrated European management structure; platform-based and parallel production; learning processes on the part of EWC actors; US origins; and adversarial industrial relations within the company. Dehnen and Rampeltshammer (2010) come to similar conclusions.

where problems cannot be resolved at plant-level; and secondly, when the difficulties experienced within the company are seen as common problems affecting all actors. On this argument, one significant factor prompting the development of the EWC at General Motors was when EWC members perceived that employees were equally vulnerable to the company's globalisation strategy (expressed, for example, in transfers of production).

The decision to establish an EWC at BMW was taken by the group works council (*Konzernbetriebsrat*) following BMW's acquisition of the Rover Group in 1994 and was motivated by fear on the part of BMW employee representatives that the integration of Rover plants might undermine the relatively high employment standards at BMW. The initially unwelcoming stance of management changed once it realised that concluding a voluntary agreement before the introduction of the EWC Directive offered a number of advantages (Whittall, 2000b: 67f). During the crisis of the Longbridge plant in 1998/99, the resources of the German group works council played a very significant role as compared with the limited powers of the BMW EWC. The main function of the EWC was to establish a basis for bilateral union cooperation (Whittall, 2000b: 78). Whittall's study indicated, firstly, that when faced with extensive structural differences (industrial relations systems, unequal distribution of EWC seats and powers), 'soft factors', such as trust-building, regular interaction and networking, grew in significance; and secondly, that where central management was located had a major influence on EWC practice, based on accustomed patterns of interaction that rested on national systems of employment regulation.

The EWC at Volkswagen was established as early as 1990 and constituted one of the first such bodies in a European vehicle manufacturer. Management's decision to recognise the EWC as a representative body was an expression of its desire to play a leading role in the construction of the European Union's 'social dimension' (Helbig, 1999: 247). Despite the dominance of German representatives within the body, the VW EWC was able to influence significant management decisions in the interests of non-German locations (Mertens, 1994; Haipeter, 2000; Müller et al., 2004a; Hertwig et al., 2008).[25]

Most of these studies employed an industrial relations perspective, in which the dependent variables or explananda were the origins and development of EWCs, their structures or types, and their effectiveness. The independent or explanatory variables were the objective framework conditions (embeddedness in industrial relations institutions at national and EU-level), factors connected with the company and its management (EWC agreement, structure of group management, and management policy towards the EWC), and operational and decision-making processes related to various constituencies within the companies. Research, following Lecher et al. (1999), is often confined to analysing the four relational dimensions already

25 Speidel (2005) has conducted a comparative analysis of international interest representation at VW and Renault. The system of international interest representation at Daimler has been researched by Müller et al. (2004a).

noted above: EWC – management; EWC – trade unions; EWC – national interest representatives; internal EWC relations. This is a schema that has also categorised some of the classic studies of German works councils (see, for example, Fürstenberg, 1958; Kotthoff, 1981 and 1994; Müller-Jentsch and Seitz, 1997).

Although there are differences between existing studies in terms of the respective significance they attribute to agency and structural elements, overall they remain within the confines of industrial relations research. As yet, EWC research has not systematically drawn on political science approaches (on multi-level governance, see, for example, Jachtenfuchs and Kohler-Koch, 1996; Schulten, 1996 and 1999; Müller at al., 2004a) nor on the debate over the convergence and divergence of national institutional systems (Hall and Soskice, 2001) and nor on work in organisational sociology and transnationalisation studies (see below in the present study). In this respect, EWC research remains in need of greater conceptual systematisation (see too Müller and Hoffman, 2002: 108, 111).

To sum up, in methodological terms previous EWC research has been conducted using either a (limited) number of individual case-studies, with sometimes extensive documentary research (such as all EWC agreements), systematic analysis of secondary material (such as annual company reports), or larger-scale surveys using standardised questionnaires to capture specific aspects. Deploying classic survey research is problematic, given the complexity of the research object, and this also means that the areas for exploration need to be commensurately restricted. As a consquence, previous surveys have focused on aspects of EWC work, their role, and styles of operation without systematically considering the structures of the internationally operating organisations in which they are established (see, for example, Lecher et al., 2002: 177ff.; Vitols, 2003; Waddington, 2003). Case-study research has often ben conducted based on interviews at corporate headquarters and one additional location (Lecher et al., 2002: 45; Telljohann, 2005: 83).[26] Given the strengths and weaknesses of previous EWC research a systematic treatment of the approaches, theoretical models and methods of studies on international organisations and, in particular, international companies would seem to be potentially fruitful.

2.2 Research on transnational organisations

One of the initial suppositions of this study is that EWCs represent distributed operational organisations that persist through time, the sub-elements or sub-organisations of which interact across the borders of a number of nation-states and which are also embedded in specific national-cultural institutional settings. Such

26 This would appear unsatisfactory from the standpoint of organisational sociology and transnationalisation research, which we argue for here, mainly because it presumes a clear centre-periphery relationship from the outset, and overlooks the diverse (and possibly decentralised) interactions between EWCs' individual national and workplace units.

distributed structures have been intensely discussed in both organisational sociology and management research since the 1960s. Transnationalisation research (Pries, 2008a) has also devoted increasing attention to cross-border organisations (Portes et al., 2002; Pries and Sezgin, 2010). Social science research on international organisations is now so extensive that we cannot begin to do it justice here. Moreover, there are also marked differences between for-profit and non-profit organisations as far as theoretical traditions and areas of research are concerned. Our aim in what follows is to highlight some of the key research findings on the for-profit and non-profit sectors with specific reference to transnationalisation.

2.2.1 For-profit organisations

Organisational sociology and organisational science more generally has an extensive tradition of developing ideal-types of cross-border and international companies.[27] The central concern has been the tension between national structures of rules, norms and institutions, on the one hand, and resource structures and mechanisms for coordination and control, as well as value and norm orientations, within cross-border operational organisations (see Dunning, 1979 and 1995). The two principal questions in research into international companies relate to the typical models of organisation and the generation of typologies, and the instruments for analysing and measuring organisations (Friedrichs, 1997; Pries, 2000).

In relation to typologies of internationally operating companies the key considerations are: 1) the spatial distribution of individual units of the undertaking; 2) specific cross-border patterns of cooperation and coordination; and 3) factors that determine (1) and (2).

As far as spatial distribution is concerned, since the early work of Perlmutter (1969), Dunning (1979) and up to Porter (1986), Bartlett and Ghoshal (1989) and Doz and Williamson (2001), it has been argued that one of the most fundamental distinctions between organisational types is whether they are monocentric or polycentric organisational structures, or, in an alternative formulation, between a centre-periphery model and a network model (Macharzina, 2003). For example, several studies have looked at the issue of the extent to which network structures facilitate the pursuit of international strategies or may even be the precondition for such strategies. In this area, a central role has been played by process-focused studies of spatially and nationally distributed value-chains (see Welge et al., 1998; Riedl, 1999; Pries and Schweer, 2004; Mense-Petermann and Wagner, 2006).

As far as patterns of coordination are concerned, a number of authors have focused on value-orientations and shared cultural perspectives (Hofstede, 1997). Others have identified personal links and networks as the crucial mechanism for integrating individual units of international firms and achieving cohesion and cooperation (Carroll and Fennema, 2002; Borghoff, 2005). Finally, non-personal

---

27 On the conceptual apparatus used here, see Chapter 3 below.

trans-organisational mechanisms, such as bureaucratic control, benchmarking, and metric-driven ('output control' or 'managing by numbers') or discursive coordination have been identified as other possible significant forms of integration (Dörrenbächer, 2000; Pries, 2000; Welge and Holtbrügge, 2003).

The typology proposed by Bartlett and Ghoshal is also a common reference point for many studies in this area, and will be deployed – with certain amendments – in the present study. Building on work by Perlmutter (1969) and Porter (1986), Bartlett and Ghoshal (1989) suggested four ideal-types of internationally operating organisation. Two of these are based on a centre-periphery relationship (global and international) and two have a multi-polar structure (multinational and transnational).[28] They argue, based on this typology, that the 'transnational corporation' is more likely to prove successful as a form of corporate internationalisation compared with the other three options. Against the background of a large number of theoretical and conceptual challenges to the Bartlett/Ghoshal typology, Harzing (2000) tested three of the four models (multinational, global, transnational) with a relatively large sample and was able to confirm these three types (multinational, global, and transnational). This is a noteworthy result, given that the Bartlett and Ghoshal had based on their typology on only nine case studies, compared with Harzing's study, which looked at 166 subsidiaries of thiry-seven internationally-operating companies (see Meier, 1997).

For Bartlett and Ghoshal, transnational organisations have a number of characteristics that render them a very specific type of international organisation: these include the cross-border dispersion and decentralised structure of material resources, locations, employees and knowledge; a non-monocentric but rather polycentric organisationally-specific culture; a more heterarchic and spatially-distributed structure of power and interests instead of sharply delineated centre-periphery relationships, but accompanied by a high degree of mutual responsiveness and interdependence – that is, strong coordination – between dispersed organisational units. These characteristics mean that transnational organisations can also be designated as heterarchies, 'global learning networks' or 'multi-centre structures'. It is precisely these processes of transnational coordination and control that allow transnational organisations to achieve dynamic embeddeing in their complex, diverse and heterogeneous environments.

In addition to shaping the flows of resources for their primary activities, a key role is occupied by the underlying processes of information, coordination and

28 Bartlett and Ghoshal (1989), as with many studies based on organisation science, make specific use of the concept of 'international organisation' meaning an organisation that operates across borders and which has a clear centre-periphery relationship and weak coordination of the activities of its sub-units. The term 'multinational organisation' is used here specifically in the sense of a decentralised and weakly-coordinated international organisation and not a category to denote all internationally-operating profit-seeking organisations, as is often the case in research into multinational organisations (for a more detailed discussion, see Chapter 3).

decision-making: these not only form the foundations for the efficient fulfilment of the organisation's primary tasks, but also the basis for learning processes – and hence also for organisational evolution. It is assumed that within transnational organisations, standard hierarchical structures and processes are not sufficient to respond to global complexity and heterogeneity. The embedding of organisational units in varying local contexts combined with strong supra-local coordination allows transnational organisations to develop emergent recursive and reflexive structures and processes.

The central issue of patterns of spatial distribution and coordination mechanisms exerts a strong influence over features of corporate internationalisation that are held to be of significance. For example, UNCTAD uses two indices – the 'transnationality index'[29] and the 'network spread index'[30] – to identify and characterise international operational organisations, and in particular international companies. However, these provide information only on the spatial distribution of international activity and do not measure networking and coordination. Moreover, these indicators also only measure the objective distribution of resources, but not regulations, routines and structures of communication and decision-making, let alone company cultures that are the prerequisite for the value-chain to function.

Research on international firms and internationalisation strategies that make use of indicators (Ruiogrok and van Tulder, 1995; Riahi-Belaoui, 1998 and 1999) has developed further approaches to ascertain the degree of company internationalisation using quantitative data. One additional option for measuring international organisations through the construction of indices is that of clustering using organisational patterns and national cultures (see, for example, Hofstede, 1997). More recent methodological approaches have sought to combine data on national cultural clusters with 'hard' data on the geographical spread of activities to produce a complex 'degree of globalisation' index reflecting both dimensions (see, for example, Fisch and Oesterle, 2003). Some studies also distinguish between global and transnational companies, and compile indices such as 'local responsiveness', 'interdependence' (from firms' headquarters) and 'organisational design' (see Harzing, 2000). Studies of processes of corporate internationalisation indicate that structures for exercising management control and organising operations can develop asymmetrically

29 This measures the ratio of foreign assets to total assets, foreign turnover to total turnover, and the number of foreign employees to total employees (UNCTAD, 2002: 88). Van Tulder et al. (2001) used the index as a combination of the three company-specific indicators to operationalise the concept of internationalisation (ibid. 47). Their study of the 100 largest ('core') companies yielded an average transnationality index of 35 per cent; in contrast, amongst companies with the most international activities, the transnationality index ranged between 50 and 55 per cent (ibid. 57f.).

30 This is calculated as the ratio of the number of foreign countries in which a transnational company has wholly-owned subsidiaries to the number of foreign countries in which it could potentially operate (that is, countries with a positive stock of foreign direct investment) (UNCTAD, 2002: 109).

in terms of their degree of internationalisation, leading to the possibility of major discontinuities in the process of development (see, for example, Schulte and Hirsch-Kreinsen, 2002; Borghoff, 2005).

Personal links, cross-shareholdings and other financial linkages, and supplier relationships between organisations or organisational units can also be ascertained using network analysis (see Borghoff, 2005; Rohwer and Pötter, 2002: 47; Wassermann and Faust, 1994). In the area of for-profit organisations, a particular focus has been on the relationships between corporate centres and business units in different countries together with their diverse roles in local networks (see Cantwell and Piscitello, 1999; Edwards and Ferner, 2004).

Overall, there is a substantial bank of studies on the international structures and characteristics of international firms, with the prime focus on the distribution of resources by country and by the location of facilities, as well as on mechanisms for coordination and linking the large number of organisational units dispersed across a large number of countries. We argue that the experience gained from this research can and should be deployed within the field of EWC research.

2.2.2 Non-profit organisations

Research into non-profit organisations has developed its own approach to transnationalisation, integrating a number of social science disciplines (sociology, political science, legal and cultural studies) relatively independently of organisational studies (Pries, 2002; 2008). In addition to questions of the coordination of knowledge and overarching value and strategic orientations, the prime focus of this research has been on the efficiency-legitimacy dilemma (Scharpf, 2000): that is, that consideration that international organisations must guarantee a minimum degree of efficiency through distributing and coordinating their operations, but must also ensure that they maintain internal legitimacy (as an overall organisation and in terms of individual units) and external legitimacy (as an overall organisation and at their various locations and national sites).

Whereas general transnationalisation research has a well-developed body of research, both in terms of theory and empirical research, covering a range of phenomena, including transnational migration, transnational families, transnational literature and media and transnational social movements (Pries, 2002; 2008),[31] international non-profit organisations remain comparatively under-researched within organisational science. Yet international non-profit organisations are confronted with the problem of coordinating spatially-dispersed units to a even greater extent than businesses, as the latter have access to 'hard' mechanisms (hierarchy, financial incentives) to promote compliance by individual units and members. In contrast, the majority of international non-profit organisations have either have strongly

31 For the field of industrial relations, see Gordon and Turner (2000) Hürtgen (2008); Pries (2010).

bureaucratic and centralised forms of coordination (such as IMF and OECD based on inter-governmental treaties) or constitute loose networks of largely independent local units (such as the NGO ATTAC). In contrast, aside from such global and focal[32] multinational organisational patterns, transnational organisations, in the sense of decentralised but strongly coordinated organisations, remain a rarity (see Keck and Sikking, 1998; Roose, 2003).

Political science research on transnational organisations has concentrated 'primarily on the scope for democratic and effective policies under conditions of economic debordering' (Jachtenfuchs, 1998: 242). The main focus of this discussion has been the consequences of the global debordering of market processes for the internal governing capacity of nation-states and the influence of economic globalisation on the modern national welfare state, and the limited social-policy options available to highly developed capitalist nation-states (Scharpf, 2000). Although interest in this area has been mainly on researching international regimes, international organisations have attracted the attention of research into processes for solving and regulating conflicts of interest (see Taylor and Groom, 1988; Neyer, 1999; Zürn and Wolf, 2000).

This links existing analyses of international interest and public welfare organisations with the study of corresponding organisations in the nation-state, in that both are focused on questions of regulatory effectiveness. Transnational interest organisations are not only able to fulfil regulatory functions in their own interest, but also in the interest of third parties, and hence function in an analogous way to the self-discipline exercised with associations at a national level (Mayntz, 2003: 11).

Irrespective of these dimensions related to how organisations emerge and develop, international interest organisations as non-profit organisations are usually notable for (1) a relatively polycentric distribution of resources and structure of interests, (2) a manifest need for cross-border regulation and interest-articulation, and (3) a constant need to resolve the efficiency-legitimacy dilemma. It is precisely this dilemma that demarcates for-profit and non-profit organisations, since, as far as businesses are concerned, efficiency (in the form of adequate profits) is usually simultaneously[33] the most important source of legitimation, whereas for non-profit

32 We adopt the term 'focal' here in place of Bartlett and Ghoshal's designation of 'international' in order to clarify the distinction between this and the general designation of 'international' or 'cross-border' organisation. In the context of this study, a 'focal' organisation is one of four organisational types. Substantively, it denotes a pattern of internationalisation that is typified by a centralised distribution of resources and weak coordination of organisational activities.

33 This somewhat cautious proposition is intended to take account of the fact that there are convincing explanatory approaches in organisational sociology that argue precisely the opposite: neo-institutionalism, for example, argues, and can demonstrate, that organisations principally structure themselves to gain external legitimacy and are not directed at organisational efficiency or rationality (see Meyer and Rowan, 1977, and for an overview Scott (2001); Walgenbach and Meyer, 2007).

organisations efficiency, as such, is not in itself sufficient to generate internal and external legitimacy. Securing a minimal degree of organisational efficiency and legitimation vis-à-vis supportive client groups represent two more or less equally importany – co-existing and counterposed – requirements placed on non-profit organisations.[34]

2.2.3 Summary

From a theoretical and conceptual point-of-view, our view is that EWC research would be enriched by applying insights and models from organisational studies and transnationalisation research. Although research from the field of management science on international and transnational business organisation is often characterised by a prescriptive and practice-driven approach – Bartlett and Ghoshal, for example, explicitly argue for the transnational organisational form as one that offers a good strategic fit for certain industries – research on international for-profit organisations, nonetheless, offers empirically-based and usable contemporary models that can help classify internationally-operating organisations. This foundation of social science research are used in this study as a heuristic. There are also good reasons to suppose that firms operating in Europe represent central factors or environments that pre-structure the operational context of their corresponding EWCs. In the absence of any form of characterisation or typology of such companies, as cross-border for-profit organisations, it would appear to be extremely difficult to understand or explain the EWCs that operate in them. We would, therefore, argue that EWC research should systematically and expressly draw on research into international companies.

From an empirical point-of-view, the four-fold typology of international for-profit organisations (global, multinational, focal, and transnational) has been shown to have both explanatory power and to be relatively uncomplicated. As a rule, studies distinguish between aspects of the spatial structure of distribution (centralised vs decentralised) and aspects of coordination and integration (strong vs weak).

Many of the theses advanced within EWC research can be related to these dimensions. For example, when Streeck (1997: 328) comments that EWCs are 'neither European nor works councils', then in effect he is denoting EWCs as focal organisations with the marked dominance of the company country-of-origin combined with weak mechanisms for European-level coordination. Implicit in this designation is that greater influence should be accorded to the home-country effect than to the international type of organisation or to the influence of the evolution or learning of the company itself.

34 The general significance of international and transnational organisations in terms of this efficiency-legitimacy dilemma has been discussed by Beisheim and Zürn (1999); this issue has been reviewed for trade unions as non-profit organisations by Schroeder and Wessels (2003).

From a methodological point-of-view, research in the fields of organisational sociology and transnationalisation offers a wide range of instruments for measuring and categorising cross-border organisational structures. Based on these initial considerations, we propose that EWCs can be characterised as non-profit organisations and the companies in which they operate as for-profit organisations.

Chapter 3: Theoretical and methodological framework

The core of this study consists of a relatively innovative perspective on EWCs that draws on approaches within transnationalisation research and comparative (international) organisational research. In this, EWCs are understood as non-profit organisations established on the basis of a unitary European institutional foundation and distributed across a number of nation-states, existing and acting both *within* companies operating across the EU as well as *externally* upon them. Whereas works councils (both at workplace and company level) can conventionally be viewed as sub-units or sub-organisations of a firm's organisation, subject to a unitary national legislative framework and institutional setting, matters are considerably more complex in the case of EWCs as these are established on the basis of a European provision that is only effective after being transposed into a multiplicity of national laws. From a formal legal point-of-view, an EWC is a European non-profit organisation in the sense of having clear membership rules, a given structure and clear aims in terms of employee representation and the establishment of dialogue with the central management of European companies.

Although internationally-operating companies, understood as 'corporate actors', must also coordinate spatially distributed operations that function on the basis of diverse statutory regulations in heterogeneous institutional and cultural settings, in contrast to EWCs, understood as non-profit 'collective actors' and interest organisations, firms are driven by the contrasting logic of for-profit organisations.[35] The problem of mobilisation (the 'transformation problem') and the issue of balancing of interests, as well as of efficiency and legitimacy (Scharpf, 2000), is posed differently for firms, which can deploy means of hierarchical control for managing organisational sub-units that are not available to EWCs.

Understanding EWCs as non-profit organisations within and counterposed to for-profit organisations leads on to the central presupposition of study: that is, that European corporate structure and organisation is a key determinant of the form of internationalisation of the corresponding EWC. The reasoning for this is twofold: firstly, the company represents the main partner for interaction and the focus around which EWC's activities crystallise; and secondly, company organisation is a central element in the situational and institutional-cultural context of the corresponding EWC, and one which exercises a profound influence on its structural forms and scope. Given that the strategies and organisational decisions of central

35 Scharpf (2000:101) distinguishes 'between "collective actors" that are dependent on the preference of their members and are controlled by them, and "corporate actors", that enjoy a high degree of independence from the ultimate beneficiaries of their actions' (see Mayntz and Scharpf, 1995: 49ff.).

managements constitute the main rationale for the existence and activities of EWCs, and that firm structures and cultures define a major element of an EWC's scope for activity, the cross-border or European-wide operating company represents both the *precondition* for EWC activity and also its *object*, the location in which it is performed and its adressee or counterpart.

This perspective also highlights the key role of a preliminary analysis of corporate structures and activities. Seeing EWCs as non-profit organisations does not imply that EWCs or individual actors within them do not possess the attributes of agents. Rather, an EWC is understood as a complex and 'constituted' collective actor, composed of sub-elements or groups dispersed as collective or individual actors across a number of national states and acting within these states' institutional and cultural contexts and developmental trajectories. Such a perspective also allows consideration of the intra-organisational transactions that always occur within EWCs. This actor-perspective is supplemented by and embedded within the structure of the relevant company as a corporate actor (see Chapter 3.2.4 for a more detailed elaboration).

One special feature of EWCs as a collective actor is that EWC members interact and cooperate with each other within the EWC, but are also active at the company's local operations, which are dispersed amongst several national societies, each with its own distinctive institutional arrangements. This perspective highlights a number of the central problems that EWCs confront as organisations. The geographical dispersion of EWC members means that particular efforts have to be devoted to integrating and coordinating EWC members and activities. These efforts are rendered more complex by the fact that EWC members originate from differing national-cultural contexts – that is, different social spaces. These diverse cultural and institutional local ties shape and mark EWC members' perceptions and interpretations, their notions of fairness and other norms, and, ultimately, their expectations of their involvement in an EWC and their assessment of the value of such a commitment.[36] In order to ensure its efficiency and legitimacy, an EWC must constantly take account of both the varying scope afforded by each national culture and structure of interest representation as well as mediate between and integrate the divergent conceptions, and expectations of EWCs rooted in different national cultures.

Against this background, three main concerns stand at the core of our study.

- Firstly, we argue that EWCs, as non-profit organisations, can be understood and characterised in the context of their respective companies, which, in turn,

36 The divergence in expectations is illustrated by the case of EWCs in French and German companies. For French companies, based on the fact that in France only trade unions may negotiate with management and workplace employee representation is intended only for information and consultation, there is no pressure to 'develop' EWCs into negotiating partners. The position is different in German EWCs, where some efforts have been made to transfer the negotiating rights of German works councils to the EWC (see Chapters 4 and 5).

can be assigned to a typology a profit-seeking organisations. This, in turn, raises the issue of the explanatory validity of the selected typology of global, focal, multinational and transnational organisations. And further, it raises the question of whether there is a dominant type of EWC or a general movement towards a particular type?

- Secondly, and subject to establishing an appropriate typology that embraces companies *and* EWCs, we engage with the issue of the *effectiveness* of interest regulation in and through EWCs – in particular on the issue of employment guarantees and commitments to retain existing operations.
- Thirdly, and finally, we intend to explore factors that might explain the emergence of particular types of EWC and their effectiveness in regulating interests. In particular, on the issue of employment guarantees and retaining operations, is there a link between an EWC's negotiated outputs and its location in the typology?

The following sections set out the theoretical and methodological starting point and approach of our study. Drawing on transnationalisation research and research into international firms, in the first section we propose a typology of international organisations that can be applied both to for-profit and non-profit organisations (Chapter 3.1). This will then be used in the empirical section as an analytical heuristic and also to enable companies and their EWCs to be depicted in a condensed form based on actual company and EWC structures and activities as ascertained through research. In doing so, we apply the typology initially proposed by Bartlett and Ghoshal (1989)[37] using two dimensions – the *spatial distribution* of resources (material and personnel), power, culture, and knowledge, and the *coordination* of organisational activities. Secondly, we develop a theoretical approach that models the varying (potential) factors that influence the EWC type and its effectiveness in regulating interests (Chapter 3.2). This draws on a number of aspects that have customarily played a part in EWC research (home-country effect, pattern of interaction between actors) as well as additional elements from organisational studies that have, as yet, been somewhat overlooked in this field (situative and institutional environment, cultural context of EWCs, developmental paths, and inter- and intra-organisational processes). Chapter 3.3 elaborates the methodology of the study.

3.1 Company and EWC typology

The main aim of our study is to investigate EWCs as European non-profit organisations from the perspective of organisational studies and transnationalisation research and, on this basis, to assign companies and their EWCs to ideal-typical clusters of factors. At the same time, we have endeavoured to avoid the difficulties of inductive categorisation seen in some EWC research, in which EWC typologies are proposed based on a small number of case-studies and a large number of factors

37 The current edition of this text is Bartlett, Ghoshal and Beamish (2008).

(see Lecher et al., 2001; 2002; Kotthoff, 2006a). In addition to the problem of a lack of transparency in data collection and analysis, such approaches are also vulnerable to Goldthorpe's (1997) criticism of studies that operate with few cases and too many variables. In order to avoid the problems inherent in an inductive and descriptive typology, we have adopted an *ex ante* deduced typology of international organisations based on the ideal-typical distinction between international organisations as global, multinational, focal and transnational business organisations (see Figure 1). This is intended to direct attention to two central aspects of internationally-operating organisations relevant for characterising EWCs as pluri-local non-profit organisations: the spatial distribution of EWC structures and the coordination and integration of spatially-dispersed activities and structures. It also allows us to identify and characterise, through a process of abstraction and summarisation, specific patterns of dispersion and coordination that would appear to apply to all internationally-operating organisations, including companies and their EWCs.

Figure 1: Four ideal-types of international organisation.

Coordination / Dispersion	Weak	Strong
Centralised	Focal organisation	Global organisation
Decentralised	Multinational organisation	Transnational organisation

Source: authors, based on Perlmutter (1969); Porter (1986); Barlett and Ghoshal (1989); Hofstede (1997); Welge and Holtbrügge (2003); Doz et al. (2001). See too Hertwig et al., 2009b.

The four ideal-types of international organisation describe specific matters of the dispersion and coordination of organisational elements. A *focal* organisation denotes a centralised distribution of resources with weak coordination of the organisational activities of organisational units (such as production facilities localised in different nation-states). A *global* organisation is characterised by a centralised pattern of distribution, but in contrast to the focal organisation is highly coordinated. A *multinational* organisation can be said to exist where there is a decentralised distribution of resources with weak coordination of the activities of organisational elements. And a *transnational* organisation has no clear centre-periphery structure: rather, it combines a decentralised distribution of resources with a high degree of international coordination of its sub-units.

Based on the terms developed within international organisational studies, we understand 'distribution of resources' to refer to material and personnel but also to power, knowledge and culture.[38] This definition is sufficiently general for it to

38 Since in this study the structures of distribution within companies and EWCs are always seen from the perspective of the regulation of interests within companies

be applied to both companies and EWCs, and also contains the key elements for characterising cross-border organisational structures. In terms of the distributive dimension, it is possible to differentiate the spatial-social dimension from the direct material and personnel resources, power, culture and knowledge. Direct material resources for companies mostly consist of the scale of production and employment at individual locations; for EWCs these constitute the number of members or representatives of the European body. The analysis of companies, therefore, rests principally on the distribution of employees, subsidiaries and production volumes in the countries in which the company operates. The distribution of power reflects the differences in the capacity and competences for exercising influence and decision-making as between the various locations of an internationally-operating company. In analysing the distribution of cultural elements, the main issue is whether local operations are dominated by elements of the home-country culture, implying a movement towards uniformity, or whether there is scope for a more pluri-local differentiation of the company culture[39]. Finally, 'knowledge' refers to the spatial distribution of the generation of strategically innovative knowledge resources (principally research and development), which are of particular relevance for globally-operating vehicle manufacturers (see Chapter 3.3 below on the operationalisation of the resource and coordination aspects).

In the case of EWCs, 'resources' are understood principally as seats on the EWC and its steering committees and other governing bodies, distributed through various mechanisms between the different countries or operations covered by the EWC agreement. 'Power' means the scope for intra-organisational influence that can be exercised by EWC members on EWC decisions together with the opportunities to introduce issues of concern into the EWC process or to use the EWC to serve a specific set of interests. It also refers to the differentially distributed (inter-organisational) scope to influence management decisions, articulate interests and to prevail vis-à-vis the company. As with companies, the organisational structure of EWCs can also be characterised by national dominance or by pluri-locality, in which the special features of national actors are taken account of in the sense of 'local responsiveness' (Perlmutter, 1969). In contrast to the typology applicable to companies, for EWCs 'knowledge' does not refer to innovation in the area of research and development but rather to access to information about strategic decisions or planning that might be of significance for cross-border interest representation.

In terms of the dimension of coordination, the main issue is how the sub-elements of an internationally-operating organisation are steered or coordinated and their activities controlled. This involves, on the one hand, the various mechanisms and

at EU level, these elements are of interest primarily in terms of their significance as *resources* and *conditions* for processes of company-related interest regulation. We do not propose to undertake a comprehensive analysis of power relations and organisational cultures in this study.

39 We will consider the aspect of culture in the following Section, too.

instruments of organisational coordination (see, on this, for example, Schreyögg, 2000; Kieser and Walgenbach, 2003). On the other, one further critical consideration is whether there is an intensive process of coordination and a tight linkage of activities or whether sub-units of the organisation are relatively loosely coupled and subject to weak coordination of operational processes and management of interests within the overall organisation. In the case of the vehicle manufacturers considered in this study, tight coordination could be said to be present if there is intensive coordination and internal agreement on supplier relations, setting profit-margins and investments, control over human resources strategy, and the generation of product and process innovation, with demonstrable regular and frequent communication and interaction within management and close control and supervision of the operations of individual facilities. In contrast, close coordination for EWCs could be said to occur when there is a comparatively high frequency of communication and meetings of the whole EWC, other governing bodies and between individual members (see too Chapter 3.3).

In previous studies, the capacity of an EWC to represent employee interests has often been measured either in material or formal attainments, such as the number of agreements concluded. This study adopts a more nuanced approach towards the effectiveness of interest representation – which we subsequently term as an output – which is *not* measurable purely in terms of the number of formal agreements. Firstly, we consider, in addition to the quality of processes of information and consultation, the significance of other opportunities for participation – such as participation in negotiations and the conclusion of binding agreements. The results of these are, however, always interpreted in the light of the need for regulation, as perceived by employees in a company. A greater need for regulation (as with parallel production or inter-plant competition) can lead to a much higher level of activity on the part of an EWC that, in some cases, can be externally highly visible (as with the EWC at GM). However, this needs to be distinguished from the actual successes in terms of securing the continued existence of particular plants and employment opportunities.

And secondly, in addition to these more formal aspects, we also consider the actual structures of coordination and communication and other 'softer' elements of a shared EWC culture or identity as an output of interest representation as these often lead to an improvement in employees' scope for representation and are also usually a precondition for achieving success in interest representation, both formally and substantively.

3.2 Explanatory factors for EWC types and effectiveness

In order to explain the EWC types established through empirical research, together with their effectiveness in the practice of interest representation, we adopt a theoretical model that combines a number of approaches to organisational research, industrial relations and transnationalisation and integrates these with the findings of a large number of existing EWC studies (see too Chapter 2.1). Four analytical dimensions can be identified from the research contexts already outlined that are relevant for explaining and understanding EWCs, their internal structures and dynamics, and their effectiveness in interest representation. These are:

- the type of internationally-operating company;
- developmental paths and critical events;
- institutional and cultural (country) contexts;
- actor strategies and the role of individuals (see Figure 2).

3.2.1 Type of internationally-operating company

The previous sections noted the central significance of the internationally-operating company within which an EWC is constituted and in relation to which it acts. Company structures and managerial strategies are not only the object for its representative activities: as a social system, the company also constitutes (with its specific configuration of spatial distribution and coordination activities) a major part of the situational, institutional and cultural contextual conditions for the existence of the EWC and its scope. One central assumption of this study is, therefore, that the type of firm (the specific configuration of the distribution of material resources and personnel, decision-making power, culture, and knowledge together with the coordination of resource flows, activities and communication within an international company) exercises a major influence on the type of EWC – its patterns of distribution and forms of coordination. This is also linked with the contention that EWCs are not independent of the structural and situational context set by the company in terms of their own structures and activities. We have therefore incorportated such a structural component, which is often not systematically taken into account in EWC studies, into our explanatory model.[40] That is, we argue that the type of internationalisation that characterises the firm is likely to exercise a direct influence on the structures and scope of the EWCs and, with this, the effectiveness of the EWC in terms of the regulation of interests: in other words, there is an *organisational fit* between the company and EWC.

The assumption of a correspondence between company and EWC rooted in an 'elective affinity' embraces two principal propositions. The first is related to the influence of the form of corporate internationalisation on the type of EWCs – that is, on the degree of centralisation of its structures and the strength of coordination of its activities. The second is linked to the effectiveness of the EWC and states that the probability of a high level of output (in terms of 'hard' indicators, such as retaining operations and employment guarantees, but also as regards 'soft' aspects,

40 Examples of where structural aspects have been considered include Marginson et al. (2004); Müller et al. (2004a); Fitzgerald and Stirling (2007); Speidel (2005); Waddington (2003, 2006).

such as communication, solidarity or identity)is greater when there is a 'fit' between the type of company and the type of EWC.

Figure 2: An explanatory model of EWC type and effectiveness.

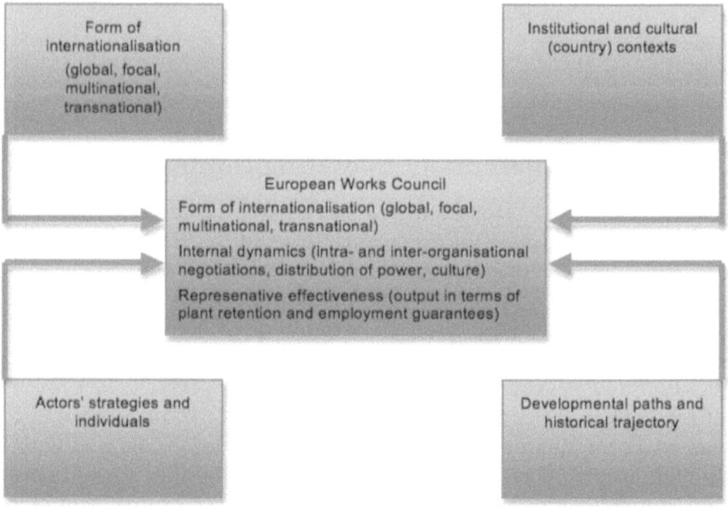

Source: Project Team

The thesis that there is a 'fit' between an organisation and its environment is hardly a new one in organisational research. Contingency theory is based on the assumption, firstly, that the formal structures of an organisation are necessarily influenced by its environment or 'situation'; and, secondly, that an adaptation of formal organisational structures to environmental contingencies then takes place in order to produce the degree of efficiency required for organisational survival (see, for example, Pugh et al. 1963; Pugh and Hickson, 1976; Pugh and Payne, 1977; Miles and Snow, 1984. For an overview, see Brown, 1992, Chapter 3; Kieser and Walgenbach, 2003).[41] For contingency theory, organisations that are not, or poorly, fitted would experience problems in surviving in the market. Some variants of evolutionary theory (on population ecology, see Hannah and Freeman, 1977;Aldrich, 1977; McElvey and Aldrich, 1983) and neo-institutionalism (DiMaggio and Powell, 1983; Scott, 1987) also assert the significance of organisational adaptation to environmental circumstances or expectations in order to secure the resources, legitimacy and, ultimately, the survival of the organisation.

41 However, the concept of 'fit' has a number of connotations. For Miles and Snow (1984), for example, it refers to the link between management strategy, firm structure, and market conditions.

How does, then, the form of internationalisation of a firm influence the type and effectiveness of an EWC? What mechanisms effect this adaptation? In order to tackle this issue, we make a number of further assumptions. Firstly, we assume that EWCs' structures and activities are *not* simply automatically and spontaneously derivable from firm structures and uniformly determined by these. On the one hand, it would be reasonable to suppose that EWC structures and activities are structured purposively and, at least to some extent, with a strategically rational intent (Child, 1997; Simon, 1957) in order to realise the aims of the actors' concerned. As such, the establishment and configuration of an EWC can be understood as a 'high cost situation' (Schimank, 2000) in that all the agents direct considerable attention to the decisions that must be made, given that there is a good deal at stake both in terms of potentially high costs and high benefits – for example, management anxiety that the EWC might acquire too much influence or fears on the part of national employee representatives that they might not be able to negotiate sufficient scope to exercise influence or obtain resources. On the other hand, the structures and activities of an EWC arguably represent a compromise, an outcome of inter- and intra-organisational negotiating processes (Walton and McKersie, 1965; McKersie and Walton, 1992) between management, employees, workplace employee representatives and trade unions at various levels of interest regulation (local, national, EU, globally), and into which these agents bring their differing expectations and power resources (Pries, 2005; 2010). The assumption of organisational fit can be broken down into the four aspects of the pattern of distribution (material and human resources, power, culture, and knowledge).

(1) *Distribution of material and human resources.* As far as the distribution of resources within a company is concerned (employees at operations, operations in countries, production volumes at operations) and in the EWC (members in countries, resources for EWC work), there is often a direct connection as the distribution of EWC members is closely aligned with the distribution of employees across countries in which the firm operates. However, there may be scope for deviation from a rigid numerical rule, if, for example, key actors consider that it is important for all countries to be represented on the EWC or to accommodate the fact that some countries have particular arrangements in terms of trade union pluralism.
(2) *Distribution of power.* In many instances, institutions for interest representation at a firm's headquarters have much greater scope for exercising influence as compared with employee representatives from foreign operations based on long-standing relationships with corporate management and the benefit of direct access to senior managers (see Streeck, 1997; Hancké, 2000). If one assumes that the employee side has an interest maximising its influence over management via the EWC, it would be reasonable to suppose that the distribution of such scope within the EWC would correspond to the distribution of power within the company. In a company with a decentralised power structure (multinational or transnational), individual operations have a greater role in making

decisions on production and retaining or changing facilities. As a consequence, a relatively large number of organisational units are likely to exercise roles of central concern to EWCs and it would be advantageous for the work of the EWC if the various distributed power centres were also appropriately reflected in this body. In contrast, in a global company (centralised resources and strongly coordinated) an EWC would be likely to be more effective in terms of interest regulation if it also had a recognisable power centre to match the company's power centre.

As a consequence, from a rational perspective, it would seem advantageous for EWCs to configure their structures to correspond with those of the company (that is, either distributed power or a power centre) in order to gain access to decision-makers, secure scope for influence and be consulted on company decisions. In practice, however, structures and cultures of interest regulation within a company might promote a concentration of power in representative bodies located at the company's decision-making centres, irrespective of any theoretical rational fit. In this sense – and in addition to the argument based on organisational fit referred to above – cultural and path-related factors might be needed to explain an EWC's structure.

(3) *Distribution of culture.* As far as the cultural dimension is concerned, we assume that the company culture exercises a major influence on the culture of the EWC, whose working practices and modes of interaction and communication reflect the cultural particularities of the regime of employment regulation of the home country, the company's industrial relations, and dominant groups within the EWC (see too Gilman and Marginson, 2002; Waddington and Kerckhofs, 2003). Since organisational cultures develop over long periods of time and invariably reflect cultural elements from their environment (national culture, employment relations system etc.), it is difficult for them to be configured intentionally, and if so only in marginal areas (see Schein, 1995; Hofstede, 1980).

Nonetheless, more recent studies indicate that, over time, EWCs may develop their own cultures and can break free of the culture of their company and its country-of-origin. This process of cultural formation refers to the emergence of common expectations and aspirations in interest representation, and the strategic objectives and modus operandi of the EWC, that are probably shared by EWC members and which can manifest themselves as an autonomous EWC identity (see Telljohann, 2009; Whittall et al., 2007; Hürtgen, 2008).

(4) *Distribution of knowledge.* The distribution of knowledge in an undertaking can initially be seen in the context of research and development activities: as a rule, knowledge work takes place in a small number of R&D centres, usually located at a company's headquarters. Because of short product cycles (of less than a decade of market presence for a single model type and a development period of almost equal length), in addition to product development (from initial design and concept vehicle to readiness for mass production), production and process development (from design of manufacturing plant to initiating normal

operations) is also an extremely significant field of knowledge production, application and dissemination.

As a consequence, familiarity with a company's strategic development plans are of relevance for EWCs. Knowledge constitutes an important resource that (co)determines the strategic capacity and power of EWC members. As such, the distribution of R&D centres and the locations of R&D management that are of relevance for Europe are an important indicator of the distribution of decision-making power and channels within a firm. It is reasonable to assume that the type and effectiveness of an EWC are significantly affected by the pattern of distribution of knowledge, even if this connection is more implicit and operates over the longer term.

In addition to aspects of organisational fit between firm structure and EWC structure noted above, an additional factor also influences the type and effectiveness of EWC. We deal with this under the dimension of the *coordination* that is characteristic of the firm's mode of internationalisation and have denoted it 'regulatory need'. One central assumption of our study is that the demands placed on an EWC are influenced by the firm's business situation and dynamics, together with management policies, and are relatively independent of the pattern of resource distribution in an internationally-operating business. This applies in particular to the field of guarantees on employment and the retention of plants and operations. Irrespective of the mode of corporate internationalisation, what is decisive is whether a vehicle manufacturer is doing well, in terms of growth and expansion (such as Toyota up until the 2008 crisis) or suffering contraction (as with General Motors).

Strong coordination within a firm, based on platform strategies, parallel production and internal competition, leads to the emergence of a functional regulatory need for the EWC to coordinate its own activities to anticipate the consequences of such corporate strategies – such as mutual undercutting on employment conditions, threats to close plants seen as uncompetitive. Amongst other things, the strength of coordination of the company induces the EWC to initiate an intense exchange of information and regular meetings, to create time to develop common strategies, and to intensify the development of behavioural norms that span countries and individual operations. A weakly coordinated firm – indicated in a 'one plant, one model' strategy (such as Daimler and Toyota), moderate inter-plant competition and relative low intensity of cost pressures (as was the case for a long period in the case of Daimler) – will tend to impose a lesser burden on EWCs, and place commensurately fewer pressures to develop their own strategies for preserving plants and employment in opposition to management strategies.

The regulatory performance of an EWC – its effectiveness in interest representation – therefore depends, in large measure, on the identified regulatory need. It would reasonable to expect that strong coordination of a company, in the form of parallel production (simultaneous manufacture of a model at a number of plants) and inter-plant competition to win investment and production volumes, generates a correspondingly strong need for regulation that functions as a strong motivation for EWC development (see also Hertwig et al., 2011 and Hertwig et al., 2009a).

Neither the organisational fit between European company and EWC structures nor regulatory need alone determine the type and effectiveness of EWCs. For example, a strongly-coordinated, highly interactive and effective EWC may emerge even if the regulatory need is low. For some EWC actors, working with others in the EWC might be driven by political concerns or a concern to retain an operation. Conversely, a high regulatory need might not yield a strongly-coordinated and effective EWC: this could apply if the prior existence of well-developed cross-border interest representation arrangements in the form of a company or world works council serves as the functional equivalent of an EWC. As far as EWC effectiveness is concerned, a significant role will be played by the subjective perception of regulatory need by relevant actors[42] and a corresponding organisational capability, understood here as the capacity of an EWC, as a collective actor, to aggregate possibly divergent interests on an intra-organisational basis to a sufficient degree to permit inter-organisational negotiation with European management. Despite a high regulatory need, such a capability can founder on the weakness of its central figures (such as the EWC coordinator, secretary or chair), the disinterest of dominant coalitions within the EWC, or a hostile stance on the part of management.

3.2.2 Developmental paths and historical trajectories

Explanation of the specific type and effectiveness of EWCs also rests on a further factor: path-dependence (or trajectory) (Pierson, 2004; Beyer, 2005; Djelic and Quack, 2007). Organisational structures and patterns of culture typically reflect, as 'crystallised' or 'congealed' process, prior outcomes or developments. Although the historical trajectories of organisations, seen as their 'biographies', do not uniquely determine their futures, they form corridors within which development is possible and probable. As such, developmental paths preconfigure the spectrum of current and future options for action and for structural evolution and change for agents. They structure the actions of actors inasmuch as they render certain patterns of action more probable, at the same time making other developmental options less likely.

If the notion of path-dependence is employed not merely in the sense of 'history matters', then a number of mechanisms can be considered that stabilise organisational paths or that can lead to their change or dissolution. Beyer's (2010) critical review of social science path-dependence models identified seven different mechanisms of path dependence, each with its own 'continuity ensuring logic'

42 'Bounded rationality', to which EWC actors and decision-makers are subject, can mean that this need is perceived as high (or low) when considered ex post. There are many examples where an EWC has not been able to develop an appropriate coordination strategy despite a substantial need for regulatory intervention.

(Beyer, 2010: 9).[43] These differing logics in part relate to the economic advantages of adhering to paths that have been previously embarked on or the high costs of revising a path (such as increasing returns on the existing path, functionality etc.). The path-dependence literature lays considerable stress on the primacy of technology decisions as paths that permanently constrain the freedom of organisations to choose or shape future options (see too David, 1986; Ackermann, 2003; Schreyögg et al., 2003; Ortmann, 1995). Other sources of path-dependence have also been located in the field of culture and tradition as well as power and interests (legitimacy of certain patterns in the organisational environment, reducing uncertainty, sequences). The stability of paths is also held to vary, depending on the underlying mechanism, with differing degrees of susceptibility to interruption and change.

In the context of our study, considerations of path-dependence apply to both firms and EWCs. For example, the choice of a particular corporate strategy[44] not only shapes the scope for management in terms of freedom of decision-making, but also renders improbable any abrupt shift in the strategic direction of the company based on the structuring power of the 'industrial model' adopted (on this, see the comprehensive literature on the trajectories of automotive companies: Boyer and Freyssenet, 2002; Boyer et al., 1998; Freyssenet et al., 1998; Freyssenet, 2009c).

For EWCs, it is also reasonable to suppose that these follow particular developmental paths in terms of structures and processes. This concerns, firstly, the foundational conditions of an EWC (the initiative to set it up, management's stance, the role of unions, the provisions and regulations in the founding agreement) and, secondly, events in the further development of the EWC, and in particular, crises, acute inter- and intra-organisational conflicts, divestments and mergers or acquisitions. Learning effects and the circumstances for the emergence of trust, solidarity and, possibly additionally, a distinctive EWC identity and culture are also of significance since – as a number of studies have indicated – an EWC requires a certain amount of time to develop in order for patterns of interaction, communication routines and agreement, common perceptions, expectations and visions to emerge (see, in general, Berger and Luckmann, 1968; Telljohann, 2007; Whittall et al., 2007).

There is strong empirical evidence for the importance of the specific circumstances under which an EWC was established (see Chapter 2.1: of particular relevance is whether an EWC was established before 1994, between 1994 and 1996, and after 1996; under Article 13 or 6; in the face of management hostility, with its toleration, or support; constitution of an employee-only forum or a mixed composition; reference point in term of national legal system etc.). A number of studies have also shown that particular events in the life of an EWC – most notably, European-level

43 Beyer lists increasing returns, sequences, functionality, complementarity, power, legitimacy, and conformity (Beyer, 2010: 9).

44 On different 'profit strategies' and 'industrial models' in the international car industry, see, for example, Boyer and Freyssenet (1999), Boyer and Freysennet (2002), and Boyer et al. (1998).

restructuring and associated conflicts – will influence its operational style, functioning and self-perception. As a consequence, this study assumes that, in addition to the forms of corporate internationalisation discussed in Section 3.2.1, to be established through current and cross-sectional analysis, the developmental path and trajectory of the EWC, which we term the 'trajectory effect', and which is established through historical analysis and longitudinal study, will also have an impact on the nature and effectiveness of an EWC.

3.2.3 Institutional and cultural country contexts

A third important factor that can influence the type of EWC[45] is constituted by its institutional-cultural framework conditions. National contexts and institutional-cultural conditions have already been conceptualised in previous EWC research as the home-country effect,[46] and organisational science has also generated a large number of studies and conceptualisations of the significance of the country-of-origin or business-system effect (Crouch, 1993; Hollingsworth and Boyer, 1997; Maurice and Sorge, 2000; Tempel, 2001; Whitley, 1992b). One of the basic suppositions as far as this explanatory dimension is concerned is that the EWC Directive, as a supra-national EU-wide institutional given, does not determine EWCs' specific organisational structures and patterns of activity (that is, their type). We do not assume here that the EWC Directive has a standardising and long term – isomorphic – effect within the EU. Rather, our supposition is that the influence of supra-national, European regulations and institutions is imbued by national, local, and even sectorally-specific institutional settings as international firms and their EWCs always act in a context of embeddedness in technical and institutional environments (Scott, 2001; Granovetter, 1985). As for- and non-profit organisations they are both an active element in and object of the impact of cultures that contain typical patterns of practices, perceptions and belief systems, norms, and values (see, for example, Schein, 1995).[47] The ways in which actors in international firms and EWCs act are significantly affected by cultural and institutional framework conditions.

---

45 These national contextual factors also influence the form of corporate internationalism itself, an aspect that is beyond the scope of this study.

46 The influence of the company's home-country effect has been shown in a number of EWC studies (see, for example, Lecher et al., 1998b; Müller and Hoffmann, 2002; Kotthoff, 2005). Gilman and Marginson confirmed a major impact of the country-of-origin on the nature of EWC agreements (Gilman and Marginson, 2002). Whittal also noted that the high level of resources available to the BMW central works council as a result of the German system of workplace interest representation was an important explanatory factor for the inability of management to implement its plans to close the Rover Longbridge plant (Whittall, 2000a).

47 According to Hofstede, culture is 'the collective programming of the mind which distinguishes the members of one group or category of people from another' (Hofstede, 2001: 9). On this account, culture is a commonly-held and learned 'code', under which

The systems of employment regulation, and with it the legal and cultural basis for EWCs' activities, diverge markedly between EU countries. For example, there are major national differences in the way in which the EWC Directive was transposed. As far as the national characteristics of employment relations are concerned (for example, juridified vs voluntaristic systems, adversarial vs consensual etc.), the participation rights of workplace institutions for employee representation (information and consultation, up to codetermination and veto rights), the structures and roles of trade union systems (non-political or political unions, pluralism etc.) and, not least, national custom-and-practice in the field of employment relations, the EU constitutes a heterogeneous landscape of national systems of governance (Keller, 1997; Ferner and Hyman, 1999; Hyman, 2004; Whitley, 1992a).[48]

Institutional and cultural influences can be discerned at a number of levels.

- Firstly, and based on the country-of-origin effect, it would be reasonable to assume that national cultural systems that shape interactions together with the institutional settings that prevail at the company's home country will influence forms of (supra-national) interest regulation and representation via EWCs. One key factor in this respect will be the employment regulation regime in the company's home country, understood in this context principally as the formal statutory provisions that regulate interest representation together with national cultural custom-and-practice in this area – that is, established routines, norms and values (Pries, 2010). Some work in the management research literature has also focused the significance of the national cultures and cultural contexts of organisations' foreign affiliates (Ferner et al. 2001; Rosenzweig and Singh, 1991; Wächter et al., 2003).
- Secondly, and additionally, it would be reasonable to suppose that the institutional and cultural circumstances of those countries in which a company is active outside of its home country, and from which employee representatives are delegated to the EWC, also exert an influence and characterise the perceptions, expectations and potential activities of EWC members.
- And thirdly, internationally-operating firms and their spatially distributed affiliates also have their own cultural configurations. The fact that firms and EWCs are subject to a range of influences (EU Directive, national institutional settings, culture of the international company) raises the question as to how these institutional givens and the specific recombination of existing and new institutional elements become 'translated' into organisational life (see Czarniawska and Joerges, 1996; Sahlin-Anderson, 1996).

individuals perceive, think, feel and act. Organsiations also possess a distinctive culture with its own particular 'code'.

48 See in particular reviews of EWC research in various countries in Hertwig et al. (2009b); Rudolph and Stegemann, 2009; Rehfeldt, 2009; Köhler, 2009; Martinez Lucio, 2009; Rampeltshammer and Wachendorf, 2009.

3.2.4 Actors' strategies and personalities

The fourth dimension that can be drawn on to explain the type and effectiveness of EWCs relates to the strategies, interest-based actions, and views of management and employee representatives in relation to the EWC as well as the individual inclinations and personalities of the main actors. One of the key explanatory factors identified in earlier EWC research was the interaction between and strategies of EWC actors. For example, Lecher et al. (2001; 2002) investigated the interactions and relationships amongst EWC members as well as between the EWC as a collective actor and management, trade unions and national workplace representatives. The core of this approach was the issue of the interests of the different groups of actors in relation to the EWC, their strategies, and the specific patterns of interpretation, expectations and norms that this strategic choice rested on.

Although agents' activities are always embedded in social relations and operate against the background of existing institutional orders, workplace social systems (Kotthoff and Reindl, 1990) and historically-developed structures and networks of relationships (Granovetter, 1985) – and as such any explanation must be linked with path-dependence and institutional settings – actors, nevertheless, can choose to act differently to the option most favoured by institutional and historical circumstances (Giddens, 1984). Indeed, individual and collective actors enjoy a high degree of autonomy within institutional frameworks. National cultural institutional contexts offer a corridor within which agents move and act (that is, they both facilitate and constrain). Despite institutional limits and restrictions, groups of actors have scope to engage in strategically calculated and situation-specific action, and can behave in ways that diverge from those actions most favoured by the institutional context (see, for example, Giddens, 1984; Schimank, 2000; Crozier and Friedberg, 1977).

The fundamental stance or inclinations of groups of actors towards interest regulation (at workplace, national, and EWC level) has a particular significance in this context. There are a large number of studies in the sociology of work and industrial sociology on management strategies and their views of collective employee representation and the perceptions of managers (Bosch et al., 1999; Dilger, 2002; Fischer, 1998; Hauser-Ditz et al., 2008; Minssen, 2006; Trinczek, 1987, 2004). A number of studies have also explored different types and strategies of collective interest representation (Kotthoff, 1981, 1994; Osterloh, 1993; Hauser-Ditz et al., 2008; Müller-Jentsch and Seitz, 1998).

The main questions for an analysis of EWCs concern the issue of whether the EWC is seen as a meaningful institution for interest representation by workplace representatives in the firm's home country, whether central management accepts the EWC as an equal partner, and the strategies pursued by groups of actors as far as participation in the EWC is concerned (instrumentalisation, conflict, marginalisation, cooperation). As far as management strategies are concerned, previous studies have identified a wide range of positions, from a proactive and open stance towards the EWC to a more defensive-repressive strategy (Bartmann and Dehnan, 2009; Whittall et al., 2009; see too Lecher et al., 1999). These differences in strategy and behaviour are not all explicable in terms of objective circumstances but are rooted in subjective preferences, norms and broader ideological perspectives. As a consequence, we make explicit reference to such biographical and other directly personal factors when considering this analytical dimension.

As far as actors' strategies are concerned, EWCs, and the contexts that are relevant for explaining the type and effectiveness of EWC, are treated here as multi-level and multi-agent systems. The EWC and management, and also beyond them any trade unions or employer associations involved, are seen as collective actors subject to differing dynamics of action and legitimation at local, plant, national and European level. At the same time, neither management nor the EWC constitute groups that are necessarily unitary. An EWC brings together a wide range of employee representatives from different countries, and hence differing institutional contexts. Under the EWC Directive, the main counterparty for the EWC on the management side is the so-called 'central management'. However, national and local (plant) managers are also actors, each with their own perceptions, interests, conceptions and strategies in the context of cross-border interest regulation throughout the entire group. Both groups of actors – EWC and management – are, therefore, not only engaged in inter-organisational processes of interaction and negotiation with each other, but also act in a context in which intra-organisational processes of interaction and negotiation are taking place within the EWC (depending on the national system of industrial relations between EWC members, local employee representatives, trade unions, trade union members and employees) and within management (consisting of central management, divisional and functional heads, local management etc.). Moreover, these actors also have access to differing power resources that can be mobilised to secure their interests. These differing power resources are not only or simply the product of immediate material and personal resources but also flow from their educational background, their level of knowledge, and the extent to which they are networked with other actors.

The conditions for intra- and inter-organisational processes and strategies of negotiation were first conceptualised by Walton and McKersie (1965) in a schema that has been used mainly in industrial relations research to analyse collective bargaining processes and the various sub-elements and modes of negotiation (inter-organisational bargaining as integrative and distributive bargaining, intra-organisational bargaining, attitudinal structuring). Walton and McKersie's focus was the analysis of individual negotiations and the historical development of negotiating relationships between trade unions and firms. The core of their analytical schema consisted in sub-dividing negotiations into four sub-processes, which were then deployed to investigate negotiations (Walton and McKersie, 1965: 4f).

Distributive bargaining denotes a mode of negotiation in which the negotiating parties have opposed aims. The object of negotiation is a contested good, and the negotiating situation is viewed by the actors as a zero-sum game in which one party can only gain at the direct and corresponding expense of the other. Collective bargaining between trade unions and employer associations or individual firms often fall into this category.[49] Negotiating tactics that typify distributive bargaining include the use of threats and industrial action.

In contrast, integrative bargaining represents a mode of negotiation based on mutuality and cooperation. It usually occurs where there is a common (workplace) problem, and where the two sides each have an interest in coming to a solution. Integrative bargaining is based on mutual trust, in which the actors are open about their motives, aims and objectives. From the standpoint of game theory, this mode is most likely to yield a win-win situation as both parties gain from solving the problem. Attitudinal structuring is not a mode of negotiation as such but rather embraces actions intended to influence the positions of the other side in order to shape the framework of negotiations and – depending on the negotiating situation – lower resistance, create trust, or achieve a consensus. Both integrative and distributive bargaining can be accompanied by varying tactics of attitudinal structuring. In the case of integrative bargaining one party, for example, might be open about their motives and room for manoeuvre, whereas subterfuge, strategic manoeuvring and open conflict are more likely in distributive bargaining.[50]

Walton and McKersie also encountered 'mixed bargaining' (*idem*, 1965: 373), where both approaches were used in negotiations. For example, workforce cuts can be defined as a distributive issue, and the subject of intense conflict; at the same time, they can also raise integrative elements, such as training and social benefits (ibid. 379).

'Intra-organisational bargaining' sits obliquely in relation to the first two categories. As a rule, the main negotiators are groups or individuals acting on behalf of their organisation, and the aims, strategies and outcomes of negotiations must be referred back to the organisations that they represent or their main decision-makers (the 'principals'). As a consequence, processes of negotiation and agreement take

---

49 Negotiations at workplace or establishment level in countries with workplace bargaining may also constitute distributive bargaining in many instances. In Germany, or other countries that have comparable dual systems, there can be restrictions on the topics over which workplace bargaining can take place, with an express intention to remove distributive bargaining from the immediate workplace, reinforced through the obligation on both sides not to engage in industrial action. However, even here workplace negotiations between works councils and local management, on issues such as grading, which falls within the scope of works councils in Germany, are also defined by the parties as distributive issues.

50 Although each of these negotiating approaches might lead to the same outcome, the consequences of negotiations can differ. If a particular outcome is obtained through distributive bargaining, then the losing party might attempt to influence how the outcome is implemented to their advantage or even to sabotage it. Negotiating outcomes achieved under pressure tend to have high follow-on costs (control and monitoring, implementation) for each organisation. If an outcome is seen by both sides in terms of integrative bargaining, then it is more likely that the actors will have an interest in implementing the result in line with what was formally agreed.

place between these and the negotiating parties (for example, over whether an offer should be accepted or rejected) and these influence inter-organisational bargaining. Individual factors can also play a role (for example, if the lead negotiator has other, or even opposed, aims and motives to those of the organisation or seeks to gain personally through their conduct in negotiations).

For Walton and McKersie, the ways in which negotiators act, and the strategies and tactics that they use, are influenced by three main aspects. The first are the aims of the organisation in the name of which negotiators act. The aims and motivations of the negotiating parties (that is, the organisations and not those individuals sitting at the negotiating table) are seen as given by Walton and McKersie. They are not concerned with the origins of these aims, but rather the conduct of the actors in negotiations against a background of established motivations. Secondly, the situational or contextual circumstances – the negotiating situation – exercises an influence over the choice of tactics and the approach of the negotiators (Walton and McKersie, 1965: 9f). A third aspect, noted by Walton and McKersie more or less in passing, has already been referred to: the negotiators (as 'agents' of their organisation) also have interests that might not always fully coincide with those of the the 'principal', may diverge from them, and might even run counter to them.

Walton and McKersie's framework offers a useful basis for our analysis of inter-organisational bargaining (management v. EWC) and intra-organisational bargaining (between local, national and European groups of actors on both management and the employee side). In relation to negotiating relationships in European automotive undertakings, during the 1990s a 'gradual shift [took place] in approach from formerly *distributive* collective bargaining to a greater emphasis on *integrative* bargaining around issues of job security and competitiveness' (Speidel, 2005: 175f; emphasis added) (see too Sisson et al., 1999). In view of the structural and conjunctural problems of the car industry since the 1990s, growing competition and the rising threat of plant closures, an 'all-in-one-boat' mentality has developed in which workplace parties have been more willing to work to achieve solutions that offer benefits to both parties.

The contextual conditions in which bargaining takes place also embrace a wide spectrum of social relations and structural aspects that can also be assimilated to the approach used here, with its focus on the distribution and coordination of material and human resources, knowledge, culture, and power. Walton and McKersie's supposition that bargaining is influenced by the situational context can be concretised in three respects in relation to these elements.

- Firstly, structures of distribution and established patterns of coordination as well as paths of interaction and communication are relevant aspects that influence bargaining and the bargaining strategies of both employee representatives and management at individual locations within international organisations. These include the established culture of interaction and the regulation of interests in the company, the channels of communication that operate between management and employees, or their representatives, and the influence of affiliates on

strategic management decisions. The structural conditions and historically-established structures of interaction can be viewed as a corridor or path, within (or upon) which bargainers can move and which preconfigures, facilitates and limits their activity.
- Secondly, in line with Walton and McKersie, it is reasonable to suppose that those collective actors engaged in bargaining have differing interests, aims, inclinations and perspectives that influence their negotiating tactics. However, rather than assuming that these aims and motivations are pre-given and fixed, we contend that the parties are embedded in and subject to national (or socio-cultural) contexts of relationships of interest regulation that have developed over time and are also a product, in part, of social and cultural influences. As a consequence, which mode of negotiation will prevail – distributive or integrative bargaining, the definition of a common problem or antagonistic interests – is influenced both by the interests and aims of the actors, their historical experiences and established routines, as well as the structural socio-cultural contexts of relationships of interaction and communication.
- Thirdly, actors also deploy their power resources to prevail in negotiations. Here we can assume that the degree to which a party can prevail over its counterparty is a function of the degree of dependence between the two actors (Emmerson, 1962; Peffer and Salancik, 1979). Parties thus have differential capacities to mobilise power resources.[51] It is also possible for actual (informal) power structures in an organisation to deviate from power structures that are formalised and codified by the organisation's rules, and which may be sanctioned by law (hierarchy, managerial prerogative).

Moreover, internationalisation, or the prospect of this as a strategic option, does not automatically endow companies with an additional power potential. Rather, internationalisation can open up new sources of power for the employee side as a result of the uncertainties that flow from it – limited capacity to plan corporate restructuring, fragility, complexity and the inherent risk of international business activity (Simon, 1957; March and Simon, 1958; Pries, 2002: 47). Because internationalisation strategies and projects involve fragile, complex and incompletely predictable plans, their successful realisation depends to a considerable degree on the fact that employees and their representatives are willing to 'play along' or be incorporated by management.

51 For Crozier and Friedberg (1977), this power is based on the ability to control zones of uncertainty. This involves particular organisational spheres or processes, control of which and whose reliable functioning is of existential significance for other actors in the organisation. Four central zones of uncertainty have been identified: expert knowledge, environmental relationships, flows of information and communication, and the use or organisational riules (see Ortmann, 1995: 52).

3.3 Research methodology

Our theoretical model is operationalised in three steps. The first consists of establishing criteria for assigning companies and EWCs within the four-fold typology of international organisations (global, focal, multinational, and transnational). Secondly, we propose a number of indicators of EWC effectiveness in interest regulation and outputs. And thirdly, we locate and make explicit the corresponding operationalisations of the factors in the four dimensions of the theoretical model.

3.3.1 Typology of firms and EWCs

The advantage of a four-fold typology is that it enables both firms and EWCs to be assigned to a type of internationalisation and, through this, to indicate, in a shorthand way, their principal characteristics. This requires determining whether the patterns of distribution in the organisations under consideration, in terms of material resources, power, culture and knowledge, should be characterised as centralised or decentralised. As far as the dimension of coordination is concerned, this entails establishing the strength of structures of coordination in companies and EWCs.

The features that we establish through empirical research are then located on a four-point ordinal scale. The axis for patterns of resource distribution ranges from highly centralised, somewhat centralised, somewhat decentralised to highly decentralised. The coordination axis ranges from very strongly coordinated, somewhat strongly coordinated, somewhat weakly coordinated, to very weakly coordinated. Such an ordinal scale is appropriate in this context as it allows the variance in the sample to be accurately depicted without implying that it is possible to achieve a high degree of quantitative precision, which is not possible given the qualitative nature of much of the data. As such, whether an organisation was assigned to a category was based on a comparison with other organisations in the sample. For the pattern of distribution, we defined variables that allowed for the measurement of the distribution of material and human resources, the distribution of power and scope for decision-making, and the distribution of organisational-cultural elements and knowledge.

The basic reference point for looking at the companies in the study is the geographical scope of their EWC: operations have only been included if their employees are represented by the EWC. Since the EWC only includes some European countries, we do not take the overall worldwide configuration of the company as the basis for assigning it to one of the forms of internationalisation identified in the typology: rather, we consider only those parts of the company that are subject to an EWC. As a rule, these are European operations. Two problems arose with this approach, however. Since only the European parts of a company could be included, the European 'home country' was not always the actual country-of-origin of the whole group (as was the case with Ford and GM, both from the US, and Honda and Toyota from Japan). In the case of non-European manufacturers, therefore, the European 'home country' was defined as that country in the EU with the most employees. In the cases of GM and Toyota, this meant that the European 'home country' was not the country in which the official European headquarters was located. Toyota's European management is located in Brussels, and employs some 1,000 staff. However, the largest plant is in the UK with 4,000 employees: as a consequence, the UK was deemed the European 'home country'. Similarly, GM's European centre in Zurich employs some 300 staff (as of 2008), and represents more of a bridgehead for the US parent; in contrast, the real (and future) headquarters of Opel, the largest employer in Europe in GM's brands, is in Rüsselsheim, near Frankfurt in Germany.

Many studies of internationally operating firms make use of a number of indicators to measure the pattern of distribution (see, in particular, Ruigrok and van Tulder, 1995; UNCTAD, 2002; 88, 109; Riahi-Belkaoui, 1998, 1999; Fisch and Oesterle, 2003; Pries, 208a; Dörrenbacher, 2000; Welge and Holtbrügge, 2003). The fact that these parameters always relate to companies' global pattern of distribution, but our interest was confined to Europe, meant this data could not simply be ported over. As a consequence, we calculated new indicators with an EU focus, although these lean heavily in conceptual terms on the indicators used in research into organisational internationalisation (typically indicators on the pattern of distribution of employment, output and the location of affiliates).

The degree of centralisation of the distribution of resources in internationally operating firms was measured using three indices: (1) the ratio of employees in the European home country to total EU employment; (2) the ratio of the number of production facilities in the European home-country to the overall number of production facilities in the EU;[52] and (3) the ratio of the volume of production in units in the home-country to overall output in the EU.[53]

---

52 'Production facilities' includes only manufacturing operations – that is, plants carrying out final assembly or manufacturing parts or sub-assemblies. The reason for this is that these operations account for the bulk of employment and, therefore, have a corresponding weight within the EWC. The inclusion of distribution centres, for example, would have led to a ballooning in the number of operations but would have added only a small number of employees. We have also only looked at manufacturing locations as a whole, and not individual plants or sub-operations within sites. Locations with a number of individual plants (in some cases legally independent units), as at VW Wolfsburg or GM Bochum, are counted as one site (and usually referred to as a 'plant') for calculating the site index as this always is only concerned with the spatial and social unit of operations.

53 For items (1) and (2) the main sources were companies' Annual Reports, usually with 2008 as the reference year. Since the financial year of Japanese companies for this periods ended in spring 2009, the 2009 Annual Reports were used for Toyota and Honda. Earlier data was used where developments in the recent past were of particular significance for the structures and activities of collective representation, and have been noted as such in the individual case-studies. Data for item (3) (output) were taken from the statistics produced by OICA (2008).

As far as the distribution of power and decision-making capacity was concerned, the frame of reference chosen was the European level. The distribution of power was measured along five variables.

1. Distribution of strategic competence: this was based on whether the European HQ had sole decision-making rights over strategic decisions, whether there were negotiations between the HQ and affiliates in which affiliates acquired a reasonable degree of influence, or whether individual affiliates – as it were at the end of the scale or scope – were able to make strategic decisions autonomously and without the involvement of the HQ.
2. Decision-making on the distribution of production volumes as between plants: this was measured in terms of whether the HQ was the sole decision-maker over the distribution of production volumes and to what extent affiliates were involved in these decisions.
3. and 4. Distribution of competence on investment and use of personnel: this was measured using a similar approach to (2). We investigated whether affiliates could determine their personnel policies independently (for example, whether heads of departments could hire staff without needing the consent of the corporate centre). We also asked whether there were standardised HR policies and practices developed by the corporate HR department and transferred to affiliates. In the case of investment decisions, we sought to ascertain the extent to which, and within which budgetary envelope, affiliates could make independent investment decisions.
5. Scope for plant managers to influence strategic decisions made by HQ. The range of this scope extended from a centralised arrangement, in which plant managers were not involved at all in decisions, to a broad decision-making scope and opportunities for involvement, in which managers could exercise discursive influence on HQ's decisions or those of top management.

The analysis of the corporate culture was mainly focused on the degree to which the typical modes of activity and operational routines, the system of norms and values, expectations, and patterns of interpretation characteristic of the home-country operations of a company, are also characteristic of its subsidiaries and foreign locations. An organisation in which the cultural features and patterns of the HQ dominate the organisational culture of foreign affiliates and displace local cultural elements has been denoted as having a centralised company culture. In contrast, a decentralised culture is characterised by the fact that foreign affiliates bring their own cultural features into the group and retain their own cultural profile. One initial variable in this area is whether the company has a culture that is officially externally communicated. In the area of vehicle manufacture, this might include the 'Toyota Way', the specific Toyota production system with its aspiration to establish a uniform production culture throughout the company's operations. A second point relates to human resource management practices, and in particular how staff are deployed and the transfer of managers between head-office and subsidiaries.[54] The central issue here is the transfer of standardised HR policies and practices developed at HQ to subsidiaries. We also asked whether foreign plants were managed by host country nationals or always managed by home-country nationals. The third aspect relates to management training. Management training can be carried out in a standardised way at corporate hedquarters or on a more decentralised basis and adapted to national and local practices and traditions, with training provided at local affiliates. A fourth significant aspect concerns the official internal language of the company, and in particular whether the language of the home-country predominates or, as an indicator of the decentralised distribution of cultural elements, foreign affiliates retain their own national languages with English used a form of 'neutral' international language for management communication. Fifthly, we investigated the extent to which functional designations are standardised across all European subsidiaries and, in addition, whether these reflect the specific features of organisational life in the company's home country. One central field for research into the automotive sector concerns the identity of individual brands produced and marketed by a group. While some companies have a plethora of marques that have retained a local or national identity (such as Vauxhall in the UK for General Motors or SEAT in Spain for Volkswagen), other companies adopt a centralised brand approach (such as Ford).

As far as the distribution of knowledge is concerned, our research confined itself to the issue of the distribution of R&D operations within a group. A concentration of strategically significant functions for generating technical innovation in the home-country or at the corporate headquarters was categorised as a centralised distribution. A more even distribution of R&D operations throughout Europe was classed as a decentralised knowledge structure. The issue here was to establish whether strategically significant functions were centralised, with more derivative activities (such as localising design elements to meet national requirements) assigned to foreign locations or, in contrast, whether there was a decentralised distribution of strategically significant R&D operations and areas of work.

Operationalising the dimension of coordination of sub-units within a company proved to be tricky. Initially, we attempted to gain an overview of the relative significance of various instruments of coordination within a company, as – we assumed – that in principle we would encounter a large number of forms of coordination (Kutschker and Schmidt, 2006: 986ff). However, it did not prove possible to ascertain and weight all the individual means of coordination. In addition, it emerged that the use of various instruments of coordination was not, in itself, a reliable indicator of the strength or weakness of coordination within a company. We therefore undertook only a broad analysis of the set of instruments used for coordination, and determining the strength of coordination was concretised through variables more amenable to empirical research.

54 See too Tempel, 2001: 129ff; Ferner and Edwards, 1995.

Initially we investigated whether companies used 'soft' plans or broadly-defined objectives, or whether the amount of elbow room for actors within a firm was stringently controlled through precise plans, directives and programmes. A second variable was the significance of internal supplier relationships. We began with the supposition that where a large number of internal plants for sub-assemblies and components carried out critical operations for final assembly, this would induce a high level of coordination within the firm. The focus of the third aspect was personnel strategy. In this case we investigated whether the exchange of managers and specialists played an important role for the enterprise as a whole. Two further variables concerned decision-making processes on future production volumes and manufacturing orders. In this case, we investigated whether a major role was played by parallel production and whether individual plants competed for production and investment. A further aspect was related to communication within management. Here we distinguished between the frequency and regularity of management meetings, whether there were fixed routines, and who attended meetings. The final aspect was the issue of control. Here we set out to analyse whether there was an internal reporting system, how often the affiliates had to provide standardised reports and key quantitative indicators, and the regulations that applied in this area for foreign and home-country operations.

The analysis of the distribution of resources within the EWC also made use of a quantitative procedure to obtain the basis for advancing propositions about the pattern of distribution and to allow comparison between the EWCs in our sample. For this purpose we developed a number of indices and parameters not previously applied in EWC research. The distribution of resources within an EWC was measured with three items. The first related to the ratio of EWC seats occupied by representatives of the home country to the total number of seats on the EWC. In instances in which home-country members occupied a comparatively high number of seats, this was taken as an indicator of a somewhat centralised distribution. If the home-country members had a relatively low share of the seats available, this was seen as indicating a somewhat decentralised distribution.

Since the distribution of seats is not usually independent of the distribution of employees across countries, it was necessary to obtain information about the share of home-country EWC members in relation to home-country employees in the overall EU workforce. In order to capture this, we developed an EWC representativeness index. This index expresses the home-country share of EWC seats in relation to the home-country share of employees represented by the EWC.[55] A value of one indicates that EWC seats are distributed in proportion to the distribution of employment. A value of less than one indicates a disproportional distribution in favour of host-country employees (or plants), whereas a value of greater than one

55 As a formula, the index is calculated as follows:.

$$\frac{\text{Home-country EWC seats}}{\text{Total EWC seats}} : \frac{\text{Employees in European home-country.}}{\text{Total EU employment.}}$$

means that the distribution is unequal to the advantage of home-country operations. As a third indicator, we took the share of home-country seats in the steering committee (or equivalent) of EWCs. The values (which, in theory, can range from 0 to 100 per cent) of the EWCs in our sample provide an additional item of evidence on the degree of centralisation of this forum.

Finally, and thirdly, we investigated the extent to which the EWC had access to resources (staff, use of external experts, finance for training and advice, access to trade unions etc.), and how this scope for access was distributed between EWC members at the home country and other EWC members (Waddington, 2011). This also involved ascertaining whether there was a secretary at the headquarters of the company and, by implication, an individual more accessible to home-country employee representatives. Overall, we assumed that the distribution of resources based on these variables was unequal if the European home country had a higher number of seats than the average of our sample, both on the EWC as a whole and its executive committee, and if the access of the home-country members to resources was markedly more favourably arranged than for host-country EWC members.

Closely related to the distribution of resources within the EWC is the issue of competence and decision-making power on the EWC.[56] For this we defined three variables. Firstly, we asked who determined the issues that were to be dealt with by the EWC. This was seen as highly centralised if the home-country EWC members (or another centre) were, in practice, able to determine the issues for consideration. It was classed as somewhat centralised if these decisions were made in the select committee (or equivalent). Finally, power in this areas was seen as decentralised if all EWC members enjoyed comparatively equal scope to participate in these decisions.

The second variable was the nature of decision making in the EWC. This could range from discursive-democratic to unilateral-authoritarian. The third variable was concerned with the question of who functioned as the interface to management. In this instance too, it was conceivable that central functions were exercised by home-country EWC members, which would indicate a centralised distribution. The distribution would be decentralised of, for example, posts were rotated, and the role of acting as the interface to management would be occupied by a series of EWC members in turn.

As far as the distribtion of cultural elements was concerned, our aim was to establish whether the practices of interest representation, expectations and interpretations from the home country determined and dominated the EWC (centralised

56 In reality, there is a substantive connection and a positive correlation between the distribution of material and staff resources, power, and knowledge. However, we initially assume here that a large number of seats on the bodies (which, at least theoretically, correspond with the distribution of voting rights on the EWC) and the availability of financial resources (for training, advice, travel etc.) as a material resources, access to informal social networks as power potentials, as well as privileged access to information (knowledge) should be investigated separately as determinants of the structure of distribution.

culture), or whether there was a diversity of cultures or any independent culture that embraced all EWC members and which reflected the elements from several of the cultures represented in the EWC (decentralised culture).[57] A number of specific aspects were looked at. Firstly, we investigated whether national features, in terms of institutions of employment regulation, were taken into account within the EWC. This included whether scope was made to accommodate trade union pluralism, as in Belgium, France, Italy and Spain, in the composition of the EWC. While these characteristics are expressly referred to in some EWCs, with the aim of ensuring that all countries and operations feel represented, others are governed by a principle of simple proportionality based on workforce size.

As a second aspect, we looked at the languages used in the EWC. The fact that official meetings are now usually interpreted, as provided for in most EWC agreements, led us to look instead at the languages used in everyday communication. As with companies, it is possible that the language of the home country dominates the EWC, or that English has been adopted as a *lingua franca.* Thirdly, we considered the role of uniform (cultural) practices (cultures of communication and meetings), symbols or important individuals that guide the EWC as an organisation (Hofstede and Hofstede, 2005).

In contrast to companies, the distribution of knowledge within EWCs could not be defined in relation to strategic R&D know-how. Rather, for an EWC relevant knowledge includes information about the activities of the company and its strategic planning. We have supposed that knowledge could be defined as centrally-distributed if strategically relevant knowledge is monopolised by home-country institutions, without information being distributed to, or reaching, host-country EWC members. A second aspect concerns the compilation and distribution of the minutes of EWC meetings and meetings of the EWC's governing forums. There is a wide spectrum of possibilities here, ranging from a swift and comprehensive distribution of the minutes (translated into all the languages used in the EWC) to a complete lack of any minutes.

The issue of the coordination of EWC activities was depicted using six variables.

1. The number of regular EWC meetings of the EWC as a whole.
2. The number of meetings of the steering committee (or equivalent).
3. The number of extraordinary meetings held.[58]

57 In order to determine the type of internationalisation, we adopted a simple centralised/decentralised dichotomy. We were able to pursue the question of the strength – and hence the force guiding action, or the homogeneity, multiplicity or contradictoriness, spread and degree of internalisation – of cultural elements (see Schreyögg, 1999: 451ff.) in some of the case-studies: however, we did not investigate it sufficiently systematically to be able to incorporate it as a dimension in the typology.

58 We asked about the number of actual meetings held, not the number provided for in the EWC agreement.

4. The role of informal communication between EWC members was seen as significant, as this also revealed the internal structure of communication. Coordination was seen as strong if there was a high density of interaction and communication between EWC members or, at least, between some members. We distinguished between different forms of coordination and communication: communication can function on a networked and decentralised basis between individual EWC members; it can also radiate out from the home-country centre, which coordinates communication.
5. Whether there was technical support for communication within the EWC in the form of contact details for members, an e-mail list or an intranet. We asked how well individual EWC members knew each other, and whether the body was, more or less, an anonymous one, in which making contact was difficult as EWC delegates changed so often.
6. Finally, we examined the role of working groups within EWCs that met on occasions in addition to regular meetings of the body. A high frequency of such groups would be interpreted as an index of stronger coordination.

3.3.2 Effectiveness, outputs and level of EWC activity

In order to arrive at a reasonably nuanced assessment of the effectiveness of interest regulation by EWCs, we distinguished between two dimensions: the level of activity and the output of interest representation. Whereas the level of activity can be read off, for example, from the number of extraordinary meetings held or formal agreements concluded with management, the output of interest representation denotes actual results in terms of how well EWCs succeeded on our two key measures for employees: maintaining employment levels and securing the continued existence of plants.

Distinguishing between these two dimensions of EWC effectiveness seemed necessary for several reasons. Firstly, the strength of an EWC, in terms of its capacity to represent employee interests, can only be judged in the context of the problems and challenges it faces. There will be less need for an EWC, and hence less motivation, to engage in regulatory activity in a company that is economically successful. The absence of formal agreements between management and EWC in such a case would, therefore, be a result of the fact that there is simply less call for such provisions. Although a 'symbolic EWC' might be characterised by a low level of representative effectiveness, this needs to be interpreted and understood in comparison with other EWCs in terms of context and situation – how the company is structured, the economic situation, management strategies, and the regulatory need that follows from this. Conversely, a high level of activity can be the result of serious business difficulties that have generated high levels of conflict in a company but without this necessarily leading to employee interests being taken account of in company decisions or being effectively represented at European level.[59]

Secondly, EWCs, especially in large groups, are not the sole institution for the representation or regulation of interests. The scope for the EWC to establish a profile as an independent actor in this area varies from company to company. It is likely to be lower where (prior to 1994) independent institutions for interest regulation were established between management and collective employee representation or where other collective actors, such as trade unions (possibly rivalrous), have aspired to determine the dynamic of negotiations at European level.[60] An EWC as an independent collective actor at European level can get into difficulties, for example, where there are strong company-related institutions for interest regulation at national or world level (such as national group works councils or world company councils). As a consequence, analysing the level of activity and regulatory effectiveness of EWC must consider the role and function of an EWC in the overall set of arrangements for interest regulation throughout a whole group as well as the corresponding institutional environments.

3.3.3 Investigating influencing factors

One of the main contentions of this study is that research and approaches from organisational sociology and organisation theory can be profitably adopted for research into EWCs. As a consequence, and compared with other influences (country effects, developmental path and actors' strategies), we have placed particular stress on, firstly, the dimension of 'company type' as an influencing factor (that is, the form of internationalisation) and, secondly, in line with main supposition of our research, on the proposition that there is an organisational fit between the type of firm and the type of EWC Correspondingly, this dimension has been operationalised using a much wider range of variables and indicators than the other three dimensions, which were dealt through a consistent approach in all the case-studies (analysis of critical events and turning-points on a developmental path, role of key individuals) but with fewer and less specific variables and characteristics.

On the issue of the institutional setting and country effects, information was collected on the regulatory regime for employment in a number of selected countries

---

59 In contrast to works councils in large German companies, for a variety of reasons most EWCs are some way removed from being able to provide ongoing interest representation. The resources they have available (time and financial) and their fundamental logic of activity do not allow them to conduct interest representation on an everyday basis as a well-functioning works council might.

60 In many companies, there is a system made up of a number of different, but functionally closely-interwoven, institutions of interest regulation. Change in the external (legal) framework, such as the EWC Directive, does not necessarily lead to the dissolution of old institutions, and the installation of new arrangements – but rather, probably, over the longer term to the transformation of established structures.

(Belgium, Germany, France, UK, Poland, Spain, Japan) using secondary sources (EIRO, 2006; Ferner and Hyman, 1999; Hertwig et al., 2009; Morley et al., 2006; Traxler, 2003; Traxler and Huemer, 2007). We were interested in particular in systems of workplace interest regulation and interest representation outside of the workplace through trade unions, but also wanted to understand custom and practice, expectations and perceptions of 'the norm' on the part of actors in relation to collective interest regulation in these countries.

Aspects of path-dependence for companies were explored through an analysis of their historical development and changes in production systems and corporate strategies. There are a number of comprehensive and richly detailed studies in the literature on the automotive industry dealing with the trajectories of individual manufacturers (Boyer et al., 1998; Freyssenet et al., 1998; Freyssenet, 2009c). We were also able to outline the influence of critical events in the recent past on EWCs or relationships between management and the EWC by means of interview data. For the EWC, we looked at the circumstances prevailing when they were first constituted and important events in their history. Where possible we attempted to reconstruct the conduct of the EWC (or those actors involved in it) in crisis situations. The main issue was an heuristic understanding of the situation, interests and perceptions of the actors. Information for this was collected both through interviews as well as through secondary analysis of the relevant literature.[61]

The strategies, views and perceptions of EWC members and management representatives were also researched through questions posed in interviews. For example, interviews with managers asked about whether they considered that EWCs should develop into a negotiating partner, and the actual and prospective role of their own EWC in processes of interest regulation. EWC representatives were asked about the conduct, motivations and strategies of other EWC members in order to be able to investigate the diversity of perspectives and interpretations within the EWC.

3.3.4 Data collection methods and analysis

The research project, the main results of which are presented in this study, was divided into two phases. In the first, between March 2007 and February 2009, six manufacturers were studied: Volkswagen and Daimler with their headquarters in Germany; Renault and PSA Peugeot Citroën in France; and the two US-headquartered firms, Ford and General Motors. In the second phase, between March 2009 and March 2010, the two Japanese manufacturers Honda and Toyota were included, and an overall comparison made of all eight companies.

The automotive industry offers especially favourable circumstances for the study of our research questions. Firstly, the car industry is characterised by a very complex

61 There are many studies of crises and conflicts at EWCs: for Renault (Rehfeldt, 1998); Volkswagen (Haipeter, 2000; Müller et al., 2004a: Speidel, 2005); GM (Bartmann and Dehnen, 2009; Banyuls et al., 2008).

product produced through and by means of a highly articulated value-chain that extends not only within Europe but across the globe (Canzler and Schmidt, 2003; Pries and Hertwig, 2005; Pries and Bosowski, 2006; Freyssenet, 2009c). The complexity of the value-chain, which is inherent in the nature of the product, creates a need for a high level of integration between a number of – differing – production facilities and sub-units, with corresponding demands on the negotiation and coordination of interests at European level. In fact, plants are distributed across a number of EU countries in the case of virtually all manufacturers in Europe, with only a few exceptions.

Secondly, the typical five to ten year product life-cycles in the car industry produce regular intensive internal processes of negotiation and coordination on which (European) plant will produce which model and in what quantities. In this, plant benchmarks as well as bargaining power and, ultimately, long-term agreements between management and employee representatives can play a central role. This involves both inter- and intra-organisational negotiations between the plants of the final assembler as well as (in the context of outsourcing or relocation decisions) between final assembly plants and suppliers.

Thirdly, the European car industry is one of the most significant and innovative in terms of the dynamic of its development and its sheer size. Since the 1990s, it has seen a number of major mergers, restructuring and extensive transfers of production (in particular to the newly-acceded EU member states in Central and Europe), which have been the occasion for negotiations and the resolution of interests at European level between plants. Along with the issue of innovative working time models (as seen at VW and BMW), negotiations around the subject of employment guarantees and retaining operations offer an especially favourable terrain for case study research, and this area has seen the most far-reaching European agreements between managements and EWCs. Finally, the organisation of employees and trade unions in the European car industry exhibits a comparatively high level of Europeanisation, so that the European-wide contextual embedding of EWC structures and negotiating dynamics is further advanced than in other branches (Platzer and Müller, 2011).

Time and resource limitations meant that it was not possible to collect primary data (mainly in the form of interviews) in all countries in which the companies in our sample operated. As a consequence, six countries were chosen for data collection at the plants of the eight companies: Belgium, Germany, France, UK, Poland, and Spain. The selection of plants was guided by a theoretical sampling approach, aimed at the capturing a high degree of variance in the contextual conditions in which manfacturing operations were carried.[62] In particular, we set out to include countries with differing systems of employment regulation (such as Spain and

62 The manufacturers operating in Europe in the study bring together all relevant constellations of companies with headquarters in an EU member state, and companies headquartered in the USA and Japan.

France with a pluralistic union structure and adversarial traditions of regulation; and Germany with a more consensus-based model). As an Eastern European country, Poland was chosen in order to encompass the dynamics of transfers of production, which can create conflicts of interest, and the significance of EWC work for a new EU member state.

Table 1: Interviews with management representatives from home-country and foreign plants

	Management	EWC
Home country	10	32
Foreign	8	41

The initial method for data collection was a systematic documentary analysis. This included company sources (annual reports, company publications), EWC installation agreements (initial, extension, renewal) as well as other relevant academic and press publications. In addition, we were also able to draw on previous studies of selected companies and EWCs for information, some of which proved extremely significant for our research. Secondly, we conducted ninety-one structured interviews[63] with management representatives, EWC members, experts and advisors, consultants or research staff of EWCs. In addition, we held interviews with representatives of trade unions and employee associations.[64]

In addition to these interviews, we were able to attend preparatory EWC meetings and a select committee meeting for the employee side as observer.

63 The references to interviews in the case studies that follow are indicated as follows: DE01, VWM03, PSAE02 etc. The first letters represent the company (D = Daimler, VW = Volkswagen, PSA = PSA Peugeot Citroën, R = Renault, H = Honda, T = Toyota, F = Ford and GM = General Motors. This is followed by a letter indicating whether the interview was with an EWC member (E) or a management representative (M). The number indicates the number of the individual interview.

64 Interviews were transcribed and analysed using a schema: the findings were then progressively summarised. The basis was operationalising the typoplogy and the influencing factors and contextual conditions envisaged in the theoretical model as well as EWC interest representation outputs outlined above.

Chapter 4: Daimler

4.1 The Daimler AG Group

4.1.1 History and characteristics of Daimler AG

Daimler AG, with its headquarters in Stuttgart, is one of the oldest car manufacturing companies in the world. The company was founded under the name Daimler Benz AG in 1926 through a merger of the Daimler Motoren Gesellschaft (established in 1890) and Benz & Cie Rheinische Gasmotorenfabrik (established in 1883). The company has produced cars, commercial vehicles and diesel engines since the early twentieth century. From 1933 up until the end of the Second World War, the company was heavily engaged in armaments production. Following the Second World War, the company undertook a number of acquisitions that eventually led to its becoming the largest German industrial undertaking.

The internationalisation of the group took place in varying forms in each of its individual business areas with markedly different internationalisation profiles for the two divisions that currently dominate the company, Mercedes-Benz Cars and Daimler Trucks. From the 1950s onwards, the commercial vehicles division has pursued an ambitious acquisition strategy, not only across Europe but also in North and South America. For example, during this period Daimler Benz bought Hanomag-Henschel, Steyr-Puch, the Mexican manufacturer FAMSA, and the US American commercial vehicle producer Freightliner (see Köhler, 2003: 74). The acquisition of Freightliner in 1981 led to the integration of a major independent international brand into the group (see Pries, 1999b: 45). By contrast, up until the 1990s the cars division pursued a global strategy under which luxury-class vehicles were manufactured using a production model based on German skilled labour, with the entire world market serviced by cars exported from plants located in Germany. In 1964 Daimler sold Auto Union to Volkswagen and after that point the cars division focused exclusively on the premium class with vehicles manufactured almost exclusively in Germany.[65] During this period, measured in terms of the shares of foreign investment and employment abroad, the Daimler Benz group as a whole exhibited a much lower level of internationalisation than other major car manufacturers (see Riehle, 1996: 254). The group's international presence was concentrated almost wholly exclusively in the commercial vehicles division and sales operations. For example, by the late-1970s Daimler had more than 160 sales subsidiaries throughout the world.

---

65 The exceptions were CKD joint ventures with local partners in South Africa (1966), Indonesia (1971), and Austria (1979): see Köhler, 2003: 74.

In order to reduce the risks of an exclusive focus on cars, exposed by the oil crisis of the late-1970s, Daimler Benz embarked on a strategy of widening the scope of its operations to embrace financial services, electronics, and aerospace. During the 1980s, a number of acquisitions were made in these areas, including AEG, Dornier, Fokker, MBB and MTU. Against all expectations, in 1992/3 this restructuring process ultimately propelled the company into a serious crisis that also enveloped the company's core business – the cars division (see Köhler, 2003: 74). The strategic response, aimed at securing the company's position in the face of the challenges of an increasingly globalised market, was to aim at becoming a global car business, a 'World Plc', which would operate and be active in all key markets. This approach, which was initiated and driven forwards under the leadership of the new CEO Jürgen Schrempp, reached its apogee in the merger between Daimler and Chrysler in 1998.

The period after 1990 witnessed a number of fundamental changes within the group as Daimler began to transform its product and marketing strategy and abandon its concentration on luxury cars. The small car segment, and with it younger consumers, was addressed by the introduction of the SMART car and the A class in 1997. A sports utility vehicle, the M class, was introduced and produced exclusively in the United States. The production system was also changed through a modernisation programme aimed at raising productivity, which had lagged behind its competitors since the 1980s: the main thrust of this strategy was a lowering of the level of vertical integration ('manufacturing depth') in the company's manufacturing operations and closer cooperation with suppliers (Pries, 1999b: 47ff.). In contrast to other car manufacturers, the company has pursued a 'solitary factory' approach, under which one plant produces a single product and product line, and Daimler has not adopted the platform strategy pursued by other manufacturers (see Köhler, 2003: 77).

In the mid-1990s, the company embarked on a globalisation offensive aimed at internationalising its production arrangements by installing new products in new markets and drawing on existing globalised production structures in its commercial vehicle and bus business, such as the complete knock-down facility (CKD) in Mexico. Other CKD assembly plants were opened during the 1990s in Africa and Asia (see Pries, 1999b: 47ff.). The cars division was returned to its status as the core area and Mercedes Benz AG was reintegrated into the overall group. In addition, a number of companies acquired during the 1980s were either sold or closed. Overall a recentralisation of the group took place.

> The hierarchies and business divisions were reduced, the reporting and communication channels were shortened, the headquarters staff numbers reduced, competencies bundled, and the company passed through a dynamic concentration and recentralisation process (Köhler, 2003: 75f.).

In May 1998 Daimler merged with the US American car manufacturer Chrysler. The whole company was renamed DaimlerChrysler AG and became the fifth largest car manufacturer in the world. The group CEO, Jürgen Schremm, stated that the merger would lead neither to plant closures nor mass redundancies. As both manufacturers produced complementary product lines (Daimler – premium and luxury cars; Chrysler intermediate class cars, vans and SUVs) only modest synergies from rationalisation were expected. Although touted as a merger of equals, in reality the exercise was more accurately described as a takeover of Chrysler by Daimler. The nine-year history of DaimlerChrysler AG was characterised by a slew of acquisitions and disposals. After years of losses – according to the company, amounting to €500 million[66] – in May 2007 the Chrysler Group and its affiliated financial services company was sold to the American finance investor Cerberus Capital Management L.P., with Daimler retaining merely 19.9 per cent of the shares. In October 2009 the remaining group was renamed Daimler AG (see Köhler, 2009). Since its separation from Chrysler the Daimler group has consisted of four divisions:[67] Mercedes-Benz Cars; Daimler Trucks; Daimler Financial Services; and Mercedes-Benz Vans, Daimler Buses and other activities (VBO – vans, buses, other). In addition, the company also has a sales and distribution organisation. With around two-thirds of global employees, the cars and trucks divisions are by far the largest business areas, followed by the sales operations, which itself employs just short of 50,000 people worldwide. The sale or closure of a large number of divisions – such as AEG in the technology area or Debis Air Finance in the financial services area – has meant that since 2006 the cars division has returned to its status as Daimler's core business.

> DaimlerChrysler thus returned to its origins as a company focused on the automotive business leaving behind the former dreams of a diversified technology corporation and integrated mobility and transport systems company (Köhler, 2009: 320).

The brand portfolio currently consists of ten brands: Mercedes-Benz, Smart, Maybach, Freightliner, Sterling, Western Star, Mitsubishi Fuso, Setra, Orion, and Thomas Built Buses. In 2008, Daimler had seventy-two manufacturing operations worldwide (Daimler, 2008, 222), and sold a total of 2,078,922 vehicles (2007). The capital structure of the company is widely dispersed: 58.4 per cent of the company's equity are held by institutional investors, with 22.1 per cent held by private investors. The two largest shareholders are the Emirates of Kuwait with 6.9 per cent and, since 2009, Aabar Investments with a share of 9.1 per cent. The company holds 3.5 per cent of its own shares.[68]

---

66 See <http://www.spiegel.de/wirtschaft/0,1518,482790,00.html> accessed on 30 May 2010.

67 In 2010, the VBO division was broken up into two separate divisions, vans and buses.

68 Daimler, Annual Report 2008. Also <http://www.daimler.com/dccom/0-5-7196-49-70868–1-0-0-0-0-0-8-7164-0-0–0-0-0-0-0.html#bm1236086862> accessed on 31 May 2010.

4.1.2 Distribution of resources, power, culture and knowledge in Daimler AG

The distribution[69] of resources, power, culture and knowledge within the Daimler AG group is notable for the high level of centralisation on all these dimensions. In particular, measured in terms of the distribution of resources – employees, plants and production volumes – Daimler is the most centralised company in our sample (see too Figure 21 in the Appendix). However, there are marked differences in the degree of centralisation in individual divisions (Daimler, 2008: see too Köhler, 2009: 317). Whereas the cars division remains highly centralised, Daimler Trucks and Vans and Buses are more decentralised. Most vehicles produced by Mercedes-Benz Cars in 2008 were manufactured in Germany. There is only one non-German plant in Europe, located in Hambach in France.[70] Daimler Trucks is a much more internationally organised business than the cars division: only seven of its thirty-three global plants are located in Europe. Most of the products of Mercedes-Benz Vans and Buses are manufactured in Germany. Of the total of twenty-two plants, eleven are in the EU.

In terms of the distribution of employees across all divisions, Daimler continues to exhibit the highest level of centralisation of all the companies in our sample: 86 per cent of the 194,233 employees in Europe were employed at home-country locations. For VW this ratio was 77 per cent, followed by Renault with 73 per cent and PSA with 62 per cent. In terms of employment globally, and despite the relatively high level of internationalisation of some of the divisions, 61 per cent of all employees are located in the home country: this compares with 53 per cent at VW, 55 per cent at PSA, and 47 per cent at Renault. The company's largest plant, at Sindelfingen near Stuttgart, on its own accounts for 15 per cent of all employment in Daimler's European operations.

69 Since the scope of the EWC embraces the entire group in Europe, the following discussion of the structures and coordination processes of the company always relates to all Daimler AG's divisions.

70 Worldwide there are other Mercedes-Benz Cars plants, including in the USA, South Africa, Argentina, and China, with smaller plants in Vietnam and India assembling vehicles for the local market.

Figure 3: Distribution of Daimler AG operations in Europe, 2008.

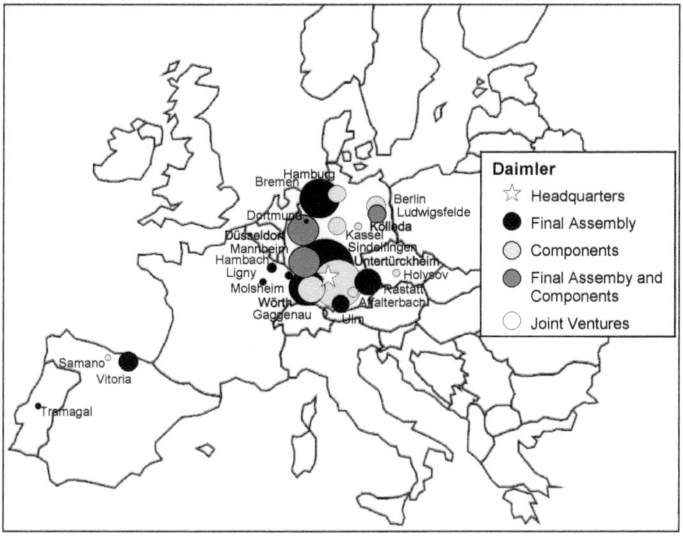

Source: compiled by the authors based on Daimler's Annual Report 2008; symbol sizes are proportionate to the number of employees at each site.

The geographical distribution of operations is also centralised. Globally Daimler had seventy-two plants in 2008 (see Daimler Annual Report 2008): twenty-two of these (and hence 31 per cent of the world total) were located within the European Union. As the home country, Germany had fifteen manufacturing facilities, accounting for 21 per cent of the global total – a value broadly the same as VW (22 per cent) but far exceeded by Renault (34 per cent) and PSA (39 per cent). However, in relation to plants within the EU, Daimler takes first place with 68 per cent of its plants in its home country, followed by Renault and PSA (each with 63 per cent). In comparison, Ford (20 per cent), GM (25 per cent) and VW (31 per cent) are much more decentralised.

Of the more than 2.174 million units produced in 2008 in its own global manufacturing facilities (OICA, 2008), 57 per cent were made in German plants. If the production volume of the home country plants is compared with the output of all EU plants then the proportion rises to 83 per cent. In contrast, VW has a value of 56 per cent, a seventeen percentage point difference, followed by PSA (54 per cent) and Renault (47 per cent), with the latter having a much more decentralised structure of production.

Table 2: Distribution employees, plants and production, Daimler AG (2008)

	Employees	**Plants**	**Production**
World	273,216	72	2,174,299
EU	194,233	22	1,505,505
EU Home-country (Germany)	167,753	15	1,244,334
Largest plant	28,804	–	–
Share EU/world	71%	31%	69%
Share EU home-country/EU	86%	68%	83%
Share EU home-country/world	61%	21%	57%
Share largest plant/EU	15%	–	–

Source: author's compilation based on Daimler AG Annual Report (Daimler, 2008) and OICA (2008)

The distribution of power within Daimler AG also seems to be more centralised than in the other companies in our sample. The most important strategic decision-making powers within the group lie with the group management board and within the individual divisions. For example, decisions about setting up new plants or the allocation of production volumes are made by the boards of the divisions. Decisions in the car division are relatively independent of those in the commercial vehicles division.

> Decisions are made in each operatiional unit. Those responsible for the truck area decide whether we will open a factory in Russia or whether we will no longer produce a product at a plant. The head of the cars division decides whether we'll build the successor to the A class in Rastatt or in Eastern Europe (DM01).

Investment proposals are cascaded from individual plants via the divisional head of the business unit. (cars, trucks etc.). However, the group management board makes the final decision centrally, approves the financial resources requested, and specifies the required returns. The application and deployment of investment are, however, planned and decided by the divisional boards.

> The management board clearly has the final say on investment decisions, and nothing will shift that. Plants and business units have to do the necessary preparatory work and they must be able to justify these and then they develop them and make their application. However, the management board has the final say on any investment decision (DE03).

Individual plants have a right to be consulted but not to make a decision. However, individual divisions have a comparatively high degree of independence as the financing of investments is an issue that barely crosses divisional lines in terms of planning and investment appraisal.

There has also been a centralisation of power in the human resources area in recent years and the extensive autonomy previously enjoyed by plant-level HR managers is now much more constrained. Although decisions on the deployment of personnel can still be made with a reasonable degree of autonomy at individual plants, the head of HR at an individual plant has only limited powers to hire personnel on indefinite contracts of employment: rather 'they have to consult with headquarters and the head office can also reject the proposal' (DE03). Staffing decisions made locally in plants – also against the background of commitments to agreements on headcount between management and the group works council – are always controlled and checked at corporate headquarters.

> In terms of personnel, although local plants have some decision-making scope, this is always subject to firm control by corporate management on questions about how many staff we use, changes in the total level of employment, and whether we hire on a fixed-term or indefinite basis or use agency staff (DE03).

These limits were highlighted by a member of the works council in terms of the shifting competencies and distribution of decision-making power between head office, plant management and local HRM.

> The plant manager and head of personnel used to be the key decision-makers in the plant. And if I had to deal with them about a problem, such as an important works agreement or some other issue, then they were the two main people I went to. That's no longer the case. My HR head has now been downgraded in the management hierarchy and he has a chief at headquarters who he has to clear everything with. So if I think that something is a very fundamental question, that is there's a basic disagreement on an issue, then I usually just pick up the phone and call the head of personnel at *corporate headquarters* because *he's the boss of my boss and I might as well speak with him right away* (DE02, emphasis added).

As far as the *cultural* aspects of the company are concerned our research suggests that in the overwhelming number of cases can also be regarded as 'somewhat centralised' in terms of the ordinal scale employed. However, the deployment of managers can be characterised as 'somewhat decentralised'. Both the share of foreign managers in German plants as well as of German managers in foreign plants is low. Foreign plants mostly employ local managers on this basis that they better understand local culture and lifestyle differences than German managers. 'It's claimed that if you were to put a German in South Africa then you'd have even more problems in the event of disputes. It must be someone who understands the locality' (DE02).

Nevertheless, previous studies have suggested that there was a very active interchange and use of German managers in foreign affiliates and therefore a comparatively high export of German cultural elements. Following the Chrysler merger, top management of Chrysler was replaced in 2000 by a management team dominated by Germans – with a German CEO and COO –to this extent 'Germanising' Chrysler's management (Köhler, 2009: 313). The same took place during restructuring efforts at Mitsubishi and Freightliner (ibid. 316).

Management training is usually centrally devised at the Daimler Academy in Stuttgart but delivered locally.[71] The Daimler Corporate Academy was founded in 2006 and 2007 and consists of two major divisions: the Leadership Academy and the Business Academy. The Leadership Academy delivers training for all levels of management. The Business Academy is responsible for specialist training for finance, purchasing, HR and compliance and any training that crosses technical functions throughout Germany. This central facility enables training to be delivered to a common standard.

Other elements of the corporate culture also indicate strongly centralised elements. For example, the Daimler brands and management positions are categorised using the same terminology worldwide. Although, following the merger with Chrysler, the organisational language became English, German continues to be spoken at management meetings if the majority of participants are German-speaking.

The distribution of knowledge is fairly highly centralised at the home country, where strategically important research facilities are located. Daimler's knowledge resources have been centralised since 2006 and, for the most part, located in the cars division (Sindelfingen and Untertürkheim) (Köhler, 2009: 313). In 2008, of a total 18,900 employees in R&D in the whole group 11,600 were employed by Mercedes-Benz Cars. Overseas R&D operations employed only 3,600 staff (Daimler, 2008: 61).

However, in some divisions local operations play a very significant role in R&D. Although most activities take place in the R&D centre at Untertürkheim, responsibility and control of these activities rests with the divisions with a major role played by the manufacturing plants.

> We've got a central focus in Untertürkheim. [...] *But responsibility always rests within each of the business areas.* Although there is a central board member for R&D, responsibility lies with the divisional boards. And within the divisions, the divisional head is responsible for design and development of their own products. The focus is on central development and then additional activity here at the local operation (DE03) (emphasis added).

4.1.3 Coordination of business activities

Our research into coordination within Daimler AG suggests that the strength of coordination processes varies. There is very strong coordination within each of the individual divisions, but generally rather weak coordination within the group as a

71 'Some 1,800 managers at more than 60 locations participated in Leadership Academy programs in 2007, and more than 12,000 employees attended the Business Academy. In addition, in 2007, some 2,500 interdisciplinary qualification events attracted more than 25,000 participants' (Daimler Sustainability Report, 2008: 55).

whole, which is the reference point for our study. Individual business activities are integrated and 'pillarised' within each of the divisions.

There are efforts at group-level to standardise HR policies and practices. For example, in line with pressure from the group works council, issues of employment policy are always centrally regulated. Specific directives and guidelines, which are negotiated between corporate management and employee representatives, apply for all divisions and locations.

> Jointly we have managed to establish that many basic decisions should apply throughout. One quite interesting issue is the question of employment policy: that is work organisation, and teamwork. However, the group works council is very eager for such issues to be uniform. That is, we don't want a completely different philosophy of teamwork in the cars division compared with commercial vehicles. This idea has been more strongly argued for by the group works council than by management. And in the area of gainsharing we've got no difference between buses and vans and cars and lorries (DE03).

In terms of production, individual business areas operate relatively independently, with no cross-divisional supply relationships. However, intensive relationships exist with suppliers within individual divisions. For example, each division has its own – separate – range of component manufacturers.

Management meetings take place at various levels of the hierarchy. At the level of plant manager, heads of operations regularly communicate through personal meetings and teleconferences with their chief operating officer. There are regular meetings of the management boards of each brand. R&D takes place both divisionally and cross-divisionally. Since product development is distributed between central R&D and each of the main specialist departments at individual production operations, strong coordination is vital (DE03).

4.2 The Daimler EWC

4.2.1 Establishment and main features

Following negotiations between the German central works council and central management, the Daimler EWC was constituted on 25 July 1996 under the provisions of Article 13 of the EWC Directive, as transposed into German law. International employee coordination has a long tradition at Daimler extending back to the 1980s (see Müller et al., 2004a: 163ff.).[72] A European employee forum was established in 1992 for the sales organisation, covering national marketing and sales offices and showroom staff. Although this was an informal body, company

72 'Unofficial' relationships between German trade unionists and, principally, trade unionists in Brazil have continued to exist parallel to and largely independently of the 'official' international representative bodies (works council, central works council, EWC, World Works Council): see Müller et al., 2004a: 164ff.

management acknowledged and acccepted that it met. This body can be seen as a precursor of the EWC as it was the first cross-border employee representation arrangement within the company. When the EWC was established, employees in the sales operations were incorporated into the EWC in the form of a formal working group.

> There has been a European sales and distribution working party since 1992. These are the European works councils in the sales and distribution operations: that is, works councils from subsidiaries in Europe. Since that time there have been regular meetings to exchange experiences and engage in joint discussions with management. This is a type of forerunner of the EWC (DE01).

The ultimate initiative for setting up a European employee interest representative body was taken by management, which wanted to make use of the Article 13 provisions to create a forum that was 'company specific' (DE01). As a purely employee body the formal structure of the EWC corresponds with the German works council model. In addition, the EWC can also be characterised as a 'group-level EWC' for Daimler AG, in that it embraces all the group's business areas (with representatives of all the Mercedes-Benz divisions, trucks, buses and vans, and distribution). The initial agreement was signed by two representatives of the German group works council, two representatives of group management, and the designated members of the EWC Presidium. Following the takeover of Chrysler, the EWC agreement was renewed on 1 May 2002 and adapted to the new situation.

4.2.2 Distribution of resources, power, culture and knowledge in the EWC

Over the course of its development the composition of the EWC has changed several times. Initially, and up until the merger with Chrysler, the EWC had thirty members and exhibited by a clear dominance on the part of the German employee representatives. A total of twenty seats, in all 67 per cent of the total, were reserved for German works council members, with only ten seats for the then ten other European countries in which Daimler Benz had either production or distribution operations.

Figure 4: Distribution of seats on the Daimler EWC (2008)

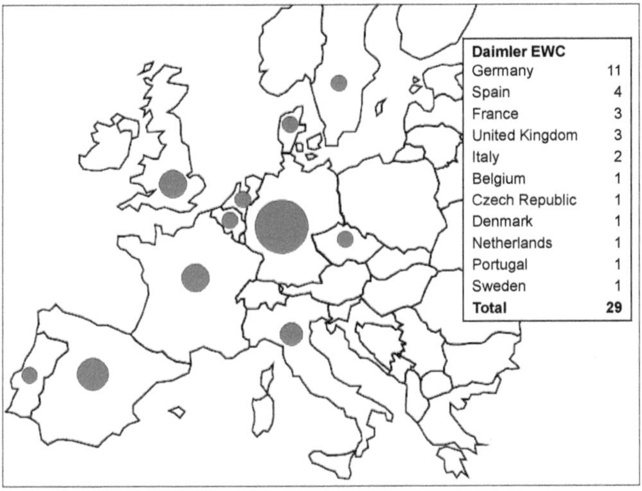

Source: authors' compilation based on Daimler Annual Report 2008.

Since the renewal of the EWC agreement in 2002, the EWC has had twenty-eight members, almost halving the number of German representatives to eleven seats (equivalent to 39 per cent). This has led to a clear shift in the balance between home-country and non-German representatives. As a result, in terms of the relation to employment, German employees are now clearly underrepresented. The EWC representative index[73] at 0.46 is the lowest after General Motors (0.44). The EWCs of the non-European manufacturers (Ford, 0.58: Toyota, 0.63) and of VW (0.53) have slightly higher values (see Figure 25 in the Appendix). EWCs in similarly centralised companies – primarily Renault and PSA – have indices of 0.78 and 0.92 respectively, markedly higher than the Daimler EWC. According to one German EWC member, the distribution of seats reflects the EWC's particular culture. In allocating mandates the key issue has been to integrate foreign operations.

> This is completely in line with our tradition, that we try and make sure that our foreign colleagues are also included. This is nothing new and as a result this distribution of seats also came about in the EWC. In fact, we also did this for the company's supervisory board. We gave up one of our seats on the supervisory board. Initially there was also a representative of the UAW for Chrysler. And after the separation has been carried out we have not taken this seat back but made it available to another foreign colleague (DE03).

73 On the method of calculating this, see Chapter 3.3.1 above.

In this respect the Daimler EWC also resembles the VW EWC and is strikingly different from those of Renault and PSA in which home-country interests dominate – mainly attributable to the pluralistic and competitive trade union system.

Although the share of German EWC members has fallen since 2002, German representatives, with more than a third of all the seats, remain the predominant single contingent. As far as the distribution of EWC seats on a country basis is concerned, the installation agreement specified a formula for calculating this.[74] The selection of foreign EWC members is left to national custom and practice. Of the eighteen non-German members, eleven represent sales subsidiaries and only seven production operations.

The financial resources of the EWC are unequally distributed within Europe. The main outgoings of the EWC are covered by the German central works council. The EWC does not have its own budget: according to a German member of the EWC the company pays for 'everything that is necessary' (DE01). For the German EWC members who are also works council members, and who have time off in full ('facility time') for their duties, there is no problem with getting access to the necessary resources. The costs of travel for foreign EWC meetings are paid for by each local operation (DE01). This arrangement not only means that the bulk of resources for European employee representation are controlled by the company's headquarters, but it can also disadvantage foreign EWC members.

> That is, we can have a conflict if a European member who doesn't have full-time off says 'I need more time off'. Then they have to go to their personnel manager and say 'Hi, I need more time off for EWC work'. That goes on the French budget but not on ours. It can be that the personnel manager says 'Yes OK, but when are you going to do something for the company' (DE01).

The EWC presidium has four members: a chair and two deputies, of whom two are from Germany (central works council chair and their deputy) and one each from France and Spain. This composition can be explained by the fact that only the largest units are entitled to representation on the presidium. In contrast to the EWC as a whole, this clearly reflects the dominance of the German operations, which account for 50 per cent of the seats in the presidium. The presidium meets when necessary and otherwise meets once a year jointly with the EWC.

There is no independent secretariat to organise communication between EWC meetings or prepare annual meetings. These tasks are taken on by an employee of the central works council who is responsible for both world employee representation and the EWC. Their tasks include managing the meetings (meeting organisation,

74 There is one seat per country for between 500 and 1,500 employees. For a workforce of 1,500–3,000, there are two seats, and between 3,000 and 4,500 three seats. There is a further seat for each 3,000 employees beyond this. Some countries in which Daimler has operations are not represented on the EWC because of these thresholds.

compiling, translating and distributing minutes), and supporting the EWC throughout the year: they also represent the main contact point for EWC members.

As far as the distribution of power and scope for influence is concerned, the Daimler EWC is one of the most centrally organised bodies in our sample, most notably through the dominance of German EWC members and the central role played by German codetermination institutions – the works council and central works council. Which issues will be dealt with by the EWC is largely decided by the central works council. Although the agenda for EWC meetings is prepared by the presidium, in which there are two foreign representatives alongside German members, the draft agenda is drawn up by a member of the central works council, who works with the presidium and finalises the agenda in conjunction it.

> We supply the draft. There are a number of regular agenda points that are always the same: report from the chair, that is what took place over the previous year; report of the presidium, what happened and what took place; reports from relevant meetings that are relevant – that is the global employee representative body or supervisory board, whatever is important. Then you've got reports from different countries, and then everyone has a chance to speak (DE01).

The fact that the topics for discussion have been pre-determined by the German employee representative bodies, and that foreign EWC members tend to be more passive, endows the home-country representatives with comparatively high degree of influence.

However, some EWC representatives emphasised that the EWC presidium is a working body – not a decision-making one. Since 'managing EWC business' is a key function of the presidium, the fact that it selects topics for the EWC and arranges them for the agenda is generally seen as positive and supported by the members. Any final decision on topics or strategies is made by the plenary body. In practice, there have been few controversies, and resolutions are usually supported by all present.

> *The presidium makes proposals, and in fact the body expects that.* However, matters are discussed by everyone before a decision is made – which as a rule is also unanimous. Most topics are initiated by Germany, but this does not mean that foreign members cannot put forward their ideas or that they are not considered. It's often the case that the proposals that come out of our German camp are *often seen positively by the foreign members.* They simply don't have our access to information (DE03)

Although all EWC members have a right to propose topics, this option is used to a very different extent by representatives from foreign plants. In many cases they raise topics or problems that are purely national in scope, discussion of which is not allowed within the EWC. Such issues are, therefore, typically dealt with outside the formal annual meetings (DE01).

> The biggest problem continues to be that as long as we have only a right to information and consultation many of the foreign representatives find this difficult to deal with – the fact there are only limited possibilities for the EWC at present. This then leads them

> to try and bring up problems at the EWC for resolution that they cannot solve locally. We often notice that they arrive with pockets full of problems and they say 'Now we've got the EWC we have to make sure that we get everything resolved' (DE03).

In such cases the presidium will choose topics for the EWC in line with the provisions of the installation agreement. Moreover, management will not discuss questions affecting only one site at EWC meetings.

> It's often very disappointing for them when our side has to say 'No' because our management board is not willing to negotiate about what is happening in Portugal, for example, due to the legal position (DE03).

The German EWC members also have a major advantage over other members due to the high level of professionalism fostered by works council activity, which is mainly a result of the statutory provisions for time-off and resources as well as the skills developed by German works council members. The central works council not only has several members with full facility time and a budget, but also employees whose main role is to coordinate the work of employee representation. As with the other companies considered in our sample, VW, Ford and GM, in which German works council members at the companies' head offices play a key role, German employee representatives in the Daimler group also have privileged access to centres of decision-making. The main reason for this is that the German EWC chair, Erich Klemm, is also a member of other decision-making bodies within the group (see Müller et al., 2004a: 176f.): he is not only the chair of the central works council, the group works council and the works council at the company's largest plant in Sindelfingen, but he is also a member of the company's supervisory board. As well as many years of experience and professionalism, he also has the necessary access to top management. As such, the EWC chair serves as an interface to management for the EWC as a whole, based on these multiple roles and privileged access to the most senior managers in the group. He also has numerous contacts with regional and national policy networks.

> There are huge differences, and I mean this without being judgemental, in the level of professionalism. Erich Klemm has been in office for years, he has been the chair of the works council at Sindelfingen, also for many years, and has been a works council member with full facility time for many years. He has a network, links to politicians, to business and to the wider society. To put him on the same level as a local employee representative, perhaps new in office, and who does not appreciate the range of codetermination rights that they are entitled to and may not even have any – you simply can't compare them. It's just not possible to require someone like that to be on the same level, to undertake strategic tasks straight away. There have been many asymmetries from the beginning and you just can't wish them away (DE01).

The asymmetry of power between German employee representatives – and in particular the chair of German central works council – and foreign EWC representatives also generates a culture of representation in which the EWC chair acts as advocate and representative of the foreign members, and the champion of their interests, and is expected to do so by them.

> On the other hand a foreign EWC member will also say 'Well look, you're at the headquarters, you must be able to say what's going on. So tell us, from your perspective, what the problems are. I don't know what's going on in my own country and I need someone to tell me what's happening. And I also need someone who works for me because I can't do everything myself' (DE01).

As far as the distribution of cultural elements is concerned, the Daimler EWC represents a rather centralised forum. However, although the culture of employee representation of the home country exerts a strong influence, there are aspects that point to a more European perspective.

The German features are particularly pronounced in the composition of the EWC, which, in line with German practice, is a purely employee institution. The Daimler EWC is headed by a strong chair, who is viewed as a significant individual with substantial influence over the operations and culture of interaction within the EWC based on his personality and relationship to management. The fact that the bulk of EWC work takes place within German institutions or bodies dominated by German employee representatives – the EWC presidium and the central works council – also points to the dominance of German cultural patterns of employee representation.

A further element that is indicative of the dominance of the home-country culture is the selection procedure for EWC members, as codified in the EWC installation agreement. Although the delegation of EWC members from non-German plants is required to be in line with national custom and practice, and it is up to individual countries to agree locally who should be sent as a member to the EWC, national features of other European employee representative systems, such as trade union pluralism, have not been taken into account due to the limited number of EWC seats. In the UK, this has led to serious conflicts between trade unions and the British subsidiary, which has occupied two of the UK three seats with members of an 'Employee Forum' that is not controlled by the trade unions.[75]

The European element, and hence the more decentralised aspects, of the culture are reflected in the EWC's communication style. The official language is English. All official documents are drafted in English and, if necessary, translated into the national languages of EWC members. In contrast, meetings are held in German. However, simultaneous interpretation is always available for all the languages

75 Up until 2006, British unions appointed three shop stewards to the EWC. The introduction of the Employee Forum at the UK operations meant that this body acquired the right to delegate EWC members. This led to a protest by the unions, as they were no longer the sole determinants of who would be EWC members, culminating in six British EWC members attending the 2006 annual EWC meeting instead of the three provided for by the agreement. Because it was impossible to change the allocation of seats to suit the UK subsidiaries, the unions and the Employee Forum finally agreed that the unions would have one seat and the Employee Forum two seats.

represented. Although the EWC agreement did not provide for language training, this was provided following the merger with Chrysler for both the group works council and the central works council.

The EWC has operated a mentoring system for some years, mainly aimed at promoting communication and lowering cultural barriers. However, the fact that German EWC members are responsible for one or two foreign colleagues, and that there are no working parties without German participation, promotes the spread of cultural elements derived from the home country, such as forms of communication, typical patterns of communication and 'forms of discourse', and perceptions of workplace events and contexts. It is also an indicator of the means through which the EWC centre has been able to assert its conception of how an interest representation forum should be coordinated that is rooted in German experience.

The more centralist tendencies of the EWC not only affect the distribution of resources, power, and culture but also shape access to sources of knowledge of strategic significance for interest representation. Within the EWC the German members have a clear advantage in terms of the knowledge they acquire through the German system of codetermination. Since all German EWC members are also works council members, they have a statutory right to the comprehensive information provided for in the Works Constitution Act.[76] In addition, they also benefit from the fact that they share the same language as corporate management as well as the existence of procedures that have been tried and tested within interest representation bodies in the Daimler group. As such, the EWC does not offer a 'European value-added' for German EWC members. This is further reinforced by the fact that events at foreign Daimler plants have no or only a minor impact on the working conditions or stability of German plants. 'The German works council does not need the EWC to get information and also not for negotiations. In fact, EWC meetings contain no surprises for German works council members' (DE01).

The situation is different for EWC members from foreign plants. In contrast to German employee representatives, they benefit from the communication and interaction within the EWC. Firstly, they have access to important current information between annual meetings, either through the presidium, the central works council staff, or their mentors. Minutes are prepared after every EWC meeting. Internal minutes are drafted in English and translated into national languages if needed. Minutes of meetings with management, which are seen as much more important by EWC members, are translated into all the languages. Both are sent to all EWC

76 For example, there is an obligation on the employer to inform and consult on the design of jobs, the working environment and basic operational matters (Section 90, Works Constitution Act; on staff planning (Sect. 92); on business developments and financial matters, including proposed investments, rationalisation and reorganisation (Sect. 106); and any changes or alterations to operations that might impact on employee interests (Sect. 111).

members as soon as they have been translated. In addition, there is an intranet giving access to information for download.

Secondly, the EWC provides an opportunity for an annual meeting with central management, not only giving access to important information disclosed directly by management but also allowing them to put questions and discuss problems. The foreign EWC members also benefit indirectly from German codetermination provisions, as the EWC always holds its meetings concurrently with the meeting of the German economic committee (*Wirtschaftsausschuss*).[77] And since the issues that have to be reported on in this committee are stipulated in German law, this gives foreign EWC members an opportunity to gain a detailed and comprehensive picture of the economic and financial condition of the company. The knowledge available at EWC meetings often means they know more than their own local management.

4.2.3 Coordination of EWC activities

Compared with other EWCs in our sample the Daimler EWC may be characterised as 'somewhat weakly coordinated' in terms of the ordinal scale adopted. For example, in contrast to some other EWCs and steering committees in our sample (such as those at Ford, GM, VW, Toyota) the EWC presidium at Daimler meets only once a year. Although the agreement provides for special meetings in critical situations, these have only taken place twice during the history of the Daimler EWC. The first occasion was an extraordinary meeting in 2005 over the issue of the 'New Management Model'. The second was the separation of the Chrysler sales operations from Daimler in 2007. However, the fact that this only affected the sales division meant that the meeting was confined to the distribution working group. Both of these extraordinary meetings led to negotiations with management and the conclusion of corresponding European framework agreements. As yet there have been no extraordinary meetings of the presidium. The main reason for the low frequency of meetings has been the perception that have been no issues that have warranted a need for the EWC to become active.

> The presidium meets when it needs to and only when it must. The fact is, though, that in the past there's never been an issue. The structure [of the company] has meant that no conflicts have come up, and *therefore no meeting was necessary.* You meet once a year and that's completely sufficient [...] There's e-mail and telephone, and that's been enough. It's never been and still isn't necessary for the presidium to hold particularly long meetings. *There are just no issues that need to be intensively discussed.* (DE01; emphasis added)

---

77 The 'Economic Committee' is a separate body established under the Works Consitution Act in all *companies* (not workplaces) with more than 100 employees. Members are appointed by the works council, and its role is to consult with the employer on financial and business developments and report to the works council.

The annual EWC meetings last three days and, as well as the one-day meeting with management, include a preparatory meeting and a follow-up meeting. As a rule the internal meeting contains the standard agenda points, such as the report of the chair, report of the select committee, report of relevant meetings (World Employee Committee, supervisory board) and country reports.

There are two forms of working group within the EWC, informal and institutionalised. The informal working group is the mentoring approach initiated by the German side, which mostly benefits foreign EWC members. Under the mentoring system, matched German EWC members mentor foreign members either from the same division or if there is close geographical proximity. For example, there is a pairing of Evobus representatives from France, Czech Republic and Germany and of the van assembly plant in Spain with the German van plants in Düsseldorf and Ludwigsfelde. The EWC members from Hambach (France, SMART production) and Rastatt (A and B class) do not have direct links in terms of the products that manufacture but have been matched because they are located near each other.

> We've tried this out and used a mentoring approach on and off. That is, German members were told you're now responsible for X and Y: please make sure that you exchange with them, make sure that you contact them between meetings because EWC meetings only take place once a year. This has not been institutionalised. But we've said 'Please look after this and please keep in touch on topics of common interest through the year. Because once a year is not enough, so please [keep in] regular touch' (DE01).

Within the pairing arrangements, the German EWC members act as mentors and are responsible for maintaining exchange and contact between meetings. As a rule, communication between meetings takes place through phone calls and occasional meetings. However, contact between EWC members depends very much on the situation. 'There are, of course, situations and then there's a lot more contact. But as long as business hasn't been collapsing then the mentors only meet once a quarter' (DE03).

Within the van division, mentoring has been developed to the extent that EWC members meet once a year with divisional management outside formal EWC meetings. However, these are voluntary meetings and depend on the initiative of EWC members and the willingness of management to take part. Even if the mentoring groups only meet or communicate sporadically, the mentoring system contributes to integrating the EWC, with the prospect that it might become both more strongly and decentrally coordinated between annual meetings.

As noted above, there is an institutionalised arrangement for the representation of employees in the company's sales operations: this was established before the EWC and subsequently integrated into it as working group. It facilitates experience exchange by employee representatives in European sales operations and meets regularly with management. Within the EWC it became active when the Chrysler sales network was separated and concluded a framework agreement with group management.

4.2.4 Critical events and EWC outputs

Two major events can be identified in the history of the Daimler EWC that had a significant influence on its development: the establishment of the World Employee Committee (WEC)[78] and the separation of the Chrysler sales organisation from the Daimler group.

World Employee Committee

Almost six years after the establishment of the EWC, on the 17 July 2002 an agreement was concluded between management and employee representatives of DaimlerChrysler AG to establish a World Employee Committee. The forum was initiated by senior members of the German works council and representatives from the UAW and IG Metall with the aim of institutionalising global cooperation between Daimler employees, in view of the leap in the international character of the company following the merger. An international working party of employee representatives had been established in 1998. Management initially was negative towards this body, as it feared an extension of the German codetermination rights to other countries. However, agreement was rapidly reached on establishing a corresponding forum, albeit in the form of a four-year test phase and with an express concern to avoid the designation 'works council'.

The World Employee Committee (WEC) is a formal global representative body for employees and trade unions, intended to improve information exchange between employee representatives from different countries and between employee representatives and management. It is also intended to facilitate the building of personal relationships, and with these mutual trust, between employee representatives from countries involved. It is also an institutionalised forum for dialogue between management and international employee representatives, with employees receiving information at the annual meeting on issues affecting the group at global level. As a consequence, the WEC might be regarded as a type of 'global economic committee' (Müller et al., 2004a: 173). However, management does not envisage the body taking on more far-reaching functions.

The WEC currently has thirteen members: six representatives (works council members) from Germany, three trade union representatives from the United States[79] and one employee representative each from Canada, South Africa, Spain and Brazil. The chair, at the time of writing, was Erich Klemm, as head of the group works council and

78 Daimler management was eager to avoid the term 'world company council' (which usually translates as 'world works council' in German). The body was initially called the 'International Automobile Workers' Group' and subsequently the 'World Employee Committee'. We use the terms' World Employment Committee' and 'World works/company council' synonymously.

79 In contrast to GM, cooperation with the UAW has been positive (se Köhler, 2009).

European works council.[80] The composition of the body was negotiated with group level management by the German works council. Rather than seeking to include all the group's operations, in part on cost grounds, the main emphasis has been placed on establishing a body able to operate effectively (see too Müller et al., 2004a: 172).

Given the significance of Daimler's international activities, and the existence of the group works council and World Employee Committee, the EWC finds itself at constant risk of becoming the 'fifth wheel on the wagon'. For example, the company's recent proposals to transfer production of the 'C' class from Sindelfingen to the United States (and Bremen) highlights the potential significance of institutions for interest representation beyond the European level.

Separation of the Chrysler sales network

The separation of the Chrysler sales network constituted a second critical event in the history of the EWC, as it represented the first time that the EWC engaged in negotiations with management. Overall, some 400 employees were affected by the decision, the largest single group of which, around 120 individuals, came from Germany. The remaining 280 employees were distributed across the European operations, with a maximum of fifty at each. The initiative for negotiations came principally from management, which wanted to secure a binding arrangement affecting all employees in as short a time as possible. 'The company was interested in doing this quickly: "Come on let's get on and conclude a European agreement"' (DE01). Management announced the separation of the Chrysler sales network to the EWC at an extraordinary EWC meeting. Since this only affected the sales area, there was an extraordinary meeting of the 'sales and distribution working group' at which management set out the problems and its proposed solution. Following this, for the first time in the history of the EWC, a European negotiating committee was constituted, consisting of the German chair of the sales and distribution working group and a Belgian and a Dutch EWC member. The negotiating committee discussed management's proposal and, following consultation with the wider membership, proposed a draft for a framework agreement to management.[81] Although this agreement was ultimately signed by the EWC at an extraordinary meeting, the real driving force was the distribution working group: 'The working group recommended signing, and the EWC said "OK, if that's what you want then we'll go along with it"' (DE01).

80 See <http://www.eurofound.europa.eu/eiro/2002/09/inbrief/de0209204n.htm> accessed on 30 May 2010.

81 'The negotiating committee gave some thought to the provision, negotiated, and, of course, kept the working party informed about the state of developments during the course of the negotiations. Then it said "That's it – is it OK?" Always by e-mail. And then a final draft was prepared [...] The negotiating commission said "There's no more to be had, it's OK as it is". Then the working party said "OK, then we'll agree with that" (DE01).

The agreement provided for all non-German employees to receive a welcome bonus of €7,500 during the transition to the new company. EWC members also agreed with this provision. Given that there already was an agreement that ruled out compulsory redundancies for German staff at the company until the end of 2011, a separate agreement was concluded for the German employees that promised a bonus of €15,000 for employees on transfer to the new company. This led to some serious protests within the forum from some representatives of foreign operations, but these abated relatively quickly.

Outputs

As far as the strength of interest representation is concerned, the Daimler EWC has moved from being a service provider for information (Lecher et al., 2000) to a body with a capacity to take action – if only on limited and as yet few occasions – in negotiations with management. In terms of the effectiveness of interest representation, the development of the Daimler EWC can be divided into two phases. The first phase embraced the period following the establishment of the EWC up until the separation of the Chrysler sales network in 2006: during this phase, the forum acted purely as an information and consultation body. In the ten years that followed its establishment, the EWC undertook no major activities and had a generally low profile. Its main task consisted in providing foreign EWC members with information, giving them access to top management, and offering scope for consultation during annual meetings (see Müller et al., 2004a). One of the main reasons for this was the absence of inter-plant competition that meant that no situation arose in which the EWC had to seek negotiations with management or initiate other activities.

> At VW, GM and Ford you've got *a European structure of production, which we don't have. We have not had any competition between plants.* That's tended to turn our EWC into a kind of talking shop, as there are no joint problems or conflicts within the body. There just isn't any conflict. (DE01)

In addition, the merger with Chrysler did not generate any particular need for the EWC to take action, given management's emphasis that it would not lead to any rationalisation that might have put pressure on the Daimler workforce. Rather, expanding the group's activities was expected to have positive outcomes for employees.

The second phase of the EWC's development was initiated by the separation of the Chrysler sales organisation in 2006. This marked the point at which the EWC began to show signs of advancing beyond information and consultation, and the forum was able to initiate negotiations with management and conclude an agreement.

One important indicator of an EWC's output or effectiveness in interest representation is the number of formal agreements concluded with management. As yet three framework agreements have been concluded, although they differ substantially in their quality.

The *first,* entitled 'Principles for Social Responsibility at DaimlerChrysler' (2002), was initiated by senior members of the German works council without consultation with the World Employee Committee (although this took place at the same time as the founding agreement of the WEC was concluded). However, this agreement was largely negotiated by the World Employee Committee. Although the EWC was a co-signatory to the agreement, only the EWC chair and one further German member participated in the actual negotiations. This agreement follows the principles of the UN Global Compact and is based on a model agreement produced by the IMF that, in turn, is based on the OECD Guidelines for Multinational Enterprises (see Müller et al., 2004a: 174ff.).

The *second* agreement dealt with personnel and staffing issues in Europe in the context of the New Management Model. In 2005, the company announced a worldwide workforce reduction of 6,000 administrative posts, of which 3,300 were in Germany. This prompted an extraordinary EWC meeting at which management disclosed details of the planned measures. Since a large number of other European operations were affected by the planned redundancies, as well as the German headquarters, the EWC and management agreed on a set of principles to guide implementation of the proposals throughout Europe. 'The New Management Model led us to state that we will now set out at European level what should happen in the case of any workforce reduction' (DE01). In September 2006, representatives of management and the EWC signed a 'Framework Agreement on Staff Adjustment Measures in the Subsidiaries of DaimlerChrysler AG in the European Union', the main substance of which was that any workforce reductions should take place in a socially responsible way and with the involvement of employee representatives.[82]

What is notable about these first two agreements is that the EWC barely figured as an actor. As with the VW group, existing German employee representation arrangements were used to bring negotiations to as swift a conclusion as possible. In order not to delay the process, foreign EWC members were not included to avoid the need for the German negotiating partner to have to spend time explaining and justifying established procedures.

> We did the first agreement and we did the second one. We just made use of the established and tried-and-tested negotiating system. That is the chair of the EWC with the management board. We said, 'Let's just do this quickly and we use the established structures'. And that's what we did (DE01).

According to one EWC member, one reason for using established German employee representation arangements was that management was hesiant about negotiating with a body intended only for information and consultation.

> We've now concluded a first agreement at European level with management, but as long as the law, the European Directive, is not in line with that, our management has

82 The agreement provides that if jobs are to be lost at a location, attempts should be made to find comparable posts at the same site. If this is not possible for any given country subsidiary, then the search should be widened to other subsidiaries in the same country, and, if necessary, to other locations abroad.

> difficulties in going beyond that. However, one should not underestimate the agreement we negotiated (DE03).

The *third* agreement, on the separation of the Chrysler sales operations from Daimler, marked a turning point in the history of the EWC as this was the first time it figured as an actor in its own right.

> In this case we said 'Why not let the Europeans, and in this case the sales people, negotiate? It's time they took a look at how these things work'. And so for the first time we had a European negotiating committee. This consisted of the chair of the sales and distribution group, he's German, and then a Belgian and a Dutch colleague. They did the negotiations. They sat down with management and drew up an agreement. (DE01).

The participation of foreign EWC members in negotiations led to greater equality and a more even power balance within the forum, which accorded with the aspirations of a number of foreign EWC representatives. 'In my opinion it was a big step to let the Europeans negotiate on their own. Because otherwise you just catch hell if the Germans do it and then somebody comes along and says European agreement, great, where were we then?' (DE01).

Although, the EWC has been able to exercise the role of negotiator and conclude an agreement with management with the inclusion of foreign EWC members in one instance, the EWC's effectiveness rests to a great extent on German institutions of codetermination and the tried-and-tested cooperation between work councils and management at the company's headquarters, which can be made use of for European and international interest representation. The willingness of management to negotiate with the EWC in the case of the Chrysler sales organisation was mainly driven by management's wish for a single and rapidly concluded provision that would apply to all the affected regions. 'Bringing all these topics into one body made it a simpler proposition to do something that would have otherwise have had to take place at many sites, with the risk that it would all be done differently everywhere. We therefore decided, in contrast to our previous approach, to engage in a substantive discussion' (DM01).

In general, management regards the EWC as a body for facilitating the disclosure of information and company decisions to employees in Europe through a central interlocutor. It has always stressed that the EWC is principally an information and consultation forum, and that any negotiations are on a voluntary basis – and in particular that they should not be seen as creating a precedent for the EWC to develop into a negotiating body.

> If we were to make an acquisition at European level tomorrow, then there would some matters that we would need to regulate. Or if we were to reorganise and close companies, then we would probably do things similarly. However, this is not a reason to turn the EWC into a qualitatively different body. We are not prepared to change our rule on this simply because we were able to work successfully together on one occasion (DM01).

From the point of EWC members, management has distant but respectful view of the forum. Employee representatives were aware that management accepts the body as a forum for regular information and consultation, and that any movement beyond this would be regarded either sceptically or with blank refusal. 'I must say one thing: they obviously respect us. That is worth quite a lot. Meetings are held and deadlines are kept to. Even Zetsche [the CEO] himself has made time for the EWC. There is respect there' (DE03).

The significance of the EWC varies for employee groups within Daimler depending on their national background. For non-German employee representatives, it enables then to gain access to information not available in national subsidiaries as well as an opportunity to engage directly with management. The EWC offers a platform on which employee representatives from European operations can establish mutual contact and exchange. By contrast, there is no 'value-added' for German representatives, and the EWC has a subordinate status compared with other institutions for employee representation in the Daimler group. As far as German EWC representatives are concerned, the central works council is 'the sun around which everything revolves' (DE01). The high level of engagement of German employee representatives is best explained through an overarching culture of cross-border employee solidarity in the group. As the both the mainspring and coordinators in the EWC process, German works council members act as advocates for their colleagues abroad, as evidenced in the mentoring system and the scope for representation on the company's supervisory board, the strategic decision-making body for the entire group. Although the EWC may not have yet acquired the status of a regular and accepted negotiating body, it does arguably offer significant value-added through facilitating communication between employee representatives, and with this the building of trust and solidarity. As previous studies, and the findings of this research, show, (see the chapters on VW and GM), the EWC creates one significant prerequisite for effectively dealing with any conflicts and crises that might arise.

There are a number of plausible reasons why the Daimler EWC has not developed into a negotiating body analogous to that seen at Ford or GM. Firstly, there have very few issues that might have required greater EWC involvement. Despite multiple restructurings, acquisitions and disposals, the key actors did not identify any major need for regulation. One explanation for this possibly lies in Daimler's corporate structures and managerial strategies. In contrast to GM, VW or Renault, Daimler is not characterised by widespread parallel production or inter-plant competition for production allocations and employment (see too Köhler, 2009). As yet, the company has generally prospered (see Figure 23 in the Appendix). And although new plants have recently been opened in Asia, and are planned for Eastern Europe, German EWC members do not consider that this will lead to transfers of production that might jeopardise German operations: 'I have no idea whether there will be a factory in ten years in Eastern Europe. But even if there is, I do not see that this would lead to a massive shift in production arrangements' (DE01).

Greater coordination of the EWC is also impaired in some respects by the structure of the body itself. As a forum spanning all the group's divisions, the EWC is not primarily a body representing the company's manufacturing operations and includes nearly as many employees in sales, marketing and distribution. The fact that all business divisions are represented (trucks, cars, vans, buses and others) has led to a heterogeneous institution in which it is likely to be more difficult to identify common problems and issues. Questions related to production, often the main focus for German workplace representatives, are of less concern to non-German members as there are few manufacturing operations in the EU outside Germany. The real common ground for many EWC members lies in the field of sales and distribution operations, which do not compete – and for which there is, therefore, little need for regulation.

> It turns out that Europe as an issue is mainly one for the *sales area, and their issues and not ones that are classic topics for works councils.* As a result, the topics that interest the EWC are not as important as those that are discussed [at national level] in Germany (DM01; emphasis added).

One further factor lies in the considerable significance of home-country institutions for interest regulation and representation. As with the first two framework agreements, German representative institutions are also used for non-German issues within the context of the EWC. Established paths for communication and negotiation, and the immediate proximity of the German central works council and group-level management, mean that using these channels for international representative work can seem the more obvious route to take.

4.3 Provisional assessment

Despite the demerger of DaimlerChrysler and the end of the vision of a 'World Plc', Daimler remains an internationally-active company with a leading global position both in the premium and luxury car segment and in commercial vehicles. Our findings suggest that the group's divisions have an extremely disparate character: whereas employment and manufacturing capacity in the cars division are heavily concentrated in the home country (traditionally and once more following the sale of Chrysler), the trucks division is a comparatively internationalised unit. Taking the group as a whole, what stands out in comparison with all the other companies in our sample is the high degree of centralisation (see Figure 21 in the Appendix). This applies for virtually all the main dimensions considered here: the bulk of employment and production capacity is concentrated in Germany; the company culture is strongly marked by home-country practice, with cultural elements exported to foreign operations; and the creation of strategic knowledge mainly takes place at the corporate centre. Only the distribution of power can be denoted as 'somewhat centralised', given the fairly high degree of autonomy enjoyed by individual divisions, which are only weakly coordinated and controlled from the centre. Despite the high degree of internationalisation of some divisions, the company has largely refrained from parallel production or inter-plant competition. Although divisions are strongly coordinated internally, the group as a whole is weakly coordinated. As such, Daimler AG can be categorised as a *focal* organisation.

The EWC has fitted into this arrangement. For a long period, the EWC was a highly centralised service provider for the non-German operations. Internationalising interest representation was more a cultural outgrowth – exemplifying the values of international worker solidarity – than the product of a real and pressing need to take international action. This only changed with introduction of the New Management Model and the separation of the Chrysler sales operation following the demerger. Although the EWC is now more decentralised than before, it still ranks as a more centralised body than the other EWCs in our sample – but with weak coordination. As with Daimler itself, the EWC also corresponds most closely with the features of a *focal* organisation.

The coordination weaknesses of the EWC are the product, on the one hand, of the corporate structure and strategic direction adopted by management, which has, as yet, only generated fairly limited and short-lived needs for regulation. The level of Europeanisation in production is low. And compared with other companies in our sample, parallel production and inter-plant competition have been only marginal concerns. At the same time, the EWC continues to be strongly marked by the developmental path of the working group representing sales and distribution staff. The fact that production in the cars division has a low level of internationalisation means that the EWC is a relatively heterogeneous body, in which the representatives of the strongly internationalised sales and distribution operation have come to play a major role and, so far, have been the main force driving activity.

Overall, the Daimler EWC has played a minor role within the spectrum of interest representation and regulation in the group[83] – including when compared with other EWCs in our sample. It constitutes a communication platform that mainly provides an additional benefit for non-German operations by affording access to information and to management as well as an opportunity for exchange between representatives of different operations. The negotiations on the separation of the Chrysler sales operations show that, under certain circumstances, the EWC is able to conduct substantive negotiations with management on the basis of its access to a number of important preconditions, such as workforce support, the required degree of trust, and the (at least, potential) option of strongly coordinating its members' activities.

The Daimler EWC represents a rather subordinate element within the overall structure of interest representation in the group. For the actors involved, the central works council, group works council and even the WEC – along with codetermination on the supervisory board – represent much more significant instances. Its relative strength and organisational capacity, however, is evidenced in the fact that

83 Müller et al. (2004a) come to a similar conclusion.

when called on, it was able to perform successfully and function as a capable actor. Although its strength in such specific instances is principally attributable to its interplay with established German institutions for employee codetermination, its particular contribution lies in its potential for functioning as a European platform for interest regulation. The negotiating outcomes demonstrate that the EWC meets the requirements – trust and solidarity, a functioning communication system, and relationship networks – for a more active role in the future in internal processes of interest regulation in the group.

Chapter 5: Volkswagen

5.1 The Volkswagen Group

5.1.1 History and characteristics of the Volkswagen group

With more than 6.4 million vehicles sold in 2008, the Volkswagen group is the largest vehicle manufacturer in Europe. The origins of the group extend back to 1937 when the 'Gesellschaft zur Vorbereitung des Deutschen Volkswagen mbH' was established to manufacture a new car developed by Ferdinand Porsche.[84] Over the course of its history, the company has evolved into an internationally active and highly complex group encompassing a large number of subsidiaries (Eckardt et al., 2000; Haipeter, 2000: 124). Volkswagen's development has been characterised by three main features.

1. The acquisition of marques, a concomitant widening of its vehicle range, and a shift from a Fordist production strategy to a combined Ford-Sloane model.
2. Early internationalisation of sales and production.
3. Embeddedness in a legal framework, with a unique ownership structure and a governing statute that applies to Volkswagen alone (the 'Volkswagengesetz').[85]

In 2010, the group had two divisions: automotive and financial services.[86] The automotive division consists of ten brands: in addition to Volkswagen (passenger cars), it includes Volkswagen (commercial vehicles), Audi, Škoda, SEAT, Bentley, Bugatti, Lamborghini, Scania (since 2008), and Porsche (since 2010). The group is structured along the three dimensions of functions/business processes, products, and markets (regions) (Adelt et al., 2008: 44ff.).

For a long period, VW represented the epitome of Fordist mass production, centred on volume production of the Beetle (Jürgens, 1998; Boyer and Freyssenet, 2002: 58f.). This changed in the late-1960s following a global sales crisis, with the strict Fordist strategy replaced by a 'compromise between Fordist and Sloanist principles' (ibid. 285): VW became the 'German General Motors'.[87] In the 1970s,

84 The company was renamed 'Volkswagenwerk GmbH' in 1938.
85 See Section 5.2.1 below.
86 Below these broad divisions, VW is divided into business areas and a large number of subsidiaries (production, sales etc.). In 2007, there were 175 consolidated subsidiaries within Volkswagen AG (Adelt et al., 2008: 12ff.).
87 In 1965, VW acquired Auto Union GmbH from Daimler-Benz. The main motive was not initially gaining access to the higher end of the car market but also a for more capacity because of labour shortages. In 1969 Auto Union merged with NSU Motorenwerken, and in 1985 became Audi AG, a subsidiary of Volkswagen.

this approach centred on the decision that both VW and Audi should produce a high-volume model. From 1975, the Golf became the volume model for VW: the product range was extended in the small-car sector by the Polo/Audi 50 and in the medium-sector by the Passat/Audi 80, with each intended to be assembled flexibly in either VW or Audi plants. A renewal of the product range in the 1980s led to a re-allocation of operations between plants, and the adoption of the principle of 'one plant – one model'.

This changed in the early-1990s when parallel production and international competition between plants was openly adopted as a management strategy (see, for example, Eckardt, 2000; Haipeter, 2000: 352ff; Speidel, 2005: 59ff.), an approach bolstered by the decision to produce a single model at several plants, culminating in the Golf III being assembled at Wolfsburg, Mosel, Brussels, Sarajevo and also at plants in China and Mexico.

The 'automobile crisis' of the early-1990s led to serious sales problems for VW and, from the mid-1990s, prompted a range of rationalisation strategies under the leadership of Ferdinand Piëch. The group's organisational structure was altered to more closely align it with brands, combined with the pursuit of synergies across brand lines. One important element in this was the shift to a platform strategy, in which the previous eleven vehicle platforms were reduced to four to cover the entire vehicle range. This also went hand-in-hand with a restructuring of product development. Up until 1994, each brand had possessed its own R&D operation, leading to extensive functional overlap. After this point, only VW and Audi were allowed to develop vehicle platforms, with the other marques confined to designing bodies and interiors in line with their market segment and brand image. The objective was to achieve greater commonality of components, realise synergies – in procurement and supplier relationships, as pursued by the then head of purchasing, José Ignacio Lopez – reduce time-to-market, and ultimately control costs (Eckardt et al., 2000; Jürgens, 1998: 298ff; Jürgens, 2009; 231f.).

The company embarked on an internationalisation strategy at an early stage in its history. Eckardt et al. (2000) distinguish three phases: in the period up until 1972, VW is described as a 'distribution oriented' company (ibid. 45); in the second phase, extending to the mid-1980s, the internationalisation profile shifted to that of a production-oriented multinational company; in the third phase, which began in the 1990s, VW has been characterised as passing through the 'transition to a transnational firm' (ibid.; Uhl and Lavon, 1997: 217ff.).

During the first phase, VW's strategy was based on exporting vehicles manufactured in Germany. In 1967, for example, 85 per cent of output was made in Germany (Jürgens, 1998: 277). In the immediate wake of the Second World War, the British authorities stepped up the export of cars from the Wolfsburg plant, which lay in the British occupation zone in what was subsequently to become the *Land* of Lower Saxony. Nonetheless, despite the large-scale export of German-built cars, plants and sales operations were also opened outside Germany as early as the 1950s, with manufacturing facilities and sales offices opened in the 1950s and 1960s in North and South

America (Brazil, 1953; South Africa, 1956; Puebla, Mexico, 1964).[88] Volkswagen Brussels AG was established in 1971. However, these facilities were mainly intended to open new markets, not compete with VW's German plants.

The second stage of internationalisation was aimed at opening up European markets. In 1986, VW acquired a majority stake in the Spanish car manufacturer SEAT. After 1990, new plants were opened in Central and Eastern Europe, and the Czech manufacturer Škoda was acquired. In the context of 'coordinated manufacture', in which a number of plants were used to produce a single vehicle model, there was a strengthening of VW's internal division of labour and relationships with suppliers, with some foreign operations acquiring strategic functions for some models (Eckardt et al., 2000).

In a third stage, that began in the mid-1990s, additional manufacturing and assembly plants have been established in Central and Eastern Europe (Poland and Hungary).[89] The expansion of the group was mainly intended to achieve manufacturing scale, widen the product range, and obtain synergies through the cross-brand and cross-market use of vehicle sub-assemblies (see Widuckel, 2001: 334).[90] The relationship between the corporate headquarters (plus the German plants) and foreign operations has also changed significantly over time. Initially, VW was a multinational company in which foreign subsidiaries 'operated in their regions relatively autonomously from the Wolfsburg-based VW AG [...] Foreign operations were not integrated into the central functional organisation of the parent company, but simply attached to it. There was a "modernity gap" between the parent company and subsidiaries, as subsidiaries were equipped with older technologies and mostly produced older models originally developed in Germany' (Haipeter, 2000: 144). The new strategic direction led to greater operational integration within a group-wide division of labour (Eckardt et al., 2000; Uhl and Lavon, 1997: 218). For example, foreign subsidiaries were given responsibility for new models (such as the New Beetle in Mexico) and their own development capacities (Pries, 1999b).

The VW group is notable for its ownership structure and governance arrangements under the Volkswagen Law. The German regional government (*Land*) of Lower Saxony, which held 14.7 of the company's equity in 2008, exercises a high level of influence over the group. The largest shareholder was Porsche Automotive Holding SE (with 37.4 per cent). Other holdings were distributed amongst institutional investors, of which 5 per cent were German and 17.7 non-German, with a free-float of 24.4 per cent held by private investors (VW, 2008: 126). The Volkswagen

88 The plant in Westmoreland/Pennsylvania was established in 1978 but closed in 1988 (see Dombois, 1992).

89 VW also re-entered the US as a manufacturer in 2011, with the opening of an assembly plant in Chattanooga, Tennessee.

90 In July and September 1998, four further brands (Rolls-Royce [until 2002], Bentley, Bugatti and Lamborghini) were integrated into the group. VW has also had an equity stake in the commercial vehicle manufacturer Scania since 2000, and this became a wholly-owned subsidiary in 2008.

Law, passed in 1960 following the transformation of VW GmbH into a public stock corporation (AG), guarantees a continuing high degree of public influence (by Lower Saxony) over group-level decisions, as, irrespective of the actual distribution of shareholdings, no owner may have more than 20 per cent of voting rights.[91] Decisions on opening and closing plants also require a two-thirds majority of the Supervisory Board (Section 4, VW Law), which cannot be achieved without the votes of employee members, with the implication that major decisions on closures or moving the company's headquarters can be blocked. This also reveals the power enjoyed by the German plants and employee representatives, since strategic decisions about the group must meet with their approval. The German plants not only have a high level of influence over decisions but also a type of 'status quo guarantee', as a vote to close a plant is almost inconceivable, except under extraordinary circumstances or alignments of interest.

The VW group is active in all global markets, but with a focus in Europe. While 73 per cent of turnover came from foreign sales in 1967, this had fallen to 59 per cent by 1994. In 2008, the foreign share had risen back to 75.7 per cent. The single largest share of revenue, at 47 per cent, is Europe (excluding Germany). North America is a further key market (11.2 per cent), followed by South America (8.6 per cent) and Asia (7.4 per cent) (VW, 2008: 138). Between 2007 and 2008, the number of units sold rose by 2.1 per cent (following a rise of 9.8 per cent between 2006 and 2007).[92]

5.1.2 Distribution of resources, power, culture and knowledge in the VW group

The distribution of resources – production facilities, employees and production volumes – can be characterised as 'somewhat centralised' compared with the other companies in our sample. However, the individual indicators do not all run in the same direction.

In terms of the distribution of production facilities, there is moderately strong focus on Europe (see Adelt et al., 2008; VW, 2008).[93] In 2008, the VW group had some fifty production facilities worldwide, of which thirty-six were located in twelve EU countries (72 per cent).[94] With eleven plants, Germany accounts for 22 per cent of

91 On 23 October 2007, the European Court of Justice ruled that the limitation of voting rights to a maximum of 20 per cent under the Volkwagen Law was in breach of EU law. On 13 November 2008, the German Parliament removed the sections dealing with limits on voting rights and proxies.

92 Between 1998 and 2008, overall production and sales rose (see Figure 23 in the Appendix).

93 For this study, facilities that occupy a single conjoined space and a common workforce count as one site, as with Wolfsburg, even if there are formally a number of separate plants or establishments (see Chapter 3).

94 Belgium, Bosnia-Herzegovina, Czech Republic, France, Germany, Hungary, Italy, Poland, Portugal, Slovakia, Spain, and the UK (and more recently, Russia).

the global total. Outside Europe, there are plants in South Africa, Asia (one in India, five in China), Mexico (one plant), Argentina (two plants), and Brazil (five plants).

Table 3: Distribution of employees, plants and production, VW group (2008)

	Employees	Plants	Production
World	337,789	50	6,437,414
EU	230,000	36	4,124,820
EU Home-country (Germany)	178,000	11	2,326,481
Largest plant	43,500	–	–
Share EU/world	68%	72%	64%
Share EU home-country/EU	77%	31%	56%
Share EU home-country/world	53%	22%	36%
Share largest plant/EU	19%	–	–

Source: authors' compilation from VW (2008) and OICA (2008).

In 2008, total world output was 6,437,414 units (OICA, 2008). Just under two-thirds (64 per cent) of this was produced in Europe (4,124,820), of which more than half was made in Germany (accounting for 36 per cent of the world total). This was followed by Asia (16 per cent), South America (13 per cent) and North America (7 per cent) (VW, 2008: 154). In relation to the whole EU, the home-country share of production was 56 per cent. Compared with other companies in the sample, Volkswagen may be regarded as 'somewhat centralised' in this respect and broadly comparable with PSA (54 per cent). Daimler is a much more centralised company, with 83 per cent of its production in Germany. Ford and GM (each with 37 per cent) and Toyota (38 per cent) are much more decentralised.[95]

In 2008, the share of home-country employment in total world employment was 53 per cent, and for Europe 77 per cent – indicating a more centralised distribution. Only Daimler had a higher concentration (at 86 per cent). With a figure of 27 per cent, Toyota is much lower in the centralisation ranking on this dimension (taking the UK as the country with the largest number of employees in the EU). Analysis of employment by plant also indicates a more centralised distribution than other firms in the sample. In 2008, the group headquarters in Wolfsburg, with 43,500 employees,

95 Ford, GM and Honda are decentralised when looked at on a world scale. Taking the shares of output in the USA (for GM and Ford), and in Japan (for Honda and Toyota) compared with total world production, then Ford's share is 30 per cent, GM 28 per cent, and Honda 32 per cent. Toyota exhibits broadly the same degree of centralisation as VW, Renault and PSA with 53 per cent. See the concluding sections in Chapter 12.

accounted for 19 per cent of total employment within the EU. On this dimension, GM and Ford have the highest values (28–35 per cent). EU-based companies have either similar values (in the case of Daimler, 15 per cent) or lower proportions (Renault, 6 per cent; PSA, 8 per cent).

In terms of the distribution of power, the VW group is often characterised as a strongly centralised undertaking. However, this does not appear to be the case in terms of the distribution of decision-making powers and the participation of (European) operations, where the group appears less centralised. Compared with the other internationally-operating firms in our sample – and notably GM, Daimler, Renault, PSA and Toyota – VW can be characterised as relatively decentralised or, using the four-point ordinal scale set out in Chap 3.3.1, as 'somewhat centralised'. Important indices for this are the marked role of the German plants, the mechanisms for incorporating German and international plants in corporate decision-making, the high level of plant-level autonomy on operational matters in some respects, and the matrix structure, in which responsibility for global functions or processes is not concentrated in Wolfsburg but distributed across individual plants.

As the legal parent company, VW AG has a unique role in the group as a whole. However, its significance is 'underlined by the fact that the Wolfsburg plant is, simultaneously, the headquarters and legal seat of the group, and that the executive board of the AG is also coterminous, in individual terms, with the group executive board' (Haipeter, 2000: 33). Although the principal decision-making centre is clearly located in the Wolfsburg headquarters – in terms of overall product and investment strategy – decisions within the group are taken at a number of levels and involve a variety of actors.

Figure 5: Distribution of plants within the VW group.

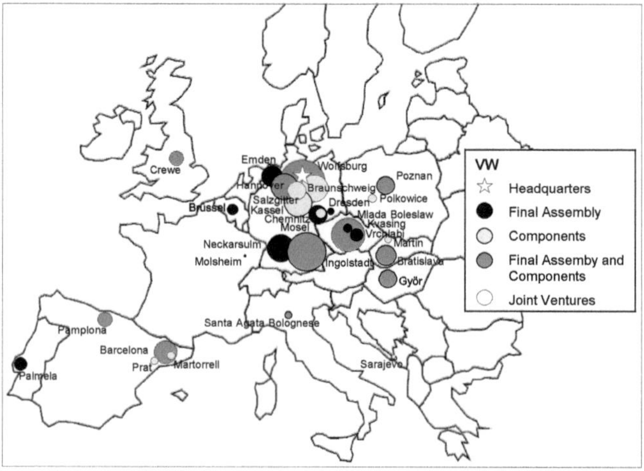

Source: compiled by the authors based on Volkswagen Annual Report 2008. Circles are proportionate to the number of employees.

For a long period in the group's history, individual brands exercised a fairly high degree of autonomy over strategic decisions. However, since the 1990s, according to the managers interviewed for this study, 'a clear trend towards group-level decision-making had taken place' on strategic issues (VWM03). As a consequence of more recent strategies of cross-brand standardisation (platform strategy) and synergies (sourcing and group-level purchasing, R&D), many important decisions are now taken by the group board. There are four particularly important group-level committees in which group-wide decisions are prepared: product planning, investments, liquidity and foreign currency, and management (see also Adelt et al., 2008: 15f). For example, the product planning committee

> Prepares a market-oriented product programme for each marque and region that constitutes the basis for the annual planning cycles. Within this committee, strategies are developed for each vehicle segment and strategic positioning models or flagship models, such as roadsters, coupés and dropheads. The committee also defines the target markets and price bands, as well as product-oriented strategies for opening and developing markets in individual regions, and develops strategies for implementing group-wide platform and modules...' (Adelt et al., 2008: 16).

However, decisions made by the group board are not taken in isolation. In particular, managers at the German plants have considerable influence on group-level decisions (see too Jürgens, 2009: 226f), based on the fact that functional heads at German plants meet their corresponding board member once a week in Wolfsburg to discuss and prepare decisions. In comparison, for example, HR heads in foreign plants have much less scope to influence decisions, whether in discussions or informal conversations, as they only confer once a week with the head of HR at Wolfsburg by video conference (VM03). Their access to group-level management is always mediated, and correspondingly limited both in range and potential persuasiveness. The special role of the German operations is not only the result of the firm's corporate strategy: as already noted, it is a formal outcome of the provisions of the Volkswagen Law, which requires a two-thirds majority of the supervisory board for plant closures. German plant managers act on the basis of this, safe in the knowledge that their operation is secure within the overall group – despite not having any direct representation on the supervisory board.

In addition to the local level (group headquarters) and the national level (participation of German plants), the global level also has a comparatively high significance as far as decisions over the allocation of production volumes and investment are concerned. By contrast, there is no clearly defined European level within the group (VWM02).

One important channel of influence for both German and non-German plants are the so-called 'strategic planning rounds'. These take place at global level once a year, usually in November, and include all plant managers in preparing and discussing strategic discussions (see also Jürgens, 2009: 235).

> At VW this is organised through annual so-called planning rounds. As of 2008, we are in planning round 56, and next year will be planning round 57. These plans look five

years into the future, with concrete investment decisions being made for the next two to three years (VWE04).

Although plant managers have quite considerable scope for influencing the strategic planning process, this is subject to quite tight limits. As far as decisions on investment, production volumes and workforce issues are concerned, plant managers have some scope for flexibility – provided this remains within the overall planning targets (one-year plan and five-year plan). However, the financial scope for individual plants is subject to stringent centrally-set parameters. In the field of staffing, plant managers have the power to appoint section heads (*Abteilungsleiter*) (VWM03). However, this is also subject to a narrow corridor set by central plans and centrally-set targets for the staff development programme.

> Someone can't just say 'I'm going to hire 500 people externally, and that we've got 500 too many here'. That wouldn't make sense. That is, this sort of staff planning is always properly coordinated (VWM03).

However, a number of areas of relatively substantive autonomy continue to exist at plant level. For example, interviewees from SEAT management stressed that the SEAT board could make comparatively autonomous decisions on the choice of suppliers or investment – within the corridor of the strategic guidelines on products and plants set by the group management board. Although SEAT is closely integrated into the group's internal supply relationships, within this overall context individual marques have fairly extensive autonomy within 'decision cascades' (VWM04/05).

Decisions on the allocation of production volumes or make/buy decisions are preceded by internal tendering, often augmented by external requests for tenders (see Jürgens, 2009: 230). The significance of such 'market mechanisms' has grown as the group has stepped up its cross-brand planning and decision-making.

> It's no longer taken for granted that Audi builds all Audis or that VW makes all VWs. New products are tendered throughout the group. It might happen that in future an Audi A1 and a VW Polo will be assembled on the same assembly line at a single VW plant (VWM03).

Tenders have triggered competition between plants, with each submitting proposals or tendering for new activities. At the same time, plants participate in decision-making through the committee system. VW coordinates its decision-making processes using a variety of mechanisms and instruments, with a key role played by the multiplicity of committees (see too Adelt et al., 2008). This process consist of discussions and negotiations in which the specific aspects of tender submissions made by plants are improved on and, where appropriate, negotiated.

> The [decision-making process] takes place in committees. The plants are involved in these, and this is also discussed in advance with representatives at the plants. Plants have scope within this arrangement to submit an additional proposal [...] We also need the agreement of the local trade unions and workplace employee representatives for many of these things (VWM01).

VW is characterised by a mixture of centralised and decentralised aspects in the field of culture. In the first instance, the *culture* of the VW group is strongly marked by the home country and, specifically as the 'VW culture', by the company's own traditions. As such, it can be categorised as having a 'somewhat centralised' character (see too Helbig et al., 2001). For example, the company has set out seven 'values and guidelines' intended to guide all company activities.[96] At the same time, individual brands also have both a strong (national) identity and culture, which would indicate a 'somewhat decentralised' distribution of cultural elements.

This can be seen in the proportion of German managers in non-German plants. For a long time, it was customary for foreign plants to be managed by German staff. This began to change relatively recently following recognition of the fact that local managers often offered the advantage of familiarity with the local culture, which was especially helpful when dealing with local workforce representatives. Our Spanish interviewees described SEAT management as a largely Spanish, with some German expatriates. Around 20 per cent of the 'Gerentes/Directores' in the Spanish plants are non-Spanish, of whom around 85 per cent are German managers: these work at the top two management levels, but not at section head level, with more limited interaction with shop-floor employees.

The case of VW's acquisition of Škoda also points to mixture of centralised and decentralised aspects to the distribution of cultural elements. As is usually the case with takeovers, strategically significant management posts were immediately staffed with VW managers. In addition, some 300 'foreign service employees' were posted to the three Škoda plants: these were known as 'Tandems', with local managerial posts temporarily double-staffed by expatriates and local employees (see Klemm and Popp, 2005). The main source of problems was Škoda's strong independent culture, which has continued to the present. VW's original attempt to 'restructure' Škoda in line with VW's own philosophy failed 'due to the ideological suspicion of the Czech workforce, against the background of their prior experience with "actually-existing socialism"'(ibid. 127). Škoda continues to retain a strong independent brand identity and organisational culture that is not readily subsumable within VW's culture. Overall, the plethora of marques within the group suggests a more decentralised culture. A number of the brands have a clear national connotation and origin (Škoda, SEAT, Scania), but are also sold worldwide.

The internal symbols used in the group are also largely standardised throughout the company's operations, with uniform terminology used to denote various functions and posts. The hierarchy is also identical in all plants. As far as communication within the group is concerned, both German and English are used at management level. However, German is the main company language, and German-speakers can be found at many non-German locations within the group. There is a standardised staff development and management training programme, which is obligatory for all

96 These include 'customer orientation', 'high performance', 'creating values', 'capacity for innovation', 'respect', 'responsibility', and 'sustainability' (see Adelt et al., 2008: 21f.).

managers. This includes working in a range of departments and posts at Wolfsburg and in operations abroad (VWM03).

The distribution of *knowledge* at VW occupies a midway position in terms of centralisation. For a long period, R&D activities were organised on a relatively decentralised basis. Up until 1995, each marque had its own product development organisation or department: although these were coordinated, this function was strongly tied to its own brand and retained a high degree of autonomy. This overlap in product development competence was steadily reduced in subsequent years as a result of the new platform strategies. A further step towards centralisation in this area also took place when VW and Audi were given responsibility for most development work, with the role of the marques limited to body design (Jürgens, 1998: 301f.).

However, strategically important knowledge is not strongly centralised within the group. Although Wolfsburg is the largest R&D centre – with some 9,000 employees operating across brand lines[97] – the individual marques retain development capacities at their own headquarters. There is also a high degree of coordination between development locations as engines are developed across brand lines (VWM03). As such, there is a relatively low degree of concentration of knowledge at the group's headquarters.

5.1.3 Coordination of activities within the Volkswagen group

VW has always been a highly networked (in terms of internal supplier relationships) and integrated undertaking (see Marshall, 1991: Pries, 1999b). The degree of coordination within the group has changed markedly over time and has been progressively strengthened, especially following the establishment of the Volkswagen Group in 1994 as the overarching organisation (Jürgens, 1998). Although individual marques are highly coordinated internally, the new strategies in place since the 1990s, aimed at achieving cross-brand synergies, have also bolstered coordination throughout the group as a whole.

Coordination within the group is based on a complex matrix structure that integrates the three dimensions of products and marques (coordination between their assembly plants and component plants); markets and regions (between regions and across regions); and functions and business processes. This is managed by a number of 'central departments and object-oriented multi-disciplinary committees' (Adelt et al., 2008: 45), which bring together members from various divisions and which serve to prepare subsequent management decisions (ibid. 45). Coordination is also effected through plans, of which there are various types (one-, two- and five-year), and which are developed by a number of group-level managers. These set out fairly strict guidelines for plants and functional areas within the group as 'in essence they stipulate production volumes, staffing and investment for each plant' (VWE01).

97 For an overview, see <http://www.volkswagen-karriere.de/de/wie_wir_arbeiten/unternehmensbereiche/forschung_und_entwicklung.html> accessed 26 January 2012.

Internal supply relationships, in which there are well-established links between assembly plants and component plants, are also strongly coordinated (VWM03). There are a number of different methods of coordination, each with varying degrees of centralisation and decentralisation. On the one hand, the headquarters in Wolfsburg is the principal focus of coordination for the group as a whole. On the other, coordination also takes place in a networked pattern through the matrix structure. For example, Kassel is the lead plant for all foundries throughout the group and international coordination and control is managed from Kassel for this area (VWM03). Communication related to this takes place without any major involvement from Wolfsburg.

Decision-making within the group can be denoted as strongly coordinated, reflected in the high density and varying forms of communication (personal meetings, phone calls and e-mail) within management, between the corporate headquarters and local operations, and between management and workforce representatives. In addition to the annual planning rounds, there are large numbers of other meetings.

> Before [the planning rounds] there are, of course, a lot of discussions. And no papers go up to the supervisory board without employee representatives being involved, for example. In relation to one planning round, there will be regular meetings at that level, and also distributed over the year, depending on progress against the plan (VWE04).

Whereas there is evidence of strong coordination of decision-making at the German plants, direct communication with other EU operations, and especially with non-EU operations, seems to be less intensive. Heads of function at non-German EU operations have face-to-face meetings in Wolfsburg every eight weeks, but those outside Europe only twice a year. Foreign operations are integrated on personnel issues with the help of their own corporate-level manager – the head of International HR – whose task it is to ensure that information flows between headquarters and foreign plants.

Control of local activities mostly takes place through the corporate centre. Departmental heads at the plants report once a week directly to the appropriate member of the management board. In addition, there are monthly standardised reports that provide defined data and reporting systems which headquarters-based managers can use to observe global developments in real time (VWM01). It was emphasised the issue is less that of 'control' in the narrow sense but rather a mutual exchange of information, views and ideas (VWM03).

5.2 The European Volkswagen Group Works Council

5.2.1 Establishment of the European Volkswagen Group Works Council

The European Volkswagen Group Works Council (referred to for simplicity in this section as the 'Volkswagen/VW EWC' or simply 'EWC') was constituted on 30 August 1990, and was the first EWC at a vehicle manufacturer, anticipating the adoption of the EWC Directive by some four years. It was set up on the independent initiative of workforce representatives at Volkswagen AG, Audi AG and SEAT.

One important motive was the strong tradition of international union cooperation between plants and firms in the VW group and the emphasis on international employee solidarity adopted by the group works council (*Konzernbetriebsrat*). 'The essence of this approach was its moral and political aspiration to secure uniform humanitarian and democratic standards and trade union rights throughout the entire Volkswagen group' (Haipeter, 2000: 259).

In addition, the establishment of a cross-border body for interest regulation was also a response to the expansion of the group that had been in train since the mid-1980s, and the threats that been perceived in the introduction of parallel production and cost-based inter-plant competition (see above and Jürgens, 2009: 237; Widuckel, 2004: 61).[98] The 1988 SEAT crisis, when management decided to transfer some Polo production to Spain, leaving Wolfsburg dependent on a single model (the Golf), was also an experience that gave further impetus to these efforts.

Official management recognition of the EWC took place in February 1992 and the installation agreement[99] was signed in public at the European Parliament. Observers emphasised that the industrial relations climate at VW, characterised by cooperative and trust-based relationships between management and employee representatives, played a major part in concluding the formal agreement.

> Recognition of the European Works Council by corporate management in February 1992 was a product of the many decades of personnel management philosophy at Volkswagen, which aimed at achieving common standards in dealing with freely-elected employee representatives. That is, respect for trade union organising, recognition of trade unions at the workplace, and recognition of trade unions as a negotiating partner (Uhl and Lavon, 1997: 222).

In recognising the EWC, VW also ignored the negative view of employee participation in cross-border companies that prevailed amongst employers. VW's aim was to lay down a marker on the issue of social standards, explicitly adopt a pioneer role, and provide a positive signal for the legislative process on employee rights at European level (Klebe and Roth, 2000: 751). Concluding an EWC agreement at this early stage meant that it could continue, as negotiated, under Article 13 of the 1994 Directive. The EWC is an employee-only body (the 'German model') and the agreement reflects the specific VW culture of codetermination. In effect, the mode of cooperative agreement – 'cooperative conflict management' and 'social responsibility' (Haipeter, 2000: 266f.) – between management and employee representatives was translated to the European level. 'Social dialogue and competitiveness constitute the pillars of a productivity pact at European level between corporate management

98 The first steps towards cross-border employee coordination were made in 1966 when a VW world company council was established on the initiative of the International Metalworkers' Federation (see Speidel, 2005: 207f.).

99 'Agreement on Cooperation between the Management of the Volkswagen Group and the Volkswagen European Group Works Council' (7 February 1992), Preamble.

and the European Group Works Council' (ibid.). Management and employee representatives agreed to work 'together at European level in the spirit of constructive dialogue and cooperative surmounting of economic, social and ecological challenges and for jointly solving any conflicts which may arise'.[100]

It is hard to gauge the role and significance of the VW EWC without taking into account the complex and interwoven 'system' of codetermination institutions that have grown up in the group over many years (see too Koch, 1987; Mertens, 1994). The most important pillars of this are board-level codetermination through employee representation on the supervisory board and the VW works council. Both these strands have operated over a long period under the framework of the 'Volkswagen Law' (see above): this granted the *Land* government of Lower Saxony a high level of influence over group-level decisions through a blocking minority and limited the voting rights of some shareholders to a maximum of 20 per cent, irrespective of their actual shareholding (see the Introduction to the English Edition, in this volume). The VW EWC and the VW Global Group Works Council (established in 1998) are also a product of the development of employee participation and cooperation and are closely linked with the Wolfsburg works council and group works council (Haipeter, 2000; Helbig, 1999; Speidel, 2005; Müller et al., 2004b).

In turn, the VW EWC's integration into the 'VW system' and the long-standing traditions of international employee cooperation mean that its achievements cannot be considered in isolation. For example, two European agreements concluded under the aegis of the EWC – the 2002 'Social Charter' and the 2004 'Agreement on Workplace Safety' – were formally signed not by the EWC but by the Global Group Works Council. And both participants and observers ascribe the EWC a central role in negotiations with management during the conflict over the closure of the company's Brussels plant, in which it acted way beyond the usual framework of EWC activity (see the section on 'Outputs' below).

5.2.2 Distribution of resources, power, culture and knowledge within the VW EWC

In 2008, the Volkswagen EWC comprised thirty-four members from eleven countries. With fourteen members, the German contingent was by far the largest single group. Other countries had far fewer seats each: Spain had five; the Czech Republic three; and Belgium, Hungary, Sweden and Poland each had two. There was one seat each for the UK, Italy, Portugal and Slovakia. Members of these delegations corresponded in some cases with constituent companies of the group. In the German contingent, for example, eight members were from Volkswagen, and two from Audi and VW Sachsen (with plants in Zwickau and Chemnitz in Saxony). There is a

---

100 'Agreement on Cooperation between the Management of the Volkswagen Group and the Volkswagen European Group Works Council' (7 February 1992), Principles.

delegate from Sitech GmbH, the seat design and manufacturing subsidiary, and one member represents the 'Committee for Financial Services and Sales'.[101]

The allocation of places has undergone a number of changes since the EWC was established, as documented in the various amendments to the installation agreement. While the EWC had only seventeen members in 1992, this had risen to twenty-five by 1999. The share accounted for by German members rose by four by 2008. In 1992, the German operations had ten seats in all, eight from VW AG and two from Audi. This was added to in 1995 by a member from VW Sachsen. In November 1995, two members were added from the Czech Republic and one from Slovakia (VW Bratislava) following the acquisition of Škoda. These members had participated unofficially in EWC meetings since 1992 (Haipeter, 2000: 267). As such, VW was the first company to formally include its Eastern European operations in an EWC. The growth of the EWC largely benefited the new companies integrated into the group, for the most part outside Germany: this also led to a fall in the quantitative German dominance of the forum.

Figure 6: Distribution of seats in the Volkswagen EWC, 2008.

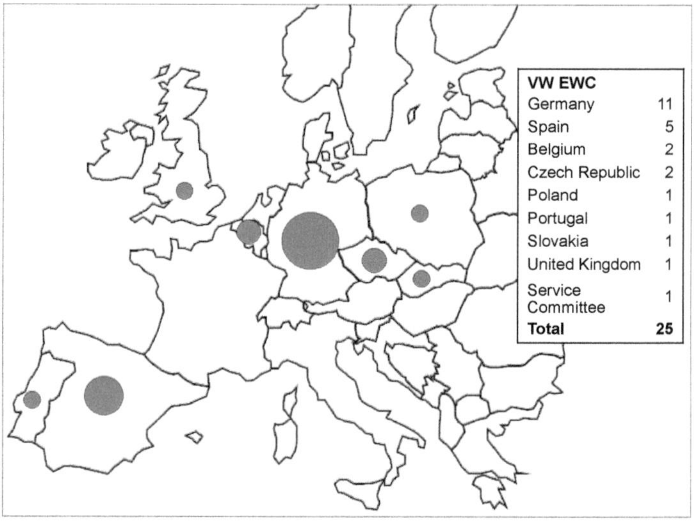

Source: authors' compilation based on VW Group Annual Report, 2008

The distribution of seats has never corresponded with distribution of the workforce by location or country. And in determining the allocation of seats, there has never been any attempt to reflect the proportion of the workforce at particular plants or

101 This committee has sixteen members in all (see below).

operations. Rather, all products and brands in a country are to be included: 'For example, Spain is represented by a total of five delegates (three delegates for Seat and two for VW Navarra), while the Czech Republic and Škoda "only" have two delegates despite a similar sized workforce' (Eurofound, 2006: 4).

The arrangements for the distribution of EWC seats were also chosen with the aim of strengthening the morale and identity of the EWC and promoting cooperation between the large number of national actors, with their diverse trade union traditions and divergent approaches. It was clear to the initiators from the outset that the EWC could only acquire an effective capacity to act through voluntary cooperation and consensus, not by pushing through majority decisions that might simply have reflected German concerns (Uhl and Lavon, 1997: 223f.).

Compared with the rest of our sample, the distribution of seats on the EWC can be denoted as 'somewhat centralised': only 41 per cent of places are occupied by German members (compared with a home-country share of 57 per cent at PSA, 53 per cent at Renault, 21 per cent at GM, and 28 per cent at Ford). The EWC representativeness index[102] – which expresses the relationship between the home-country share of EWC places and the represented workforce – is 0.53,[103] with a clear advantage to non-home country locations. On the other hand, with 41 per cent of the total, the German members continue to be the largest group, able to overrule other national contingents not only through this numerical dominance but for other reasons discussed below (see also Figures 24 and 25 in the Appendix).

The issue of the resources available to the EWC was regulated by the installation agreement.[104] The costs of supporting individual members are borne by their respective subsidiary. This includes the costs for everyday EWC activity together with travel, translations and external experts. Although the EWC appears to grant equal access to resources to all members, in practice those located at the group's headquarters can draw on a wider resource base due to the link with German representation bodies (local works council and group works council) that can be mobilised for EWC work.

German codetermination arrangements give local employee representatives access to formal training opportunities. In comparison, according to the Spanish EWC members, there is no comparable provision in Spain: it was also reported that no resources were made available to attend meetings (VWE08). However – as with a number of other locations – there are staff with German language abilities able to translate material for EWC members.

102 For the calculation of this, see Chapter 3.3.1 above.

103 The calculation is based on German and EU employee numbers and the distribution of EWC seats in 2008.

104 This was subsequently expanded by the 1992 'Agreement on Cooperation between the Management of the Volkswagen Group and the Volkswagen European Group Works Council (7 February 1992), Enclosure 3.

The governing group within the EWC – the presidium – is elected by EWC members. Under the EWC agreement, each country must have at least one representative. In 2008, the presidium had fourteen members. In addition, there is a general secretary, who is also elected by EWC members. Compared with the remainder of our sample, this body – with three German members and 21 per cent of the seats – is extremely decentralised in nature: only Toyota has a lower proportion of home-country members. The EWC is also supported by an international office, which is also responsible for the VW Global Group Works Council.

The main tasks of the presidium are to manage the EWC's business and prepare for meetings. It also decides on the choice of an external trade union expert. Based on agreement with the EWC as a whole, the presidium can conduct negotiations with management on issues that require consultation.

In addition to country-based EWC seats and the presidium, two committees have also existed for some time. The Audi Committee (1999–2005) and the Service Committee. The main aim in establishing these was to represent all employees in the group – the chair of each was also a member of the EWC – but without making the EWC itself so large that it would become unwieldy (VWE02). The Service Committee was set up in 2002 as the successor to the Finance and Sales Committee, which had been established in 1996 with the aim of including staff from the financial services division and the VW sales network.[105] This committee has since been assigned to the Group World Council, and in 2008 had sixteen members. It meets at least once a year independently and is represented by one representative on the EWC, with a rotating membership. It is organised on a decentralised basis, with just four members from Germany (finance, logistics, retail, and Audi sales) and countries are also represented, even if they have no manufacturing operations (France, Netherlands, Austria).

As far as the distribution of power and scope for exerting influence is concerned, German employee representatives enjoy a structural advantage compared with their colleagues from abroad. Previous studies have highlighted the inequality of power on the VW EWC, which in essence is product of the German system of employment regulation, the configuration of codetermination arrangements at VW, and the accumulation of posts by a number of important office-holders.

> Firstly, under the German law on stock corporations the supervisory board of Volkswagen AG – and hence the employee side of the supervisory board – is not only responsible for appointing the group management board and for oversight and control of the business of Volkswagen AG but also has competence for the entire group, given that in practice the German parent company is also the financier of other brands and regions within the group and the centre for corporate-level decision-making. Secondly, the German central works council of Volkswagen AG is located at the level of

105 '4th Protocol Note Concerning the Agreement on Cooperation between Volkswagen Group Management and the European Volkswagen Group Works Council' (21 November 1996), Article 1.

> the company as a whole, and its management board, which is coterminous with the group management board. As such, German employee representatives have privileged access to Volkswagen at group level. Thirdly, the location of the group headquarters in Wolfsburg, also the location of the German combine works council, creates both geographical proximity to the group management board and ease of communication, as well as to other central group business functions that are also located at the same site (Haipeter, 2000: 33).

The accumulation of roles and posts also allows German employee representatives, and in particular the chair of the EWC – who is also chair of the group works council and a member of the supervisory board – to have a headstart in terms of information and influence (see too Dombois, 2009).

> The VW EWC is strongly rooted in the German system of codetermination and also strongly influenced by this culture in a direct way: both the EWC president and general secretary are from Volkswagen Germany; at the same time, the EWC president is also the head of the company's central works council, president of the WWC and a member of the Volkswagen management committee of the supervisory Board (Eurofound 2006: 4).

The privileged position of the EWC chair and general secretary is also due to the fact that employee representatives are based at the group's headquarters, the site of decisions affecting the business as a whole. As such, VW's group organisation – with a clear, centralised decision-making centre – also promotes the power of the German group works council, and in particular employee representatives in Wolfsburg. Although other companies in our sample have similar arrangements, such as Ford, PSA and Renault, the long-standing and deeply-embedded position of home-country representatives at VW and its workplace culture stands out by comparison. Not only is there a close local fit between decision-making and centres for employee representation; German employee representatives have also traditionally had close contact with central management via the group works council. Such access to group-level management level also opens a channel of possible influence for the EWC.

Other German EWC members also have privileged access to management through their membership of the group works council, a body that is frequently described as the real working forum and the 'centre for employee representation' within the undertaking.

> The fact is that the tune gets played in Germany before decisions are made – via the supervisory board, and, in a much more amplified version, in the group works council. [...] Ongoing work takes place on the group works council or its committee, and that's where real discussions take place. As far as agreeing positions is concerned, all the same people are involved: group works council members are all represented on the EWC and the World Works Council, so that there is a complete pass through of information (VWE04).

From the standpoint of the German employee representatives, the fact that some EWC members have a privileged status is not seen as problematic as long as the necessary transparency is maintained and the actors involved do not exploit the situation for their own benefit.

> On the other hand, we elect the people to these functions so that they can coordinate and prepare. If there is transparency and we do not have the feeling that we're kept in the dark, then this is fine (VWE04).

The standard topics at EWC meetings are the financial situation, sales, products and staffing. Topics for discussion at meetings, or those that should be addressed in the management presentation, are agreed between management and the presidium (VWE02), with the EWC usually beginning by stating which information it would like to have. As well as the EWC's regular agenda items, particular topics might also be identified for consideration.

> There is a detailed presentation by the management board that is very comprehensive, as a far as I can see. Topics for discussion are agreed beforehand and the works council says what it would like and we then look at what the agenda should be. There can be specialist topics – last year we had work organisation in VW AG – and an extra topic, the company's components strategy (VWM02).

One German EWC member emphasised that, in principle, all those involved have an opportunity to participate and that all concerns were taken up by the presidium. However, the presidium itself noted that the option of proposing agenda items was rarely taken up by non-German EWC members.

> They always have the opportunity [to raise their own interests]. If someone were to come along and say 'I'd like that item on the agenda' then we could do that: but it never happens! (VWE02).

One further source of power flows from the existence of an international office specifically responsible for the EWC and Global Group Works Council. This serves as the 'powerhouse and coordinator' of activities (VWE02). The position is usually staffed on a long-term basis, leading to a close relationship with EWC members. And since the individual concerned participates in all meetings, they also develop a high level of information and rich contacts (VWE02). In addition, there is an almost permanent exchange with HR management: 'We're in constant contact – that's our everyday work' (VWE02). The same applies for cooperation between the EWC general secretary and the head of international HR.

Compared with our findings on the issue of the pattern of distribution of power and resources, which mostly suggest a somewhat centralised structure, a more decentralised arrangement would appear to prevail in the area of culture. In the first instance, our interviews with German and non-German EWC members gave no indication that the German representatives might attempt to impose their views on non-German colleagues or the EWC as a whole. Rather, it appeared that there was an explicit effort to take account of national cultural features and traditions as a type of 'local responsiveness'. This was attributable, in turn, to a shared aim by the initiators to create a body that was both efficient and effective. This required acceptance on the part of all those concerned. An attempt by one party to dominate the other – in cultural terms – would have put 'Project EWC' at risk from the outset.

> Criteria that have played a role were, firstly, the diversity of trade unions, as in Belgium, that allowed all to be represented. [...] Achieving an effective working body was clearly an objective (VWE02).

The distribution of EWC seats also points to a decentralised culture, in which the trade union pluralism that characterised some countries is expressly recognised. Spain and Belgium, for example, which had a number of competing unions at a single plant, were granted additional seats. The process through which country seats were allocated was also not standardised but left to national custom and practice.

> If this had been carried out proportionally, as far as I understand, it would have led to an under-representation of the smaller operations. In addition, the different traditions of representation and legislation, the representation in Spain, for example, by trade union representatives and up to three or four competing unions at a plant, would *have felt entirely unrepresented* (VWE04: emphasis added).

In contrast, the use of languages within the EWC points to a partly decentralised and partly centralised structure. Although there is simultaneous interpretation at all meetings, and minutes are translated into national languages, most EWC staff have a high level of language ability and are able to function as 'coordination centres' for many locations directly in the local language (VWE04). However, German has a greater significance in everyday business. This is shown in the fact that in many plants, employee representatives have access to colleagues who speak German and who can translate in the event of immediate enquiries. However, this also means that in some cases there is no direct communication between the centre and local operations. According to SEAT representatives, they only communicated with the centre via an EWC representative who spoke German (VWE08; VWE09). There was no direct contact between them and Wolfsburg: however, they did communicate by phone directly with Spanish-speaking representatives from Argentina, Brazil and Mexico. One further example is the central works council intranet, which is also accessible to employee representatives from outside Germany. However, the fact that content is in German means that effective access depends on having translation support.

Access to knowledge resources, needed to develop strategies, is also easier for home-country representatives than for non-German EWC members, given the group structure and their inclusion in the German group and central works council arrangements. Non-German EWC members are reliant on the communication undertaken by the presidium, which selects the information to be distributed and also excludes what it considers is not of relevance.

> The fact that we regularly have meetings with the chair in the central works council committee and the group works council committee, in addition to the EWC meeting cycle, means that we are in the flow of information on an ongoing basis and also in a position to shape opinions. This is certainly more difficult for the colleagues in Spain, who only receive information from time to time from the office and who are not situated in the flow of information (VWE04).

For the non-German EWC members, the EWC also represents a source of information that is usually not available through other means, such as from local management. On occasions it was emphasised that membership of the EWC meant that employee representatives had access to more information than their local managers (VWE03). As such, the EWC's open approach to information contributes to a more even distribution of knowledge within the group.

5.2.3 Coordinating EWC activities

The high level of coordination of EWC activities can be read off from a number of indicators. The EWC meets fairly frequently as a plenary body. In addition, regular, almost fixed, dates are set for meetings, with one plenary meeting each year.[106] A further meeting is held as a meeting of the Global Group Works Council. Although not all EWC members are members of the Global Group Works Council – in order to keep this forum 'slim and trim' (VWE02) – in practice they are all invited and attend. As such, the Global Group Works Council meeting is also, in effect, an expanded EWC meeting. Additional meetings are held should exceptional circumstances require it, as with the threatened closure of the Brussels plant (VWE02). The presidium also meets twice a year in addition to the regular EWC/ Global Group Works Council meetings, with scope for further ad hoc meetings if needed.

The frequency of communication between official meetings is fairly high. There are also numerous decentralised communication links between individual EWC meetings or groups. For example, meetings are held between SEAT representatives and Audi works council members (VWE05, VWE06).[107] Working parties have also been set up to deal with particular problems. EWC members from different sites also maintain direct contact, depending on the issue. One EWC representative reported on a visit from foreign colleagues.

> We clear some cases independently, dependent on what we are supposed to do. [...] we talk to each other. In fact, the guys from [the foreign plant] are coming over at

---

106 Following the VW corruption affair, all EWC and Group World Council meetings were initially held in Germany in order to counter the perception that such events were 'pleasure trips'. Since 2007, some EWC meetings have begun to be held outside Germany.

107 The close contact between Audi and SEAT representatives is due to the fact that SEAT was managed via Audi for a period after 2000'; SEAT operations have since been brought back within the direct scope of the VW group.

> the end of this month. They are going to visit me. [...] They are coming to see Bentley and Bentley will put up a tour for them to attend a football game and so on (VWE03).

Although our interviewees at Wolfsburg stressed that most EWC members knew each other, and that in principle could all communicate with each other, contacts were often initiated through the EWC centre. There are a number of reasons why the flow of communications is focused on the centre. Some are simply pragmatic, given that the group works council at the group's headquarters centralises all information of relevance for the EWC. 'Much of the information arrives here and is then distributed from here. And many of the enquiries from colleagues also arrive here' (VWE02).

> The EWC official is the coordinating centre and known to everyone. They coordinate if requests come in, and asks whether there has been a response, and whether this is still outstanding. We also receive information there, and if there is a conflict somewhere [...] We are more likely to receive from them via the central office than directly (VWE04).

In addition, efforts are made to standardise channels of communication within the EWC, at least as far as official or generally relevant issues are concerned. There are agreements within the EWC under which the centre should be notified about any communication between individual EWC members. The context for this is the view that the EWC should respond in a unified way, which presupposes a consistent foundation of information.

> If internal matters touch on our work, we are more inclined to [communicate] through official channels. *In terms of information, we've arranged matters so that we do not build up independent channels*, but rather we communicate with each other in a coordinated way. That's why the office was created [...]: Q: 'If you write an e-mail, would you CC Wolfsburg?'. A: 'Yes, they go in CC' (VWE04).

This provision means that, even if there is no language problem to impede direct communication, such communication only takes place between individual operations on less important matters. Whether there is direct contact between EWC representatives can often turn on personal relationships and trust. Given that the type of information that might be exchanged can touch on highly sensitive and contentious matters, the decision to pass information through the EWC centre seems a reasonable one.

5.2.4 Critical events

The history and development of the VW EWC has been punctuated by a number of notable events, in addition to other influences. The most significant of these have been (1) the 1993/94 SEAT crisis, (2) the establishment of the Global Group Works Council in 1998, (3) the VW 'corruption affair' in 2005, which led to the resignation of the long-standing head of the groups works council and EWC, Klaus Volkert, and (4) the conflict over the proposed closure of the Brussels plant, in which the intervention of the EWC played a major role in retaining operations with some 40 per cent of the workforce.

(1) The SEAT crisis 1993/94

The SEAT crisis represented a milestone in the development of the VW EWC in that it was the first time that there was a clear and urgent need for transnational coordination between employee representatives following the severe impact of the crisis of the early-1990s in European car markets on SEAT. The rationalisation programme not only envisaged substantial financial flows from VW to its Spanish subsidiary, but also a loss of some 10,000 jobs. The EWC made a major contribution to the fact that the restructuring programme that followed the crisis was resolved without conflict through its success in balancing a number of diverse interests – including German top management, and Spanish, German and other European employee representatives (see Haipeter, 2000: 449ff.). The German works council members played a particularly important role in that by dealing with top management – as it were as advocates of their Spanish colleagues – they helped extend the principle of socially-responsible restructuring and workforce reductions to the company's foreign operations.

> In fact, the EWC emerged strengthened from this crisis, as the actors succeeded in retaining the principle of a solidaristic approach to how risks and opportunities should be dealt with and because the European level of bargaining gained in significance in the management of the crisis (Haipeter, 2000: 450).

However, the successful resolution of the crisis at the same time revealed an 'open flank' in the EWC's policy of international solidarity, as, while the EWC's scope was confined to Europe, including by that stage Eastern European operations, VW's growing internationalisation and new production strategies suggested that the task of employee representation would be faced by much wider international challenges.

(2) The Establishment of the VW Global Group Works Council

As early as 1996, meetings took place between trade unionists and workforce representatives from VW operations in Brazil, Argentina, Mexico and South Africa in the context of EWC meetings. The Global Group Works Council was set up in 1998, and an agreement was formally signed with management in 1999 (Klebe and Roth, 2000). The forum is based in Wolfsburg and chaired by the head of the EWC and group works council. There are forty-four seats, with fifteen countries represented (as of 2008). The information and consultation provisions in the installation agreement closely match those of the EWC. There are two meetings a year, with a plenary meeting in the summer and a meeting of the steering committee in the autumn. Most EWC members also have a seat on the Global Group Works Council, and those who do not have a seat in their own right are always invited to meetings: an EWC meeting is always held at the same time.

Since its foundation, this body had emerged as a significant actor within the company. Firstly, the group's structure and decision-making processes mean that the international level is now more significant and – in contrast to the EWC which has no equivalent level of management – the Global Group Works Council has an international management level as a counterparty at the same level within the group. And secondly, guided by their commitment to international solidarity, German employee representatives have sought to extend their achievements in the field of representation to international operations. This also indicated a clear trend towards going beyond the limits of European interest representation and focusing more consciously on the global level.[108]

(3) The 'VW affair'

The 'VW affair', which emerged in 2005, began with revelations about corruption at Škoda but soon widened out to involve the head of personnel at VW, Peter Hartz, when details of a scandal over 'pleasure trips' became known, in which works council members were given a range of inducements to adopt a cooperative line with management (Dombois, 2009).[109] The former chair of the works council and other works council members had used their position over many years to obtain financial benefits for themselves and other works councillors.

The scandal, which prompted the resignation of the chair of the works council, marked a turning point in the work of international employee representation, and eroded the confidence of ordinary employees and many trade unionists and workforce representatives in the company's operations outside Germany.

> It was during a time in which colleagues already had a lack of trust in the leadership of the EWC and Global Group Works Council. Re-establishing it and putting it on a new foundation required a high level of transparency, and it is on such a basis now: everyone knows it's changed. If I say something, it's now recorded in the minutes and I'll get an answer; there is discussion and support for a solution (VWE04).

While German works council members, in particular, feared a serious loss of trust and support for the institutions of codetermination at VW, and possibly for IG Metall's reputation at the plant, in fact those who stood for election on the IG Metall list emerged with very good results in the subsequent works council election (see Dombois, 2009). EWC members are now fully aware of the serious consequences and risks of such a loss of trust and confidence for the work of international interest representation. One result of the scandal can be seen in the efforts to ensure that representation is transparent (VWE04).

(4) The conflict over the proposed closure of the VW plant in Brussels

In 2004, overcapacity and the satiation of European markets led to the prospects of job losses throughout the group. The largest losses were at the German plants, where there was a reduction of 20,000 jobs, mainly through early retirement and voluntary

---

108 The VW Social Charter, adopted in 2002 and signed by the Global Group Works Council, codified the provisions set out in ILO norms.

109 See too <http://www.spiegel.de/wirtschaft/0,1518,449888,00.html>.

redundancy. In 2006, VW announced that it intended to close its Brussels plant, with a loss of 5,400 jobs. This was part of a reorganisation of Golf production, in which assembly would no longer take place at three sites but be concentrated in Wolfsburg and the Mosel plant in East Germany. The express reason for this was that, following the cuts already made at the German plants, other non-German operations needed to be brought into the restructuring programme.[110] From the EWC's point of view, there was criticism of the untypically poor level of information disclosure by management. For example, the issue was not raised at the EWC meeting held just a month before the announcement of the decision: 'Even when the issue was raised, no statement was made about the Brussels plant' (VWE02). For the EWC, the reason for this was attributable to the then head of the Volkswagen brand, Wolfgang Bernhard (ibid.).

In response to management's plans, the EWC presidium held an extraordinary meeting. On 12 December 2006, it adopted a common position criticising management's approach and called for a 'pain-sharing' strategy – an equal distribution of risks and opportunities – within the VW group. Management was asked to present a detailed restructuring plan covering all European plants, to include alternative strategies for securing their continuing operations and to indicate any scope for developing new areas of employment.[111] The decision to close the plant completely was eventually withdrawn under pressure from the EWC and trade unions, with 2,000 of the original 5,400 jobs secured.

Assessments of the outcome and role of the EWC in the conflict vary as between those involved. Whereas many – and not only German – employee representatives viewed the outcome in positive terms, others did not regard it as a success.

> 3000 jobs [lost], that's not a victory. That's just the way you look at it, isn't it? Then he [the EWC member] said to me: what if it would have got closed? And I said yeah, maybe you should have closed it (VWE03).

The Slovakian EWC representative expressed himself in similar terms, given that retaining the Brussels plant implied transferring production to Brussels that had to be offset at other plants by cutting numbers of temporary agency staff (VWE02: 18). This had a severe impact on the Slovakian operations, where there was a high proportion of such employees. This approach led to open conflict between employee representatives from different countries at the EWC meeting. The British representatives reported that an exchange took place that culminated in the Slovakian member leaving the meeting.

> They took cars from Slovakia to Brussels and laid off temporary contracts. And [the Slovakian representative] said 'I understand what you are saying to me. But still I have got to worry about my plant and say it to my workers, even though they are temporary' [...] So he walks out of that meeting. He was pretty much angry (VWE03).

---

110 VW Press Release (21 November 2006): 'Restructuring of Volkswagen Brussels'.

111 'Joint Statement of the Volkswagen European Group Works Council' (7 December 2006).

The presidium viewed the events as a successful example of a 'pain-sharing' strategy that achieved a fair balance between different plants on the basis of mutual solidarity, and in line with the objective of an equable distribution of risks and opportunities.

> I think we were able to survive even in difficult times because from the outset we maintained that we had to make sure that *opportunities and risks within the group were shouldered equally.* So far we have succeeded. It should also be said that, of course, the German operations have given up very many vehicles to support other European plants. [...] It's easy to see what balancing has taken place over the past decade for reasons of solidarity (VWE01).

German managers also saw the Brussels case as an exemplary success for the EWC, and highlighted the interaction between the EWC as representative of the workforce and group management.

> Was that a success for the EWC? Quite clearly, yes it was. Of course, a change in the management board helped. [...] I'm convinced that this led to the fact that this is now an Audi plant, where we'll produce the Audi A1 in the future. It would not have turned out like that if there had not been a European Works Council, and they had a lot to do with this (VWM03).

Analysis of the conflict suggests that the (contested) outcome was brought about through a number of important elements; on the one hand, the *organisational fit* between the EWC and the company played a large part, as did other factors, such as the developmental trajectory of both the EWC and the company and the culture of their interaction, relationships between the actors, and solidarity. One major contributing factor was the engagement of a number of key individuals. Bernd Osterloh, the chair of the group works council and EWC, took a strongly proactive role in order to retain the Brussels plant: this was not a completely self-evident stance, as closing the plant would have lifted the pressure on Wolfsburg, and hence his own constituency.

> Yes, of course it all ran via Mr. Osterloh. He played a major role and fought hard for Brussels, although in fact he could have used this to get something for Wolfsburg. He really was wearing a European hat and not a Wolfsburg hat. And he really involved himself to make sure that a solution was found (VWM03).

One important factor was the specific culture of codetermination, in which management and employee representatives had traditionally aimed to resolve problems in a cooperative way: this marked out a path that set out a limited range of options for the actors. In addition, the fit between the structure of codetermination and decision-making structures at VW offered some scope to put pressure on management. In addition to his roles in the EWC and group works council, Osterloh was also a member of the group supervisory board and therefore participated in all significant group-level decisions. One subtle form of pressure that this can facilitate rests on the fact that Osterloh is also co-responsible for extending the contracts of management board members (VWM03). Management was also aware that, based on the long period of trust and solidarity built between different plants through involvement in the EWC, the workforce would stand behind the decisions of the EWC and be prepared to take further action. The final outcome of the Brussels conflict led to a process of learning within the EWC that highlighted the possible significance of the EWC for both German and non-German participants.

5.2.5 Effectiveness of interest regulation and outputs of the EWC

The specific outputs of the EWC in terms of representing employee interests at VW companies are hard to evaluate. The main problems relate to being able make an unambiguous allocation of the results of interest regulation to the various institutions that undertake this function within the VW group, given that the EWC is only one element in a wider system of codetermination and certainly not the most dominant. As a consequence, it is hard to isolate its achievements from those of other institutions for employee participation, and in particular the group works council and Global Group Works Council.

Two agreements were negotiated and concluded with management through the EWC: the 2002 'Social Charter' and a 2004 agreement on workplace safety.[112] However, both were ultimately signed by the Global Group Works Council, which is, in practice, an extension of the EWC. In the case of the Brussels conflict, the EWC was universally seen as having played a crucial role in securing the retention of the plant with 40 per cent of its original workforce. However, in this case too it is not entirely clear who – that is, which actor in the VW codetermination system – this outcome should be attributed to. For example, Bernd Osterloh, the chair of the EWC, played a clearly important role. However, he did not act as an individual but had the support and access to channels of codetermination available to him as the chair of the group works council and the Global Group Works Council, as well as a member of the company's supervisory board.

These findings suggest that Osterloh mobilised political and social capital for the purposes of European interest representation via the EWC – capital that he had acquired through his functions as a member of the supervisory board and chair of the group works council. As such, the EWC gained from its embeddedness in the VW system of codetermination. On the other hand, the EWC also achieved its own value-added as a coordination platform for European plants, contributing

112 The 'Charter on Labour Relations' (also termed in draft form the 'Codetermination Charter') was adopted for all locations represented by the Global Group Works Council and the EWC in late-2009. It is intended to extend elements of employee participation to non-German operations by codifying binding and extensive minimum standards for the participation rights of workplace employee representatives for all operations within the group.

significantly to generating trust and solidarity, which in turn strengthened other codetermination institutions – including the German group works council and even employee representatives on the supervisory board.

The group works council plays a central role in interest regulation in the group, given its location at group level and status as the primary employee counterpart for management at this level. In contrast to GM and Ford, there is no such European-level counterpart at VW. VW's group organisation, the proximity of the group works council to group management and the evolved relationship between group management and the groups works council mean that the EWC plays a relatively subordinate role.

In addition, in terms of international interest regulation, and despite the VW group's high degree of Europeanisation, the EWC does not have a significant function for VW given the particular importance of the global level in addition to the EU. Provisions in the field of interest regulation that are intended to apply to European operations are usually transferred to the global level, as was the case with the Social Charter and proposed Charter of Employee Rights, as an expression of the values of international employee solidarity. However, in this connection it is the Global Group Works Council and not the EWC that is the competent forum.

Despite these difficulties in assigning 'representational success', a number of effects on the scope for interest representation and in particular for the internationalisation of employee representation can be uniquely attributed to the EWC. Previous studies of the VW EWC have noted a range of factors that suggested that the EWC offered added-value for employee interest representation. The most significant of these was the fact that the EWC represented a means for employee coordination, within which employee representatives from different plants could build relationships based on trust and mutual confidence. 'The established institutionalisation of the EWC opened up a structured context for the coordination of employee representation. It held out the prospect of developing relationships of trust between employee representatives' (Widuckel-Mathias, 1993: 146; translated from German)

The EWC created an additional source of information and an instrument of control for both German and non-German employees that allowed them to check the accuracy of management information disclosed on a bilateral basis. 'Information about conditions at other plants provided by local management can be checked. Key elements of competition between plants, such as Saturday working, overtime provisions, breaks or the use of temporary work, must be disclosed' (ibid.: 148) Within the framework of the strategic planning rounds, the EWC is informed and consulted about any decisions that emerge. The EWC agreement covers investment, models, and capacity usage at plants. The EWC allows non-German plants an opportunity to obtain additional information and data on important elements of group strategy; in addition, they also obtain, for the first time, access to and, at least in principle, influence over group-level decisions. This, in turn, enables them to raise problems with local management (see too Widuckel-Mathias, 1993).

> For the foreign plants, this is often their only opportunity for access to the management board and to engage with directly on issues over which there is conflict or about the situation in their operation (VWE04).

Non-German EWC representatives often receive information before their local management (VW03). It is also frequently reported that there are positive feedback effects at local level. In the case of the UK, changes induced by the EWC have led to greater respect for and recognition of employee representatives by management. One non-German EWC representatives compared his current situation with that of his predecessor of a decade before. During this period, the role of the representative had changed from 'supplicant' to those of an accepted counterparty.

> They [HR-Management] normally would not talk to us. My predecessor [...] had to hang around outside managers' officers trying to stop them as they were passing. He had no other means, nothing. He had to just try to stop him as he saw him. It's difficult, isn't it? He was trying to get contact to the manager [...] – he did not return his calls and did not invite to any meeting. Imagine that. Now I see [local HR manager] every day. I walk into his office every day (VWE03).

Interviewees from outside Germany considered that the EWC was, in the main advantageous, as far their concerns went. However, there were varying levels of participation by non-German representatives. As already noted, the scope to raise issues or initiatives on the EWC was scarcely made use of by non-German members. One reason for this is the fact that local employee representatives are unwilling to surrender their role, power (and raison d'être) to a central institution. On the other side, any expansion of the role of the EWC was held to imply a considerable increase in workload.

> I did not know whether the colleagues were interested in transferring their local bargaining opportunities to another level. I think, in terms of work, that would just about kill us here (VWE02).

As a rule, non-German members did not express an aspiration to use the EWC as a negotiating body. For example, the Spanish representatives viewed the EWC as a forum whose main role was to serve as a means for spreading information between individual national employee representatives; secondly for consultation between these representatives; and thirdly for codetermination or greater influence over management decisions (VWE05, VWE06).

The main focus of disagreement between our interviewees was over whether the EWC can be seen as a *negotiating forum*. The fact that the EWC did not have a formal negotiating mandate was confirmed by employee representatives. 'That is really not necessarily a negotiating forum' (VWE02). Management also stated: 'There is no legal position that requires anything to be negotiated [...] We have no need to negotiate' (VWM02). However, in terms of the agreements that had been concluded and the interest representation outcomes of the EWC, the role of the EWC as a *negotiating partner* was confirmed.

We also say that the EWC has been a co-negotiator, that the closure of Brussels was prevented. We have agreements [...] where both [sides[have signed (VWM02).

The employee side also confirmed that they considered that negotiations were held in conflict over the Brussels plant, with the main actors for the EWC side being the president and the general secretary. However, which actors can be regarded as being assigned the role of negotiator for the employee side is unclear, as access to top management is basically via German codetermination institutions.

De facto, of course, it appears like this as the body does not meet on a continuous basis with the other side with negotiations taking place. Rather, this is done through the president and general secretary *because this gives an opportunity for access to top management* (VWE02: emphasis added).

From the standpoint of one management representative, the EWC is a negotiating forum, but one which is restricted to clearly-defined levels and narrowly-circumscribed issues: but in doing this it also lays down a framework for local employee representative bodies.

They conduct negotiations but I would say that these deal with major policy issues: what additional benefits we offer, what we do in the field of vocational training in other countries – but they are not as specific as they would be locally [...] The political line is agreed in the Global Group Works Council or EWC, and then this is negotiated on locally (VWM03).

The Brussels case illustrates that the VW EWC only took on a crucial role when it had to prove its worth in practice and could act as a negotiating partner in a crisis. This does not mean it was previously seen as a valueless institution by EWC members: on the contrary, it was valued for the fact that it was available as a forum for international cooperation and as a potential negotiating actor, as well as for the direct added-value derived from its access to relevant group-level information. This change in the role and significance of the EWC illustrates that an EWC can exist purely as an information body in one phase and as a forum capable of taking action and negotiating in another. This latter aspect highlights the significance of *organisational capacity* as a prerequisite for effective EWC work.

Explanations for the comparatively important role of the EWC have been offered, firstly, in terms of the high need for regulation (pressures due to competition between plants, functional necessity for joint action) and, secondly, the high organisational capacity (operational capability, trust and international solidarity) of employee representatives. The first set of factors have been related to the fact that for the central EWC actors there is an objective – and subjectively perceived – functional necessity for interests to be represented through an EWC. The second set suggests that establishing and making use of an EWC could be seen as a self-evident development, given the paths and values (international solidarity) of employee representatives, and in particular those from Germany. This latter aspect is interesting as it has been argued that in functional terms there is no need for an

EWC as an institution located 'between' the group works council and Global Group Works Council as these latter two bodies offer functional equivalents to the tasks performed by the EWC.

The objective need for regulation can be viewed as comparatively high, given the group's strategic orientation since the mid-1980s. Individual plants have been competing to win production allocations for some time. The form of coordination in the group, and in particular the use of internal market mechanisms, therefore exerts a major influence on the scope for problems that will have to be addressed and resolved by institutions for interest regulation. Parallel production and a further weakening of the facility-brand-link (the classification of facilities within the group in accordance with existing brands) is likely to reinforce the trend towards greater internal competition over capacity and jobs as plants belonging to different brands develop the capability to produce the same model (as with Audi and Škoda) (VWM03).

The subjective need for regulation is reflected in the views and expectations of the actors concerned –EWC representatives of various plants and their workforces. That the EWC is seen as an important body by the German side in its own right is indisputable – aside from its role in the overall canon of representative institutions. The EWC can also be seen as an additional power resource for employee interest representation in Wolfsburg, rooted primarily in the institutional cooperation and international solidarity of VW plants. How this resource is used depends very much on the representative strategies adopted and the individuals involved. 'Bernd Osterloh plays the EWC and Global Group Works Council cards very intensively [...] There is certainly an additional input' (VWM03).

The VW EWC's high level of organisational capacity is mainly a product of the strong coordination of the forum (frequent and regular meetings, close cooperation in the presidium, and connections maintained between official meetings through the Wolfsburg 'coordination office'), the high level of material resources available (finance, information, organisational know-how), and trust and solidarity. Over the course of the history of the EWC, there have been a number of occasions when the EWC has emerged as an active institution.

Cooperation between management and the EWC follows on, in a 'path dependent' way, from the tradition of joint problem solving between employee representatives and group-level management. In addition, our management interviewees cited a number of advantages that the EWC brought to the company, such as minimising the scope for conflict.

> I'll tell you, I know this from [another company], where there's hardly a day without an e-mail turning up: in Italy there was a spontaneous downtools and in France and Spain they set fire to the dustbins. I think we also benefit as a company from this way of working [...], that we are able to work relatively peacefully locally. [...] As a rule we do not have situations like the workers in Spain saying 'We are not going to work' [...] Because we discuss things reasonably ahead, we don't need this type of escalation. [...] And that is a benefit for us. It clearly makes sense (VWM02).

EWC meetings also serve management as a source of information about the situation and problems in foreign plants.

> Management also gains in that the group board gets to hear what's concerning employee representatives at individual plants (VWM02).

Not least, the cooperative relationship between the EWC and management generates both internal and external legitimacy. Decisions made jointly and agreed with European (and global) employee representatives ensure a degree of acceptance on the part of the workforce in VW plants and convey the impression to the outside world of a 'fair' and socially responsible enterprise. The participation of EWC members and the EWC's high outputs are, therefore, also advantageous to the company.

5.3 Provisional conclusion

Our findings on VW's organisational structure and coordination would suggest that the VW group represents a 'global organisation' but with some characteristic features of a transnational one: as such it could be denoted a 'global/transnational' organisation. Overall, the group is 'somewhat centralised', albeit with some markedly decentralised elements in some dimensions. The bulk of the workforce (77 per cent) is located in Germany. Out of our sample, only Daimler (with 86 per cent) has a more centralised workforce distribution. The values for GM (47 per cent) and Ford (48 per cent), and in particular Toyota (27 per cent) are notably lower. In terms of the EU, 56 per cent of VW's vehicle production takes place in Germany. Again, only Daimler, with 83 per cent, exceeds this value, with PSA (54 per cent) and Renault (47 per cent) exhibiting broadly similar values. Only in terms of the distribution of its manufacturing subsidiaries can VW be classed as 'somewhat decentralised' compared with the other firms in the sample: only 31 per cent of VW's plants are located in the home country, against 63 per cent for Renault and PSA, and as much as 68 per cent for Daimler. In contrast, the values for GM and Ford are up to 10 percentage points lower (Ford – 20 per cent; GM – 25 per cent).

Our findings on the distribution of power within the VW group indicate a less centralised arrangement than that proposed by previous studies. Wolfsburg certainly 'is the undisputed centre of power for both management and works council' (Jürgens, 2009: 227) and the group management board is the fulcrum for strategic decisions on global investments, products and plants. There is also no global or European management level operating independently of the group headquarters in Wolfsburg. 'Compare that with Ford, which has a European structure. That's not the case with us' (VWM02). None the less, compared with the other companies in our sample, there are processes and structures, such as the weekly conferences in Wolfsburg, through which – primarily German – managers have extensive scope to influence management board decisions. Managers of non-German plants also have a comparatively high degree of influence within the annual planning rounds and through regular video conferences, although this does not nearly equate to the scope available to German plant managers.

The culture of the group is very much shaped by the German 'VW culture'. However, individual marques retain their own, often strong, brand cultures (Audi, SEAT, Škoda) and brand identities (SEAT, Škoda, Scania), often derived from their specific national origins.[113] In some cases, brands also have their own marketing organisations. Some indicators of a softening of German cultural dominance can be seen recently in the greater use of local managers in important roles in non-German plants. The somewhat decentralised configuration of knowledge resources in the group is basically due to the fact that individual brands continue to maintain their own development departments – although the Wolfsburg development function is a highly significant one. In contrast, strategic knowledge and innovation resources are concentrated in the German brands (VW cars and Audi). As such, the activities within the group, both in terms of brands as well as value-added processes and activities in the group as a whole, can be characterised as strongly coordinated. Examples include the cross-brand platform strategy, intensive supplier relationships, and strong managerial coordination.

The distribution of these elements in the EWC varies. For the dimensions of resources, power and knowledge, some aspects of the forum point to a somewhat centralised structure. For example, the EWC chair and secretariat are both located at VW's headquarters. Based on the close links between the EWC and other institutions of employee representation (supervisory board, Wolfsburg works council and group works council) local representatives have multiple channels of access to knowledge and power resources that can be mobilised for EWC activity. Although German culture is evident in a number of signs – such as the use of German at non-German plants and the particular role of Bernd Osterloh in shaping the identity, capacity and impact of the EWC – there are also indicators of a somewhat decentralised distribution of cultural dimensions, such as acknowledgement of national features of union organisation. Although the views and opinions of EWC representatives of different nationalities might diverge – as happened with the assessment of the Brussels conflict – the forum also exhibits a shared culture (based on mutual trust and a 'share-the-pain' approach) that is accepted and supported by most members. One consequence is that over its twenty-year history, the EWC has developed its own cultural pattern that, despite the continuing and in some areas unconcealed dominance of the 'German contingent', is not simply a mirror of the German culture of interest representation.

Because the EWC's activities can be characterised as strongly coordinated, given the high frequency of meetings and communication, it can be classified as a global organisation. As with the VW group, there are, however, aspects that suggest a

113 The political power enjoyed by SEAT (as with Škoda) is also based on political considerations, as whenever SEAT was faced with savings or job losses, the Spanish state has intervened.

trend towards decentralisation and, as a consequence, transnationalisation. This has been reinforced by the incorporation of other companies within the group, such as Scania (2008), Porsche (2010) and Karmann, which has also led to a change in the distribution of seats, and possibly also of power, within the group.

This type of EWC can be explained to a considerable extent on the basis of the interaction of a number of factors included in our underlying theoretical model (corporate structures, actors' strategies, developmental paths and home-country culture and institutions) (see too Chapter 3). In the first place, the somewhat centralised structure of power within the company promotes a corresponding distribution of power and resources within the EWC. The dominance of German plants within the EU means that there still is a strong German 'contingent' within the EWC, despite the underrepresentation of the German workforce (which has 44 per cent of the seats). The group's power structures, with the decision-making centre in Wolfsburg, would suggest a comparably strong power centre in the EWC, able to act in direct geographical proximity to top management and with recourse to accepted and tried-and-tested forms of influence. In addition to these functional reasons for a centralisation of power within the EWC, a number of historical and cultural factors also lead to centralism. The strong works council and group works council have meant that the power centre for employee representation has traditionally been located in Wolfsburg (developmental path). This has coincided with the emergence of close relationships and an almost collegial style of interaction between employee representatives and top management. Management's strategy of accepting of the EWC as a negotiating partner, together with the strong German and specifically VW institutions of codetermination, also serve to stabilise existing EWC structures in that they open up scope for a high degree of influence over corporate decisions in comparison with other companies in our sample, albeit mediated to a considerable extent through established VW employee representation arrangements.

Strong coordination within the EWC is a reflection, firstly, of the structures of the VW group and its own strong coordination, and secondly, the culture (and path) of interest regulation at VW. The wide distribution of plants across European countries and strategies of parallel production and inter-plant competition have produced sufficiently intense pressures for the EWC, so that representatives perceive it as a useful instrument and coordination platform for employee interests (regulatory need). And finally, the existence of the EWC also bolsters the position of local employee representatives, creating a win-win situation for both foreign and home-country representatives. Moreover, irrespective of any specific problems, the culture of interest regulation at VW also supports a strategy of compromise, balance and international solidarity. As such, a strong and effective EWC also has value in itself as an expression of the identity of employee representatives within this culture.

Considering the outcomes of the activities of the EWC purely in terms of formal agreements, the EWC can only be assigned a comparatively modest effectiveness as an representative body. By 2008, only two agreements – on 'soft' issues – had been ratified, and in neither of these was the EWC the signatory body as their scope was extended to the Global Group Works Council. There have been no 'substantive' agreements on retaining operations or production allocations. In contrast, the perception of numerous actors involved with the EWC – its members, management representatives, and external observers – is that the EWC is very much an 'effective' organ of interest representation and represents a significant negotiating partner in a variety of situations (see Jürgens, 2009: 237). For example, the outcome of the Brussels conflict, viewed as a success by most of those involved, was also attributed to the EWC by many of those involved.

Analysis of the structures of both the VW group and its arrangements for employee participation also reveals, however, that the EWC is not a 'lone combatant' in the dense and complex jungle of European and international corporate structures. On the contrary, its effectiveness can only be brought to bear when combined with other established codetermination institutions within the VW group and the German system of employment regulation. As such, the representative successes of the EWC are successes for the overall system of interest regulation at VW, and would scarcely have been possible without the other employee representative institutions. This was very clearly the case in the Brussels conflict, where the primary activity of the EWC consisted in adopting a joint opinion that set out international representatives' disapproval of the proposal and expressed their solidarity. However, the main negotiating partner was the chair of the EWC who, in order to lend weight to the EWC's demands, drew on the power resources available to him through the key representative institutions in the company (group works council, Global Group Works Council and supervisory board). Although this makes it difficult to gauge the specific role of the EWC, it is, none the less, apparent that it is the overall machinery of codetermination at VW and its organisational fit with the company's group-level structures that facilitates such a high degree of employee influence.

Within this, however, the specific role of the EWC as a 'European platform' for interest regulation should not be underestimated. The foundations for deflecting representatives from pursuing exclusively national strategies and enabling them to become engaged on a realistic basis in implementing a 'share-the-pain' strategy (the approach long favoured by the works council) could only evolve over several years of interaction and communication, and the growth of relationships based on mutual trust and solidarity between its members. As such, the EWC has shown itself able to deliver a 'European value-added' to the overall mix of employee representation.

The key factors impeding further 'transnationalisation' and a more substantive role for the EWC within the 'VW system' lie in the group's structures and in the paths of tried-and-tested, and comparatively strong, institutions for interest regulation at VW. The fact that there is no European management and that global group level management is located in Wolfsburg means that the EWC lacks a direct 'counterparty' or negotiating partner on management's side. On the other hand, the group works council and Global Group Works Council both represent robust structures for interest representation that are able to fulfil the functions of a strong EWC and, given the conditions offered by the German system of codetermination and the even stronger codetermination traditions at VW, might even be able to exceed expectations.

Chapter 6: PSA Peugeot Citroën

6.1 The PSA Group

6.1.1 History and characteristics of the PSA group

PSA Peugeot Citroën is a globally operating automotive company, headquartered in Paris, that manufacturers cars, commercial vehicles and motorcycles. In addition to the Peugeot and Citroën marques, the group includes Faurecia (components, 70 per cent stake), GEFCO (logistics), and Banque PSA Finance and Peugeot Citroën Retail. Over its 100-year history, PSA has undergone numerous episodes of restructuring and strategic change. In 1976 PSA was constituted from the previously independent Peugeot SA and Citroën. Prior to this, in 1974, Peugeot had acquired a 38 per cent stake in Citroën. Shortly afterwards, the company took over Chrysler's European plants, subsequently renamed 'Talbot' (1978). During the 1970s Peugeot changed from a Fordist company that, up until the mid-1960s, had concentrated on producing a small range of mid-size models to a more complex 'Sloanist' mass producer pursuing a 'volume and diversity' profit strategy (Loubet, 1998; Freyssenet, 2009a). 'From 1979, PSA management had to organize a company comprising more than 30 factories that produced 26 models [...] with a workforce of nearly 220,000, maintain three sales networks, and above all ensure that each of the three marques, Peugeot, Citroën, and Chrysler-Europe [...] would have distinct and separate characters' (Loubet 1998: 344).

Sales fell rapidly in the wake of the second oil crisis (1979/80), necessitating a switch in strategy. In order to adjust output to declining demand and lower costs, the workforce was cut by 27 per cent, several external plants closed, the Talbot marque discontinued (in 1985), and the Peugeot and Citroën vehicle range narrowed. Peugeot and Citroën have shared common platforms and technologies since the mid-1980s. After 2000, there was a plan to move to three platforms only: this proved unfeasible given the strategy of widening the model range and entering new market segments (Freyssenet 2009a: 259).

PSA's international activities extend back to the 1950s (Loubet, 2003) when plants were established in adjacent countries: Vigo (Spain) opened in 1958 and Mangualde (Portugal) in 1962. For a long period PSA pursued a global strategy, with models exported from a single location. While Peugeot focused on Africa and America, Citroën was traditionally strong in Spain and Portugal, and later Eastern Europe. The group's international activities grew further from the 1980s: PSA Japan was set up in 1988, and the group has been active in Latin America since the early-1990s (Brazil, Argentina). There has been a cooperation agreement with the Chinese manufacturer Dongfeng Automobile since 1992. In order to strengthen its presence in Central and Eastern European markets and take advantage of lower costs, PSA opened a plant in Trnava (Slovakia) in 2008 and began a joint venture in Russia.

The British Ryton plant, which assembled the same models as those envisaged for Trnava, was closed in 2006 (Freyssenet, 2009a: 261f.; see below). There are numerous cooperation arrangements, including Ford (diesel engine development), Fiat (Sevelnord, from 1994) and Toyota.[114] In 2008, PSA had sixteen assembly and fifteen component plants. Growth is focused on markets in Central and Eastern Europe, China and the Mercosur region. Despite this, some 70 per cent of PSA vehicles are still sold in Europe. Output grew steadily from the mid-1990s, reflected in rising employment in France and internationally until 2004/5, after which the workforce in France fell (Freyssenet, 2009a: 265).

Although PSA is a global undertaking, it is still described as a family business in which the Peugeot family continues to exercise considerable influence. The family holds nearly a third of the shares, with 45 per cent of voting rights.

6.1.2 Distribution of resources, power, culture and knowledge in the PSA Group

As far as the distribution of resources in the group is concerned, PSA is a *centralised* company. Within Europe, there are plants in Spain, Portugal, Italy, the Czech Republic and Slovakia.[115] Compared with other firms in the sample, PSA has a high share of home-country production facilities, with 63 per cent of its plants in France (as with Renault). This is only exceeded by Daimler, with 68 per cent. Outside Europe, there is a PSA-owned plant in Brazil (2,800 employees in 2007) and two plants in Argentina (with a total of 5,500 employees in 2007). In Germany, the group's activities are confined to a sales network established in 1973 and managed from Saarbrücken.

In terms of the distribution of employment, PSA occupies a midway place in the sample. In 2008, more than 62 per cent of EU employees were located in France.[116] The other three manufacturers in our sample with their corporate headquarters in the EU have a much more centralised structure (Daimler – 86 per cent; VW – 77 per cent; Renault – 73 per cent).

The group has a more decentralised aspect only as far as the concentration of employment at individual plants is concerned. The largest (Sochaux) with 14,300 employees, only accounts for 8 per cent of the total workforce. The largest combined – Sochaux, Mulhouse and Vigo – employ 19 per cent of the total workforce. In contrast to VW in Wolfsburg or Ford in Cologne, there is no clear centre in this respect.

---

114 Since 2005, the Peugeot 107, Citroën C1 and Toyota Aygo have been produced in a joint venture with Toyota at the Kolín plant in the Czech Republic.

115 Vehicles are assembled under licence a five locations (Turkey, Iran, Nigeria, Morocco and Thailand).

116 If non-EU operations are included, the share drops to 55 per cent.

Table 4: Distribution of employees, plants and production, PSA group (2008)

	Employees	Plants	Production
World	207,800	31	3,325,407
EU	182,200	19	2,477,812
EU Home-country (France)	113,700	12	1,348,866
Largest plant	14,300	–	–
Share EU/world	88%	61%	75%
Share EU home-country/EU	62%	63%	54%
Share EU home-country/world	55%	39%	41%
Share largest plant/EU	8%	–	–

Source: authors' compilation from PSA Annual Report (2008) and OICA (2008).

As far as the distribution of production volumes is concerned, non-French plants account for 59 per cent (OICA, 2008) – which can be characterised in terms of our scale as 'somewhat centralised' (see Chapter 3.3.1) compared with the other companies in the sample. Only Daimler, with 43 per cent, has a higher degree of concentration. One reason for this 'disproportion' between home-country output and employment is that a number of component plants as well as other functions, such as R&D, which do not contribute directly to production volumes are also located in France. In terms of units produced, the largest plant is in Spain, where the Vigo plant, which manufactures Citroën vehicles, produced 547,000 units in 2007, a rise of 74,000 compared with the previous year. Altogether, however, the French plants produced more than 1,300,000 vehicles, putting France far ahead of all the other European plants (PSA, 2008a; PSA 2008b).

In order to research the distribution of power, information was collected on competencies at the various levels within the group (headquarters, production locations) and on issues (decisions on allocating production volumes between plants). The findings suggest that strategic competencies are comparatively strongly concentrated at the group's headquarters.

> Strategic decisions as to where particular models are to be built are not made by the plants. Global production is decided at headquarters [...] Within the structure of PSA there is a strong focus on France. [...] The corporate centre sets out the production programme as this is not only a matter for a single plant but for several. The centre has the responsibility for harmonising and allocating production (PSAM01).

Figure 7: Distribution of plants in the PSA Group in Europe, 2008.

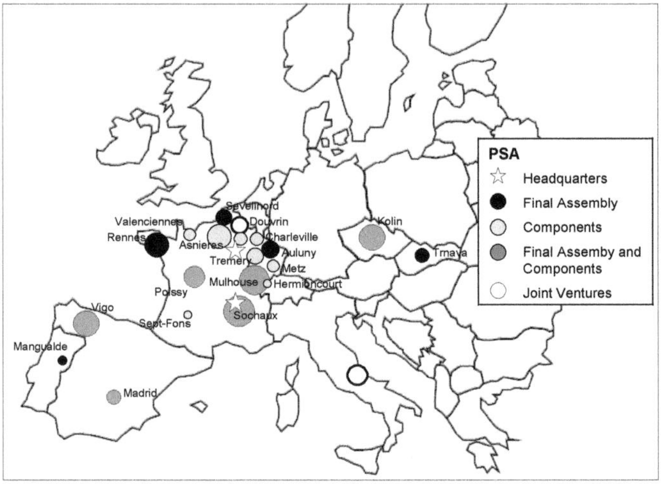

Source: authors' compilation based on PSA Annual Report 2008; circles are proportionate to employee numbers

Although plants are integrated into a multi-level decision-making procedure, the main mechanism of coordination is not discussion or negotiation between central management and plant managers but a process of consultation with plants in the context of an internal market and tendering process in which plants compete for production allocations. Final decisions over the allocation of models and production quotas is then made by the corporate centre.

> A decision on production is made as with other decisions with the inclusion of plant management, taking into account the individual circumstances of the plant, such as structural conditions. Plants let us know about their context and the pressures they are under. Proposals are then made for plants and these enter into the decision-making process. However, the final decision is made by central management, but before that the circumstances, special features and wishes of individual plants are given a hearing (PSAM01).

As far as budget responsibilities are concerned, plants only have a limited scope for independence. Plants must submit a budget proposal to the corporate centre, and this has to be approved.

> Plants can suggest a budgetary framework. This goes to the headquarters. In the final analysis, it is the corporate centre that decides on the exact figure. And plants must respect their budget (PSAM01).

The budgetary framework serves an envelope within which small 'projects' or investments can be carried out. For their part, larger elements of expenditure are always centrally planned and decided.

The [budget for investment] depends on the scale of the investment. Each plant has an investment budget. However, these tend to be small projects, such as evaluating production processes or if a section of the assembly line has be reworked. That is done locally. However, if the paintshop has to be renovated or renewed, that counts as a major investment that cannot be decided locally but by central management (PSAM01).

Industrial relations are managed on a more decentralised basis, with the group opting for local provisions: there is no form of standardisation based on French regulations or a model prescribed by the corporate centre. Employment terms and working conditions are negotiated and regulated in accordance with local legal frameworks. The scope for international negotiations, which might affect the EWC, is seen by management as being a very limited.

Each country negotiates locally on those issues that can be negotiated at that level. There are only a few issues that could be negotiated at European level. In most cases, the national framework is sufficient. The EWC is informed about such negotiations (PSAM01).

The strongly French character and paternalism of PSA's corporate culture is highlighted by a management representative in the following terms.

Nowadays PSA's culture is a Peugeot culture. This is a family business, and the Peugeot family has the majority at PSA. Although there are number of foreign plants, for PSA the *home market region is important.* Renault is different, for example. *Peugeot is a French company,* Renault is a global undertaking. [...] There is strong emphasis on France in PSA's structure. This is slowly changing because our production is becoming increasingly international, but the thinking in the company remains predominantly French (PSAM01; emphasis added).

The strong emphasis on the home region is also a major factor in the high significance accorded to French culture and values, which are also transported beyond France's borders. There are a number of major PSA operations in the Northern and Eastern industrial districts of France. One significant indicator of the cultural dominance of the home-country culture is the use of French as the company language at all levels of the hierarchy.[117]

All top managers speak French. Plant managers and central management speak French (PSAM01).

The cultural dominance of the home country is also evidenced in the organisation of management exchanges. In contrast to comparable companies, PSA does not operate a formalised programme of management exchange through expatriation in which employees in management roles have to occupy a series of positions in

117 This is also revealed in the fact that in addition to the EWC secretary, all the management representatives interviewed asked for the interview to be conducted in French.

foreign subsidiaries in order to gain promotion. When inducting new host-country managers in foreign plants, it is always French managers in these operations who are required to ensure that PSA principles – centrally developed and standardised – are implemented. PSA also carries out standardised training for its non-French managers, most of which is delivered in France.

> One can work abroad, but it is not compulsory. However, there are a few French experts who work on short assignments in other countries – to install new systems, for example. They also induct local employees and managers (PSAM01).

Most plants outside of France are managed by host-country nationals, as they have much more intimate knowledge of national-cultural practices and customs that can be difficult for foreign managers to learn.

> There are French managers who work in foreign plants. However, most are local managers. We want to have managers in plants who are familiar with the country, the mentality, and the workforce (PSAM01).

In place of a specifically French personnel department, there is an international HRM department responsible for the entire group: operational personnel management takes place locally. One centralist element in this is the fact that the company has a 'corporate HRM' department, located at the company's headquarters and which controls and standardises all important personnel functions.

> One peculiarity of PSA is that there is a 'corporate HRM' department, and no French personnel department. Corporate HRM is responsible for all parts of the group, and has a French section, in order to avoid duplication. That is, there is an international personnel department, the task of which is more synthesis and integration. Operational matters are dealt with national personnel departments (PSAM01).

As far as the culture of individual brands is concerned, PSA has undergone change as a result of combining different cultures through the merger of Peugeot and Citroën and the acquisition of Chrysler's European operations, with its SIMCA heritage (renamed Talbot). As such, it is hard to speak of a consistent PSA culture. However, the two current marques, Peugeot and Citroën, have a strong French brand identity. The model range is highly uniform across all markets, with only limited adaptation to local markets (as with the Peugeot 206 SW and C4 Sedan for Mercosur, or the 307, 307 Sedan, C2 China or Xsara Picasso China (PSA, 2008b: 52ff).

Knowledge resources are concentrated in R&D operations in France, with six development centres that conduct research and product development for the whole group (PSAM01: 6, 8). There are also regional development centres, whose task is to anticipate special features of local markets: there is one operation in Brazil, for the South American market, and a further centre in China. While important know-how resources are controlled centrally, PSA has cooperative arrangements with other manufacturers, such as Toyota at the Kolín plant in the Czech Republic.

6.1.3 Coordination of activities in the PSA Group

As with most of the companies in this study, PSA is also a highly coordinated and strongly integrated undertaking. As far as the coordination of production operations are concerned, the large number of internal supplier relationships calls for a high level of coordination: PSA has fifteen component plants and an internal supplier company through its stake in Faurecia. Close coordination between the corporate centre and individual plants also applies to the allocation of production volumes. This takes place in the context of inter-plant competition for models and production allocations, attributable also to the use of parallel production. For example, in 2007 the Peugeot 206 was assembled in Mulhouse, Poissy, Palomar (Argentina) and Porto Reale (Brazil); the 207 was built in Poissy, Madrid and Trnava (Slovakia) (PSA, 2008b: 32). 'Certain models are produced in parallel at two or three plants. Production can be rebalanced between these plants if needed' (PSAM01).

There is a regular mechanism for coordination at management level that includes both corporate and plant managers. All plant managers (and heads of functions) meet once a month in Paris, with the scope for exchange by phone and e-mail between the formal meetings.

Coordination appears to be radial at PSA. The corporate centre is the real initiator and crystallisation point for communications. Decentralised horizontal communication between plants does not appear to be significant. This is also evident in control and reporting systems. Functional heads at plant-level report direct to the corporate centre; there are also regular quality checks/audits, during which quality managers from the plants meet at the headquarters (PSAM01). This form of control would appear to be much more centralised than at Volkswagen, for example, where plant managers are seen as 'participants in a discursive process'. This also supports the finding of a somewhat centralised distribution of power between the corporate centre and local operations.

The strong and centralised coordination of the group is also evident in the standardisation of the 'PSA Production System', which is intended to raise quality at all the group's plants.

> One other important area is the PSA production system, which has been introduced to cover the entire group. The ideal factory is organised in accordance with this production system. The system operates such that those areas at each site that operate particularly effectively are evaluated and then adopted by other plants. Once one has adopted all the elements, then a plant is operating in line with 'System PSA'. This is used to raise quality and promote competition between plants (PSAM01).

6.2 The PSA Comité de Groupe Européen

6.2.1 Establishment and main features of the Comité de Groupe Européen

The PSA Comité de Groupe Européen – subsequently referred to as the EWC or European Committee – was established on 10 July 1996 under an agreement between the PSA Group and six French trade unions and the European Metalworkers' Federation (EMF). As such, the EWC represents an Article 13 EWC, where the agreement was concluded prior to the adoption of the Directive and which was allowed to remain in operation as originally agreed for the duration of the agreement. Its formal structure was in accordance with the 'French model', under which the chair of the EWC was the chief executive of the PSA Group. In contrast to the German model, there is no employee-side chair who also conducts the EWC's business. This function is assumed at PSA by the EWC secretary: however, this individual is not employed on a full-time basis for the EWC but works in a technical capacity 'for some hours a week in the establishment'. In addition, this person is also an official of the FO Metalurgie trade union and chair of liaison committee between the EWC and PSA management. As far as the scope of the EWC is concerned, it is a group forum encompassing all the PSA divisions.

Article 1.2 of the EWC agreement deals with the relationship between the EWC and the French *comité de groupe*, a body broadly corresponding to a German group works council. Under the agreement, the EWC is understood as an extension of the *comité de groupe*. As a consequence, all members of this body also sit on the EWC. This construction was also included in the revised EWC agreement concluded on 3 November 2003.[118]

6.2.2 Distribution of resources, power, culture and knowledge in the EWC

The distribution of seats on the PSA EWC as between individual countries has changed several times since the EWC's initial constitution. From the outset, members of the French *comité de groupe* were automatically members of the EWC. As a consequence, since 1996 there have been thirty French members. The number of EWC seats for the other countries was set out in the EWC installation agreement, with Spain having three seats, Germany and the UK two each, and with one seat each for Austria, Belgium, Italy, the Netherlands and Portugal. Although PSA also had employees in Denmark and Switzerland, these countries were not represented on the EWC. And in contrast to the requirements of the Directive, the number of EWC seats – totalling forty-two – far exceeded the number envisaged when the forum was initially established. One reason for this was the specific EWC construction as an 'extension' of the *comité de groupe* and prevailing trade union pluralism in France and at PSA: all six trade unions active at PSA insisted on representation.

In the revised EWC agreement, concluded in 2003, countries' seats were not longer specified in absolute terms: instead a procedural rule was established for calculating the number of seats that each country was entitled to. With the exception of France, any country with more than 500 PSA employees has at least one

118 'Agreement Regarding the PSA Peugeot Citroën Group European Works Council', 23 November 2003.

seat; each additional 5,000 employees leads to a further seat (and a further seat with more than 50,000 employees). According to our survey, the EWC has grown by five seats since 2004. In late-2008 it consisted of forty-seven members, of which twenty-seven were from France, six from Spain, three from Germany, and two from Poland. The UK, Austria, Switzerland, Belgium, Italy, the Netherlands, Sweden, Slovakia and Portugal each had one seat. In addition, two countries – Argentina and Brazil – had observer status, which allowed them to participate in the annual meetings. The number of seats for France was reduced by three in 2006 as a result of a fall in the French workforce (PSAE01).

Figure 8: Allocation of EWC seats on the PSA EWC, 2008.

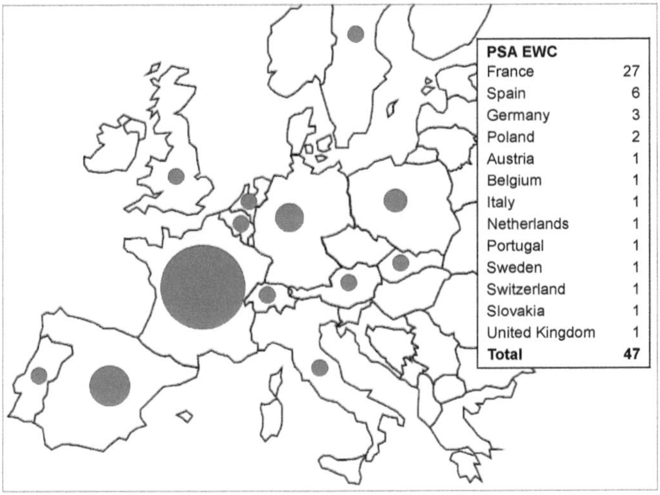

Source: authors' compilation.

Unlike comparably organised groups, the PSA EWC almost perfectly mirrors the distribution of employment within the EU. The allocation of EWC seats always corresponds to the distribution of employment in the individual countries in which PSA operates. The EWC representativeness index – the home-country share of EWC seats in relation to its share of employment – had a value of 1.11 in 2004 (based on ETUI 2006 data), which indicates a balance in favour of the home country. In contrast, in 2008 the value was 0.92, indicating a shift to the advantage of non-French plants (authors' calculation; PSAE07). This was a result of the introduction of the procedural rule, an expansion of PSA operations, and the inclusion of 'new' plants. However, the quantitative dominance of France has remained undiminished. In contrast to the other EWCs in our sample, the PSA EWC – with some 58 per cent of home-country seats – is the most centralised forum, just ahead of Renault (with 53 per cent) but far ahead of VW (41 per cent) and Daimler (39 per cent).

Problems in terms of a 'balanced' representation of employees have emerged as a result of the fact that the group's six divisions are all brought together under the umbrella of one EWC. In countries with only one seat, the EWC member is often required not only to represent the concerns of different plants but also of different divisions.[119] This problem raises a specific difficulty with 'group EWCs': in the case of PSA it has led to several country seats rotating between divisions. For example, the Polish representatives change once a year. 'However, we have four group divisions in Poland that should be represented, including Faurecia. Therefore each year we have another person who does this' (PSAE08). However, this lack of individual continuity has serious consequences for the integration – and hence also of the capacity – of the EWC ('coordination') as it is difficult for members to build up relationships based on mutual trust and confidence.

At the time when the PSA EWC was established there was no presidium or secretariat, as provided for in many EWC agreements as well as in the EWC Directive. The liaison committee was first instituted in 1999 through a separate agreement. It is the 'permanent representative of the EWC' (PSAE01). In late-2008 (the date of our research) it comprised eleven members, of which six were from France, three from Spain, and one each from Germany and the UK (PSAE01; PSAE07). The committee is located at the group's headquarters in Paris. In addition to the committee, the EWC also has a permanent office with a secretary (see above), who conducts the forum's business and organises communication between the various actors involved – the EWC centre (liaison committee, *comité de groupe*, French trade union and EWC delegates) and EWC members in different countries and plants. His task is also to prepare and chair the annual meeting with PSA group management (PSAE06; PSAE01).

There is 'no set budget' (PSAE01) for EWC expenses. However, the costs for the work of EWC members are borne in full by the group – in line with the EWC agreement: 'Management pays whatever we need as members of the EWC' (PSAE01). This covers the cost both of EWC meetings – travel, accommodation, simultaneous interpretation – as well as provision for experts or consultants. In principle, these resources are open to all EWC members. In practice, they are not drawn on outside the group headquarters.

As far as the distribution of power is concerned, the PSA EWC can be characterised as 'somewhat centralised'. The dominance of the French EWC members is a product of a number of factors. In the first place, it results structurally from the distribution of seats within the EWC and liaison committee, as well as the scope for participation for French representation institutions (*comité de group comité d'entreprise* etc.) available through the French legislation (see Rehfeldt, 2009). And secondly, it is based on the engagement of the French EWC members and trade

119 Of the three German EWC members, one originates from the PSA Bank, one from Faurecia, and from the sales division. A Faurecia employee was represented for a long time on the liaison committee, but was replaced by an employee from the PSA Bank in 2008.

unions in interest representation and the passivity of EWC members from non-French plants.

The liaison committee constitutes the interface between the EWC and central management. One of the main reasons why management wanted to establish this body was to create a single counterparty for European employee representation. Because of its proximity to management, together with the rights and procedures that flow from the French system of employment regulation, the committee has fairly frequent direct contact with management. Information exchange, discussion and coordination usually take place within a small group of people, principally the secretary, liaison committee members and management. Those EWC members that are not on the committee have comparatively limited scope for contact with management. The pattern of communication between management and the EWC was depicted by a management representative in the following terms:

> We [personnel management] have a good deal of contact with Mr. [Secretary], more than with the others. [...]. We have little direct contact with the members of the EWC. However, if there are additional questions/enquiries or contacts, all members are treated in the same way (PSAM01).

The EWC secretary has privileged access to top management:

> Q: Who do you turn to in management if you have questions? Those responsible for international employment relations? – A: Yes, either him or I go direct to top management. I can speak to anyone there (PSAE01).

One reason is the fact that the main language within the group is French. The EWC secretary also prefers to speak French rather than English. Close contact between the EWC secretary and top management is also promoted in organisational terms by the fact that the company has set up a complementary institution to the EWC secretary on their side:

> Management has set up a contact point, with a representative for international employment relations issues. This is currently undertaken by M [...] and its job is to sustain contacts with the liaison committee (PSAE01).

The scope for influencing management is seen as adequate by a range of actors. For example, the liaison committee was described by a German EWC member as the 'permanent committee' that 'discusses with management' (PSAE01). The numerous, and sometimes informal, contacts with management were seen throughout as 'negotiations':

> It's the same as in politics, in the preliminary discussions – they're also negotiations, if you want. The [secretary] has initial talks, meets the head of personnel in France at lunch or for a working discussion, and gets information and tries to exert some influence from the employee standpoint. Those are negotiations, if you want. On the day of the [annual EWC] meeting, not a great deal is negotiated. But in the preliminary discussions, yes (PSAE06).

Strategic responsibility for the choice of topics for the EWC is also centred on the liaison committee: 'The [development of strategy] takes place amongst those on the *comité de liaison*. We decide that' (PSAE01).

Issues and questions for the agenda for the annual EWC meeting are agreed between management and the liaison committee (PSAE01). Other EWC members also have an opportunity to raise issues or topics for discussion during the course of the year and at the preparatory meeting of employee representatives held with central management the day before the EWC meeting. According to EWC members, scope to propose items for the agenda is open equally to all participants.

> They are invited and can also ask beforehand. However, this mostly takes place in the preparatory meeting. This is done the day before, and the meeting often runs until 10 o'clock in the evening. The secretary coordinates this and then puts the questions to the manager concerned (PSAE06)

In this instance also, coordination of the main activities both before and in the follow-up to the meetings takes place via the secretariat:

> I can ask to speak and can say that I don't think this or that is right in Germany. And the General Director will listen and write it down, it's minuted and the questions are answered. [...] There [at the EWC meetings] you can certainly speak to one or another [top manager] who is there – *but this is a purely French affair.* What can three out of fifty do? [This refers to the three German EWC representatives.] They [the managers] do respond to our questions: last year it was a German problem that the sales situation was difficult – *but one has very little influence* (PSAE06; emphasis added).

This limited scope for influence on the part of non-French EWC members can become especially evident in the event of crises. During the single most serious crisis – the closure of the British Ryton plant (see too below) – the EWC prioritised French interests in stabilising their own plants and employment levels. The most that was achieved within the EWC was the adoption of a resolution. The closure of Ryton was accepted by the French members, in oppostion to the interests and votes of the British EWC members. For some EWC members the aim of retaining remaining production capacities for the Peugeot 206 in France also played a role (PSAE06):

> A [solidarity strike] was proposed, but this was turned down! It was turned down in particular by the French because either they or the Spaniards were worried about their jobs. And in this case it was a matter of the 'skin is nearer than the shirt' and the French labour lawyers were also of the opinion that if Ryton was closed then we would have more to secure our jobs (PSAE06)

> Previously the 206 was our volume model, built in Great Britain and France. And, of course, the French trade unions managed to ensure that now all 206s that were going to be manufactured would be produced in France. And that's why this plant was closed (PSAE06).

As with the PSA Group, the EWC is also strongly imprinted by the culture of the home country. In formal terms, this is evidenced in the fact that the composition of the EWC corresponds to the 'French model', as a joint body of employee representatives and management. As a consequence, there is no chair or presiding figure appointed by the employee side who – as is often the case in Germany – can act as a strong advocate of the EWC based on their individual personality, their support amongst the workforce, and their relationships with management. The official head of the PSA EWC is the group chief executive. However, the conduct of the EWC's business is not dealt with by the company side – as is the case with Toyota or Honda – but by the secretary of the employee side. Although this individual is comparable with a German works council chair in terms of their *functions* (coordinating EWC work, discussions and consultation with management), this is not the case in terms of their *power*.

The French nature of the EWC is indicated, firstly, by the allocation of seats: here emphasis is placed on the fact that all French trade unions have to be represented on the EWC. And secondly, it is reflected in the fact that the official EWC language is French: 'On the EWC French is spoken officially. This is also set out in the *Accord Mondial* [the PSA Social Charter]' (PSAE01). Also in practice, the home-country language is used for communication between EWC members: '[...] if the EWC writes to me, then it writes in French' (PSAE06), according to a German EWC member.

The marginalisation of other languages has also in part contributed to the fact that knowledge of French has even been seen as an important criterion for delegation to the EWC (according to one German representative on the EWC). In contrast, official documents, such as minutes or management documentation, are translated into English. At the EWC annual meetings, there is simultaneous interpretation into all the languages of those attending.

The stress on the home-country culture is also evidenced in the lack of familiarity with the cultural characteristics of other countries in which PSA has plants and for which there are EWC members. This relates, for example, to other systems of employment regulation and the procedures through which national representatives are appointed to the EWC. The EWC secretary admits their own lack of knowledge of other mandating procedures: 'In France, the *comité de groupe* must be represented on the EWC. [...] The other countries delegate members to the EWC, but I don't know how' (PSAE01).

Conversely, EWC members often have little precise awareness of the structures and arrangements in which the EWC is involved. Because of the large number of members, the fact that meetings only take place annually, and the fact that some countries rotate their delegates (either because of pluralist union arrangements in some cases or the need to ensure that different PSA divisions can participate), EWC members are not usually personally acquainted.

> Quite honestly, I have to admit that I can't precisely describe all fifty-four (*sic*) people – that is, what they do or don't do. However, as far as I know management is separate.

> The management of the PSA Group – there's a General Director and a head of personnel and an auditor who checks the books on our behalf, but that's it – they're not on the EWC, and they don't have voting rights (PSAE06).

The extensive 'anonymity' of EWC members, by making it more difficult for them to understand and gauge each other, also makes it difficult for them to engage and work cooperatively within the EWC. The lack of mutual knowledge can lead to misunderstanding and ill-feeling should the conduct of a more reserved member be interested as a lack of interest, although the main reason is that they might be new arrival on the EWC with little information about its custom-and-practice and the expectations placed on them. The lack of systematic participation by non-French members in the work and concerns of the EWC has also meant that the forum's cultural centralism has passed largely unchallenged.

The fact that one of the basic tasks of EWCs is to receive and then distribute information from and about the company means that the issue of processes for generating and circulating knowledge have a particular significance. The fairly marked centralism that characterises the distribution of resources, power and culture, by implication, also characterises access to sources of knowledge within the group. The close relationships between the secretary and liaison committee and management, the fact they share a common language, together with their shared experience of the tried-and-tested employment relations procedures within French employee representation arrangements, also means that French EWC members enjoy a substantial advantage in terms of knowledge compared with their non-French colleagues. This also undoubtedly applies in other companies (such as the EWCs at VW, Daimler and Renault looked at in this study), and is not simply the outcome of a centralised distribution. As numerous interviews confirmed, one important feature as far as processes of distributing knowledge within the PSA EWC are concerned is the poor coordination of the circulation of information by the EWC centre to plants as well as between individual EWC members. In the period prior to our research, neither the liaison committee nor the secretary had pursued a strategy of involving or consulting with EWC members. This was evident in very basic procedures, such as circulating the minutes of meetings, which usually took place after a considerable delay.

> Minutes, for example, from June arrive in October. Q: That is quite a long time. A: Yes, that's how it is, and I've always complained about it. We can't get minutes four months later (PSAE07).

In addition, questions put to the secretariat by EWC members are often either not answered or only after a long delay. This is a problem also experienced by French EWC members: 'Mr [...] never replies to e-mails that you send' (PSAE03).

Some statements by our interviewees suggested that EWC members who were not represented on the liaison committee were either forwarded information only after a delay or did not receive it at all. In fact, there was an impression that the liaison committee deliberately made it difficult for communication to take place within the EWC or between individual EWC members. The EWC's coordination bodies had neglected to create the prerequisites for effective communication. For example, the leading bodies of the EWC appear to have given no thought to the issue of how to improve coordination and the distribution of knowledge within the EWC. Although the EWC agreement provides for technical and procedural measures to be taken in this area, such as an intranet or an e-mail contacts list, which would allow EWC members to maintain contact on a *decentralised* basis (without the intermediary of the secretary or liaison committee), those EWC members interviewed were not aware of them. One German EWC member, who had been recently delegated to the liaison committee, noted:

> It was very difficult to obtain a list [of EWC members]. When I was not on this body [the liaison committee], it repeatedly tried to make contact with the secretary. And when I asked him a question, he always said 'I'll send it'. But nothing ever went beyond 'yes, yes' and nothing ever arrived (PSAE07).

This was contradicted by the EWC secretary, who was evidently unaware of the problems that EWC members had in making contact.

> Aside from personal meetings [we communicate] by phone and e-mail. We all have each other's e-mail addresses. As such, there is no problem in contacting a colleague (PSAE01).

The opportunities for an EWC member to obtain information were clearly highly dependent on their status within the EWC. Members of the liaison committee had an evident advantage over 'normal' EWC members. This was demonstrated in the 'promotion' of an EWC member. The election to the liaison committee in 2008 immediately gave a German EWC member access to information that had been either hard or impossible to obtain beforehand – or if it was made available, after repeated requests, was not in a satisfactory form (such as incomplete contact details).

> Today I got a list of everyone. It is always difficult, and when I wasn't a member of this committee it was impossible to get information. [...] All I have in this table [provided by the EWC chair] is country, member, branch, substitute. That's all. I will be able to contact my people with country and name, that's not a problem. However, they could have taken the trouble to provide the phone number and address. But why make so much work – that's what annoys me (PSAE07).

Those EWC members who were not on the liaison committee were even obliged to obtain basic information – such as contact details of other EWC members – either by themselves or from third parties. In some cases, whether information was forwarded might turn on a fortuitous conversation; in others, a manager might unexpectedly send company reports that other EWC members did not have – including in one instance French EWC members who were not on the liaison committee.

> What I've now found out is that there is always a summary of these meetings. I had not been aware of this. This year, the summary was sent to the personnel manager in Germany, and he then forwarded it to the various local general managers in Austria, Switzerland, Germany and Poland. At the moment, the general manager at PSA Service is not particularly open. I became aware of these minutes or summary, so that I know what

was on this paper. Funnily, the colleagues in the Eastern countries were aware of it, but not those from France. And because I met a colleague a couple of weeks later from the French side, and I said 'Did you get it?' and she replied 'No, we don't know about that' (PSAE07).

6.2.3 Coordination of EWC activities

Coordination within the PSA EWC can be summarised in two propositions: (1) the EWC can be characterised as 'somewhat weakly coordinated' and (2) observable communication takes place largely on a centralised basis via the secretariat, and to a much lesser extent directly between the various sub-elements of the EWC.

Meetings between the EWC and central management take place annually within the PSA Group. In this respect, the frequency and regularity of meetings are in line with the requirements of the Directive and the PSA EWC installation agreement. However, they do not match the practice of comparable companies, where meetings are typically held more frequently (for example, VW, Toyota and Ford). As yet, no extraordinary meetings have been held to respond to critical events. The Ryton crisis, for instance, was discussed in a normal EWC meeting.

Meetings are prepared for by the EWC secretary in cooperation with the corresponding section of the corporate HR department established to liaise with the EWC. There is a preparatory meeting of employee representatives on the day before the meeting with management to agree on the agenda and confirm any common line to be adopted in relation to management.

All members of the EWC and managers from a range of functional areas attend the joint meeting. Officially, the annual meeting is chaired by the group CEO. In practice, however, it is led and chaired by the EWC secretary. Meetings consist, in essence, of an information session and a consultation session. During the information session, management gives a presentation on the company's financial and business position and its plans for the future (PSAE01). This can be an important source of information for many non-French EWC members as they only receive information on an irregular basis via the liaison committee, as noted above. The presentation usually lasts for two to three hours.

The consultation session gives EWC members an opportunity to put questions to management and address problems. The issues dealt with cover a wide spectrum, from maintaining existing operations and employment to product market questions, such as problems in particular countries and company strategies to respond to these (PSAE06). Questions are answered immediately by the relevant manager or minuted and responded to in writing later if no immediate answer can be given. Both managers and EWC members interviewed emphasised that the EWC's rights were confined to information and consultation, with the EWC alloted the role of the body for 'controlling management' (PSAE06), which had to explain itself to EWC members at the annual meeting.

The liaison committee meets three times a year, with scope for additional meetings to deal with specific events.

> The comité de liaison meets in the spring, with a plant visit, in the autumn and prior to and in preparation for the annual EWC meeting. [...] Meetings are held more often for particular issues or if problems crop up. We met several times, including in Brussels, when the closure of Ryton was imminent (PSAE01).

The fact that EWC members meet only once a year and members of the liaison committee three times means that (informal) communication *between official meetings* is particularly important. This takes place in a number of contexts.

Within the PSA EWC there are a number of working parties on particular issues. The most recently-constituted one of these, proposed by the Spanish members, is a cross-country group on workplace stress; previously a group existed to deal with integrating young people and creating training places (PSAE01). There are also country-specific working parties, one of which consists of German employee representatives in the group. Its main role is to promote information exchange between representatives in PSA's German operations. This working party also chooses the German EWC representative, and therefore includes members of the works councils in the various PSA divisions.

> There is a loose body, a 'conference' in Germany, where the German side can meet. Based on our 10,000 employees, we have three seats and this body can decide who is delegated [to the EWC] (PSAE06).

This body was established in 2003 following an initiative of a member of the works council at the PSA Bank. Prior to this, there was no exchange between works councils in the German PSA subsidiary.

> This European group works council was an unknown quantity and when I was elected to the works council in 2002 I could not understand why PSA branches in Germany were not in contact. I set this body up in 2003 so that all works council members and chairs at Peugeot Citröen and Bank could meet regularly. Before these meetings, it was rumoured that PSA had got in touch with the personnel managers of Peugeot [in Germany] and said 'Send someone over' (PSAE07).

The group meets twice a year 'at the start of the year, when we discuss how the previous year went, and in October, when we discuss the results of the European group works council, [and] what we've done' (PSAE07).

Although the working parties suggest regular and strong decentralised coordination by groups on the EWC, overall our findings on informal communication processes suggest that the PSA EWC is a comparatively weakly coordinated body. Most EWC members are only included in the EWC's communication processes on a sporadic basis. Where communication does take place, if at all, it is initiated by the secretary and takes the form of forwarded information or questions.

> No, there is no communication between the [members]. For example, on the 18th there was a little discussion beforehand [...] There were translators or interpreters, and it worked. However, after this meeting there was no mutual contact. Everybody just left and did not want to talk. [...] But the problem is that they don't speak French (PSAE06).

For the most part, actual communication takes place through the EWC centre, that is the secretary and the liaison committee.

> However, I do not have any link with the Spanish colleagues. Q: Do you sometimes send them an e-mail or call? A: Not as yet. Q: If so, would you do that through the secretary? A: Yes. That is, the e-mails go to Paris and Paris then says that the Spanish colleagues want this or that, do you agree? Then that would go, for example, from Spain to Paris, and then on from there (PSAE06).

The EWC secretary also conceded that there was no significant contact between EWC members. '[Contacts]. There might be, but I don't think so. As a rule, everything runs through me' (PSAE01).

A number of factors might be adduced to explain this coordination weakness and the relatively marked centralisation. Aside from language problems, our interviewees identified a lack of interest on the part of EWC members as one of the principal causes.

> That's how it is, there is no exchange. Each of us dozes away in our corner and nobody takes the initiative to say, it wouldn't be a bad idea if we got together and exchanged ideas, what's going on with you, what problems have you got, what agreements have you got, how many of you are there. That's what annoys me with this European Committee. People talk, but they don't know what the company is like abroad: how many of us there are, how does the works council function, nothing. It's just talk, very superficial. (PSAE07). Q: Why is that? A: I don't know. It's either got something to do with the language, when you can't speak it, or the lack of interest from colleagues from abroad. [...] It always depends on the individuals who are on the works council. You've got some people who really put themselves out, who'll tackle anything. And others are just pulled along. That's a shame as I think that if you've been elected to a group and you've asked colleagues to put you into a particular office, you should make something happen (PSAE07).

One reason for weak engagement of many EWC members lay in the perception that the 'value-added' for interest representation achievable through the EWC was comparatively low. The EWC is neither informally nor officially a negotiating body, and the liaison committee has shown no sign of wanting to move it in this direction. As a consequence, some EWC members decided to come to terms with the minor role played by the EWC and did not entertain any particular hopes that it might be able to support their representative role.

> It's just the same with the big strategies, the EWC has no power; we have no influence over management. All we can say is that we don't like this or that. And if problems are turned up, then we'll pursue them. But influence over production or decisions about where it takes place? [shakes head] (PSAE06).

This weakness in coordination and the shortcomings in the internal management of information by the leadership bodies of the EWC was pinned on particular individuals by our interviewees. These either had insufficient time or did not view maintaining links with other EWC members as their central task.

> No, the [lack of distribution of information] is due to our representatives. I've often given him a kick and say [German member of the liaison committee], give us information! What's going on? And it seems he doesn't have enough time. And I see that I've got information from Paris since I was there in June; I've had quite a bit of information in the meantime that I automatically forward. [...] And now I'm on the liaison committee, I'll be able to give my colleagues more information because up until now we've never had information. We got the impression that although there's a body in Paris, we're unknown (PSAE07).

Other EWC members from non-French subsidiaries also identified one of the main causes of the problems as lying with the secretary, who did not properly exercise his role in the areas of coordination and information.

> I have to make a small criticism here. I've not found that the role of secretary is efficiently performed. I think that the secretary's task is to establish and organise contact between representatives. My experience is that I ask questions, write e-mails to the secretary, need documents and information – after all, I am the chair of the works council in Germany – but never get a response (PSAE05).

> I remember when we had sales problems, I never had an opportunity to talk with other EWC members and I got very little response from the secretary. There are no synergies between members (PSAE04).

6.2.4 Critical events

Four major events have occurred during the history of the PSA EWC that appear noteworthy because each can be seen as representing an important developmental step that either led to a change in the EWC or might still do so in the foreseeable future: (1) The establishment of the liaison committee, (2) the adoption of the Social Charter, (3) the conflict over the closure of the British plant at Ryton and (4) the inclusion of the liaison committee into the strategic committee of the PSA Group.

(1) The agreement with management to establish the liaison committee marked a significant evolutionary step in the history of the EWC in that the constitution of this body was the first time that a smaller leadership group was created that was capable of efficiently managing the EWC's business. This change in the EWC installation agreement was adopted on 7 July 1999, three years after the official establishment of the EWC. Since then the committee has taken on a number of central tasks – together with the secretary – ranging from communication with EWC members, preparation and follow-up for meetings, and maintaining close contact with management.

As our findings on the coordination of EWC activities show, the establishment of the liaison committee led to an rise in the volume of communication within the committee. However, coordination of the EWC as a whole appears to have increased either not at all, or only a little.

(2) In 2003, the PSA group joined the UN Global Compact. The PSA 'Global Framework Agreement on Social Responsibility' ('Social Charter') was adopted on 1 March 2006.[120] The liaison committee played a major role in developing this. Although it was read over by the whole EWC, the Charter was formally ratified only by the two international trade union federations concerned – the IMF and EMF – together with the liaison committee. In the agreement, PSA committed itself to exceed ILO core labour standards and apply these enhanced norms to its suppliers worldwide. In addition 'in each of the major countries, local social observatories will be set up.... . made up of human resources divisions and labour unions' (ibid. 8). The EWC was given the role of assessing compliance for the annual meeting.

In addition, the Charter included a declaration of intent about the prospective establishment of an employee 'Global Council', in which both sides confirmed that 'the parties of this agreement feel that the creation, in due time, of a Global Council is beneficial'. In order to prepare for this, countries with a substantial share of employment, such as Brazil and Argentina, were to have observer status at the EWC's plenary sessions. It was decided to examine whether a Global Council should be set up three years after the signing of the Charter (ibid. 9).

(3) On the 18 April 2006, just one month after the adoption of the Social Charter, PSA announced the closure of its Ryton (Coventry) plant in the UK, which it had acquired when it took over Chrysler's European operations in 1978, together with the relocation of the plant's output to Slovakia. Under management plans, half of the 2,300 employees working on Peugeot 206 assembly would lose their jobs within four months (by July 2006). The plant was to be closed completely by mid-2007. This announcement met with particular scorn from some employee representatives as the procedure evidently breached the spirit of the recently agreed Social Charter,[121] as neither the British employee representatives nor the EWC was informed adequately or within a reasonable timeframe.[122]

After the closure plans had been announced, steps were taken to hold an extraordinary meeting of the liaison committee and an additional meeting of this committee and the EWC. However, no extraordinary plenary EWC meeting was held, although

120 See < http://www.imfmetal.org/files/06041112011079/ifa_psa_english2006.pdf>, accessed 15 August 2012.

121 One section of the Charter is entitled 'Provide employees with the means to participate' and contain PSA's commitment 'to providing employees with regular information on the company's operations and on issues likely to affect working conditions and employment, both directly and indirectly. This will be ensured through the local employee representative bodies and unions, in particular' (ibid: 5).

122 However, the sources diverge to some extent on this point. The EWC secretary noted that the EWC and liaison committee had not been informed; however, the British unions already knew about the closure. In contrast, the German EWC Newsletter states that no employee representatives had been 'consulted' about the closure (EBR-News 2/2006).

the case was raised and intensely discussed at the annual regular EWC meeting. There were major divergences within the EWC over the strategies that the EWC and trade unions should adopt in response to the plans. At some meetings, this led to serious disagreements between the British employee representatives and the majority of French and other EWC members. 'There were arguments and furious speeches, as the English colleagues were understandably livid' (PSAE06). The main interest of the British representatives, who were supported by the French Communist union the CGT, was to retain the Ryton plant, and they called on the EWC to initiate solidarity strikes and boycott vehicles produced at Ryton as a means of securing this (see too Kessler, 2006). However, the French EWC members in particular feared that the Peugeot brand would be 'damaged' by a highly-publicised strike that would have an uncertain outcome. Finally, in May 2006 there was a 250-strong demonstration at the PSA shareholders' meeting, at which the British unions put forward an alternative plan for the plant (EBR-News, 2/2006). However, their task[123] was made more difficult by the stance of their own workforce, which rejected a strike in a ballot by 516 to 440 votes. Rather, many employees wanted to take advantage of the extensive severance package on offer.[124] The British unions then decided to embark on a boycott campaign on their own, at considerable financial cost.

The outcome of the Ryton conflict makes sober reading from the standpoint of an external observer. The EWC adopted a resolution officially condemning the closure; however, at the same time the employee side was engaged in negotiations with management over severance terms and support for employees to find fresh employment – with the strong support of the unions. Finally, a comprehensive severance package was agreed that was approved by many EWC members and trade unions (and the bulk of the workforce).

The EWC's passive and generally non-confrontational stance was the product of a number of factors. The dominant view within the EWC was aligned with the economic and market interests of the company, and used different arguments to justify the activities of the EWC. For some (French and non-French) EWC members, the closure was due to economic exigencies as the plant was no longer profitable: 'Production was not profitable there and many parts had to be supplied for manufacturing' (PSAE01).

> Q: Was there any alternative to the closure? A: I don't believe so. The Ryton plant was subsidised. The 206, that was built there, production had ended and is still cost €500 per car. One has to think a bit in economic terms. What is the point, in my view, of keeping a plant if the company is making a loss (PSAE07).

---

123 Transport and General Workers Union and Amicus (which merged to form Unite in May 2007).

124 The overall package, costed at €7 million, was so attractive for the majority of employees that not enough staff was available in the final month before the official closure to maintain production (Kessler, 2006: 4).

There were also concerns about the damage to their image if they initiated stoppages or an EU-wide boycott, leading to lost sales and consequent risks to employment in other plants.

> We knew that we could not do anything against the closure. The English colleagues wanted to push for a boycott of Peugeot products. Or to recommend a boycott, but we said, just a moment: that will affect us. We don't want to run down the brand. And we would suffer then too. [...] To reverse the closure, no one could have done it, it would have been madness (PSAE06).

In particular, the French EWC members thought that the closure of Ryton on economic grounds was unavoidable, possibly even reasonable and justified: the appropriate strategy was, therefore, to try and get the best deal possible for the English workers who were to lose their jobs. The commitment by the then PSA CEO that the company would try and find employment for these workers also certainly contributed to this assessment (PSAE01). The EMF took a similar position. Although it wanted to show solidarity with the English workforce (the boycott was supported by the EMF, for example), it also wanted to avoid negative consequences for the group and other PSA plants. Highly-visible actions, according to the unions, might have worsened the position of the workforce in the expected negotiations over a redundancy package. The decision to abandon Ryton and obtain the best outcome for the employees also meant that the threat of industrial action needed to be maintained to enable problems in the negotiations to be overcome.

> The English wanted a European strike. No one was really against that, but people said 'Careful – see what management offers'. [...] We then discussed this with management and it took a good deal of work to get management to commit itself to finding a new job for each worker. A European strike would have harmed that. It would have been bad for PSA Peugeot's image, not only for the English operations but also for other European states. [...]. *Our strategy is first to negotiate with management and not strike immediately. We only strike if management doesn't listen* (PSAE09; emphasis added).

Aside from the economic case, a number of interviewees referred to the serious significance of different interests within the group and the EWC. In particular, those EWC members interviewed emphasised the contradictory interests of British and French employee representatives during the Ryton conflict.

> That's how it is, the French colleagues sometimes don't agree because of their interest in their jobs. For example: the closure of the Ryton plant naturally had some benefits for the French plant where this car was produced (PSAE06).

At that the same, the rejection of a strike or boycott by the French employee representatives was justified by the economic consequences and the 'unwarrantedness' of confronting their own company.

> We just saw the strike as wrong. And the boycott of the Peugeot brand. For us the impact would have been too severe, in Europe. We have to realise, we aren't just in

England. And I can't expect a French works council member to destroy his own brand. That would be stupid and he wouldn't do it. They've all been at Peugeot for years – nobody would do that. Solidarity doesn't – can't – stretch that far (PSAE06).

The decision of the majority of those involved that the EWC should not initiate any form of militant action can also be explained by the role assigned to the EWC by its stakeholders. Most saw the EWC as a purely informational body and not as an actor with powers to call and direct industrial action. The French industrial relations tradition prescribes a strict division of labour between the trade union sphere, characterised by collective bargaining, and workplace and company information and consultation (see, for example, Goetschy, 1999; Goetschy and Rozenblatt, 1992; Rehfeldt, 2009). Initiating negotiations and strikes is a trade union activity. This emphasis on the legally-prescribed role of the EWC as an information body and reference to the 'competence' of the trade unions therefore constituted a further argument to justify the EWC's restraint.

The EWC is an information body. Management informs us. If someone doesn't agree, it's possible to get together and start some action, such as occupying a plant. However, EWC meetings just involve an exchange of information. Action is left to the trade unions (PSAE01).

For the French and German EWC members, the Ryton case was – in overall terms – a success for the EWC, measured primarily in terms of the level of severance payments and the agreement to place former PSA employees in new employment.

All you can do is mitigate the consequences. On that, we did quite well. We were able to improve the redundancy scheme. That was right. So much money has never been paid out before. You can only try and make sure that these are dealt with in a socially-responsible way (PSAE07).

From the trade union side it was emphasised that accepting the closure of the plant was not a straightforward decision for any of the French trade unions. However, in the final analysis it was mainly the comparatively generous severance package – transition to new jobs and financial compensation – that induced the French unions to not take more assertive action against the closure.

(4) On 6 April 2007 a 'strategic parity committee' ('comité paritaire stratégique') was established by an agreement between PSA management and five French trade unions. The committee was described as an 'additional forum for dialogue and exchange' at PSA. It consists of equal numbers of management and trade union representatives and aims to provide for a 'more in-depth consideration of the issues on the company situation and short- and medium-term policies' (*L'accord PCA France sur la Gestion Prévisionelle des Emploi et des Compétences).*

The committee's task is to look at future tasks and fields of activity. Are there areas that we need to look at, and are there areas that are no longer important? What are the new technologies that need to be developed? The committee also has the task of monitoring and developing the social aspects of the company (PSAM01).

Given the growing significance of cross-border issues, PSA management proposed that non-French trade union members should also be included in the committee. According to this, all members of the liaison committee would also be members of the strategic committee. A corresponding agreement widening the scope of the strategic committee was concluded on the 19 June 2008. At the time of writing, it was noy yet clear whether this innovation has led or might lead to a fundamental change in processes of coordination.

6.2.5 Effectiveness of the EWC in interest representation

Considered in terms of its interest representation effectiveness or outputs, as yet the PSA EWC constitutes a body that is not highly effective and is confined, in essence, to an information function. Scope for exercising influence beyond this – such as consultation, let alone negotiation – is only evident to a relatively minor and initial degree. Consultation consists of little more than management responding to questions posed by EWC members at the annual meeting. There are no official negotiations – and nor are these are desired or intended by any of the parties involved. At most, those agreements that have come about, and the informal coordination meetings between management and the liaison committee and/or the EWC secretary, might be interpreted as outcomes of negotiation or forms of discursive influence over management.

Contacts between the EWC as a whole and management are largely confined to the annual meetings and the information and consultation that take place ahead of these. In contrast, more frequent meetings occur between management and the members of the liaison committee and/or the EWC secretary. There are differing perceptions of management's stance towards the EWC. As far as the fundamental position of management is concerned, the EWC secretary noted: 'There is an EWC, because the law provides for it' (PSAE01). In contrast to other companies in the sample (such as Volkswagen and Ford), PSA management does not expect any positive effects from the operation of an EWC.

However, the EWC secretary gave a positive assessment of practical cooperation with group management and management's approach to information.

> They inform us systematically. [...] Cooperation with management is really no problem. [...] The EWC is now well established and discussions with management are good. Contact with management is very good (PSAE01).

However, it should be noted that the regular contacts with management mean that EWC secretary is in a special position in terms of privileged access to information. Non-French EWC members who are not included in communication arrangements were often critical of the fact that information made available before EWC meetings either came late or was incomplete.

> You know, the French have a different idea about what making information available in a timely way is. They decide and when everything is already fixed, they say we've got this and that to so. And that's what gets carried out (PSAE07).

The secretary expressly cited the regrading of employees in the PSA logistics subsidiary GEFCO. Restructuring was carried out by management without informing the EWC or liaison committee (PSAE01).

The procedure for consultation is confined to the 'question time' session of the annual meeting. Following management's presentation, EWC members can put questions to those managers attending the meeting. The issues are compiled over the course of the year or during the preparatory meeting. However, spontaneous questions can also be asked and statements may be made. Aside from the way in which management responds, the main criticism turns on the organisation of the session.

> Beforehand we get the information for the session and have questions to put forward. In our experience, however, we send the questions in but do not get an answer. We repeatedly complain about this. It's understandable. The presentation goes on for a long time, and those colleagues who've come from England and Poland have to get their planes at around 18.00 and they have to leave at 16.00. [...] About half have left and the meeting is then ended (PSAE07).

Early departure by some EWC members is itself indicative of shortcomings in the organisation of the event; above and beyond this, it also suggests that the forum does not enjoy a high level of esteem. Rather, it confirms the suspicion that most members only accord it a fairly marginal significance. For example, the information presented at the meeting is simply 'taken away' and not linked to any expectations or hopes in relation to the EWC – let alone any notion of making strategic use of it or developing it into a centre for joint strategies.

In contrast, there are a number of agreements that can be seen as the concrete output of the EWC and the result of 'negotiations' – in practice, discussions with management rather than formalised bargaining. Aside from the extensions to the EWC installation agreement, this mostly relates to the agreement of the liaison committee, the Social Charter, and the agreement to extend the 'strategic committee'. In addition, the EWC has also adopted resolutions, as with the closure of the Ryton plant.

Using the schema set out in the theoretical section, the causes for this low level of output and effectiveness of representation can be analysed at various levels (impact on company, country of origin, foreign operations) and in terms of differing dimensions (need for regulation, organisational capacity, management strategy).

For the company, the EWC mainly has a symbolic function: it legitimates the firm in terms of compliance with established requirements of European law. Overall, however, the significance of the EWC is low. This reserved stance adopted by management also coincides with the view of the French trade unions that – as illustrated in the Ryton case – is primarily directed at the situation of their own employees. The EWC does not represent any form of advance for home-country employees: in essence, it represents an extension of the group level works committee through the addition of foreign employee representatives, but is not seen as having any enhanced potential for improving their own representational activity.

The EWC has also only been of limited use for PSA's foreign operations. Because the company's approach to information does not offer a great deal of scope for including employees from the company's foreign operations, the EWC could provide a means for expanding the information available to non-French employee representatives. Although the EWC is primarily a 'service EWC' (Lecher et al., 2001), this role is not undertaken by a strong chair acting as an 'advocate of the diaspora' (Kotthoff, 2006a) for peripheral employees. French employee representatives evidently do not see themselves as obliged to raise the standing of the EWC for reasons of international solidarity. Beneath the surface, the dominant strand of thought remains one of competition between plants and countries. The 'dominant coalition' is constituted by the French EWC members – and these do not need the EWC for their own interest representation, and nor do they see any necessity to lend it any strength.

One of the EWC's fundamental problems is that, as yet, only a small number of actors have sufficiently high expectations to inject the additional impetus it needs to enable it to develop into a medium of cross-border representation within the PSA group. Most of its members do not think that the EWC has any particular contribution to make to resolving their problems and the need for regulation is correspondingly seen as fairly low. This view is all the more remarkable given the numerous objective indicators that point to a high need for regulation. For example, the change in management at PSA in February 2007[125] was accompanied by a shift in strategy under which the existing social compromise was terminated and the main means of restoring competitiveness became cutting the workforce and expanding production in low-wage countries (see Freyssenet, 2009a: 262f.). Not least, the Ryton events demonstrated an increased need for regulation through the EWC. French trade unions are well aware of the movement towards relocating production in the automotive industry. 'Today, a lot of assembly work is carried out in Central Europe, in the Czech Republic, in Slovakia and in Poland, where wages are five, six, seven or eight times lower' (PSAE01). Seen objectively, therefore, inter-plant competition and experience with previous restructuring exercises within the group would suggest a greater need for regulation, and particularly so for foreign EWC members.

One reason for the low output and lack of mutual consultation between EWC members is the forum's low level of organisational capacity. This is mainly the result of the comparatively weak position of the EWC secretary. In contrast to the chair of a works council in Germany, the EWC secretary is neither the chair of the EWC nor does he or she work full-time for the EWC. They are also not represented in other central group-level bodies. Although the secretary attends meetings of the works committee, they are not an elected member of this body (PSAE01). The criticisms

125 Jean-Martin Folz was replaced as CEO by Christian Streiff: in turn he was replaced by Philippe Varin in June 2009.

expressed by some EWC members during the course of this research also suggest that the problems are not only structural (a result of the construction of the 'post') but may also be related to the secretary as an individual. Our findings also point to very divergent perceptions between the secretary and ordinary EWC members as far as the level of integration within the EWC and current problems are concerned. While some EWC members see the lack of cooperation as a problem, other EWC members and the secretary take a different view.

The dominance of the French delegates together with the culture and structure of employee representation in France would also appear to have held back the development of the EWC into an effective forum. From a French perspective, the EWC does not create any real 'added value'. For the French members, it represents an 'extension' of French structures of interest representation. The dominance of French representatives is legitimated through the structure of the PSA group itself. One the one hand, the PSA EWC is not marked by any noticeable culture of international solidarity. In contrast to VW, for example, there are no actors that consider themselves under an obligation to use the EWC to support employees at the company's foreign operations. On the other hand, immersion in the French system of employment regulation also means that it is difficult for French unions to imagine that the EWC might conduct negotiations, as this remains unambiguously a trade union concern. As such, a negotiating EWC might find itself in a competitive relationship with trade unions, whose prerogative in this area is a key element in their legitimacy and rationale. In addition, the logic of union action in France is shaped by competition between employee representatives, which compels them to raise their own profile and justify themselves to their members, workforces and potential members – and ultimately to negotiate agreements that are in their members' interests. However, this logic also induces national-level fragmentation of interest groups within the EWC.

One obstacle to achieving a more effective body has been the various lines of cleavage within the EWC. In some respects, these are aligned with national borders: for example, the majority of EWC members rejected British employee representatives' call for a strike or boycott of the Peugeot brand over the Ryton closure. In some cases, they are aligned with political differences.[126] One principal reason for this, again, is the fragmented union landscape in France – trade union pluralism – that frequently makes it impossible for EWC members to agree a common position. 'Yes. With all of us together. One can arrive at a position with the Spaniards or the Germans. It's just difficult with the CGT' (PSAE01). These political differences not only delay and hamper internal agreement on the employee side, but also negotiations with management, as often no unified demands can be agreed.

One further aspect is resignation over the prospects for employees to influence management decisions – whether as a member of the German works council or the EWC. This pessimism was reflected in a lack of engagement in the EWC. At the same time it also legitimised lowering their personal efforts, with a fatalistic

126 For example, the CGT took the side of the British and advocated a European strike.

outlook confirmed by the view that not much could be achieved. This was set out very clearly by a German member of the EWC in the case of the Ryton closure.

> We have no scope [to influence management]. Of course, you can call for a resolution to look at all options to retain the plant. But the works council here, or anywhere, cannot decide whether a plant will be closed. That's a decision for management. One can simply mitigate the consequences. We have done well on that, and we were able to improve the redundancy plan. That was right. So much money has never been paid out before. You can only try and make sure that these are dealt with in a socially-responsible way (PSAE06).

6.3 Provisional conclusion

Based on the typology of international companies used as the basis for this study, PSA, with its combination of a somewhat centralised distribution of resources, power, culture and knowledge and strong coordination of internal processes, can be characterised as a global organisation. A number of recent developments suggest that the degree of centralisation might weaken in the future, primarily as a result of the group's growing internationalisation. 'The strategy is to produce locally for the markets in which there is a demand for vehicles' (PSAM01).

Should the level of foreign production, the cultural specificities of local markets and the generation of market-specific knowledge become more significant, PSA might begin to move towards a more decentralised organisation in terms of these dimensions.

However, there are strong inertial forces impeding any rapid and consistent move to decentralisation in the near future. The long-established PSA culture and influence of the Peugeot family certainly number among these. Both represent strongly entrenched structures that exert a major influence on the thinking and practical options of top management. Moreover, it is likely that in periods of crisis, a company that it already heavily focused on France will tend to opt to retain its home-country plants if capacity and jobs are to be cut, in part under local union pressure. As already noted, it is highly probable that the interests and operational logic of the French trade unions would tend to promote such a development.

As with the company, the PSA EWC is also a comparatively centralised organisation. However, our findings indicate that the EWC can be characterised as relatively weakly coordinated. Using our typology of international organisations, it can be denoted a 'focal' organisation. The form of internationalisation of the EWC can be largely explained through the interplay of a centralised corporate structure, the culture and structures of the system of industrial relations, and the history of PSA as a traditional family undertaking.

The EWC is influenced by these corporate structures inasmuch as the high proportion of French employees provided for under the formula in the EWC installation agreement leads directly to a dominance of home-country delegates. However, this also indicates a cultural phenomenon: within the French 'multi-union' system, none of the six trade unions is willing to give up any of its rights as each has to prove and legitimate itself to its members and supporters. As a result, French EWC members also dominate the scope for influencing management. The EWC is located near the company's power centre, with French employee representatives having 'direct access' to decision-making centres and knowledge resources within the firm through the medium of French employment legislation. In comparison, the scope for participation by non-French EWC members is minimal. This situation is also reinforced by the coordination weakness of the EWC secretary and liaison committee, which leads to non-French members receiving either no information about important company developments or only receiving such information at the annual plenary meetings – in effect, wholly excluding them from decision-making processes.

The EWC's weak coordination is in stark contrast to the very strong coordination of the company, which raises an objective need for regulation as a consequence of corporate strategies of parallel production and inter-plant competition. This weakness is the result, on the one hand, of features of the French institutional system. In contrast to a number of other countries, there is no strong employee EWC chair working full-time for the EWC or employee interest representation, and supported by administrative staff and resources (as with VW). On the other, it is also the product of the stance and strategies of the 'dominant coalition' within the EWC and the majority of actors involved in it. For most participants, there is either no major perceived need for regulation or the prospects for resolving interest representations problems through the EWC are seen as extremely remote. As yet, no strong individual – such as a chair or strong trade unionist – has emerged to press for a strengthening of the EWC as a means of promoting or, at the minimum, acting as advocate for the company's foreign operations.

The culture of plant-based interest representation and inter-union competition not only leads to a centralised pattern of distribution, which secures the dominance of the French unions in terms of power and representation, but also imposes tight constraints on any strategies to develop the integration and participation of the delegates from foreign operations – and leaves little room for international solidarity. This fragmentation of national interests became especially apparent during episodes of crisis, as revealed in the case of the Ryton closure. The low level of interest and engagement on the part of French *and* foreign EWC members, the limited resources of the EWC and coordination weaknesses have, to date, prevented the development of trust and solidarity, the emergence of an authentic EWC identity, and a culture of risk and burden sharing.

Finally, there are only a few signs that more decentralisation – of resources and power – and greater coordination might occur in the near future. As far as the distribution of seats in the EWC is concerned, a number of different developments can be observed. Although there has been some movement to the advantage of non-French delegates, the allocation of seats still points to a somewhat centralised body. The principle of distributing seats in proportion to the share of employment of a country automatically leads to the – long term – dominance of French employee representatives. This dominance is also bolstered by the fact that the EWC, in practice, is an extension of the *comité de groupe*, and, as a consequence, of second-order importance for French trade unionists.

In contrast, there are some signs of decentralisation in terms of a shift in the allocation of seats to benefit foreign plants, the inclusion of countries with observer status, and the establishment of a strategy committee, one of the key functions of which is to improve access to information and influence on corporate decisions for non-French members. Finally, and more recently, the election of individuals who want to 'get something going' within the EWC has raised the pressure to improve its effectiveness and serve as a true 'organ of interest representation' for non-French plants. For example, information that was previously monopolised, is now forwarded at the appropriate time and comprehensively to EWC members (and non-members). Given the unbroken dominance of the French representatives and the deteriorating global economic context, only time will tell whether these developments might release forces within the forum that might raise the EWC's status and standing.

Chapter 7: Renault

7.1 The Renault Group

Renault is an internationally-operating automotive group with its headquarters in Paris (Boulogne-Billancourt). The company was founded in 1898 under the name 'Renault Frères' by the two brothers, Louis and Marcel Renault. In 2008, the Renault group (Renault SA) included Nissan Motor (43.4 per cent), Renault s.a.s. (100 per cent) and Dacia (99.4 per cent). In turn, Renault s.a.s owned stakes in AB Volvo (20.7 per cent), Renault Samsung Motors (80.1 per cent), RCI Banque (100 per cent), and the Russian car manufacturer AvtoVAZ (25 per cent). In addition, there was a division encompassing finance, sales and service companies (Renault Annual Report, 2008: A3).[127]

In 1999 Renault entered into an alliance with the Japanese manufacturer Nissan.[128] Renault and Nissan each have a 50 per cent shareholding in Renault-Nissan b.v., which mainly exercises strategic functions related to the alliance between the two companies (Freysennet, 2009b: 274). Renault-Nissan B.V. also includes Renault-Nissan-Purchasing Organisation (RNPO) and Renault-Nissan Information Service (RNIS). The aim of the Renault-Nissan Alliance is to identify and pursue synergies by developing common platforms and systems as well as combining purchasing activities (see too Schmid and Hartmann, 2007). Jointly developed vehicles on the 'B' and 'C' platforms use up to 85 per cent of common parts. RNPO accounts for 92 per cent of the purchasing volume of the group and 64 per cent of suppliers supply both Nissan and Renault (Renault, 2008: 17; Renault Annual Report, 2008: A17).

With a total production of 5.96 million vehicles, the Renault-Nissan group was the fifth largest vehicle manufacturer in the world in 2007 (Renault Atlas 3/2009: 4, figures from OICA 2007). Renault's own output of 2.38 million vehicles put it in ninth place. Renault's most important markets are in Europe. However, by 2007 the share of non-European markets in group sales had risen to 35 per cent (compared with 17 per cent in 2000). In 2008, Renault sold 1.507 million vehicles, or 63 per cent, of its total 2.382 million output in the EU (see Renault Atlas 3/2009: 37). The Central and Eastern European market is also fairly significant, accounting for 16.4 per cent of sales. Based on the division of labour with Nissan no new Renault vehicles are sold in North America, where Nissan sold 576,000 vehicles in 2007. Whereas Renault's sales

---

127 We have not considered the Nissan relationship in our research. Renault's 43 per cent holding means that Nissan continues to be an independent company. In addition, Nissan employees are not represented by the Renault EWC but have their own EWC (ETUI, 2009). In order to retain as a high a degree of congruence as possible between the structure of the company and that of the EWC we therefore excluded Nissan in these respects.

128 Nissan has only a 15 per cent stake in Renault and no voting rights.

had fallen dramatically due to the crisis at the time this study was conducted, Dacia saw a very substantial rise in sales (Annual Report, 2008; Freyssenet, 2009b: 280ff.).

One notable feature of Renault was the long phase of government control that continues to influence the company. In the immediate wake of the Second World War, the company was expropriated and put under state management. Up until its reprivatisation in 1996, the group bore the formal title of 'Régie Nationale des Usines Renault' (RNUR). As a nationalised company, Renault enjoyed a long period of prosperity that saw a number of social innovations. 'For many years, Renault served as a testbed of industrial relations and a "social shop window" for France' (Rehfeldt, 1998: 451). For example, in 1955 an agreement was concluded with the Communist CGT union for an additional third week of holiday. Renault was also seen as an innovative employer in the field of employment regulation (see Freyssenet, 1998). Since 1996, the group has been progressively privatised. In 2008, the state held 15 per cent of the shares, equivalent to 18.2 per cent of voting stock as Nissan has no voting rights. Most shares are now owned by private and institutional investors (64.2 per cent with 77 per cent of voting rights). Employees owned 3.1 per cent of the shares with 3.8 per cent of the voting rights (Renault, 2008: 15).

The company began to internationalise in the 1920s, with plants opened in Belgium (1926) and the UK (1927). However, internationalisation at Renault has not charted a direct course and has been punctuated by phases of recentralisation. Overall, however, foreign operations have become more strategically significant over over time (see Speidel, 2005). In the first post-war phase of internationalisation, from the mid-1950s to the mid-1970s, Renault pursued an export-oriented growth strategy that included establishing CKD plants abroad.[129] By 1965, Renault operated twenty-three plants abroad, assembling 27 per cent of the company's output. As with other car makers, this phase was marked by a pronounced hierarchy and division of labour between the corporate centre and subsidiaries, in which the centre exercised strategic functions (business strategy and product development), with the subsidiaries typically confined to assembling parts made in Europe from CKD kits (see Pries, 1999a).

During this period, Renault introduced restrictive Taylorist methods and had a very hierarchical and centralised corporate structure. In return for a growing intensification of work, Renault offered comparatively high wages and employment standards. During this phase, the company began to implement a platform strategy. Six models were built on three platforms by the mid-1960s. By the mid-1970s, the company had passed through a phase of strong economic growth in which the number of employees in its French plants rose from 63,000 to over 100,000 between 1965 and 1973.

The true foundation for Renault's advance during the 1950s and 1960s was a particular pattern of interaction between the main actors in the company's industrial relations system (the 'système Renault' (Loubet, 1998). This rested on an initially

---

129 This strategy foundered on growing import restrictions imposed by its target markets. In order to raise the number of cars sold abroad, Renault had to set up manufacturing capacity in these markets (Speidel, 2005: 132).

extremely stable workplace compromise between management and the CGT, for a long period the strongest trade union at Renault. This implicit accord between the two sides consisted in turning Renault into a competitive and innovative company able to set high social and employment standards and take on a particular responsibility for the 'needs' of France in the fields of industrialisation, exports, and regional planning (see Freyssenet, 1998: 369).[130]

The crisis of the 1980s led to a cut in the workforce of 50 per cent in the company's French plants and of 15 per cent at its foreign plants between 1988 and 1997. The causes are attributable to a number of structural factors. Over a long period, profitability had taken place second place to volume. Renault had introduced a large number of only superficially different models, and acquired a reputation for poor quality. Investment in automation lagged and was partially abandoned in the second half of the 1980s (Freysssenet, 1998; Hancké, 1998). In view of the crisis, internationalisation during this period was focused on raising efficiency, with the aim of creating better linkages between international operations.

From the mid-1980s a process of primarily cost-driven recentralisation took place. Following the sale of its US subsidiary AMC to Chrysler in 1987, production was concentrated largely in Western Europe. This phase coincided with a weakening of the CGT, whose share of the employee vote fell to 47 per cent so that the majority of members of the works committee was made up of the four reformist unions (CFDT, FO, CGC, CFTC) (Rehfeldt, 1998). New participation rights under the Auroux legislation and stronger works committees reduced the influence of workplace union sections and enabled management to introduce highly conventional Japanese methods of participative management aimed at forging 'productivity coalitions' (Windolf, 1989) directly with employees, and excluding unions from decision-making. This constellation pushed the CGT to the margins (see too Speidel, 2005: 81f).

The literature cites a number of factors behind the weakness of trade unions and employee representation arrangements at Renault. Initially, the specific combination of a weak statutory basis, the expropriation of the company in 1945, and the long period of vigorous economic growth – with high and growing sales – hampered the emergence of strong union organisation. In addition, the government also stood behind the company, which represented a model of labour and employment regulation without any need for active intervention by the trade unions. As a consequence, over a long period trade unions had no great need to press for greater influence over company policy. After 1985, the company moved to a more systematic policy of marginalising unions. The weakening of the CGT and the strategy of incorporating the other unions into a workplace coalition re-established industrial peace

130 The initial post-war decades were marked by 'compromise' between the company and the CGT, which had a strong position but did not follow a classically adversarial course (Loubet, 1998). However, this compromise was not sustained. Between 1968 and 1973 there was no year in which there was not at least one major industrial dispute in each of its plants (Speidel, 2005: 72 ff.).

at Renault. However, the phase of radical workplace modernisation initiated by the 'Accord à Vivre' (a framework agreement between the company and unions on modernisation) was only possible with the – at least formal – agreement of the unions because the CGT was ultimately isolated and had lost its hegemony over other unions. The CGT subsequently confined itself to a policy of refusing to sign agreements (as was also initially the case with the EWC installation agreement).

In contrast to VW, internationalisation at Renault was a 'management-driven process' from which employee representatives were largely excluded (Speidel, 2005: 5). The long-standing compromise between the company and unions allowed management to restructure the company to achieve and maintain competitiveness. Although representatives were formally consulted to win workforce acceptance, they had no real involvement in shaping employment conditions (Speidel, 2005: 4f.).

After a long period during which the company followed a strategy of 'one plant – one model', it shifted to the widespread adoption of parallel production. For example, in 2007, the Clio III was assembled in two French plants and one Spanish plant. The Clio II was assembled in Slovenia, the Megane II in Douai (France) and Palencia (Spain) (Renault, 2008). The express aim of management has been to force plants into mutual cost competition.

> We know that there is a price difference of €900 between a Clio built in Turkey and one assembled in France. These days management considers that the competitive situation is important for plants' productivity and for the competitiveness of the whole company (RM01).

Figure 9: Renault operations in Europe, 2008.

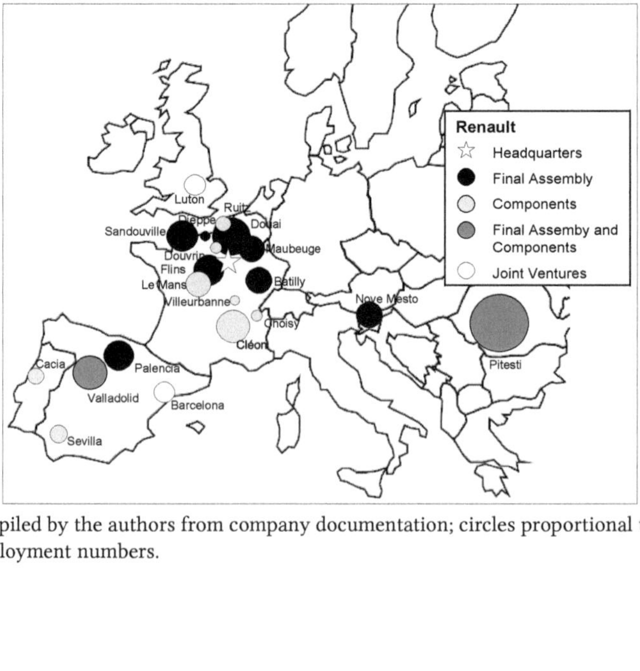

Source: compiled by the authors from company documentation; circles proportional to employment numbers.

7.1.1 Distribution of resources, power, culture and knowledge in the Renault group

In 2008, Renault operated plants – including through its Alliance with Nissan – in all world regions. There were twelve plants in Europe (vehicle assembly and parts), four in Spain and one each in Portugal, the UK (Nissan) and Slovenia. Six of the French plants were for final assembly, with the remainder manufacturing parts. France accounted for 63 per cent of all European plants. This value, exceeded only by that for Daimler (68 per cent), indicates a highly centralised distribution in this dimension. Aside from PSA (also 63 per cent), all the other companies in our sample have lower values (VW, 31 percent; Ford 20 per cent. See Figure 21 in the Appendix).

The figures for employment yield a similar picture. In late-2008, Renault employed 129,068 people, of whom 73 per cent were employed in France.[131] This is a centralised distribution when compared with other companies in our sample. Only Daimler (86 per cent) and VW (77 per cent) had a more concentrated distribution. In contrast, on this measure, PSA (62 per cent), Toyota (27 per cent), Ford (48 per cent) and GM (47 per cent) were much more decentralised. Although the distribution of employment is strongly tilted to France, no one French site constitutes a central or main plant.

As far as the distribution of power is concerned, Renault would appear to be a comparatively centralised group. Important strategic decisions – such as production allocations or assignment of models to plants – are taken at the corporate centre. 'Strategic planning is undertaken by top management' (RM01). Individual plants participate in strategic decisions through a committee. However, not all plants are represented on this body. In addition, for central management it is essentially an advisory forum. There are separate managers for four regions on the group management committee: France/Europe, Pacific, Euromed (Southern Europe) and America. There is no specifically European level of management.

The degree of centralisation in the group is also illustrated in a number of cultural aspects, of which brand identity is especially important. There is a close mutual relationship between the Renault group, the Renault brand and France as a nation in terms of tradition and their respective identities. As a traditional French undertaking, Renault is closely associated with France and French culture; conversely, the group and the Renault brand constitute an important element and focus of identification within French culture. Although Renault may have other brands, these do not have parity of status. The Renault brand is at the heart of the company. 'Our identity rests on the Renault brand. Renault has a culture that is identified through the brand' (RM01).

131 Of these 42,000 worked for the Renault brand.

Table 5: Distribution of employees, plants and production, Renault (2008)

	Employees	Plants	Production
World	129,068	35	2,417,351
EU	83,768	19	1,510,977
EU home country (France)	60,791	12	716,979
Largest plant	5,071	–	–
Share EU/world	65%	54%	63%
Share EU home country (F)/EU	73%	63%	47%
Share EU home country (F)/world	47%	34%	30%
Share largest plant/EU	6%	–	–

Source: Renault Annual Report, 2008; Renault Atlas, March 2009: 15, 30f.; OICA (2008)

One further important aspect of the cultural dimension is the use of language within the company. Despite the European and international activities of the group, the dominant language is French – including top management. The fact that French is spoken at many Renault plants can be seen as an indicator of the fact that in some respects French cultural elements are imposed on the business practices of the subsidiaries.[132] At business meetings 'amongst equals' – such as with Nissan representatives, according to one interviewee – English tends to be spoken, even at Renault.

> At the level of personnel managers [communication] takes place in French. However, there are meetings where eighteen languages have to be interpreted. Managers at non-French plants also speak French. If we have meetings with Nissan, these are held in English as many managers speak English (RM01).

There are some less centralised elements in the field of staffing, when employees move between plants. Management positions are also not centralised in the sense that appointments go solely to French managers. According to management there are non-French managers in senior roles as well at management levels in some French plants – in this case a person of Spanish descent. 'The HRM manager for Europe is Spanish. The production director at one French plant is also a Spaniard' (RM01).

Staff development programmes for training future managers are also not indicative of centralised standardisation and control by the group's headquarters. Specific training for management is provided within the group, some of which is held nationally or locally and some centrally in France.

132 One indicator of the high significance of French (Renault) culture can be seen in the fact that both the managers who we interviewed (from the HRM department) and some employee representatives, including the EWC secretary, preferred to conduct the interviews in French rather than English.

R&D takes place all over the world. In addition to Paris, there are development facilities in Spain, Romania, Brazil, India and South Korea (Renault, 2008: 25f.). Nonetheless, there is a strict functional division of labour between the centre and local operations. Whereas core R&D functions are localised in France, R&D in foreign subsidiaries mainly adapts designs to local market requirements.

> The research and development centres for European model production and high technology are in France. Alongside these there are smaller research centres in Romania, Brazil and Korea (RM01).

Strategic know-how for the development of new models or for product and component innovation is, therefore, centralised in France. The coordination of R&D in the group is also managed from France.

7.1.2 Coordination of activities within the Renault group

As far as internal supplier relationships are concerned, Renault is a highly coordinated organisation, with component plants closely coordinated with assembly plants. Parallel production of several models also requires tight coordination between the allocation of production volumes between international plants. As already noted, it is a declared company strategy that all models should be produced at a number of plants in order to make use of cost advantages. The high turnover of the purchasing organisation (RNPO) point to high level of coordination and integration of the group's activities.

Little information was available about contact and communication within management and between headquarters and managers in manufacturing operations. According to one of our interviewees from the HR department, there are regular monthly meetings at management level, sometimes related to the group as a whole and at others within a division or brand.

> There are personal meetings and also regular telephone and video conferences. Meetings take place once a month. There are also regular meetings at divisional level and also with management as a whole. There are also regional meetings, where all the divisions and business areas in a regional meet together (RM01).

Communication between official face-to-face meetings generally takes the form of video conferences and the company intranet.

7.2 The Renault EWC

7.2.1 History and characteristics of the EWC

The Renault EWC was established on 5 April 1993 as the 'European Group Works Council'.[133] Compared with other internationally-operating French undertakings,

133 Because the EWC was an extension of the 'comité de groupe', it continues to be referred to by that name in France. It is also referred to internally as the 'European

in which such bodies had been constituted in the 1980s, the EWC at Renault was a rather late creation.[134] The reasons for this are, firstly, the wait-and-see approach adopted by management, which was only willing to negotiate an agreement with the more reformist trade unions once the CGT had lost its absolute majority in the company (Rehfeldt, 1998: 452). In addition, Renault's internationalisation strategy did not envisage any large-scale internationalisation of production up until its merger plans with Volvo in the early-1990s. As such, for the employee side there was little need to coordinate interest representation internationally (Speidel, 2005: 241). The EWC installation agreement, initially concluded for two years, was signed by the eight trade unions represented at Renault: four French trade unions (FO, CFTC, CGC, CFDT), two Belgian unions (the socialist FGTB/ ABVV and Christian CSC/ACV), and the two Spanish unions (the socialist UGT and the Communist CC.OO). The CGT, which had lost its absolute majority in elections for the group works committee in 1992, refused to sign.[135] Signing the agreement was not without controversy among union representatives: the main issue of complaint was the lack of any obligation on the company to engage in information and consultation on planned restructuring, as provided for under French law. Ultimately, trade unions affiliated to the European Metalworkers' Federation (EMF) were persuaded by its officials that simply concluding an agreement took priority over any specific content as this would step up pressure on the European Commission to press ahead with a Directive (Rehfeldt, 1998: 453). The initiative to establish the EWC was taken by management, whose main aim was to marginalise the Communist-affiliated CGT (Speidel, 2005: 241).[136] Under the EWC agreement of 6 March 1998 the legal basis of the EWC was stated to be Article 13 of the EWC Directive.

In line with French practice, the EWC is a joint body of management and employee representatives. It is chaired by the company's chief executive. The conduct of the EWC's business is entrusted to a secretary, elected by the employee side.

7.2.2 Distribution of resources, power, culture and knowledge in the EWC

The distribution of seats between the countries in which Renault has operations was specified in the EWC installation agreement. Of the total of thirty members for the employee side, sixteen were taken by French representatives, four for Spain, two each for Belgium, Portugal, the UK and one seat each for Germany, Italy, the

---

Group Works Committee' as well as the 'European Works Council'. We mainly use the term 'EWC' here.

134 The PSA EWC was even later, being established in 1996.

135 In contrast, the subsequent agreements (1995, 1998, 2003, 2007) were signed by CGT representatives.

136 For a detail on industrial relations at Renault, see Freyssenet (1998), Hancké (2002), and Speidel (2005).

Netherlands and Luxembourg. Two observer places were reserved for representatives from Volvo. This allocation was changed in subsequent agreements, of which the most recent, concluded in 2007, provided for the following distribution of the thirty-four seats now available: France, eighteen;[137] Spain, four[138]; and one each for Germany, Austria, Belgium, UK, Hungary, Italy, Luxembourg, the Netherlands, Poland, Portugal, Romania and Slovenia.

In 2000, the EWC was extended into a de facto world group works council, with different levels of participation (full member and observer) through a merger between the EWC and the French Renault group works committee (Rüb, 2001: 262). This allowed observers from non-EU countries to attend, with one observer each from Argentina, Brazil, Korea and Turkey. In 2007, an observer place was established for a representative from Russia.

Figure 10: Distribution of seats on the Renault EWC, 2008.

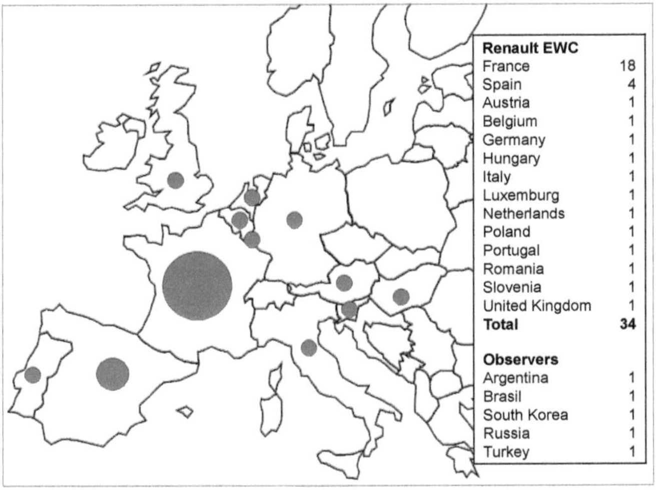

Source: compiled by the authors from company data.

> The special feature of Renault is that we have an EWC that has been extended to the world. There are thirty-nine members of the Renault *comité de groupe*: eighteen from France and twenty-one from abroad (RE01).

The agreement specifies a formula that allocates seats in relation to workforce size. However, account was taken of trade union pluralism in Belgium and Spain, with

137 Of the French members, six are from the CGT, five from CFE-CGC, three from FO, two from the CFDT, and two from the CFTC.

138 Of the Spanish members, two were from the UGT and two from CC.OO.

Spain initially allocated four and Belgium two seats. Over time, there were plant closures in Belgium (Vilvoorde), Portugal (Setubal) and the UK (Dunstable), which led to a reduction in the number of seats for Belgium and the UK and an increase in the number of French delegates to eighteen. Romania, which has the second largest workforce, remains markedly underrepresented, with just one delegate. Significant production operations in Morocco and Iran have no representation. Overall, the allocation of seats continues to provide for a significant French dominance. This was seen as a problem by a number of actors.

> There are a number of things that we need to change. Romania and Poland are becoming more significant. But, of course, management does not want an EWC with forty members. The number of places for Spain and for France will therefore have to be reduced, and the number for Romania increased. We also manufacture in Morocco, and this is not represented on the EWC at all. So, you can see that if the *comité de groupe* is to continue to be a representative forum the composition must be altered (RE01).

As yet, changes have foundered on the fact that group management is unwilling to raise the number of seats and neither the French nor the Spanish trade unions have been prepared to relinquish any.

The concentration of employment in France is also reflected, albeit in a more diluted form, in the composition of the steering committee. Of its ten members, four are from France (one member each from the CFDT, CGT, FO and CGC), two from Spain (UGT and CC.OO), and one each from Austria, Slovenia, Romania and Belgium.[139] When constituting the steering committee, it was decided that only trade unions affiliated to the European Metalworkers' Federation could send delegates.[140]

The organisation and substantive leadership of the EWC between meetings is performed by the secretary, elected by all the employee representatives, and nine deputies. In the initial EWC agreement, the secretary was granted 150 hours time-off a year for EWC activity, with 100 hours for the deputies. In 2000, under the revised agreement, the secretary was granted full facility time, with 200 hours for deputies that was raised to 400 hours in 2003.

The EWC installation agreement also stipulated the budget for current expenditure and travel for the secretary and deputies: in 1993, this was initially set at FF 260,000 (approximately €39,620), and in 2007 this was raised to €100,000. In future the budget will be indexed to the inflation rate. It was also agreed that members of the steering committee would be given computers and access to the internet and company intranet. Costs for EWC meetings (rooms, travel, accommodation,

---

139 Because there was still some remaining activity at the Vilvoorde plant, a provision was agreed in the EWC that one representative of the plant should stay on the steering committee.

140 As the CGT was not represented within the EMF at that time, it could not be represented on the steering committee, and therefore rejected the EWC installation agreement (Speidel, 2005: 241).

translation and interpretation) are borne by Renault. There is simultaneous interpretation at meetings for all languages represented.

The power of the EWC secretary at Renault falls some way short of that enjoyed by EWC chairs of companies headquartered in Germany. The main reason for this is that the latter are tightly integrated into wider arrangements for company-level employee representation. In addition, in Germany these roles are occupied by elected chairs of representative bodies at various levels (works council, central and group works councils, EWC, WCC): these are long-standing postholders and also have a strong position within IG Metall. In contrast, the EWC secretary at Renault, who was not a member of one the largest union when this research was conducted in 2008, mainly serves as an administrator, with the post held on rotational basis by the French unions.[141] Their main task is to organise the EWC, maintain direct contacts with member and regional groups, and forward information, as well as acting as the interface with management.

The main factor inhibiting the emergence of a dominant individual leadership for the employee side is the existence of trade union pluralism in French companies and the tensions and frictions between unions. As a consequence, although the current distribution of seats leads to some concentration of power in the hands of the French delegates and trade unions (as is the case with the German companies in our study), union competition can also produce a type of power vacuum. While there is very little scope for important decisions to be influenced by EWC members from non-French operations, the development of common strategies is hampered by the fact that there is no strong centre able and willing to carry out the necessary strategic work.

The steering committee supports the secretary. It usually meets once a month – quite frequently compared with other firms in the sample – at the EWC secretary's office in Paris. As well as discussing any ongoing problems, these meetings are also intended to prepare the agenda for the annual EWC meeting and discuss working and employment conditions at the different sites. Some of the meetings are also taken up with discussing current problems with management. There have also been a number of extraordinary meetings in recent years (closure of a warehouse in Austria in 2003, outsourcing of the accounts department, closure of the Vilvoorde plant): in all twenty-two such meetings were held (cf. Rehfeldt, 1998: 453).

However, including in the view of a number of those affected, this large number of meetings held does not reflect the EWC's comparatively low need for regulation.

> We sometimes struggle painfully to find subjects to justify our existence (RE03).

> No one ever comes up with any really serious topics, especially given that we meet once a month . It might happen that there is sometimes nothing topical to discuss at all, and

141 At the time of writing, the secretary was a member of the CFDT, and their predecessor was nominated by the FO. This agreement applies when no union has an absolute majority in the company.

it's good that the chair [in fact the secretary] suggest the topics and always finds something. We have to show a lot of initiative. The EWC itself often has little to offer (RE02).

The number and dates of regular meetings of the steering committee and the annual meeting of the EWC are decided at the beginning of the year. Topics can be proposed by any member, and any member can also call for an extraordinary meeting. The agenda for meetings of the steering committee is usually proposed by the EWC secretary, sometimes in association with management.

If there is a problem in a country, we assume that this is a fairly topical issue. [...] There is then, as we call it, a network, and e-mails will be sent to everyone. However, it is really the secretary who proposes the issues, sometimes in cooperation with management (RE02).

Resolutions or decisions are made in a variety of ways within the EWC, but not usually by consensus. Although some EWC members would prefer a consensual procedure, decisions are often taken after a vote. 'Decisions in the EWC should be unanimous if possible, but mostly there is a vote. If there is a majority in favour, the resolution is adopted' (RE01). As a rule, this concerns elections for office. 'There are only votes if someone is to be elected' (RE03). When the post of secretary was open for reappointment, there was a ballot as a number of candidates had put themselves forward.

Last year there was something of a disaster as several individuals wanted the post of secretary, and this was yet another a French union story, where someone had either promised something or not. I still don't understand it. [...] Then there was even a secret vote; up until then, it had always been done by a show of hands. This was a major disaster, and we lost a lot of time. It did not make a good impression (RE02).

In allocations for EWC places and the steering committee, consideration was given to the specific features of union pluralism in France and Spain, and originally also Belgium, and an effort was made to include the most important trade unions represented in the plants. The strategy of the EWC secretary and the steering committee consists in allocating seats to trade union members. However, this did not always work out, so that some delegates were represented on the body without a union mandate.

The cultural focus on the home country is also indicated in the use of language. Although interpreters are available to translate at all meetings, knowledge of French is an important prerequisite for membership of the steering committee.

The distribution of *knowledge* within the EWC is centralised, in part as a result of the structures noted above. However, there have been a number of structural innovations intended to improve the distribution of information and coordination of the forum. One example is the introduction of an innovative communication structure within the EWC, the so called 'binom structure' Under this, two members of the steering committee are responsible for a geographical area. This is intended to allow all Renault's subsidiaries in Europe scope to receive information and forward local problems to the EWC.

> There are ten members in the office, of which five are binomes. These are responsible for South America, for the Mediterranean states, one for Asia-Africa, one for Central Europe and one for Northern Europe. It's important for me that there are these regional responsibilities, as management has worked up a development strategy that is also based on regions. [...] So that is important. We want the regional responsibilities in the EWC to become something that keeps the regions up-to-date and can respond in the event of action. In addition, all countries should be represented on the EWC via the binomes. We are working on this at the moment in the *comité de groupe* (RE01).

The relatively wide distribution of seats in the steering committee is also intended to ensure that EWC members and plants involved receive information. Minutes of steering committee meetings are always translated and sent to all EWC members.

7.2.3 Coordination of EWC activities

The Renault EWC can be described as a somewhat strongly coordinated forum. Under Article 3 of the EWC installation agreement, the EWC is required to meet at least once a year. Although no scope for additional meetings was provided for in the agreement, this was subsequently included in the 1998 revision. EWC meetings have so far always been held at the company's headquarters at Boulogne-Billancourt in Paris. Minutes of the meetings are sent to all participants. There are regular meetings of the steering committee, which meets once a month. In addition, in recent years there have been a large number of extraordinary steering committee meetings, especially when workforce reductions were imminent. Although interpretation is provided for the steering committee, in practice the dominant language is French.

There are seven working parties within the steering committee, which meet in connection with the monthly meetings of the steering committee and deal with issues such as the charter of fundamental social rights or comparisons of working and employment conditions at Renault plants.[142] The aim is to ascertain and compare working hours, working conditions, pay and trade unions in European countries with Renault operations.

> This is also very interesting – that is, to compare working conditions at four locations: France, Spain, Romania and Slovenia. There's a chance to go in to this in depth and it often takes some time (RE02).

Actual communication within the EWC takes place in a dual radial form. At the first level, the members of the steering committee communicate with the EWC secretary; there is only rare direct contact between foreign EWC members and other members (French or non-French). At the second level – communication between members of the steering committee and other EWC members – direct communication takes place through the binomes.

142 Of these, only two meet regularly (RE01).

Members of the steering committee are in telephone contact at least once a month with the plants for which they are responsible. Each member maintains contact with other EWC members in the region and, if needed, can provide feedback to the steering group. It is intended that regular and direct contact should be established between employee representatives in plants that assemble the same models. As well as regular telephone contact, there is also an internal EWC e-mail distribution list, with circulars, newsletters and video conferences.

7.2.4 Critical events and EWC outputs

The first real test for the EWC was posed by the closure of the Renault plant at Vilvoorde (Belgium). In February 1997, management announced that it would close the plant in the summer of 1997 as part of a broader restructuring programme, make 3,100 employees in Belgium and a further 2,800 in France and Spain redundant, and allocate the Vilvoorde output to other plants. The – just recently established – EWC was neither informed nor consulted ahead of these decisions.

Employee representatives responded in two ways. Firstly, the EWC applied to the District Superior Court in Nanterre for an injunction to halt the move as its information and consultation rights had been evidently disregarded. And secondly, the trade unions mobilised the workforce to protest against the announcement. The aim of the EWC was to force management to rescind the decision to shut the plant. The judge decided that Renault has not complied with a requirement to inform and consult the EWC and that the company's decision was therefore void: a decision to close the plant had to be preceded by information and consultation (Lorber, 1997: 136). This judgment, later upheld by an appeal court in France, was unique in that it was the first occasion on which a court in the European Union imposed financial sanctions on a company for failing to comply with an EWC's information and consultation rights.[143]

The Belgian trade union responded to the announcement of the closure with an immediate strike at the Vilvoorde plant. A union coordination meeting also agreed to hold strike and protest actions on the 7 and 11 March in France, Belgium and Spain. On the 7 March 30–60 per cent of employees in France and 90 per cent in Belgium stopped work; Vilvoorde employees had been on permanent strike and occupation of the plant since 27 February. On 11 March 1997, around 10,000 Renault employees (4,000 from France, 6,000 from Belgium and several hundred from Spain) marched around the Paris ring round, the *boulevard periphérique*, and protested outside the company's headquarters in Boulogne-Billancourt, where the EWC was meeting. On 16 March around 100,000 people demonstrated in Brussels against the closure (Rehfeldt, 1998: 455; Bruyninckx, 1997). There was also harsh criticism from

143 The court forbade the company from implementing its decision until it had met its information and consultation obligations. On the implications of the judgments, see Bruggermann (1997) and Dorssemont (2006).

Belgian politicians and the European Commission, which was especially critical of the company's disregard of the requirements of the EWC Directive.

Management, visibly taken aback by this reaction, agreed to commission an independent study of Vilvoorde's viability and to retain some industrial activity at the site. The study confirmed management's position that the closure was necessary on cost grounds, but recommended that 400 employees should be retained. On this basis, a social plan was negotiated between the Belgian unions and management that provided for the retention of 400 jobs, with 600 early retirements and financial compensation and other provisions for workers losing their jobs. The EWC was not involved in the negotiations as the Belgian employee representatives wanted to use national institutions and not bargain at European-level.

The main aim of the EWC – retaining the Vilvoorde plant – could not be achieved, despite the mobilisation and a wave of international solidarity (Weber et al., 1997). Although the protests led to the management concession to provide work for 400 employees at the plant, which continued to exist in formal terms, vehicle assembly ended as planned. In response to the de facto closure of the plant, and the parallel restructuring of the company, local employee representatives across the group concluded a number of uncoordinated workplace agreements. In this process, management was able to pit individual plants against each other and attain extensive concessions on working time flexibility (Speidel, 2005: 235). In this respect, the Renault EWC developed in precisely the opposite way to the EWC at General Motors, where local agreements were seen as increasingly problematic and a European strategy was developed. In contrast, following the failure of a European solution, Renault workplace employee representatives aimed to conclude local agreements to secure their own operations.

Despite this retreat to plant-specific agreements, the conflict over the Vilvoorde plant was of considerable significance for the development of European interest representation at Renault. It was this conflict that made French employee representatives aware that the strategy of 'produisons français' matched with a focus on interest representation in France, as advocated by the CGT into the 1990s, was no longer appropriate for the future given the growing internationalisation of the group.

As yet, only one substantive agreement has been concluded between Renault and the EWC: five other agreements related to the constitution of the forum – the EWC installation agreement, signed on 5 April 1993, and four subsequent revisions to this (1995, 1998, 2000, 2003). These revisions dealt with the distribution of seats, including observers,[144] and the mechanism for allocating seats between the French delegates, the budget, facility time for the EWC secretary and their deputies,

144 In the first agreement, there was provision for two observers from Volvo; in the second agreement, concluded in 1995, two observers from REVOZ were included; and in the 1998 agreement, there were observers from REVOZ, KAROSA and OYAK. No observers were included under the 2003 revision.

members of the steering committee and the EWC.[145] In addition, the EWC was enlarged to include representatives from non-European countries. Observer status was given to Argentina, Brazil, Romania, Slovenia and Turkey.

One response to the court judgments in France on the company's non-compliance with its information and consultation obligations during the Vilvoorde affair was the inclusion in the 1998 EWC agreement of a provision (Article 3.2) for extraordinary meetings of the EWC to be held to obtain information and have dialogue and an exchange of views 'in the event of a planned exceptional decision which has transnational consequences and is of a nature such as to affect significantly employees' interests'. Such meetings should be held at a time that allows the results of the exchange to 'still be taken into account in the decision-making process'.

A subsequent revision to the agreement, concluded on 4 April 2003, further specified the company's obligations:

> The council receives statistics information on a yearly or half-yearly basis. Moreover, a summary board with the main collective agreements concluded within the Group's companies will be prepared on a yearly basis and given to the Council members' (EWC Agreement, 2003, Article 2.2).

Under this provision, documents for the annual EWC meeting must be made available at least fifteen days beforehand in order to give members opportunity to prepare. For the steering committee, it was agreed that it would be regularly updated about the ongoing progress of business at Renault.

The only substantive agreement concluded so far between the company and the EWC was the 'Declaration on the Fundamental Rights of Employees in the Renault Group', signed on 12 October 2004. This declaration, agreed on within the framework of the UN Global Compact, not only covers employees in the European Union but all the group's workers worldwide. The declaration deals with nine areas in all. For example, Renault commits itself 'to protect jobs' and to 'to train workers for other jobs or, wherever possible, to find other jobs for them within the Group' in the event of reorganisation or restructuring. On the issue of remuneration, Renault recognised the principle of 'fair compensation for work' and the provisions of ILO convention No. 100 on equal pay for equal work.[146]

Although the agreement was negotiated with the involvement of the EWC, it did not pass without criticism. For example, it was held to be unclear how breaches of

---

145 In the 2000 revision, the preamble referred for the first time to ILO Convention 87 on freedom of association.

146 The declaration also included issues such as health and safety at work, a ban on child labour and forced labour. Renault's management also stated that it would strive to ensure that employees are represented in all Group companies either by elected employee representatives or relevant 'labour organizations'. It expressly recognised Convention 87 on freedom of association and Convention 98 on the right to organise and the promotion of collective bargaining.

the agreement would be dealt with, and what the formal status of the agreement was, and in particular, whether it could be enforced by the courts.

The EWC is seen by its members as an important body for gaining information and providing an opportunity for dialogue and exchange. Non-French members notably gain from the information they have access to through membership of the steering committee. Meetings with top management are principally viewed as an opportunity to address local problems. The EWC sees itself as a means for dealing with the problems of Renault employees throughout the world. One example of this were the problems in Brazil between local employee representatives and local management, where EWC representatives called on the EWC to take the issue up.

> The Brazilian representatives really turned to us in desperation. This was then completely rejected by management – management in Brazil and France said that wasn't right. But, in short, we had the financial capacity, and two people from France went there. They could speak Portuguese and we were very successful although management was absolutely opposed. There was then some correspondence as they did not want us to fly there. But we did anyway, and everything turned out well (RE02).

What is interesting about this incident is that is was concerned with a plant outside Europe. It shows, therefore, that – at least in the view of some EWC members – that there is some movement towards the forum becoming a worldwide representative of employee interests at Renault. Drawing on the typology proposed by Kotthoff (Kotthoff, 2006a), the EWC could be seen as an 'advocate of the diaspora' (Kotthof, 2006a: 64).[147]

However, further development of the EWC has foundered on the aversion of management to any further powers: in line with the French system, management views the EWC as purely an information and consultation forum and not as an actor able to negotiate.

> The EWC is not a negotiating body, but a forum for exchange and dialogue. [...] The role of the EWC is not that of a mediator. There is good dialogue and exchange takes place. [...]. The EWC does not have a mandate for this, nor to take on mediator functions (RM01).

> We are really an information body. [...] But to be quite honest and open, we are not really consulted (RE02).

As far as the effectiveness of internal discussion within the EWC is concerned, the views of some EWC members suggest a degree of modesty in this respect.

---

147 Kotthoff (2006) originally conceived of this type as the 'German works council chair as advocate of the diaspora' but this logic can also be extended to the French case.

The problems are in fact addressed, but they are never really talked through. A problem is broached, gets looked over, but there is not subsequently a solution. The meeting ends and this situation is accepted, but without any further questioning. If you ask subsequently, you'll get five answers and you can choose any one of those you want (RE02).

This reveals the fundamental dilemma that flows from the establishment of pluri-local solidarity, especially at international level. Although there is a general view that there should be cooperation between plants on the employee-side, this often takes a back seat when the issue turns on retaining job and operations at representatives' own plants. This is reflected by EWC members.

Everyone fights for their own people in the first place, and something like solidarity takes second place. [...] Our weakness is quite simple, and I'll say it quite openly: we are often disunited because there are more individualists when we're dealing with each other, and we should really put own interests in second place (RE02).

In the view of some EWC representatives, the fragmentation of national or workplace interests reflects the outlook of national workforces, for whom the EWC plays only a minor role.

They know that there is an EWC. It's possible to bring the EWC a little closer to workers through solidarity actions, such as when money was collected in the French plants for a strike fund for Romania. But employees also ask what the fate of people in other plants has got to do with them, along the lines of 'they're taking our work away' (RE01).

7.3 Provisional assessment

Our findings indicate that Renault can be characterised as a comparatively centralised and strongly coordinated group. In the context of the analytical framework used for this study, Renault can most appropriately be denoted as a *global organisation.* As far as the pattern of the distribution of resources, power, culture and knowledge is concerned, the indicators point to a centralised structure. The bulk of the company's employees are concentrated in France. Production capacity is also heavily localised in France (although there is no single dominant plant). In analysing strategic decision-making, there is also a marked concentration on the home country and on group-level management. Knowledge resources in the group – and in particular strategic knowledge in the field of product and process innovation – also appears to be centralised. Renault has a strong cultural identity that is both strongly influenced by its home country and is also an element in France's national identity: this is also transferred to its subsidiaries abroad – albeit with a few exceptions. One illustration is the high importance accorded to the French language, including in its foreign operations.

In order to obtain cross-brand and cross-national synergies, there is close coordination of the immediate value-creating process. The activities of the Renault-Nissan Alliance and the purchasing organisation, through which some two-thirds of all group purchasing takes place and which manages most supplier relationships, are indicators of a high level of coordination. Inter-plant competition within the group, effected through platform strategies and parallel production, also points to a high level of operational coordination. The processes used for coordination also indicate a high degree of centralisation. For example, in central functions, such as strategic decision-making and R&D, coordination is not through a network but through a centralised structure, in which headquarters staff and top management figure as the dominant centres of decision-making, planning and control.

Our analysis of the structures of distribution and coordination of the Renault EWC reveal a similar picture. As such, the (somewhat) centralised pattern of distribution and strong coordination within the EWC also point to a global form of internationalisation. In essence, the EWC is an extension of the French *comité de groupe*. As with PSA, the forum is unambiguously dominated by the French members. In contrast to PSA, however, the Renault EWC is a strongly coordinated body. On the one hand, there are actors who are highly motivated to progress the work of interest representation within the EWC (the secretary); on the other, there are structures, such as the binomes and regular meetings, that facilitate strong coordination.

Although the competitive situation of individual plants, and the widespread use of platform strategies, would suggest a high regulatory need on the part of European employee representatives, a number of factors hamper the EWC from taking on a more assertive role within intra-company processes of negotiation and interest regulation. One central aspect is certainly the EWC structure itself, which in turn is due to the centralism that characterises the Renault group more generally. Centralisation of resources, power, culture and knowledge on the French EWC delegates makes it harder for foreign EWC members to raise concerns and set in train their own strategic initiatives. At the same time, pluralism within the French system of employment regulation – union fragmentation along political, ideological and confessional lines (Boulin, 2001: 158) and the concomitant competition between them – has compromised the EWC's organisational capacity. It would be hard for a stable, capable EWC centre (as at VW, Daimler or Ford) or network (as at GM) to emerge due to the structural logic of the system – and one problem is certainly the rotation of the EWC secretary.

In addition, the traditional structure of employment relations in France provides for elected workplace employee representatives (*délégues du personnel* and *comités d'entreprise*) only to exercise an information and consultation role (Goetschy, 1998). Negotiations are conducted by trade unions at sectoral, multi-sectoral level and also – crucially – at workplace level in France. These actors view the EWC neither currently nor prospectively as a negotiating partner. And reasons of self-preservation – trade unions would run the risk of losing their bargaining monopoly and hence an element of their legitimation – mean that no one would aspire to allow the forum to develop such a role. Management also sees the EWC solely as a body equipped with information and consultation rights: and a significance within the internal system of employment relations that might go beyond this has so far not been openly considered.

Chapter 8: Honda

8.1 The Honda Motor Company Ltd and Honda Europe

Honda is seen as a special case even amongst other Japanese automotive companies (Shimokawa, 2003). The company is notable for its unique corporate culture, which continues to embody the spirit of its founders, and a long-standing commitment to technical innovation. Studies of Honda have noted the particularly crucial roles of the company founder, Soichiro Honda, who began as an engineer and enjoyed success in implementing a number of adventurous technologies, and his head of finance, Takeo Fujisawa (see, for example, Shimokawa, 2003: 163). The company culture, which both of these individuals enshrined and which represents an important element in the Honda Production System (HPS), is strongly marked by its entrepreneurial spirit, rejection of conventional solutions and imitating the status quo, and organisational flexibility and innovation. The HPS remains anchored in innovative products and flexible mass production (Luethge and Byosière, 2009; see also Mair, 1998: 100).

In 2008 the Honda group consisted of three segments as well the cars division. These were motorcycles, financial services, and power products.[148] The company operates through a matrix structure with a functional and regional division, based on six geographical clusters (Japan, North America, Latin America, Europe/Middle East and South Asia/Africa, Asia/Oceania and China). In addition to the four product divisions there are also units for customer service, procurement and production. Shares in the company are dispersed, with no single large-scale shareholders. The largest, the Japan Trustee Services Bank Ltd, had only 5.2 per cent of the shares in 2008. Overall 44.9 per cent of the shares are held by a variety of Japanese financial institutions, followed by foreign banks and financial institutions and individuals (32.9 per cent) as well as a substantial Japanese free float (10.8 per cent) (Honda, 2009:89).

The European headquarters (Honda Motors Europe, HME) is located in the UK and reports directly to Honda Motor Regional Operations in Japan. Since early-2010 the European headquarters has controlled all the activities of Honda's European affiliates.[149] Honda has a production facilities distributed throughout the world. The largest production capacities are located in the United States. In Europe the

---

148 This latter includes a variety of powered products, such as outboard motors, lawnmowers, water pumps, and generators <http://world.honda.com/power/> accessed 22 October 2009.

149 Up to this date, there were three regional clusters as organisational units below the level of the European HQ. Honda Motors Europe North GmbH (HME-N) was headquartered in Germany (Offenbach am Main) and was also responsible for Austria and the Benelux countries. Honda Motors Europe South (HME-S) was managed from Paris, and covered France, Italy, and Spain. Honda Motors UK (HUK) was headquartered in the UK and also covered Scandinavia and Eastern

only automotive production operations are at the British Swindon plant which manufactures both vehicles and engines. There is a further automotive operation in Turkey, which is a unit within the HME.[150] However, this only produces 20,000 units a year for regional markets. There are other non-car manufacturing operations in Ormes/France (power products), Atessa/Italy (motorcycles, power products, engines), Barcelona/Spain (motorcycles) and Aalst/Belgium (motorcycles, parts). With the exception of the Turkish plant, all five operations are in the European Union. There are also units dealing with distribution, logistics and research and development in Europe (HM01).[151]

8.1.1 History of the company

The path to becoming a global successful car producer was initially one paved with considerable barriers and obstacles for Honda. As early as 1946, Soichiro Honda had begun to produce motorised cycles. By 1947 he had achieved a market share of 60 per cent. The Honda Motor Company Ltd was founded in 1948 and soon began to develop and manufacture motorcycles and gain its first experience of industrial mass production based on its rapidly rising sales. By 1960, Honda was the largest producer of motorcycles in the world. Honda's success in motor sport, and in particular the Isle of Man TT, characterised and promoted a youthful and sporting image of a dynamic company.

Honda only began to design its own cars in the early-1960s, including a sports car and a small pick-up (T360). There were many problems in gaining a foothold in the Japanese car market. In the mid-1960s Honda was a newcomer in a sector already crowded with indigenous competitors such as Toyota, Mazda and Nissan, some of which had several decades of experience in the business. In addition, Honda lacked its own ('keiretsu') network of suppliers, financiers and distributors, a precondition for a successful entry into the market (Shimokawa, 2003: 168f.). The problems confronting Honda within Japan forced the undertaking to move to a strategy based on sales and production abroad very early on its history. Initially Honda pursued an intensive export strategy, motorcycles shipped to Taiwan and the USA from the 1950s. Following the start of mass car production, exports rose from 6 per cent of total output to 70 per cent between 1977 and 1980 (Mair, 1998: 113). There was also an expansion in the number of models. In 1965 Honda manufactured one car on one platform: three years later there were three models based on two platforms, and by 1972 four models on three platforms (ibid. 115).

Europe as well as independent distributors and joint ventures (see too Kawabe, 2004). These were mainly sales clusters, which gave way a flatter structure in 2010.

150 However, because the Honda EWC does not include Turkey, we do not deal with it in the analysis of the company's organisational arrangements (see too Chapter 3 above).

151 See <http://world.honda.com/business-overview/index.html > accessed 15 August 2012.

Honda's second response to problems in its home country was to internationalise production. The USA was and remains the most important market for Honda. In 1977/79 Honda began to operate a motorcycle factory in Ohio using the corporate vehicle of its motorcycle distribution company, Honda of America Company 'HAM', which had been established in 1959. Beginning in the early-1980s, this export-oriented production model, developed in the 1970s, was replaced by a multinational form (Mair, 1998: 120ff.). The first car production plant was set up in 1980–82 at Marysville/Ohio, near to its original plant, in response to import restrictions imposed by the US government. Sales grew rapidly in the 1980s, especially in the US. By the late-1980s further plants were opened (East Liberty/Ohio, 1986 – engines and final assembly in 1989; Alliston/Ontario, Canada 1986 – final assembly). Local content requirements also led many Honda suppliers to invest in the US. In the automotive sector, US car sales currently account for 50 per cent of global car sales, compared with just 20 per cent in Japan. As such Honda follows a strategy of 'manufacturing products where they are sold' (Luethge and Byosière, 2009: 120; see too Kawabe, 2004; HM01).

Production in Europe began in the early-1960s with the establishment of a motorcycle plant in Belgium in 1961 which began production in 1963.[152] The aim was to avoid import duties and serve the growing motorcycle market more effectively. However, there were a number of problems, some serious. Firstly, Belgian unions resisted the transfer of Honda production principles to the plant, at least in the form envisaged by Honda. Up until this point Honda had had little experience in dealing with organised employee representatives. Honda's early problems in Japan with its enterprise union, established in 1953, had been resolved within a few years. As is characteristic of the Japanese harmonious model, this union became a key element workplace regulation at Honda based on a bonus system that rewarded individual performance (Mair, 1998: 112). There were also problems of cooperation between Belgium and Japanese employees, in part due to language barriers. Problems in transferring the production system also led to quality difficulties that impacted on sales (Luethge and Byosière, 2009: 116).

The first plant in Great Britain began to assemble vehicles using knocked-down components imported from Japan. In 1981, an additional plant was opened at Cowley to produce the Triumph Acclaim model in cooperation with British Leyland (Mair, 1998: 119). The alliance with Rover, which Honda had entered into in 1979 and had led to Honda holding 20 per cent of Rover's shares, came to a painful end for the Japanese partner in 1994. In response to rising losses, the majority shareholder in Rover, British Aerospace, secretly sold its shares to BMW who then took over the company. Because Honda wanted to avoid a loss of technology to a competitor and, moreover, did not want to be the junior partner to BMW, it then sold its shares. However, this meant that in addition to losing some important technical knowledge, which BMW was able to use to develop its small vehicle programme, Honda also lost an important anchor in the European Union (Luethge and Byosière, 2009: 117).

152 Honda of Europe was founded in 1978.

One of the characteristic features of the Honda group from the outset was the organisational model developed by the finance chief, Fujisawa. This was intended to accelerate rapid and flexible adaptation to changes in the business environment and also allow for individual creativity and innovation as well as continuous improvement in processes and structures (Luethge and Byosière, 2009: 113). From the 1980s, the Honda Production System was based on several elements, some of which were original to the company, others of which had been borrowed from other car manufacturers, notably Toyota (Mair, 1998: 117f.). The key characteristics of this production system are a high level of production flexibility, flexible manufacture of a number of models, and the very early introduction of the principle of building to order (Shimokawa, 2003). Production is based on a few high volume models and a push system driven by market forecasts. Manufacturing is undertaken flexibly using standardised parts, with models manufactured in batches of around sixty units. The model is often characterised as being 'human centred', with job rotation, work on different models, and fairly short working hours (Mair, 1994).

In contrast to other Japanese firms Honda broke with Japanese cultural traditions. Instead of the well- established system of seniority, harmony and consensus, as well as a marked degree of hierarchy, Honda operated on the basis of individual performance incentives, promotion based on performance and knowledge, participation, a decentralisation of decision-making powers and assigning leadership roles to young workers open to new and innovative solutions, and flat hierarchies (Mair, 1998: 111f.; Luethge and Byosière, 2009: 113).

Honda has always taken a restrictive position towards trade unions and collective employee representation. Although the company had come to an arrangement with its enterprise union in Japan, it was suspicious of organised employee representatives at foreign sites, such as in the USA or Europe, which, in contrast to the Japanese culture were both sometimes adversarial and prepared to engage in conflict (Mair, 1998). This stance became very evident in the case of Honda of America, which did not have trade union organisation. When the American automobile union UAW attempted to organise the HAM workforce in the 1980s, the company responded with an overt anti-union campaign accompanied by wage increases. Alongside a number of employee friendly features that characterise the HPS culture, this strategy of excluding unions has also meant that the UAW has never managed to gain a toehold in the company. As far as interest representation at European level is concerned, as we set out below, similar developments could be seen (Mair, 1998: 122).

Since 1990 Honda has gone through three changes in top management – a highly uncharacteristic development for Honda related in some respects to the varying fortunes of its car division (Luethge and Byosière, 2009: 112). Takeo Fukui, the CEO in office since 2003, seems to have returned to the innovative and entrepreneurial spirit of the founders that had given way to a much greater emphasis on marketing by his predecessors. Examples are the current push for more innovation, the decision to focus on motorcycle production as well as increased exports from Japan, investments in aerospace and alternative power train systems, and engagement in new markets such as India, China or Brazil (ibid.).

8.1.2 Distribution of resources, power, culture and knowledge

In the reporting year 2008/2009[153] Honda employed 181,000 workers worldwide. Of these some 4 per cent worked in the EU. As far as the distribution of employment at EU locations is concerned, Honda is fairly highly centralised. Almost 80 per cent of EU production workers are employed in the UK. Taking all divisions into account, Honda has more than thirty-nine locations across the world, of which twenty-two are engaged in car production. Four plants, around 13 per cent of the total, are located in the EU.[154] In 2008, Honda produced 3,912,700 vehicles in total. Of total, the Swindon plant contributed 230,423, equivalent to 5.8 per cent.[155]

Table 6: Distribution of employees, plants and production, Honda (2008/9)

	Employees	Plants	Production
World	181,876	39	3,912,700
EU	7,200	5	230,423
EU home country (UK)	3,000	1	230,423
'Real' home country (Japan)	60,000	5	1,264,381
Largest plant	2,500	–	–
Share EU/world	4%	13%	6%
Share EU home country (UK)/EU	79%	20%	100%
Share EU home country (UK)/world	3%	3%	6%
Share 'real' home country/world	33%	13%	32%
Share largest plant/EU	79%	-	100%

Source: compiled from Honda Annual Report, 2009; OICA (2008); interview (HM01); excludes Turkey

Power and decision-making competence within Europe are concentrated at the headquarters in the UK (Honda Motors Europe Ltd). This coordinates and controls all the activities of Honda in Europe, and is reported to directly by the European affiliates. The European headquarters formulates its own plans and proposals for

153 Data on the number of employees and operations are taken from the 2009 annual report, as Honda's financial year ended in March 2009.

154 Because there is only one car plant in Europe, this accounts for 100 per cent of employees in the cars division.

155 Because the Honda EWC (HECCG) covers all divisions, these are all included in the analysis of the distribution of resources of Honda Europe. However, this a problem for our study as it requires data on the number of motorcycles manufactured. For comparison with other companies in the sample, we confine the analysis to data for vehicle production (see OICA, 2008).

all business areas, which must be approved by the corporate headquarters in Japan. Once plans have been accepted, the European headquarters has scope to determine how they should be implemented.

> Basically you can say that the global strategy, of course, is set up in Japan, and the translation of the global strategy in a European strategy is *agreed by Japan*, but it is proposed in Europe. The implementation of the strategy is the European responsibility. Where a certain model is made is decided in Japan (...) when this has been decided, and when the number of vehicles that have to be produced has been approved by Japan, then it is totally up to Europe to manage this. And if they need three shifts or two shifts, that is up to Europe. (HM01; emphasis added)

The close coordination between the European headquarters and the corporate headquarters in Japan is ensured through the fact that the CEO of HME is also a board member of the Japanese parent company. This linking of important functions at management level overcomes to some extent the division of labour or division of competence between operational and strategic tasks. The scope for individual European operations to participate in strategic decisions is, however, fairly meagre. They are only sporadically incorporated into planning processes.

Honda has a strong company culture, based on values and principles that are specific to the company and which, for the most part, are transferred to foreign locations. However, over the course of its internationalisation, Honda has had some very negative experiences when attempting to export cultural elements: as such, the distribution of culture could currently be denoted as 'somewhat centralised'.

The organisational model developed by Fujisawa aimed from the outset at promoting international competitiveness and the capacity for innovation. It embraced a highly entrepreneurial culture in which the company founder and engineer, Soichiro Honda, acted as exemplar for employees in the business. In addition, an expert system, which allowed for the promotion of engineers who did not want to become managers, was installed along with a continuous improvement programme in which ideas remained the intellectual property of those who discovered them. This also served to facilitate and promote individual effort. Employees in lower levels of the hierarchy were given enhanced responsibility to stimulate the creativity of young employees (Mair, 1998: 111f.). The company has had a sustained emphasis on maintaining an open corporate culture with scope for ideas and innovation. Transparent and free flowing communication processes are seen as vital in these aspirations.

Honda actively promotes a common corporate culture in which the company, managers and employees are not seen as unequal or as two sides of the undertaking. All employees at Honda are united by the fact that they work towards an overarching aim – to promote and enhance the success of the company. This community ideology is evident in many facets of the company's structure and culture, not least in the operation of the Honda EWC. For example, employees are not designated as workers but as 'associates' (as with Toyota, where employees are termed 'members'). They are seen as participants in a general project for corporate success. Managers at local operations often do not have their own rooms but share space with others in an open plan office. Managers and employees also often wear the same company clothing, which for managers is differentiated only by the fact that they wear ties.

This common culture also implies a particular view of interests and possibly conflicts of interest between the workplace parties. Because Honda regards all employees as part of an integrated whole, it does not recognise divergent interests. Conflicts are regarded as differences of opinion or disagreements due to shortcomings in communication – such as a failure to clearly set out strategic objectives and how they are to be implemented – that can be resolved through appropriate improvements to structures of communication.

Problems in transferring elements of the Honda production system became evident early on in the establishment of operations in the USA and in Belgium. Following the setting up of the motorcycle plant at Marysville, some account taken of the local features of US human resource management which stood in contradiction to Japanese and specifically Honda HR practices in some respects (see Mair, 1998: 120f.). For example, there was only one level of hierarchy within the workforce and equal pay. There was no bonus system or pay by seniority or skill level, which was untypical for the American system. Moreover, 'Western' participative elements were implemented: employees could participate in determining issues such as working time and holiday regulations. Decentralised panels were set up staffed by employees. Only the resistance of the UAW was seen to represent a counter version of American cultural elements.

Figure 11: Distribution of Honda operations in Europe, 2008.

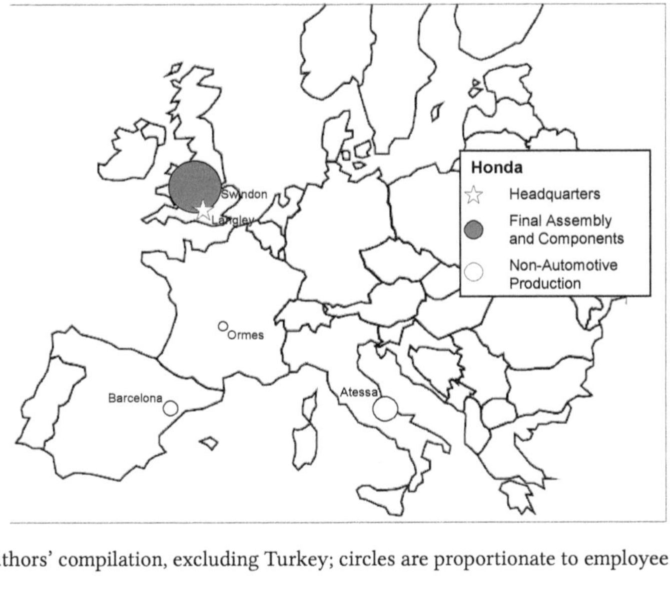

Source: authors' compilation, excluding Turkey; circles are proportionate to employee numbers.

Since 2000 Honda has pursued the strategic restructuring and standardisation of all its international production facilities. The aim of this reconfiguration is to raise the level of flexibility: ultimately all vehicle types will be constructed on a common platform (Luethge and Byosière, 2009: 120). However, this has not simply been a matter of transferring principles from Japan to affiliate operations. Rather meetings were held with employees from all parts of the world to discuss process changes and tooling modifications (ibid. 120).

Honda is seen as a company that has always been characterised by an emphasis on generating innovation and knowledge. The enduring status of the company founder, Soichiro Honda, who was responsible for a number of important developments as an engineer, continues to act as a key point of reference within the company. The significance of generating innovation can also be seen in the long-standing tradition under which CEOs of the group have generally been drawn from heads of R&D (Shimokawa, 2003: 168). Product and process innovations remain a key foundation of the success of the business, both in cars as well as other divisions. The youthful and sporting image, based on successes in Formula One and Formula Two, rests very much on internal technical innovation and development.

In 1960, the company established its own research and development company Honda R&D Co. Ltd. This organisation is noteworthy not only because it is formally separate from the Honda group but is also financially and operationally independent, with the necessary freedom to undertake technical innovation. Financial independence is ensured through the fact that Honda transfers 5 per cent of its revenues to the R&D unit, allowing Honda engineers to be insulated from immediate market pressures and 'perform research and development in a free atmosphere' (Shimokawa, 2003: 168; Mair, 1998: 111; see too Nonaka, 1991).

As far as process innovation is concerned, from an early stage Honda was one of the leading manufacturers in this area. The Honda Production System not only created scope for experiments with new technologies and production organisation; internal competition was also used to stimulate rivalry for R&D projects amongst its engineers. Since the 1970s, Honda has pursued a strategy of 'simultaneous engineering' in which the model cycle has been reduced to four years (Mair, 1998: 116).

However, the establishment of an R&D unit led to a focus on development activities in Japan. In 1975 a design centre was opened in California, given the significance of the US market. However, the aim of this was not technical development but rather 'Americanising' a model range developed in Japan – especially the Civic and Accord series – to gain access to US customers (Mair, 1998: 115f.). In that sense the function of the foreign subsidiaries was a subordinate one. This also applies to the two R&D operations in Europe (UK and Germany). The role of the approximately 180 R&D employees in Europe consists in adapting models developed in Japan to the special features of European markets.

> Implementing the local face, the local European face into concepts which are made in Japan. Japan is making concepts for the cars they [European R&D affiliates] are catching the consumer taste. The car designs in Europe and Japan are slightly different (HMO1).

8.1.3 Coordination of company activities

Honda's coordination of its car, motorcycle, and power products division can be seen as 'somewhat weak'. On the one hand, the car business gained considerably from prior innovation and the stock of knowledge built up in the motorcycle division. The company still attempts to transfer technical innovation across divisions. However, as far as internal supply relationships in Europe are concerned, individual divisions operate largely independently of each other. The sheer fact that at management level there are individuals responsible for the same areas of activity in different divisions and that divisions are responsible for their own services, such as IT and R&D, suggests a low level of integration. Business processes seem to be more strongly linked within the cars division. One example is the coordination of standardisation processes, which has been applied to all production facilities since 2000 and which brings together engineers from all over the world for coordination meetings. Some 30 per cent of components for the Swindon plant are sourced from Japan. Within the EU – and also between the British and Turkish plants – there are no particularly strong linkages (HMO1).

However, the value placed on knowledge generation means that there are horizontal and vertical information networks spanning the entire company with the aim of ensuring that knowledge exchange, and communication and coordination take place within the group (Mair, 1998: 112). Honda coordinates the production and product development divisions using its 'Digital Manufacturing Circle', its own IT application that also incorporates suppliers in order to integrate and accelerate product development (see Luethge and Byosière, 2009: 120).

8.2 The Honda European Communication and Consultation group (HECCG)

The Honda European Works Council, officially titled the Honda European Communication and Consultation Group (HECCG), mirrors Honda's corporate culture in many respects, and in particular the values of non-adversarial employment relations based on intense communication. As far as the scope for employee interest representation is concerned, the Honda EWC is the most weakly developed institution of all EWCs in our sample. According to Streeck (1997) EWCs are neither European nor truly works councils: this applies with considerable force to the Honda EWC, especially in terms of the second proposition. It is not a works council, firstly, because it is not in any sense an *organisation*: rather, it can be more accurately described as an information *arrangement* initiated, dominated, and controlled by management. In line with the wording of the EWC Directive, the HECCG embraces a *process* for employee information and consultation at its European locations. Secondly, employee representatives play a generally subordinate role in this process in comparison with management: of the overall – and extremely large – total of sixty-eight members in the forum, only twenty-eight are employee representatives. In that sense, the HECCG has great similarities with the Labour-Management

Council, an internal consultation body for employees and management representatives on the Japanese model.

The main activities of the HECCG consist in a twice-yearly meeting at which the Japanese top managers and managers from local plants and employees convene. For the employee-side this only partly involves elected representatives: for example, German works councillors (or trade union delegates) are not represented on the HECCG. As far as interest regulation is concerned, the body is almost entirely confined to disseminating information.

8.2.1 Adoption and substance of EWC agreements

With the adoption of the EWC agreement on 1 March 1995 Honda was the first Japanese company to implement the EWC Directive on establishing a European works council or a process for employee information and consultation. Although at that time the UK was not within the scope of the Directive, the initiative to set up the HECCG was taken by Honda Motors Europe, based in the UK, which controlled the Honda's European operations. In contrast to the provisions of the Directive, no negotiations took place over the EWC installation agreement, which was formulated without any involvement by employee representatives or trade unions and was not signed by any employee representative. 'The agreement was not negotiated, it was designed by the company' (HEO4). At the first meeting, held on Majorca, sixty people attended, including twenty-two employee representatives from sixteen countries and thirty-eight top managers of HME and local operations as well as twenty-three affiliates which were located within Europe (cf. *Japan Labour Bulletin*, 1995).

The installation agreement[156] does not refer to a European body – that is, an institution in the narrow sense of the term. Rather, it provides for an 'information and consultation structure which will develop a dialogue and exchange of view [*sic*] at European level' (ibid). The 1995 agreement has since been revised three times.[157] The current agreement provides for two annual meetings, the timing of which is set, according to management, to fit with the group's financial and budget planning. The planning cycle begins in March or April (first HECCG meeting), and a second meeting is held in October at which time the plans are subject to revision. The meetings have two sessions: an information session 'for the purpose of communication and clarification'; and a second session for consultation and discussion on topics of common interest and information obtained in the first session.

The HECCG is formally a joint body on the 'French model'. The agreement specifies that participants for the management side comprise all senior staff who regularly attend the 'European Presidents Meeting' as well as other European top managers. For the employee side, there is one representative for each location with

---

156 'Agreement for Communication and Consultation with Employees of Honda in Europe' (1 March 1995).

157 A fourth revision was expected in 2010, shortly after this research was concluded: see also below.

more than fifty full-time employees, but at least one representative from each European country in which there is an operation with more than fifteen full-time employees in facilities that are majority owned by the company. The HECCG covers all the company's divisions and all the European operations of these divisions. These include subsidiaries in European countries which at that time were not formally within the scope of the Directive (in 1995 this was Poland, Switzerland, Czech Republic and Great Britain) (*Japan Labour Bulletin*, 1995). Looked at in terms of these formal provisions for integrating the operations, the HECCG would appear to be a genuinely European body.

8.2.2 Distribution and resources, power, culture and knowledge within the EWC

Compared with all other EWCs in our sample, the HECCG has its own particular logic. It is the only joint body consisting of employee representatives and employers in which the employee representative group has no independent life. There are neither pre-meetings before the main meeting for the employees side, nor is there any scope for substantive exchange between employee representatives during the conference or in between official meetings. Since management controls the activities of the body, the distribution of seats by country has no influence on the opportunities that employees have to advance their interests. Rather, what seems more significant is the differentiation in the distribution of seats between management and employee representatives.

The HECCG has sixty-eight members in all, of which forty can be regarded as representing the management side. In 2009, twenty-eight members of the HECCG were local managers – 'president or senior manager' (Honda fact sheet HECCG 2010:2) – from various operations. These are chosen by the company. In addition, eleven directors of Honda Motors Europe or senior managers participate in the meetings. These are exclusively Japanese managers. The chair of the HECCG – a former Conservative member of parliament in the UK – is also appointed by the company in line with the EWC agreement. According to management the chair should be an open 'independent and neutral person' (HMO1). However, employee representatives expressed suspicion that Honda's choice of a Conservative parliamentarian for the office of HECCG chair was connected with Honda's rejection of any kind of external claim to collective employee representation (HEO1).

Figure 12: Distribution of employee seats on the HECCG, 2009.

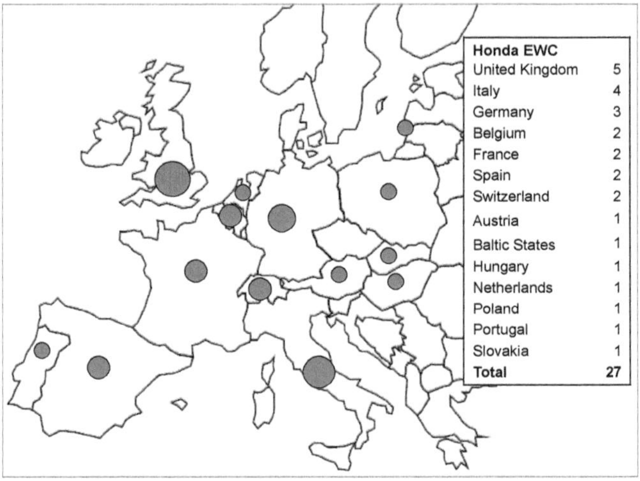

Source: authors' compilation

Of the twenty-eight employee representatives, some are elected but others have been nominated or chosen by local management. The election procedure reflects local custom and practice. 'The assignment of the employee representatives occurs in the way that is in line with local legal and conventional requirements or in line with the normal local usage' (Honda fact sheet HECCG 2010:2). In all sixty countries are represented on the HECCG including Great Britain (six), Italy (four), Belgium, Spain, Switzerland and France (each with two), Germany (three), Austria, Slovenia, Hungary, The Netherlands, Poland, Portugal and the Baltic states (each with one). Looking just at the employee side, 21 per cent (six seats) are from the UK which has the largest single number of employees in the European Union. Compared with other companies in our sample, in this respect Honda can be designated as 'somewhat decentralised'. Only in GM and Toyota do employee representatives from the home country have a lower share of the seats. The EWC representativeness index[158] has a value of 0.36, which suggests that foreign locations are over-represented. As a consequence, as far as the distribution of seats on a country basis is concerned, the HECCG is very much a European body.

The HECCG has no culture of interest representation. Processes are too strongly dominated and preconfigured by management. On the employee side, some delegates would like the body to have a stronger role. However, in view of the serious obstacles to this, there is little prospect for such a development and certainly no 'added value'. On the other hand, there also appear to be delegates who see HECCG

158 For calculation of this index, see Chapter 3.3.1.

meetings as a communication platform for issues raised by the company's product policy and who are not interested, or less interested, in being employee representatives in the conventional sense. The following quotation is drawn from an internet forum for Honda workers from a number of countries. In it, one HECCG member reports on an HECCG meeting and quotes one of the three questions which he wanted to submit to a future meeting and would like to have answered by management.

> There are periodic meetings held in EU countries where associates get together with the higher ranks on a more informal level and get to have their Honda related questions answered. Each country sends a representative which then asks the questions for all to hear and then the higher ranks answer them on the spot. I sent in *three questions for approval* and I think they will make it through to the meeting. The final questions reads like this: '*Among the actual owners, ex-owners and many lovers of the Africa twin motorcycle, there is a great hope that Honda, one day, might consider re-issue this mythical model, possibly with some revisions like PGM-FI, ABS and a more comfortable seat, but keeping its basic versatility and strong charisma. There are other brands reviving older mythical models like the Yamaha Tenere... Can Honda consider doing this?*' (emphasis added).

8.2.3 Coordination

The two meetings of HECCG each year take place in London and usually last for two to three days. The first section of the meeting is taken up with the speech delivered by the President of Honda Europe as well as a presentation by an external speaker on current business or economic topics and presentations from the heads of functions on the results, plans and future challenges in each of their areas. The second part consists of a working group phase and the so-called 'round table open session' (Honda Fact Sheet HECCG, 2010:4), at which management representatives respond to questions put by employee representatives or at which employee representatives can express their opinions and report on their experiences. According to management, this facilitates an open exchange of positions and views. All proposals and questions from delegates are taken seriously and – in terms of helpmg to raise company performance – are considered for future strategic planning.

> As the success of the company in Europe is of interest and concern of all participants [of the HECCG], every viewpoint is considered and treated as important. [...] The executive board will listen to and consider every intervention and take this into consideration when planning the direction of Honda in Europe' (Honda Fact Sheet HECCG 2010:3).

However, statements made by several HECCG employee representatives from a number of countries suggest a different picture. In particular, in the initial years HECCG meetings were notable for a desire on the part of management to exercise control. Not only were agenda points directed by management but management also controlled and monitored the substance of discussions and statements: according to a number of employee representatives, critical questions from participants were rejected (HEO1). This control went so far that the number of questions permitted was restricted to three per participant and participants were required to communicate questions to management ahead of the event. Questions deemed unsuitable were removed by management.

> [A HECCG meeting] is very much management driven and elected reps are given much lip service. In the questions and answers session the MD was very invasive to any question I put forward, I was even asked the night before if I could divulge the questions prior to this meeting in order to save any embarrassment over any questions I may ask, and I was informed that this worked well with the previous representative (HEO1).

Some employee representatives stated that questions that were raised on an ad hoc basis that management did not want to answer or was unable to answer were either avoided or not directly answered: 'if any awkward question was raised, as within my case, the MD was very evasive or pretended that they did not really understand the question and got the chair to move on to the next question' (HEO1).

According to other HECCG employee representatives the usual practice within the body had changed sometime before this. Questions did not have to be put in advance and nor were spontaneous questions forbidden: 'I have been on the meetings for five, six years, I never had to put any questions, anytime. Because when you get presentations, you can think of some questions about this presentation so you have to be able to ask questions' (HEO4).

Even if Honda management has not directly forbidden communication between employees at meetings, the entire culture of the sessions runs counter to the notion of an independent organisation of employee representatives. Moreover, management has taken a number of measures to inhibit such exchanges. For example, seating is usually arranged so that employee representatives sit with management representatives.

> The organiser distributed the seating. However, you were always seated next to your company's senior manager. The only time reps were seated alone without senior managers is the last day when you are permitted to put up to a maximum of three questions to the Japanese MD. In the evening at dinner they split you all up so you will have some senior Japanese managers seated at your table (HEO1).

By contrast, according to management, the reason for organising the seating in this way is to promote communication between delegates as well as between employee representatives and management: 'seating plans are established to encourage employees to openly talk with European executive board and European heads of product lines and functions' (Honda Fact Sheet HECCG 2010:3; HMO1). Managers argued that an informal exchange between management and employee representatives would not happen without an appropriate provision: 'What will happen is that all the Japanese are sitting together, and all the locals are sitting together because they have a reluctance to sit next to the European president.'(HMO1). In addition, breaks in the meetings would allow employees sufficient scope to meet and coordinate if they wanted to. However, the social pressure created by the constant presence of immediate superiors arguably militates against an open and free exchange by employee representatives.

During the phases of an HECCG meeting, a number of working groups consisting of employee representatives, directors and managers are formed. These discuss current problems or other issues of relevance for Honda and seek to develop solutions. Solutions are then presented by the group representative in the plenary session at which the Japanese management is present. The employee side noted that no independent issues can be raised in these group discussions and that employee concerns, in as much as they are raised at all, are not considered (HEO1). As such, the group phase has a functional element directed at promoting communication, and in that sense is entirely consistent with the basic individual participative stance of the company.

8.2.4 Critical events and outputs of the HECCG

Honda recorded growing car sales, employment and revenues over many years. Between 1997 and 2006, the number of units sold rose from 2.184 to 3.391 million, and employment from 101,000 to 145,000 (Honda Annual Report; see too Luethge and Byosière, 2009: 126). In Europe, production in this period fluctuated considerably, and fell seriously in 2001/2, but subsequently reached a new high point.

One characteristic feature of the HECCG since its inception has been that, although management has presented information on business and economic developments, they refrained from indicating to employee representatives what their position was, let alone what their strategic response might be. One example of an increased regulatory need was the relocation of a logistics centre from Germany to Poland, which led to no form of cross-border agreement between employee representatives. In 2008, management had reported on this relocation at an HECCG meeting and justified it by reference to the geographical distribution of logistic centres in an expanded EU.[159]

HECCG members have strikingly divergent perceptions and views. Management's stance strongly mirrors the Honda corporate culture: employees and managers are all 'associates' and should contribute equally to enhancing the company's success, with no fundamental conflicts of interest between the company, managers and workforce. From this standpoint, there is no logic to any form of independent European employee representative body. Differences are resolvable through open dialogue.[160]

159 A social plan was the negotiated with the German works council for the twenty-eight employees at the logistics centre in Offenbach.

160 More extensive participation rights were rejected on the grounds that they implied criticism of management (HM01). Employee or union participation would detract from the implementation of necessary managerial decisions or cast doubt on the ability of managers to make appropriate decisions. Revising managerial

When interviewed, management correspondingy emphasised the benefits for cooperation and performance offered by the HECCG, as well as its strong European orientation. For management, the aim of the HECCG is,

> [...]to have a forum, where the company can provide business information to the associates, on the one side. Secondly, it is for the company and its management an opportunity to get feedback from the associates, not only on the business issues but also on general issues, social issues and so on. So for me it's a forum to give information. Secondly to get feedback on how issues are running all over the place in Europe (HM01).

On this account, the HECCG was not set up to meet the legal requirements of the Directive but to satisfy the particular needs of the company and its employees. This was also why the composition of the HECCG (inclusion of non-EU countries) and the number of meetings went beyond the Directive's provisions. The forum was to be 'an integral part of Honda's business for Europe, not just another meeting' (statement of a former Honda CEO).

As a consequence, principles that coincided with management objectives, such as teamwork and continuous improvement, were counted as important tasks for the HECCG.[161] The main role of meetings is to facilitate communication amongst representatives and with management: according to management, an open and free exchange of opinions and positions is welcomed. Management uses the HECCG essentially as a means of information and consultation, amplified by the fact that following meetings delegates will pass on information they have received to employees at their workplaces.

In some respects employees' views utterly contradicted the official management version of the HECCG. Some German representatives did not see the HECCG as an institution capable of influencing management decisions. One works council abandoned attending HECCG meetings for some years. Despite the threat of the closure of a location, which eventually came about, they saw little point in engagement with the HECCG. One factor was the company culture: works council members know that steps to formulate their interests (collective and divergent from those of the company) would breach the implicit norms that prevail in the company and the

---

decisions in the light of employee consultation or union pressure would, in turn, either mean that the decision was wrong – essentially an admission of managerial incompetence – or could mean that correct decisions were not put into practice, inevitably damaging the company and representing a serious breach of the rules within Honda's culture.

161 To an outside observer, the official principles seem to be more directed at legitimating the HECCG: they include, for example, 'uniqueness to the business environment, maximum coverage and involvement of locations and employees, constant improvement' (Honda Fact Sheet HECCG, 2010: 2; HM01). They formulate generally accepted visions and aims, implementation of which is scarcely subject to control.

image of a 'community of interests' between company and workforce. The other was that they clearly saw the HECCG did not represent a relevant body for interest regulation. As a consequence, the HECCG represented an 'alibi event' that provided no form of information that could not have been obtained from the company's website (HE02, HE03).

In contrast, one non-German HECCG employee representative saw some 'added value' in the fact that information was provided that could be of use for interest representation.

> [T]he relevance of the issues discussed at these meetings were very important. These meetings were informing you of the direction your plants would take in the future. The last meeting I attended, the direction, due to the current climate of the car industry, was a change (HE01).

On this view, the HECCG would have some potential for development provided that management understood that the meetings should not simply be a façade to legitimise its actions and employee representatives were recognised as having an independent role. 'HECCG could become more effective if Senior Management viewed the elected reps as partners than just mouthpieces for the company. In my view they thought many elected reps were just there as a jolly and were happy for them to have a jolly as long as no awkward questions also discussions were raised' (HE01).

Two turning points of possibly longer term significance took place in the fairly recent past. Firstly, there was an initiative by some union members on the HECCG to establish their own communication network to enable employee-side exchange and mutual advice and discussion on cross-border issues of common interest. As far as we were able to discover, only sporadic exchange had taken place at the time this study was completed. One factor is that some HECCG members who had been conspicuous by their conduct – such as refusing to submit their three questions to management in advance – soon lost their place on the forum. Whether management deliberately sought to have these members replaced cannot be conclusively established. And secondly, in view of the financial crisis and its impact on the car industry, Honda saw itself as confronted with problems that prompted some parts of the workforce into action and triggered some changes in the arrangement of HECCG meetings that were, in part, codified in the draft of a new version of the HECCG agreement. According to one employee representative, the unease amongst the workforce at HECCG meetings was becoming apparent. Many expresssed an urgent need for information in order to ascertain the extent to which Honda – and their jobs – had been affected by the crisis. At the HECCG meeting in early-2010, employee uncertainty and insecurity led to a deluge of questions for management. In order to group these together, a Belgian and a British employee representative suggested that employee representatives should look at the questions before the start of the meeting and discuss their relevance of particular issues. This proposal was accepted, due to the good relationship that existed between the HECCG management coordinator and the Belgian employee representative (they both worked at the same location and were members of the Belgian works council). Employee representatives met in the lobby of the hotel where the HECCG meeting was due to take place. The two hours allotted for the session was exceeded by a considerable margin, leading to a late start for the official meeting. (A room was provided for this preparatory session at the next meeting). Over subsequent months, the Belgian and British employee representatives took on a coordinating role independently of management through contacting other HECCG members on a decentralised basis – albeit tolerated by management. Only time will tell whether this will have marked a break with management's previous strategy, and with it a shift away from the basic principles of the HECCG's culture.

8.3 Provisional assessment

In the context of our findings, Honda in Europe would appear to represent a *focal* enterprise, but one which, based on its divisional structure, exhibits certain aspects of a multinational organisation. Most of the workforce is located in the UK, with other facilities dispersed across Europe. However, the real centre of decision-making and control is in the UK, and ultimately in Japan. Based on its divisional organisation and the low significance of internal supplier relationships, Honda could be denoted as somewhat weakly coordinated.

In comparison with other EWCs in our sample, the HECCG is the weakest body. Our findings support the supposition that in setting up the HECCG, management's aim was to prevent the emergence of independent collective employee representation (see too Nakan, 2007; Royle and Towers, 2003: 362; Martin and Ross, 1999: 364). The structure, role and scope of the HECCG is set by management. Despite the history of anti-trade unionism at the company, it is highly improbable that it would officially prohibit employee interest representation through a legally supported EWC. However, the procedures and structures of the HECCG clearly represent an obstacle to such a development. The HECCG can be denoted, on the one hand, as a 'symbolic' EWC that basically serves to legitimate the company; on the other, it also has more than a symbolic purpose – that is, to foster communication and prevent the emergence of independent collective employee representation. The highly centralised nature of the HECCG refers less to any dominance exercised by British employee representatives, who account for a third of the seats and are the largest group, but rather the hegemony exercised by management. As such, the HECCG can also be classified as a focal organisation.

The nature and weakness of the HECCG's outputs can be attributed to three closely related sets of causal factors.

- The corporate culture and the consequent rejection by management of external influences and conceptions of autonomous employee representation.
- The diversified corporate structure.
- The perception of a low regulatory need on the part of employees.

Management's negative stance, for its part, is a product of the group's culture and organisation, but also the previous negative experience with trade unions. One notable feature of Honda are the internal governance arrangements, with an emphasis on individual participation and skills, an internal labour market, and an enterprise union. Honda has long been acknowledged for high levels of individual participation at all levels of the hierarchy, which has its origins in the entrepreneurial spirit of its founders. Staff are expected to enhance their capacities and potential by engaging in activities and project teams that lie outside their formal roles – and, with this, retain and develop the company's capacity for innovation. Enterprise unions, characteristic of Japan, pursue a strictly harmonious model (Araki, 2005). They not only deal with pay issues, but also skills and company social benefits. The mode of interaction is always cooperative and aimed at avoiding overt conflict. Employees and managers see themselves as members of an organisation that they wish to improve. The view of the HECCG fits with this culture, in which management and workers appear to be partners and conflicts of interests are denied.

> Our basic stance, where we are coming from, is management and employee reps gathering together as equal partners. And as a team they are coming there and discussing about business issues for Europe. [...] We think that it is very important to make those people feel together as a team. So if we start saying each one starts gathering at his side, then we are completely breaking up this principle (HM01).

Based on its previous experiences in Belgium and the US, Honda had deep reservations about European (and US) trade unions, which often formulated external demands on the company and claimed a right to involvement despite not being employees. In particular, Honda found it very hard to accept representatives of unions that organised outside the company, such as at branch level, gaining Honda a reputation for being very much an 'anti-union company' (see (Luethge and Byosière, 2009).

The divisional structure hampers the identification of common issues and areas of interest by employees.[162] Through its separation into a large number of only loosely integrated divisions, in contrast to most of the other manufacturers in our sample, Honda does not have a genuine 'core' (vehicle manufacture) able to serve as focus around which interest representation can crystallise.

The perception of a low level of need for cross-border coordination and interest representation is due, in part, to the relative prosperity of the company, with neither employees nor interest representatives seeing much reason to engage beyond the boundaries of their immediate workplace. It is also certainly attributable to the experience that there is little point in calling for a form of collective representation

---

162 As far as the divisional structure is concerned, Honda most closely resembles Daimler. The Daimler EWC is also characterised by highly heterogeneous divisional interests, and the sales group is seen as one of the main driving forces in the EWC (see Chapter 4.2).

as an employee, or group of employees, that the company is not prepared to accept or tolerate.

Unlike Toyota, for example, Honda is not willing to accept differing views expressed by employee representatives at European level. Whereas Honda locally has learned to engage with independent employee representatives, it has invested a good deal of time and money (two meetings a year, sixty-eight members) in creating a legitimating element whose usefulness for the company (in terms of disseminating information to local employees or problem-solving) is probably very low.

It is hard to gauge the prospect for the development of the HECCG, although there are several conceivable scenarios. For example, the preparatory employee meetings that began in 2010 as a result of the crisis might lead to greater autonomy on the part of employee representatives. This might also constitute a learning process for management, culminating in a realisation that a more independent EWC is not inevitably inimical to Honda's culture of internal regulation. This learning process could ultimately lead to a softening of strict management control. It is also conceivable that some groups of employees might develop their, as yet sporadic, contacts and – possibly in a more conflictual way – establish their own much more autonomous representative arrangements that would circumvent the formal structures of the HECCG.

Chapter 9: Toyota Motor Europe (TME)

9.1 The Toyota Motor Corporation (TMC) and Toyota Motor Europe (TME)

The Toyota Motor Corporation (TMC) is one of the world's leading vehicle manufacturers based on a range of measures. With more than 9 million vehicles produced in 2008, it has the highest sales figures by volume of any automotive company.[163] It also had the highest sales figures in financial terms, with a turnover of €168 billion (for the financial year 2008/9).[164] Over the past ten years, Toyota has emerged as a byword for quality and profitability. The company's success is widely attributed to its highly-advanced production system (Toyota Production System, TPS), which has become the reference standard for the entire branch (Womack et al., 1992). This is embedded in a company culture based on long-term job tenure, high investment in company-specific employee knowledge, and harmonious employment relations.

The Toyota group directly employees some 320,000 staff worldwide in more than 500 companies.[165] However, the core undertaking, with twelve plants and the development centre in Toyota City, has only 70,000 employees. The majority of the company's workforce is employed in its numerous subsidiaries, both within Japan and abroad. There are fifty-one manufacturing plants in Japan alone, either wholly or majority owned by TMC. In addition, there are subsidiaries for sales, development and logistics.[166] Although the group has expanded beyond the automotive sector – Toyota Industries Corporation is the world leader in lift trucks and initially specialised in textile machinery – the vehicles division, with the brands Toyota, Lexus, Daihatsu and Hino, accounts for more than 90 per cent of total turnover.[167]

After many years of success, the global crisis hit the company much harder than its competitors. In 2009, sharply falling sales forced TMC into a serious loss for the first time in its history. In Europe alone, the company lost €900 million (TME, 2009). This represented a major challenge to the its overall strategy, and necessitated serious cuts in employees and production capacity.

---

163 Toyota moved to first place in 2008, displacing GM which had occupied this position for 70 years.

164 The company's financial year runs from 1 April to 31 March.

165 See <http://www.toyota-global.com/company/profile/overview/> accessed on 19 April 2012.

166 As well as directly controlled companies, there are also two supplier networks that are closely tied to the group with more than 300 companies. See 'Toyota in the World' [2011] <http://www.toyota-global.com/company/profile/overview/in_the_world/> accessed 19 April 2012.

167 Including sales and finance ('Toyota Up Close', May 2007: 1).

9.1.1 History and characteristics of the Toyota Motor Corporation

The history of the Toyota Motor Corporation dates back to 1933, when the company founder, Kiichiro Toyoda, established a vehicles division within his father's weaving machinery company, the Toyoda Automatic Loom Works Ltd. The first car prototype was presented in 1935, and in 1937 an independent entity, Toyota Motor Company Ltd was established.[168] During the Second World War the company produced heavy vehicles, with civilian production resumed in 1947.

The year 1950 saw a major breach in the company's history. As a result of the deflationary policy introduced in Japan in that year, the company fell into serious difficulties. In December 1949, the founder, Toyoda, agreed a 10 per cent wage increase with the strong and predominantly Communist-affiliated Toyota trade union,[169] and undertook to refrain from any economic dismissals. As the crisis deepened in April 1950, however, some 1,600 workers – a quarter of the labour force – were slated to lose their jobs. This led to a major dispute, with frequent strikes, slow-downs and a hunger strike, between the company and the Toyota union, which became known in the company's history as the 'Great Dispute', and which has continued to shape employment relations at Toyota. The dispute ended after six weeks with the workforce reductions that the company had sought. At the same time, a number of senior managers, including the president and founder, Toyoda, resigned their offices.

One upshot of these dramatic developments was that management developed a dual strategy, centred on making organising by independent unions at the company's plants more difficult combined with, and focused on, steps to integrate the workforce and improve workplace relationships (Nomura and Jürgens, 1995: 85f.). Following internal disagreements within the Toyota union, in 1954 the company-friendly wing prevailed against the left-wing leadership. The new leadership accepted the model advanced by management, which had four main elements: (1) recognition of management's absolute managerial prerogative, (2) consultation in place of union involvement in management decisions, (3) a ban on any form of political activity at the workplace, and (4) decisions on pay to be dependent on profitability.

The new role for unions in the company was confirmed in 1962 in a joint declaration by management and the Toyota union, which set down the formal foundations for 'cooperative industrial relations' at TMC. Both sides committed themselves to a relationship based on mutual trust and respect, intended to secure long-term peace and stability in industrial relations at the company. The trade union also pledged to

168 The founder's name was changed for the new company. The company did not become the Toyota Motor Corporation until 1982 after a merger with the sales company, Toyota Motor Sales Ltd, itself established in 1950.

169 Japan Automobile Workers' Union, Toyota Koromo Branch.

support a productivity-oriented growth strategy. For its part, the company made a commitment 'to do its utmost to improve the terms and conditions of employment'.[170]

As intended, since then industrial relations can be characterised as largely peaceful, with no major disputes. Key issues related to employment and working conditions are regulated through joint bodies such as the Labour Management Council, and its various issue-specific sub-committees, in which top management and the leadership of the Toyota trade union meet. Regular consultation on current problems takes place in Joint Labour-Management Round Table Conferences, which operate at group, division, and workplace level (TE04).

The development of a number of central principles of production and management in the early-1960s put Toyota onto a highly successful growth trajectory, expressed in steadily growing exports. During the 1970s, the company enjoyed a very evident competitive advantage in terms of productivity and quality, which allowed it to offer very reliable vehicles at substantially below-average prices. The Toyota Production System (TPS), which combined the speed of mass production with the quality of craft manufacture, played a major part in its export success. The aim of the TPS was to minimise waste in production operations, in part through synchronising and standardising processes, avoiding defects, and securing constant improvement in the manufacturing process.[171] Continuous process improvements also required highly skilled and motivated employees, and the company invested heavily in staff training and development. The TPS gives assembly line workers a much greater degree of autonomy and responsibility than classic Fordist production methods based on extreme task simplification.

Toyota's development into an internationally operating company took place at a relatively late stage. Whereas the company was exporting vehicles to the United States by the mid-1950s, it took a further thirty years before it began to manufacture in its major markets. One crucial factor behind Toyota's hesitancy in establishing foreign manufacturing was the TPS, the demands of which made transplanation to an unknown socio-economic environment a potentially risky undertaking. In the early-1980s, the threat of import restrictions necessitated a change in approach. The first milestone in Toyota's internationalisation strategy was the establishment of manufacturing facilities in the United States, initially in the form of the NUMMI joint venture with General Motors in 1984, and then with its own TMMK plant in Kentucky in 1988.[172] Plants were subsequently opened in Europe and Asia. This process of expansion was an extremely vigorous one, with Toyota's internationalisation accelerating strongly in line with the expansion of its foreign production capacity. The doubling of foreign production between 2000 and 2005 meant that this almost

170 'Joint Declaration of Toyota Motor Workers' Union and Toyota Motor Company' (1962).

171 The TPS became the benchmark for lean and efficient production processes. Some of its individual elements, such as just-in-time, or *kanban*, are used in a wide variety of industrial processes.

172 New United Motor Manufacturing (NUMMI); Toyota Motor Manufacturing Kentucky (TMMK).

matched production levels in Japan, and in 2007 the total of 4.3 million vehicles assembled abroad exceeded home production of 4.2 million.[173]

As a consequence, foreign manufacturing plants have acquired a major significance for the Toyota group. The most important capacity is located in North America and in strongly growing Asian markets (excluding Japan), where some 1.5 million vehicles are produced. Europe occupies third place, with 800,000 units produced in 2006/7, just prior to the crisis.

9.1.2 Toyota Motor Europe (TME)

With more than 1 million units sold, and production facilities in four countries in the EU, Toyota is currently the third largest non-European vehicle manufacturer in the EU market after Ford and General Motors. By 2005, Toyota had sold an overall total of 15 million vehicles, and annually rising sales figures were approaching 1 million. In 2006, this target was comfortably exceeded, with sales of more than 1.1 million vehicles. The highest sales figure achieved so far, more than 1.2 million units, was reached one year later, immediately prior to the crisis. By this stage, Toyota had expanded its market share to 5.8 per cent. The onset of the crisis in 2008 led to a fall in market share, with the company more hard hit by falling sales than most of its competitors.

Toyota's European activities are managed from its European headquarters in Brussels. Toyota Motor Europe NV/SA (TME) employs more than 1,000 staff in planning and coordinating production and sales in Europe. The current structure, in which the European headquarters plays a major role, emerged over several decades of step-by-step expansion of sales and manufacturing activities. Two separate European companies were established in the late-1990s: in 1998, Toyota Motor Europe Manufacturing (TMEM)[174] and in 1999 Toyota Motor Marketing Europe (TMME). In mid-2002, both were placed into a new holding company, TME. By October 2005,[175] both companies were fully integrated into TME.

Toyota's entry to the European market took place in the 1960s and 1970s. The first vehicles were exported to Denmark in 1963 and marketed through a sales company. Sales subsidiaries were then progressively established in almost all West European countries, with the German market tackled through the establishment of Deutsche Toyota-Vetrieb GmbH. Initially, importers were legally independent

173 Developments on the Japanese home market went in a radically different direction. In the early-1990s, there was an abrupt decline in both sales and production of more than 1 million units. The 1990 peak production level of 4.2 million vehicles was not reached again until 2007, after which there was a further drop in output. Currently, some two-thirds of vehicles produced in Japan are exported, including to Europe, where 420,000 exported units were sold in 2008 (see Toyota in the World, 2009: 17).

174 TMEM was later renamed Toyota Motor Engineering & Manufacturing Europe.

175 See Ando (2005); TME (2009a: 16).

franchise holders, but were gradually converted into wholly-owned Toyota subsidiaries (in 1974 in Germany). Following the expansion of its European administrative and management structures, TMC transferred the majority of its shareholdings in national sales subsidiaries to TMME (later TME) in April 2003. This was intended to improve sales and production coordination in Europe, and also raised the significance of the European headquarters.

Although there had been a small manufacturing facility in Portugal since 1968, in which commercial vehicles were assembled under licence, Toyota's real entry to mass production in Europe took place in the late-1980s with the construction of its own manufacturing plants in the UK, where Honda and Nissan had begun operations shortly before. The motivation for this industrial engagement in Europe was mainly due to the threat of restrictions on imports from Japan.[176] At this point, the UK was viewed as offering a favourable tax regime, and the weakening of trade unions under the Thatcher government meant that Britain had become the preferred location for inward investment in Western Europe.

Toyota Manufacturing UK (TMUK) was established in December 1989 and now has two plants – final assembly in Burnaston (Derbyshire) and an engine plant on Deeside (Wales) – employing more than 4,000 (2010) Investments totalling €2.7 billion over several years have made the UK Toyota's most important European site. Production began in 1992 with the mid-range Carina (now Avensis), with a second line added in 1998 to assemble the Corolla (now Auris). When a decision was about to be made about a third model in the late-1990s, a small car specially developed for the European market (Yaris), Toyota decided against further expansion in Britain.

After protracted negotiations with competing locations, organised and conducted by the group's headquarters in Japan with only limited involvement of the European headquarters (TE05), Valenciennes in Northern France was chosen. This region, once depredated by the coal and steel industries but subsequently largely deindustrialised, allowed the French government and regional administration to offer massive regional assistance, low-cost land, and tax concessions without breaching EU competition law (Pardi, 2006: 55). In addition, wage levels were below-average for France and the site also had the advantage of being fairly close to the European headquarters.

One crucial factor in the decision to opt for a European site outside the UK was the impact of Economic and Monetary Union (EMU).[177] The substantial depreciation of the euro and corresponding rise in the value of sterling in the period immediately prior to the start of EMU led to a dramatic fall in the value of British sales in the euro area, and large losses for TMUK between 1998 and 2002 that culminated

176 It would have been easily possible for Toyota to supply Europe from Japan as its share of the European market in the late-1980s was only 2.2 per cent (c. 400,000 vehicles) and below 1 per cent in France, Spain and Italy (Pardi, 2006: 49).

177 Some 75 per cent of Toyota's sales in Europe are on the Continent, primarily in the eurozone.

in a stringent savings programme.[178] This made the establishment of an additional plant within the eurozone a likely outcome. Toyota's suppliers were also moving in increasing numbers to Mainland Europe. Once largely closed markets in France, Italy and Spain were especially interesting as possible sites for an assembly plant as establishing production activities would raise customer acceptance. The fact that the decision went to Valenciennes was also controversial within TMC as French industrial relations were viewed as challenging and the then Socialist government's proposal to introduce a 35-hour week appeared to pose a threat to the flexibility that underpinned the TPS (Pardi, 2006: 55).

Figure 13: Toyota operations in Europe, 2009.

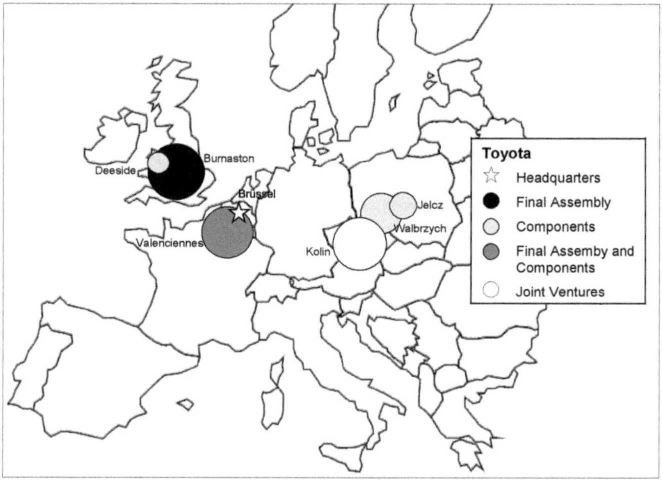

Source: compiled by the authors; circle volumes proportional to employment.

The next wave of expansion took place in Eastern Europe. In 2002, Toyota established an engine and transmission plant in Poland (TMMP, Wałbrzych), which now supplies the French and British assembly plants. In a second step, in 2005 a joint venture facility with PSA was opened in Kolín in the Czech Republic to produce a small car jointly developed by both companies and sold, with minor styling differences, as the Aygo, Peugeot 107 and Citroën C1. Toyota has a 50 per cent share in the joint venture, TPCA, but only takes 100,000 of the 300,000 units produced annually. In order to supply TPCA with small capacity engines a second engine plant was opened in 2005 in Poland (TMIP, Jelcz). TPCA has 3,500 employees (2009), TMMP 2,500 and TMIP 800.

178 A good deal of these losses were attributed to the hybridisation of the TPS in the UK (see Pardi, 2005).

One further plant of relevance for the European market was opened in 1994 in Turkey (TMMT, Adapazari). This operation is 90 per cent owned by TME and managed from the TME head office. The model has one assembly line and produces Verso[179] and Auris models. Most of the output is sold in Europe. With 3,000 employees, the Turkish assembly plant at Adapazari is the largest facility in Europe after Burnaston and Valenciennes. A small plant was opened in St. Petersburg in 2007, with some 600 employees (2009), the sole model of which is the Camry for the Russian market.

While up until 2007, Toyota's expansion strategy was successful in steadily growing its European market share the company was hit hard by the subsequent crisis. Sales fell by some 180,000 and Toyota lost substantial market share. As a consequence, in 2008 the company found itself with surplus capacity of some 200,000 units, a quarter of the total (see Table 7), plunging Toyota into a difficult financial situation. Turnover dropped by €2.7 billion, leading to a loss for TME of nearly €1 billion in 2008. The impact of the crisis varied, depending on models and with differential effects on plants. The largest models, Avensis and Auris, saw the largest falls in sales. And since both were produced at Burnaston, this confronted the most significant European plant with a major challenge. In contrast, small-car production in France and the Czech Republic was less affected, as was the Polish powertrain operation.

Table 7: Business situation and employment at TME (2005–2008)

	Financial year (April – March)			
	2005	2006	2007	2008
Net revenue (€ millions)	19.76	23.615	24.651	20.924
Operating income (€ millions)	681	916	874	-995
Sales	964,000	1,124,000	1,238,000	1,061,000
Production (1,000s)	638,000	808,463	814,093	589,794
Market share (Per cent)	5.1	5.8	5.6	5.3
Employees (production)	15,472	15,363	18,920	18,702
Employees (headquarters, sales, logistics)	6,175	6,812	7,432	8,496

Source: Totoya European Sustainability Report, 2006, 2007, 2008, 2009.

The marked drop in demand for models produced in the UK led to a number of drastic steps. Initially, there was a four-week shutdown (early 2009), followed by a one-shift cut in Auris production and a slowdown in the assembly line speed for other shifts. In addition, a pan-European savings and efficiency programme was implemented (see below). As well as freezing wages and cancelling bonus payments,

179 All Verso models sold in Europe are assembled at this plant.

there was a 10 per cent cut in working hours and pay, and a voluntary redundancy programme that reduced the workforce by 300 during May and June 2009. There were also rumours among the workforce that one of the assembly lines would be shut down completely – a step that might have sounded the death knell for the plant. These rumours were officially confirmed in August 2010. At the same time management emphasised that no further jobs would be lost and that those affected would be transferred to other production operations.[180]

In view of this dramatic situation, the plan for a new full hybrid model based on the Auris to be assembled at Burnaston with the aim of opening up a mass market for hybrid technology, announced in July 2009,[181] was a clear commitment to the future of the British assembly plant, in which Toyota rebutted growing doubts about its long-term engagement to the operation (TE09).

9.1.3 Distribution of resources at TME[182]

The distribution of employment in Europe is the most decentralised of all companies in this study (Table 8). Only 27 per cent of Toyota's European employees work in the UK, the country with the largest workforce in Europe (and therefore, on our definition, the European home country). The position is similar, if less marked, for the distribution of plants and production volumes, where the relative proportions are 33 per cent and 38 per cent respectively. This decentralised structure is also linked to the relatively rapid succession in which plants were opened in a number of European countries, not allowing any one plant to become the principal facility in the sense seen in other companies. One additional characteristic of Toyota is that European operations as a whole are not managed from a headquarters located at a manufacturing plant but from a separate administrative centre, based in Brussels, which also houses logistics management and research capacities. This distinguishes Toyota from those manufacturers that have their origins in Europe as well as Ford and GM.[183] It has the advantage of making it difficult for the main plant to pursue a clientelist policy to its own advantage.

---

180 <http://www.themanufacturer.com/uk/content/9542/Toyota_quashes_talk_of_Burnaston_cuts> 9 April 2010.

181 'Toyota to manufacture full hybrid Auris in the United Kingdom', Toyota Press Release, 17 July 2009, <http://www.toyota.eu/about/Pages/news.aspx?sd=15&sm=07&sy=2009&ed=19&em=07&ey=2009&source=All>, accessed 31 July 2012; see below on the restrictive approach to information disclosure on this issue.

182 Because of the definitions of the indicators used for analysing representational arrangements in the EWC (see Chapter 3.3.1), we excluded the Turkish and Russian assembly plants as well as Toyota suppliers in Europe.

183 Renault has ceased assembly at its traditional home plant in Boulogne-Billancourt, leaving only administration. In 1986, GM moved its European headquarters from Rüsselsheim to Zurich. However, large sections of administration and development remained in Rüsselsheim, and in 2010, the European HQ returned there.

Table 8: Distribution of employees, plants and production, Toyota group (2008/9)

	Employees	Plants	Production
World	316,121	75	9,237,780
EU (TME)	17,792	6*	561,686
EU home country (UK)	4,835	2*	213,400
'Real' home country (Japan)	65,800	15**	4,911,861
Largest plant	4,140	–	–
Share EU/world	6%	7%	6%
Share EU home country (UK)/EU	2%	3%	2%
Share EU 'real' home country/ world	21%	20%	53%
Share largest plant/EU	23%	–	–

*Deeside engine plant counted as an independent plant (but managed from Burnaston).
** Includes Toyota Motor Kyushu Inc., Toyota Motor Hokkaido Inc. and Toyota Motor Toboku; excludes other companies in the Toyota group.

Source: authors, compiled from Toyota (2007, 2009) and OICA (2008).

TME has one of the four world development centres (Toyota Technical Centre), opened in 1987 in Zaventem, only a short distance from the European headquarters. The Toyota Technical Centre houses the R&D centre, purchasing and production engineering. In early-2006, the Technical Centre was substantially enlarged in order to accommodate the expanded design and development functions. It is also planned to increase the number of largely technically-qualified staff, almost doubling the previous headcount. There is a small design centre located in Nice. In addition, some of the development capacities – for motor sport – are located in Cologne. However, this function is managed from the corporate centre in Japan and was reduced in scale following the company's withdrawal from Formula 1 (see below). If motor sport is excluded and only volume-related functions are considered, then European R&D capacities are centrally concentrated in the Brussels area.

Of all the companies in this study, Toyota has the most distinctive and Japanese corporate culture. This is deliberately styled the 'Toyota Way'[184] by the company, and rests on a number of principles: (1) Challenge, (2) *Kaizen*, (3) *Genchi Genbutsu*,

184 The 'Toyota Way' is the practical implementation of the 'Guiding Principles of Toyota', as elaborated in 1992 and 1997. Under point 7, this is as follows: 'Foster a corporate culture that enhances individual creativity and the value of teamwork while honoring mutual trust and respect between labor and management'.

(4) Respect, (5) Teamwork.[185] These are the expression of a partnership approach, the overarching aim of which is to continuously improve organisational processes throughout the whole undertaking. Employees are termed 'members'. This is not only intended to register their formal inclusion in the organisation, but also implies that they are part of the 'Toyota family' with its mutual obligation of loyalty and expectation that employees will show a high level of commitment to the company, also a prerequisite of the TPS. In return, the company professes a particular duty of care to its workforce in the form of a guarantee of long-term employment[186] and the virtual exclusion of compulsory economic dismissals. The fact the company does not simply pay lip-service to this can be seen in the most recent crisis, where, for example, a second assembly line at Burnaston was shut down without dismissals. Only in the most recent past, has there arguably been some erosion of the solidity of this promise.[187]

The comparatively centralist corporate culture is expressed in the pronounced influence of Japanese managers and specialists in national subsidiaries and the TME headquarters. In general, senior management positions are staffed by Japanese expatriates – although more recently Didier Leroy,[188] a French national, was appointed CEO of TME in a step that might indicate a change of direction.

The strength of the efforts to make employees into 'members', who can be shaped to a great extent in line with the requirements of the corporate culture, can also be seen in the very selective recruiting approaches used to hire for the new plants in Burnaston and Valenciennes, where stress was placed on taking on young people with fairly high skill levels but who had not been 'corrupted' by working in other manufacturing companies (Pardi, 2006: 52f).

---

185 '*Kaizen.* Refers to the continuous step-by-step approach that Toyota promotes internally, where even the smallest of steps leading to improved performance are recognised. *Genchi Genbutsu.* Literally means "going to the source"; it aligns with Toyota's insistence that sound decision-making is only possible when employees check the facts first-hand' <http://www.toyota.eu/society/pages/our_people.aspx> accessed 23 April 2012.

186 Although there has been extensive use of the legal options to create greater flexibility through fixed-term contracts and temporary agency employment – for example in the Polish plants, in France and also in Japan iyself, the company still maintains its guarantee of long-term employment.

187 In 2009, there were large-scale economic dismissals when the NUMMI plant in the USA was closed and also when TMG scaled back its operations in Germany (see the section on 'Output'), as well as a voluntary severance programme at the two British plants for some 300 employeees in 2009 and a further 850 in 2010 (TE08).

188 Leroy was for many years the president of TMMF before he became TME executive vice-president for sales and marketing in 2009, and in April 2010 the first non-Japanese CEO of TME.

The Toyota culture also encompasses a particular relationship to trade unions. The experience of the historical trauma of 1950 led, from the 1960s, to a tradition of incorporating pacified enterprise unions at the core Japanese plants. The advantages of this cannot always be obtained at foreign plants, where the company might encounter industry-based unions, as in Germany, or unions with a strong political identity such as the Communist CGT in France. Toyota has attempted to keep external unions at a distance, mainly in the USA[189] but also in the UK, and install enterprise-based forms of representation akin to arrangements found in Japan, such as the Toyota Members Advisory Board at Burnaston. The British AEEU (Amalgamated Engineering and Electrical Union) was unable to secure full representation at Burnaston and had to agree a framework for the TMAB in the context of a single-union agreement. In contrast, in France Toyota accommodated itself to the French union situation, and four are represented at the Valenciennes plant.[190] In Poland, at TMMP, the company made very assertive use of legislation introduced in 2006, which provides for the introduction of works councils, to establish enterprise-focused representation arrangements. However, this soon began to lose workforce support:

> Representatives are mostly from middle management, as nearly all the operatives who were elected gave up after a few months. They resigned as they had the feeling they could not change anything. There was only consultation and information, but no scope to influence anything (TE07).

The declining legitimacy of workplace representation finally led to a progressive recognition by the company of Solidarność's claim to represent employees at its plants (TE07).

Even if the central elements of the 'Toyota Way' are more evident and viable in manufacturing operations than in support services or the national sales and market subsidiaries, it is, nevertheless, possible to characterise the company culture as extensively centralised. This is also promoted by the fact that the chosen path of expansion, based on extending the company's operations through organic growth, has meant that there is no deviating brand identity in Toyota's European operations.[191]

9.1.4 Coordination of company activities at TME

The coordination of TME's production operations by the European headquarters in Brussels can be designated as 'somewhat strong'. The organisational changes noted above not only bolstered the position of the European headquarters in relation to individual operations but also to the corporate headquarters in Toyota City. This is

---

189 One exception was at NUMMI, where the plant was already unionised as a GM facility (cf. Shimizu, 1998).

190 In its official statement Toyota recognised the principle of employee representation on social accountability and on core labour standards].

191 The only exception is the joint venture at Kolin in the Czech Republic.

evidenced both in the transfer of property rights to the national marketing and sales subsidiaries (NMSC) in 2003 as well as the subsequent merger of the European sales and production subsidiary into a single structure, TME. As with other non-European groups, important decisions, such as investment in new capacity or allocations of output to plants, have to be approved by the corporate headquarters in Japan. And decisions on new locations have been made solely in Japan in the past: for example, the decision-making process to open a second plant in Europe proceeded without any major involvement of the then European headquarters (see above).

While our interviewees offered a range of assessments on the degree of autonomy enjoyed by the European headquarters on strategic product planning, the operational management of European production operations unquestionably takes place from there. As a consequence, communication between plants is centred on the European headquarters. There is an intensive exchange of information between national operations and the European headquarters, which includes the regular reporting and planning rounds of heads of departments in local operations that are held in Brussels. In the HRM area, the role of the European headquarters is seen as more supportive than directive.

> It never happens that TME is coming and saying 'You have to do it!' We say 'Tell us why.' There is really mutual trust and respect. It is rather the role of the centre to give assistance based on first hand information according to the principle Genchi Genbutsu (go and see yourself) and support the implementation of given policy guidelines taking into account local circumstances (TM04).

Within the TME, Toyota does not pursue a parallel production approach (in contrast to GME and Renault). The only exception is the parallel assembly of the Auris in the UK and Turkey. Given the small number of assembly plants, parallel production would not be an especially attractive option, and a deliberate fostering of inter-plant competition would run counter to the established practice and culturally-anchored principles of 'mutual trust'. Toyota is also known as having a more cooperative relationship with its suppliers than forcing them into price competition (see Liker, 2004). Even if overt inter-plant competition is much less prevalent than in GME, for example, this does not mean there is no competition between European plants. Instead Toyota practices permanent benchmarking with monthly key performance indicators to raise plant productivity. The NMSCs are also subject to European benchmarking competition, with headquarters regularly comparing business indicators and identifying best practice that can be transferred to other national subsidiaries.

Overall, TME appears to be a comparatively strongly coordinated group, based on the close cooperation between European assembly plants, its logistical capabilities and the NMSCs, but one which has obtained increasing autonomy from the Japanese parent. This is illustrated not least in the appointment of a European as president and CEO of TME. Although the company has a decentralised distribution of material and human resources in Europe, considering the distribution of power and knowledge between the European headquarters and operational facilities as well as the strong influence of Toyota's corporate culture, the pattern of distribution can be characterised as 'somewhat centralised'. In line with the typology set out in Chapter 3.1, TME can therefore best be denoted as a *global* type of organisation.

9.2 Toyota European Forum (TEF)

9.2.1 Origins

The EWC at the Toyota Motor Corporation was constituted on 10 July 1996, under Article 13 of the Direcive, and officially named the Toyota European Forum (TEF). The EWC was located at the headquarters of TMC (now TME), and was therefore subject to Belgian law and jurisdiction.[192]

The initiative to establish the TEF was taken by the European Metalworkers' Federation (EMF), which was given a mandate by the British[193] and German[194] EMF affiliates.[195] Negotiations were led by a full-time AEEU official, on secondment to the EMF, who later became the external adviser to the TEF. Toyota was not averse to the idea of a European information and communication platform, and this allowed negotiations to progress rapidly. Interestingly, it was the Japanese managers who were most welcoming, with British managers more concerned about growing trade union influence at the company in the light of their previous experiences with disputes at other vehicle manufacturers (TE05). However, it soon became apparent that TMC was not willing to grant the employee side either extensive rights or autonomy within the new forum. Rather, the TEF was based on the arrangements for dialogue, the Joint Labour-Management Round Table Conference, already installed at the parent company rather than any form of independent employee representation. Belgian law offered a very favourable foundation for this as the transposition provisions of the EWC Directive, which were based on national law on works councils, provided for just such a joint body of employee and management representatives.

---

192 Article 13 of the installation agreement ('Agreement to establish the Toyota European Forum', 10 July 1996). The agreement did not specify a location but rather referred to TMC's 'representative agent' in Europe. Specifying the place of jurisdiction as Belgium was only made explicit in the most recent revision of the agreement in December 2009.

193 The British trade union with representation at TMUK was the AEEU, later merged with TGWU to form Unite.

194 For the German employee side, the union was IG Metall which acted at the instigation of works councils at Toyota Deutschland GmbH.

195 The EMF had prepared a list of companies at which it was intended to start negotiations on setting up an EWC.

9.2.2 Scope, composition and structure of the TEF

At the time when the EWC was established, Toyota had only two production facilities in the UK, but operated marketing and sales companies in many EU countries. Based on this corporate structure, and in line with Toyota's integrationist management philosophy, the TEF included all Toyota's subsidiaries across the spectrum of the company's activities: production operations, development centres, national importers, logistics subsidiaries, financial services and motor sport. Geographically, under Article 4 of the installation agreement, the TEF covered all those companies controlled by TMC that had their head office in an EU or EEA Member State.[196] However, under the constitution, it is also possible to include representatives from non-EEA countries, either as observers or full members, provided there is agreement between employee and management representatives on the TEF.[197] This option was used prior to the EU's eastern enlargement. In contrast, production facilities located outside the EEA – that is, the Turkish assembly plant in Adapazari and the Russian plant in St. Petersburg – have not been included.

The installation agreement stipulates that each country with at least fifty employees and each company[198] with at least 150 employees may have an employee representative. There is an additional seat for countries with at least 450 employees or companies with more than 1,500 employees, and a further seat for each additional 1,500 employees. This original formula meant that Germany had the most seats on the TEF because of its three large subsidiaries, and not the UK, which at that time had the largest production facility. The formula was simplified when the installation agreement was revised so that seats are only awarded on a national basis, as follows: one seat for up to 500 employees; two for up 1,500; and an additional seat for each further 1,500 employees.

Employee-side TEF members are appointed in accordance with national custom-and-practice from employee representatives in local operations. Where there is no existing form of collective representation, management must organise an election for the EWC.[199] However, this does not appear to have been complied with in all cases. In particular, there have been reports from the NMSCs where the legitimacy of some representatives have been questioned.

The fact that the TEF is a joint body also led to the original formula for allocating seats being applied to management. A reduction in the size of the management contingent in 2003 (see below) meant that this arrangement gave way to a more divisionally-based system of representation in which management representatives mainly come from the European functional areas and fewer from national subsidiaries.

196 The EEA consists of the 27 EU Member States plus three EFTA members (Norway, Iceland and Liechtenstein).

197 'Agreement to establish the Toyota European Forum' (10 July 1996), Article 4.

198 In the event that there is more than one company in a country.

199 'Agreement to establish the Toyota European Forum' (10 July 1996): Article 5.

When first constituted, the TEF comprised eleven employee representatives and twenty-two management representatives – that is, a management majority. Amendments to the constitution in 2003 changed this to the advantage of the employee representatives, whose number rose to thirty (in practice twenty-nine). Management representation fell to eleven members. In addition, if deemed necessary on substantive grounds, senior management can also participate as well as HR support staff.[200] In practice, there are currently fifteen management representatives (Toyota, 2009b: 72). The TEF is formally led by a 'president', the CEO of TME who convenes and chairs TEF meetings.

As is common with joint bodies, there is a pre-meeting of employee representatives prior to the meeting with management. This is intended to facilitate an exchange of information and allow employee representatives to agree a common strategy for the joint meeting. Initially, there was just one meeting (and pre-meeting) a year. The new TEF agreement in 2003 raised this to two meetings of each kind. In addition, the agreement allowed for additional meetings.

The operational capacity of the body is provided for through a Working Committee (originally the 'Administrative Subcommittee') which consists of TEF members from both sides.[201] This is formally responsible for communication (that is, minutes and setting the agenda). The Working Committee is led by a coordinator appointed by European corporate HR. This is traditionally the HR manager for the European headquarters. Their task is to send out invitations, set the agenda and produce an (objective) summary and minutes of the proceedings. These points are then agreed in the Working Committee, which meets formally four times a year. Either directly before or just after this, the so-called 'Restricted Committee', made of up employee members of the Working Committee, also meets.

The Restricted Committee, formally set up under the 2003 revised agreement, constitutes the real working heart of the TEF, is where the employee side make the significant decisions and the site of strategic debate take place, should this take place at all. Initially the Committee comprised four employee representatives: one from the corporate centre, two from the largest production operations, and one further member elected by the TEF. In practice, it was agreed that all the company's operations should be represented as far as possible, and there is now an additional member for the NMSCs and one for the logistics division. The Restricted Committee is chaired by the representative from the corporate headquarters, who is also the secretary of the local works council. This role has emerged over the course of time with the consent of HR management, but without any formal role description, which can lead to divergent expectations – as discussed below. The role of secretary

200 Ibid. Article 5.

201 The Working Committee was initially composed of equal numbers from each side, but now consists of five employee representatives from the Restricted Committee (see below) and three HR managers (TME, production, NMSC).

('Employee Representatives' Chairperson) has only been formally cited in the most recent revision of the agreement in 2009.

The establishment of the TEF also saw the creation of the role of external adviser, with the task of supporting the pre-meeting and Restricted Committee if requested by employee representatives on the former Administrative Subcommittee. Initially, the adviser was to have an EMF mandate. However, this requirement was eased in the second agreement and adapted to the circumstances of the individual involved, who had by then left the EMF. Under the 2009 agreement, an EMF mandated representative can also attend meetings as well as the adviser. Any external representatives must be agreed with management.

In practice, the adviser plays a very active role, in particular in the Restricted Committee. He chairs and directs the meetings, which never take place without him. The fact that the same individual has held the post since the TEF was established has led to his playing a key role within the forum. As well as being familiar with the entire history of the TEF, he was also involved in negotiating the original constitution and also offers a link to the experiences of the other EWCs that he supports. As such, he can assess the progress of the TEF in relation to other forums. In some respects, the adviser was seen as exercising a dominant role in internal discussions and had strongly-held ideas about the strategic direction for the TEF that he advanced within the Restricted Committee in cooperation with the secretary – for example, in setting out a negotiating position for the revision of the TEF agreement.[202] The German works councils members, in particular, were unsure about his role and style, which was seen as overly assertive and not always positive towards alternative views. In some respects he occupied a uniquely central role when compared with other companies in our sample.

9.2.4 Distribution of resources, power, culture and knowledge in the EWC

The TEF is the most decentralised EWC in our sample. Only five of the twenty-nine employee representatives (17 per cent) originate from what we have designated as the European home country, the UK, a lower proportion than at GM. This reflects, on the one hand, the highly decentralised distribution of employment by countries, and also – as with most of the other cases considered – an underrepresentation of home country employment. As a consequence, the EWC representativeness index has a value of 0.63.[203]

However, the index should be interpreted differently for TME as compared with other companies. One of the notable features of the TEF, as already referred to above, is that the forum is not located at the largest plant or the company's central

202 Some TEF members voiced the suspicion that neither wanted the forum to develop into an instrument of employee representation.

203 On the calculation of the index, see Chapter 3.3.1.

production facility but at the European headquarters in Brussels – an administrative and R&D location. This is the base for the coordinator and EWC secretary of the TEF who are responsible for the managing the TEF meetings and sessions of the Working Committee.

Figure 14: Distribution of employee seats on the TEF, 2009.

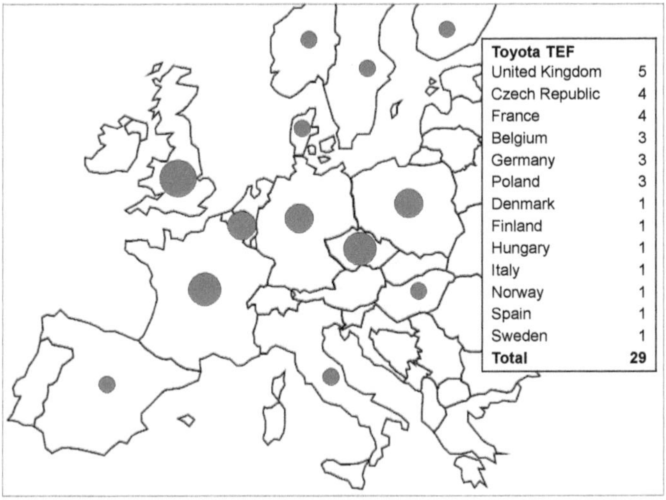

Source: TEF Agreement, 2003; compiled by the authors.

The distribution of resources to support the EWC's work is also weighted towards the European centre rather the company's main plant in the UK. In the first instance, the EWC secretary, who is also secretary of the works council (*conseil d'entreprise*) for the European headquarters, has a time allowance for the TEF that is not precisely specified. In practice, this amounts to some two hours a week. In his view, this is just sufficient to take care of organising meetings and maintaining the flow of information.[204] However, the secretary does not have formal facility time for their role on the *conseil d'entreprise*. Nonetheless, in their view, the scope that they have informally agreed with the coordinator is sufficient to allow them to make more time available for the EWC if needed.

The largest potential resources outside the European headquarters are probably those available to the German EWC members. Unlike the UK plant, there is one post with full facility time and further scope for time off for others if needed for local works council activity. The German TEF and works council members have even set

204 For criticisms of the flow of information (minutes etc.) and the use of the resources, see below.

up their own platform, the National European Forum (NEF-T). Although only some of these resources are available for the EWC, they allow larger scale activities to be mounted in critical situations (see 'Outputs' below).

In contrast, the distribution of knowledge is highly centralised, with strategic knowledge concentrated at the TME headquarters in Brussels. The EWC secretary has privileged access to both local and European management at the headquarters – and, at the least, there is relationship of trust to their direct counterpart, the EWC coordinator from the HR department.

Some members of the Restricted Committee were critical of the flow of information from headquarters, and the approach to information adopted by the secretary was seen, at times, as unreliable or strategically selective. In addition, it was suspected that on delicate matters the secretary would hold his cards very close to his chest, taking advantage of his duty of confidentiality to play an 'unfathomable game' with the adviser and HR coordinator.

> He admits he obtains information of relevance for the whole of Europe through his role on the TME works council – including business [data], only he does not forward it to us.[205] He either does not respond to questions on delicate matters, or only after a delay, and even the minutes of the Restricted Committee meetings do not arrive (TE06).

In contrast, the flow of information stipulated in the constitution to take place via the management side (agenda setting, TEF minutes and the Working Committee) seems to operate reliably, at least technically, if not always substantively (see below).

As might be expected, power resources (more knowledge, access to management) are located primarily with the secretary and the adviser, who plays a very active, and even sometimes dominant role, in meetings of the Restricted Committee and in some cases also the pre-meeting. Whereas ordinary TEF members[206] – as with other EWCs – have only limited scope for influence, members of the Restricted Committee are able to affect decisions, as can be seen in the internal differences with the Committee. For example, German and British representatives[207] aspire to a more critical, more transparent procedure with greater scope for shop-floor input. One controversial issue – but on which this alliance was not able to prevail – was on the information to be provided to 'ordinary' members on the final negotiating position for the new agreement. It was at least agreed that there would be a discussion about the addition of a further adviser mandated by the EMF at the pre-meeting, and that a candidate could put themselves forward. However, it was not possible to have a

205 This might be compared with the case of Daimler, where the EWC meets jointly with the Economic Committee (*Wirtschaftsausschuss*).

206 For simplification, we refer here only to employee-side members as 'TEF members', and not management members, as these are not the focus of our study.

207 The German representatives have access to the largest resources through the works councils. The British operations are influential because of their scale.

vote on this that would have allowed this issue to become part of the negotiating package for the new TEF agreement.

Nonetheless, the TEF culture is not dominated by the EWC centre. In particular, there have been differences between different groupings on the Restricted Committee that have reflected differing national industrial relations arrangements. For example, the German representatives in particular wanted to establish clearer structures and more democratic procedures, which became expressed in the call for the creation of standing orders for the Restricted Committee and the pre-meeting.

Membership of particular business areas has also influenced the culture of communications and trust within the forum – with production and logistics on one side, and sales (and possibly development) on the other. In contrast to the European production and logistics operations, where there is a generally high level of trade union presence, unions play no role in many of the NMSCs. One EWC member from one of the medium-sized NMSCs (TE01) described the situation in his company in terms that were not untypical for other marketing and sales subsidiaries. In his view, most of the more highly skilled employees identified unreservedly with the company, were very market oriented, and focused on sales objectives. Thinking in terms of capital and labour, solidarity between operations and regulated competition was alien to them (as it was to him).

The fact that notions of solidarity played a diminished role in the NMSCs is also very much a function of their low level of interconnection and mutual dependency. Sales and marketing organisations are exclusively focused on their respective national markets, do not depend on the neighbouring market, and do not compete with each other for customers. As a consequence, as far as economic interests were concerned, for NMSC representatives issues of competition and solidarity between plants were not part of their cognitive make-up, a consideration that would apply irrespective of the level of union organisation at these subsidiaries. However, the high proportion of non-union members amongst NMSC representatives would certainly have served to reinforce this market orientation.

The quantitative strength of the NMSCs also has an impact on the nature of discussions in the pre-meetings, which are almost exclusively concerned with business developments in national markets. Issues such as working conditions or management practices at individual operations have typically played no role. And more militant voices, rooted in a sense of employee-employee conflicts, seem to be almost unheard of – and when they are, it is solely from representatives of manufacturing operations. For example, a French trade union representative criticised the way in which capacity cuts had been effected at Valenciennes, without this having any evident impact on the further course of the discussion.

One of the factors militating against the development of a common 'identity' on the part of the TEF members, anchored in mutual trust, is also certainly the high level of instability in the individual composition of the forum. Firstly, the number of employee representatives was expanded from the original eleven to the current twenty-nine; and secondly, our interviews revealed that some employee representatives either did not turn up at all the meetings in Brussels, sent deputies or operated an internal system of rotation. The situation was different in the case of the Restricted Committee, where membership has been stable for some years.

One further reason might be, finally, that as with most EWCs, language barriers have a significant impact. Although the working language of the forum is English, there is simultaneous interpretation during the pre-meetings. And despite the fact that a good knowledge of English can play an influential role in the selection of TEF members, a number of our interviewees reported that language barriers between TEF members made communication either difficult or impossible.

9.2.5 Coordination of the TEF

Coordination between employee representatives within the TEF is comparatively weak. This can be seen, for example, in content of the pre-meetings, which are largely taken up with exchanges of information about the business situation of the various national subsidiaries. There is rarely any discussion of how the question session in the TEF should be managed and how 'delicate' issues might be raised with management. These coordination weaknesses were also evident during the economic crisis that hit the company in 2008. The failure of the plan to use the EWC to gain greater visibility over how the cost saving programme was being implemented locally was due, not least, to a lack of coordination on the part of the TEF leadership (see 'Outputs' below).

Formally, the EWC centre in Brussels is responsible for coordination. This is where the process of agenda setting takes place, and from where the minutes and other materials are distributed. In practice this does not always function satisfactorily, in part because of limited access to resources, and the fact that, for a long period, the role of EWC secretary was not specified.[208] The fact that TEF members also saw it as a joint forum also meant that many of the coordinating roles that would have been assumed by the EWC secretary or chair in a German-based EWC fell to the HR coordinator and his staff.

The lack of initiative shown by the TEF leadership is significant in that most members are dependent on communication from the centre due to the absence of horizontal networking. Although members of the Restricted Committee are in relatively frequent contact by e-mail and telephone, and can coordinate their positions before meetings, contacts between 'ordinary' TEF members tend to be confined to the official meetings, in part because of language barriers.[209] These weaknesses in coordination on the part of the TEF leadership also sometimes mean that these

---

208 This position was only formally established following the most recent revision of the agreement in 2009.

209 Some of these 'ordinary' members report that they can contact the representative of another operation direct if this person is likely to be best able to answer a specific question. For example, the Spanish representative had direct contact with other TEF members at least four times a year, and a French representative also reported occasional direct contacts.

tasks are tacitly undertaken by other members of the Restricted Committee, especially German works council members who have facility time (see below), adding to problems of legitimation for those involved as they run the risk of being seen to want to promote their own national interest.

In order to get a better handle on the highly divisionalised interests of TEF employee representatives, pre-meeting working groups were set up for production operations, the NMSCs, and logistics. However, this arrangement appeared not to be sustainable outside the meetings in Brussels. In particular, cooperation in the production group broke down due to language problems. Only the NMSC and logistics groups, which were coordinated by the German works councils, seemed to have a reasonably stable structure with fairly regular e-mail communication between the Brussels meetings (TE06).

Overall, the employee side of the TEF seems comparatively weakly coordinated. As a consequence, and drawing on our typology, in view of the predominantly centralised dimension of distribution, the EWC can be most be appropriately denoted a *focal* organisation. Given the spatial disjuncture between the location of the EWC centre (corporate headquarters in Brussels) and the European home country (in terms of employment, the UK), this focal character does not imply dominance by British employee representatives and British employees but by the EWC centre in Brussels. The fact that the TEF is also a joint forum, and that a good deal of coordination is performed by management, also means that the coordination weaknesses of the employee side might be interpreted as an expression of the fact that much of the TEF's activity is steered by management, and specifically European management. As such, the TEF's focal character has a very different meaning to that at Daimler or PSA.

9.2.6 Critical events and challenges

There have been only a few events of cross-border significance since the establishment of the TEF and which therefore fall within the scope of the forum. The main developments in this respect have been: (1) the transfer of production capacity for engine manufacture from France to Poland, (2) the sales crisis that began in 2008, which led to a pan-European cost cutting programme, and finally (3) the decision to withdraw from Formula 1 racing in November 2009, which led to collective dismissals.

(1) *Transferring production.* The opening of the Polish plants for engines and transmissions (TMMP, Wałbrzych, 2002) and TMIP (Jelcz, 2005) gave TME its first opportunity to produce parts in a low-wage cost Eastern Europe country that was about to join the EU. This led to a relocation of some French engine production, although there was no negative impact on the French workforce as it was replaced by capacity to assemble the – successful – Yaris model. Although this transfer was evidently a subject for information and consultation under the TEF agreement, the TEF was not informed. When the adviser and secretary called for the forum to be involved, this was rejected by European management with the argument that the decision had no negative consequences for the workforce.

> They said: 'There is no negative impact'. I said: 'But you have to inform and consult [...]'. So we threatened to go to court [...] and now they do [inform and consult]. (TE05).

(2) It is difficult to gauge whether management has truly developed a greater awareness of issues on which the TEF needs to become involved as a result of this,[210] as the second event, the cost-savings programme, was also clearly a cross-border issue affecting all operations, and therefore one that would require the involvement of the TEF. Following the abrupt drop in sales, in early-2009 a European cost saving programme was imposed with the aim of reducing personnel costs by 10 per cent at each site. This involved a number of central stipulations, such as limits on travel costs and bonuses, as a well as wider list of options. However, how the programme was to be implemented was left to individual locations to determine in view of the differing legal position applicable in each case.

The Restricted Committee was informed about the programme at a special meeting. It was also agreed that a further extraordinary meeting would be held when appropriate to report on how the programme was being implemented locally.

> We accepted that discussion will take place locally. But what we wanted was: don't reach agreements until you come back and report what is expected of you. But they were all pushed into reaching agreements (TE05).

In view of the fact that the TEF leadership took no initiative to collect information on local negotiations or unilateral implementation by management, the German works council members took action themselves: 'Because he [the secretary] did not do it himself' (TE06). The results were presented at a further special meeting of the Restricted Committee.

> ... the [secretary and adviser] became extremely nervous. And then suddenly the [HR coordinator] turned up at the Restricted Committee because they didn't know – and the [the secretary] did not know – what responses we had had from the operations. Otherwise there was just HR information (TE06).

The second special meeting of the TEF, at which employee representatives from the European operations were to report on local claims and how implementation was to be managed – before any final decisions were to have been made – was cancelled by management at short notice with the argument that negotiations had not been completed at all operations. Evidently, the aim of the meetings was not clearly determined, as, for the employee side, the issue was to allow for reports before measures were implemented, whereas European managers thought there might be an attempt by the TEF to influence ongoing negotiations, either directly and indirectly, and this was something that they wished to prevent.

---

210 Some employee representatives doubted this as, for example, the most recent European-wide restructuring in the software area took place without EWC participation. At the least, there continues to be no authentic shift towards greater TEF involvement by the company.

Subsequently, it emerged that the cost savings programme had not been implemented everywhere. At some operations, cost cutting had been imposed by management unilaterally, there were negotiated compromises at many locations, and some operations were almost wholly spared. The background to the failure of this pain-sharing was the fact that individual operations were affected very differently by the collapse in sales. Whereas the British assembly plant (compact and medium) had suffered a massive drop in sales, the French and the Czech plants (small and micro) were operating at full capacity and the Polish parts operation had only encountered some short-term losses. The logistics centre was also operating at full capacity due to rising demand for replacement parts for older cars.

The savings programme also had indirect consequences for the composition of the TEF. The discussion about the de facto unequal treatment of different operations and subsidiaries in the Working Committee was used as an opportunity by management to raise the issue of the EWC's representative scope, as some Toyota subsidiaries in Europe had not participated in the savings programme since they were not formally part of TME but reported directly to the parent company, TMC. Although the installation agreement expressly provided for all Toyota companies in Europe to be represented, the organisational strengthening of TME and the transfer of responsibility for units that reported to it suggested it would be appropriate to revisit the TEF's scope.[211] During the course of this renegotiation of the TEF agreement, management wanted to confine the scope of the EWC to businesses subsumed within TME. This would have had a negative impact on the German representatives as both financial services and motor sport reported directly to TMC. This made disagreements within the EWC an inevitability. The German representatives, who had long called for more powers for the EWC and felt, as a consequence, cut off from the discussions between the TEF secretary, the adviser and the HR manager, saw this as an attempt to weaken their critical stance within the TEF. In the end, a compromise was reached that provided for a preservation of the status quo for existing operations, but that only TME subsidiaries would be included in the future should new businesses be established in Europe.

(3) Toyota's efforts at global consolidation led to a dramatic shift in its engagement with motor sport – withdrawal from Formula 1. On 4 November 2009, almost simultaneously with the release of very poor results for the first half of the year, TMC management announced it would run down its Formula 1 business. Some employee representatives felt that the announcement had ben timed to coincide as with the failure of the sale of GM Europe to Magna, which dominated the business press at the time. News of the withdrawal from Formula 1 was confined almost exclusively to the sports sections of daily papers.

The decision to withdraw meant a reduction of 650 jobs at the Cologne-based Toyota Motor Sport GmbH (TMG). As there was no works council at TMG, there

---

211 To the surprise of those involved, it emerged that there was an EWC in the lift trucks division (Toyota Industries Corporation, TICO) that was not part of TME.

was no negotiated social compensation plan.[212] The severance offer made by the company voluntarily was regarded as generous by works councils at other Toyota companies on the same site. However, they were critical of the lack of transparency, as it was not possible to vet how resources had been distributed. The main target of criticism was the severity and speed of the cut: the entire planned workforce reduction was effected within just two months. This very rapid pace was also seen as responsible for the fact that no discussion was held to consider alternative employment, such as developing and manufacturing sports equipment. Finally, Toyota also departed from its own management principles that ruled out such large-scale economic dismissals. For the German works council members, this permanently damaged trust.[213] The approach to information pursued by the company was also inimical to the creation of trust: many employees first heard about the imminent job cuts by radio on their work to work.[214]

The motor sport division in Cologne did not report to the European headquarters in Brussels but direct to TMC. Nevertheless, based on the original purely geographical delineation of its scope, the TEF was responsible for TMG. However, no information was provided to the TEF before the cut in headcount, although this would have been reasonable for two reasons, if not legally enforceable. Firstly, the issue was a restructuring exercise with serious consequences for employment; and secondly, this departure from the maxim of employment security raised important questions for other operations in difficulties.

Since there was no works council at TMG and management had not initiated direct elections to the EWC, representation on the TEF took place via the works councils at other Toyota companies in Germany. These attempted to bring the case to the TEF by making use of a Restricted Committee meeting on the new agreement as an opportunity to assess the consequences of the Formula 1 withdrawal. The TEF leadership (secretary and adviser) were initially hesitant but then arranged a special meeting of the Restricted Committee and Working Committee, attended by a management representative from TMG, who reported on the position as he saw it.

> They [European management] were more cooperative as they did not want the issue to boil over at a large TEF meeting. But we then got the support of the whole Restricted Committee to take the issue further (TE10).

Finally, the exit from Formula 1 and its consequences for TMG were eventually discussed at the following TEF meeting, at which a second revision of the EWC

---

212 Under to the German Works Constitution Act (Sect. 112), a works council is legally entitled to negotiate a social compensation package (*Sozialplan, Interessenausgleich*) covering the whole work force. If no works council is elected, management will decide on any such compensation unilaterally. There is no statutory redundancy pay in Germany.

213 Cf. the information circular from the NEF-T, 10 November 2009.

214 This was possible because the news released by the agencies was broadcast before the start of work in German owing to time differences.

installation agreement was adopted. This also featured two symbolic gestures of refusal by the TEF through which they expressed their collective displeasure at how the closure of the company's Formula 1 activities had been managed. This entailed a refusal to pose for the annual group photo with management representatives, which was traditionally published in the European Sustainability Report. And secondly, the traditional tree planting outside the TME headquarters, planned to mark the conclusion of the new EWC agreement, was also cancelled. Such 'soft' forms of protest might seem rather trivial for companies with more adversarial traditions of industrial relations traditions but represented something of a scandal within Toyota with its self-proclaimed commitment to harmonious cooperation, and were taken very seriously by Japanese management representatives. 'This was so to speak a shot across the bows. And at this point all employee representatives actually acted together' (TE10).

9.2.7 Outputs of the TEF

In view of the fact that there were relatively few pressures on employee representatives in Toyota companies over a long period (no overt inter-plant competition, no parallel production, relatively high significance of non-competing sales subsidiaries) the outputs of the EWC cannot be judged using the same standard adopted for companies that had endured painful restructuring over many years. At TME there simply had not been any 'test cases', as the first true European problem took occurred with the general car market crisis that began in 2008.

As a consequence, it is hardly surprising that *not a single substantive agreement has been concluded.* However, it is interesting and revealing to consider how information exchange and transparency have functioned within the TEF – both between employee representatives and with management – as well as the degree to which there has been coordination and leadership on the employee side.

For the majority of employee representatives, the significance of the TEF is confined to the half-yearly meeting at the European headquarters. Although this is restricted to an exchange of information, its potential should not be underestimated. In the final analysis, TEF members have an opportunity to engage directly with top management and obtain first-hand information. This certainly has a value-added for many TEF members, and matches their expectations – especially those from the NMSCs. They obtain a perspective on pan-European developments as well as developments in individual national markets and operations. One NMSC representative, who did not see a need for any more extensive coordination at European level, offered the following assessment of the TEF.

> We get a very clear view, from my point of view. There's a representative coming here and he gets a clear view of the European operations of Toyota. We can ask questions of what are the plans and then we can go back and share it with our colleagues. There is a very good understanding and I think it is good from time to time to get a European perspective of Toyota (TE01).

Although some other TEF members – and in particular employee representatives from manufacturing operations – see some use in the current state of development attained by the TEF, they can also imagine an extension of its structures and powers. However, the level of awareness appears to vary considerably between TEF members. In particular, intensive discussion of strategic developments, such as negotiating a new agreement with more extensive information rights, appears to be mainly the concern of the small group on the Restricted Committee. The presentation of the negotiating position of the Restricted Committee at the pre-meeting took place without further discussion or questions from 'ordinary' TEF members, despite this being the first time that they had seen the text in its final form.

The importance of the TEF for Toyota is evident from the fact that high-level corporate representatives attend forum meetings, with almost the entire European management team taking part. As with most EWC-management meetings, the meetings consist of a detailed, structured information session with a subsequent round of discussion and questions. Meetings were initially more formalised than those in other firms in this study, aside from Honda, and questions had to be submitted in advance in writing. Because this process was coordinated by management, it was never clear whether all the questions submitted actually arrived at the TEF meeting. The process has now been relaxed to the extent that spontaneous questions are permitted, raising the degree of uncertainty for management.

For the employee representatives that we interviewed, this initially very restrictive approach was principally cultural in origin. Not to be able to answer questions was held to be a very disagreeable experience for Japanese managers, almost tantamount to a loss of face. 'This is a Japanese honour thing' (TE05). In addition, there was a need to avoid risking conflict, based both on Japanese culture as well as the traumatic industrial disputes at TME after the Second World War (TE04).

One of the core criticisms of the company's approach to information made by employee representatives continues to turn on a lack of transparency about the company's financial position. Although TME publishes a Sustainability Report, this does not include a financial report and accounts. Where data is presented at TEF meetings, this is done with an emphatic reference to the fact that the information is confidential. As a consequence, there are no minutes of any detailed financial data, broken down by country, and this information is not available in written form. According to one employee representative, it would not be possible to write quickly enough to keep pace with the slides (TE02).

In principle, no information that has not been officially authorised is confirmed in the TEF or Working Committee, nor even hinted at.

> [...] if you read something in the press then you normally put it like this: 'Well, it's not finalised, guys. We are in discussions, in early actions and we hope to succeed. And we are to 99 percent there, but we are not gonna go public until it's finalised. Yes, you are right. But it's confidential information.' That's what most companies do. [...] This company denies, denies, denies until they go public (TE05).

In the past, this approach not only applied to news that the employee side might view negatively or share price sensitive information. One example is the opening of a new assembly plant in Russia: although reports of this had already appeared in the business press, no information was offered at the TEF meeting – not even an intention to open a new plant was confirmed. A further example is the planned introduction of a hybrid variant of the Auris, which was to be assembled from 2010 at the Burnaston plant where the level of capacity usage had dropped. There were also press reports about this, but Toyota management refused to even hint at their intentions to the Restricted Committee or TEF despite the fact this would have sent a positive signal to a workforce that was very uncertain about its future. Two weeks after the TEF meeting, the news was officially confirmed.[215]

This approach to communication,[216] which was both frustrating and counterproductive for the employee side, was attributed by some interviewees to the cultural context of the Japanese parent company. In addition, carrying news that might later not be confirmed was also seen as risking a loss of face. Some employee representatives interpreted this behaviour as a sign of a lack of trust on the part of management in the employee side's ability to maintain confidentiality.

> And that means, they lack trust in us. [...] If you can't tell us you don't trust us (TE05).

Such an approach was seen as undermining the management principles of 'mutual trust and respect' that the company had committed itself to. The lack of trust in employee representatives shown in practice is also evident in the plethora of confidentiality arrangements that TEF are required to agree to. Although the general confidentiality clause in the TEF agreement corresponds to the Belgian law transposing the EWC Directive, and there are similar provisions in other EWCs, employee representatives are troubled by the amount of information that is deemed confidential, and which seems to go beyond what would be normally understood as a commercial secret. This provision has evidently been an obstacle to TEF members reporting back in their home country operations.

9.3 Provisional conclusion

Although the distribution of employment, plants and production volumes of Toyota in Europe exhibits a fairly low level of centralisation, the fact that power and knowledge is concentrated on the European headquarters and the global centre in Toyota City, together with the permeation of the Toyota corporate culture, means that the organisation can be characterised as 'somewhat centralised'. Combined with the high level of coordination of European manufacturing and logistics capacity,

215 See Footnote 212.

216 For example, participants reported the efforts of a previous TEF coordinator to induce senior TME management to be more open: 'Just tell them! You must tell them!'.

as well as the sales and marketing subsidiaries, the organisation as a whole can be classified as *global*. At the same time, as indicated in a number of organisational reforms taken in recent years and the decision to appoint a European to head TME, Toyota's European operations would seem to be gaining greater autonomy from the Japanese parent company.

These corporate structures are counterposed to those of the EWC, which we denoted as a *focal* organisation, and which is characterised by comparatively weak coordination between employee representatives combined with a highly decentralised distribution of mandates, albeit with centralised power and knowledge resources. In fact, the degree of inclusion and influence experienced by the TEF lags behind all the other companies in our sample, with the exception of Honda. As yet, the EWC has had virtually no influence on the course of events in any of the – few – developments of relevance for employees. There was no participation by the forum in the transfer of production allocations, information but no coordination on the employee side on the cost savings programme, and finally a symbolic reaction by European employee representatives to cuts in the motor sport division made after the event. The comparatively meagre outputs of the EWC are not only a consequence of the low level of preparedness of European and Japanese management to include the TEF in substantive matters,[217] and instead to use the forum as means for subsuming and integrating European operations within the Toyota culture. Weak coordination by employee representatives, illustrated in the TEF meetings, also contributes to this. Much appears to be left to chance, which in view of the challenging, and often evasive, culture of discussion that characterises management, would appear to do little to underpin a more robust approach to representation for the employee side.

One cause of the weakness of coordination on the part of European employee representatives might lie in the particular features of corporate organisation at Toyota. The separation of the European administrative headquarters from the main manufacturing operations has hindered any 'spontaneous' emergence of a powerful centre for the employee side over TME's fairly brief organisational history. While the existence of broadly equivalent production operations might assist mutual understanding between employee representatives, it also means that there is no driving force at the head of the forum – possibly also because there are no significant local employee interests tied up with the European headquarters as an operational location. The significant headstart enjoyed by the TEF secretary in terms of access to information through his position on the works council at the European headquarters and his comparatively close relationship to HR management provides him with a position of power within the forum. What is evidently a conscious strategic decision to withhold information also seems to hamper rather than help the secretary in the networking of employee representatives. It is hardly surprising, therefore, that

217 'They do not want to engage into real consultation because they think, if we consult before the final decision has been taken, they are not free to decide any more' (TE03).

the EWC (or more precisely employee representatives on the EWC) has remained largely ineffective in the few specific situations in which it might have played an active role.

The weakness of both coordination as well as the TEF's scope to exercise influence also correspond with the expectations of many TEF members – and in particular those who do not have a strong trade union background, as is often the case with some NMSC representatives. It is also an indicator of the heterogeneity of interests within the TEF, which, almost as an inevitable product of the inclusionary logic pursued by management, embraces as many business areas as possible. Seen from the standpoint of the logic of management, the TEF appears to be a platform for communication that is intended to strengthen a common European Toyota identity amongst representatives of the company's operations.

However, this needs to be qualified in some respects. As yet, the Toyota EWC has not encountered any major incidents that have placed severe demands on it. Up until the most recent crisis, the actors concerned – both management and employee representatives –experienced Toyota as a dynamic and successful company (albeit with some question marks over the economic success of the British plants – see Pardi, 2005; 2006). In contrast to GM and Renault, Toyota does not operate parallel production in Europe. As a consequence, the EWC is faced with a lower need for regulation.

Moreover, over time structural changes appear to be underway in the forum that suggest a steady increase in the standing of the employee representatives and a rise in their capabilities. For example, the first revision of the installation agreement in 2003 saw the formal introduction of a steering group composed of employee representatives (the Restricted Committee), a doubling in the number of TEF meetings to two per year, and an increase in the number and proportion of employee representatives on the TEF. This undoubtedly improved the circumstances under which employee representatives can operate. On the other hand, the company has also pursued a creeping decoupling of the central adviser position from trade union influence. Whereas the first agreement made explicit reference to the adviser having an EMF mandate, in the second there was simply the possibility of including an EMF representative as an extra member. That is, the development of independent European employee representation was not advanced.

However, as far as formal representation rights are concerned, there have been some improvements. For example, in 2009 the employee side was able to achieve a second revision of the agreement, with the support of the adviser, that provided for more consultation rights and which expressly stipulated that the Restricted Committee should be given comprehensive information and consulted in the event of extraordinary events such as collective dismissals, transfers of production or plant closures. Representatives on this committee were also given an express right to propose alternatives that, although not encroaching on managerial prerogatives, must be given consideration and cannot be turned down without justification. Only time will tell whether these enhanced opportunities will be exploited.

Chapter 10: Ford of Europe

10.1 The Ford Group in Europe

10.1.1 History and characteristics of the Ford Motor Company

The Ford Motor Company, founded on 16 June 1903 by Henry Ford and eleven other shareholders in Dearborn/Michigan, is one of the world's longest-established automotive companies. With some 179,000 employees at eighty-eight plants (2008) the company operates in 200 markets.[218] Its product range encompasses cars, vans and cross-country vehicles, supplemented by its own vehicle related financial services company. Ford Motor Company continues to be effectively controlled by the Ford family through the size of their ownership of voting stock, despite a small holding of overall equity in the company.[219]

The company's greatest innovation, which was to revolutionise the entire automotive industry, took place on 1 April 1913 at the Highland Park plant in Michigan when it initiated assembly line production, beginning the epoch of mass production. Combined with the relatively simply constructed standard car, the legendary Model T, which was produced for many years, Ford set a benchmark for industrial production in the first half of the Twentieth Century, making ownership of a car feasible for wide groups of consumers. The declared aim of building a car that would be affordable for any worker was achieved by offering a minimal level of equipment and the use of a single colour.

During the 1920s competitors – primarily General Motors – positioned themselves with higher value cars in the mass market, with purchase financed by their own credit department. This development, about which Henry Ford was initially sceptical, also ultimately became a necessity for Ford. With the acquisition of the Lincoln Motor Company in 1922 Ford gained access to the luxury car market. The establishment of the Mercury Division in the 1930s also aimed at opening the market for mid-segment cars.[220] During the Second World War, Ford was a part of the defence industry and also built military aircraft. By the late-1950s, the firm's range reached its apogee with the creation of the Ford Motor Credit Company and a specialised division for defence and aerospace (Aeronutroni).

---

218 The core brands are Ford and Lincoln (in the US). Volvo was sold to the Chinese car manufacturer Geely in the summer of 2010. Jaguar Land Rover, acquired in 1989/2000 and merged in 2002, was sold to Tata Motors in 2008.

219 In contrast to its main competitors, GM and Chrysler, during the 2007/8 crisis, Ford has never experienced a Chapter 11 insolvency nor received financial assistance from the US government.

220 Mercury production ceased in 2010.

Ford had initiated operations abroad during the interwar period, with the opening of a number of major plants outside the US. However, its internationalisation activities were significantly intensified and reorganised from in the late-1960s. For example, in 1967 Ford brought together all its European plants under a single company, Ford of Europe. Similarly in 1971 plants in Canada, Mexico and the USA were integrated into The North American Automotive Operations.

In 1970, the trend towards cooperation between manufacturers led Ford to acquire a 24.5 per cent share in the Mazda Motor Corporation (Bordenave, 1998: 229). In addition to cooperation in R&D, Ford used Mazda's Autorama sales network (later renamed as Ford) to secure entry into the Japanese market. Auto Alliance International Inc (AAI), established in 1992, is a joint venture between Mazda[221] and Ford with a plant in Flatrock/Michigan, which assembles the Mazda 6 and Ford Mustang for the American market, and two plants in Thailand.[222] Ford's raising of its stake in Mazda for 25 to 33.4 per cent changed the balance between the groups in the Autorama and AAI joint ventures.[223] The fact that a Ford manager became a board member of Mazda was seen as constituting the 'virtual takeover of Mazda' (Bordenave, 1998: 229f.). However, in late-2008 the global economic crisis forced Ford to reduce its stake in Mazda to 13.8 per cent in order to take some profits on its holding. Nonetheless, the strategic partnership has continued in the form of joint ventures and through the use of common vehicle platforms and transmissions.[224]

The operative organisation of the Ford Motor Company currently consists of two main business areas: cars and financial services. The Ford Motor Credit Company is a wholly-owned subsidiary of Ford Motor Company and is responsible for financing vehicle purchases, and leasing and insurance for the Ford and Lincoln brands. The company has a network of subsidiaries in a range of markets. Up until its sale in December 2005, the largest business segment of the Ford Motor Credit Company was the car hire and leasing business Hertz.

Ford's cars division is divided into four geographical regions that coordinate the sale and production of vehicles and components for individual marques in the corresponding regions: North America, South America, Europe and Asia/Africa (which also coordinates cooperation with Mazda).

As with other large American vehicle manufacturers, Ford has experienced a protracted crisis of both profitability and innovation since the 1980s, in particular since the rise of its Japanese competitors. The company has responded with a number

---

221 Mazda Motor Manufacturing (USA) Corporation (MMUC) is the regional division of Mazda Motor Corporation in the United States.

222 Mazda Corporate Fact Sheet: <http://media.ford.com/print_doc.cfm?article_id=21731> accessed on 4 March 2010.

223 Mazda History: <http://www.mazdausamedia.com/content/mazda-history> accessed 4 March 2010.

224 Ford Press Release, 18 November 2008: 'Ford Sells a Portion of its Stake in Mazda: Two Companies Will Continue Strategic Relationship' <http://media.ford.com/article_display.cfm?article_id=29437> accessed 4 March 2010.

of restructuring programmes such as 'Ford 2000' with which the CEO Alex Trotman sought to consolidate its global manufacturing, development and marketing capacities into a single global organisation in the mid-1990s. The divestment of the company's parts manufacturing unit, which took place in the 1990s following the example set by General Motors and which led to the establishment of the listed component manufacturer Visteon, represented a further major intervention into group's organisation. In early-2006, Ford initiated an extensive restructuring programme for its troubled North American business ('Way Forward'). The programme aimed to accelerate the development of new products through technical innovation and investment but also involved the closure of fourteen plants and a cut of 25–30,000 jobs by 2012.[225] In late-2006, the new CEO, Alan Mulally, rolled out a plan for restructuring for the entire company in the context of the 'One Ford' programme.[226] This aimed to restore profitability on a base of lower production volumes and a changed product range, shorten product development cycles through minimising complexity, and raise quality.[227] Under the 'One Ford' product philosophy, which aimed at a uniform model policy, global design and development resources were to be used more efficiently, with cost advantages obtained through manufacturing volume models on single platforms.[228]

10.1.2 History and characteristics of Ford of Europe

With a large number of production facilities and significant R&D operations, Ford of Europe, previously including the Volvo Car Corporation,[229] is the most important pillar of the Ford Group outside North America. Ford's presence in Europe dates back to 1903 when the first vehicles were sold. In 1909 an operation was opened in England and two years later the first assembly plant outside the US was opened in Trafford Park, Manchester. In 1931 Ford began to manufacture vehicles at a new plant in Dagenham, Essex, at that time the largest production complex in Europe. Following the foundation of the Ford Motor Company Ltd in 1928, Ford of Britain

---

225 Ford Press Release, 23 January 2006, 'Ford Fights Back', <http://media.ford.com/article_display.cfm?article_id=22382> accessed on 5 March 2010.

226 The full name of the programme was 'One Ford – One Team – One Plan – One Goal'.

227 Ford Motor Company, *Annual Report 2006*, p. 4.

228 This philosophy of a 'world car' was first implemented with the model change to the new Fiesta. The Fiesta, developed in Cologne and produced there from 2008, was manufactured to an identical specification from 2010 in Mexico, Spain, Thailand, and China. Ford Press Release, 20 February 2009, 'Ford Werk Köln übernimmt Schlusselrolle fur die Fiesta-Einfuhrungskampagne in den USA', <http://media.ford.com/news/fordkoelnuebernimmtschluesselrollefuerdiefiestaeinfuehrungskampagneindenusa.htm> accessed on 3 May 2010.

229 Up until its sale in 2010, the Volvo Car Corporation was directly controlled by the parent company and was not part of Ford of Europe, and therefore lies outside the scope of this study. Volvo also had its own EWC.

became the centre of Ford's activities in Europe. After the First World War a number of other plants were opened: in Belgium (Antwerp, 1922), Germany (Berlin, 1925; Cologne, 1931), and France (Bordeaux, 1916).

The next wave of expansion took place in the 1960s and 1970s with the construction of new assembly and component plants in Belgium, Germany, France, and Spain. Car assembly began at the Belgium plant in Genk under the control of the German subsidiary Ford-Werke AG.[230] A production facility for automatic transmissions was opened in Bordeaux in 1973 followed by a further plant for manual transmissions in 1976. In 1976 work also began on building a large production complex in the vicinity of Valencia, which is now one of the largest European assembly plants and also has an engine plant.

The most significant extension of production capacities took place in Germany. In 1956 Ford opened a press shop in Wülfrath, and in 1966 an axle plant in Düren. A new final assembly plant was opened in Saarlouis in 1970 and this currently manufactures the compact Focus and Kuga models. The main plant in Cologne-Niehl has remained the fulcrum of Ford's operations in Germany. In addition to assembling the Fiesta and Fusion, Cologne is also the location of the engine and transmission plants as well as forging and foundry activities. Since the beginning of the century a number of internal component manufacturing operations have been divested or placed into joint ventures (see further below).

The John Andrews Development Center was opened in Cologne-Merkenich in 1968 and since 1995 has been responsible for the development for small and mid-sized front wheel drive models as well as European commercial vehicles in cooperation with English engineers at Dunton, Essex. Since 1962 Cologne-Merkenich has also been the European centre for component and parts distribution. The Ford research centre at Aachen undertakes research into sustainable mobility and vehicle safety. Opened in 1994, it is Ford's only research site outside the United States.[231]

The most recent area of expansion has been in Southern and South East Europe. Ford has had a manufacturing presence in Turkey since 1965 in the form of a joint venture.[232] In 2002 a new assembly plant was opened in St Petersburg, and in 2008 Ford acquired a 72.4 per cent stake in a former GM plant 'Automobile Craiova SA' in Romania that had previously manufactured Oltcit, Citroën, and Daewoo models.

---

230 In 2004, the legal form of the company was changed to a GmbH: 'AG' is a public liability corporation or 'stock corporation', with an independent listing, equivalent to a British Plc; GmbH is a limited company. Ford GmbH, headquartered in Cologne, also encompasses the plants in Saarlouis (Germany) and Genk (Belgium) as well as the sales subsidiary Ford Motor Company Austria GmbH.

231 Ford Standorte, <http://www.ford.de/UeberFord> accessed on 5 March 2010.

232 Ford Otosan is a joint venture between Ford and Koç Holdings, in which each partner has a 41 per cent stake. The remaining shares are owned by public investors (Ford, *Annual Report 2007*, p. 79).

The Transit Connect has been assembled here since late 2009, with a 'mini MPV', the B-Max, added from 2012.[233]

Ford's approach to *governance and organisation* in Europe also charted an innovative course with the creation of a headquarters for its European operations in 1967 (Ando, 2005: 134). As Tolliday (2003) noted, however, the path to a single corporate centre for all the company's European activities was anything other than direct, with the company passing through alternations between episodes of centralisation and decentralisation. During the 1920s, the American parent company rejected any form of decentralisation to its new subsidiaries in Europe, despite the very different needs and institutional circumstances of national markets. From the 1920s and up until the beginning of the Second World War, the company then set out to transfer primary administration and responsibility for Ford Motor Company subsidiaries in Europe to Ford of Britain. However, the world economic crisis made it virtually impossible to control the company effectively in this due to rising protectionism and the fragmentation of European markets. Tolliday (2003:153) saw these moves towards regionalisation of production as the de facto start of decentralisation and the abandonment of integration.

The uncoordinated and relatively autonomous development of Ford subsidiaries continued after the Second World War. Ford created two centres – Ford of Britain and Ford-Werke AG – each of which manufactured distinct product ranges and operated largely independently of each other. It was not until the creation of the European Economic Community in 1957 and the European Free Trade Area in 1960 that Ford began to attempt to regain control over its European subsidiaries and integrate them into a single European organisation. The company's desire to reap the same economies of scale that were available in the United States led to a redistribution of production between existing facilities, with the aim of establishing a more efficient and specialised division of labour between plants within an enlarged market.

On 14 June 1967 Ford of Britain and Ford-Werke AG were placed into a European holding company in order to coordinate the development, manufacture and sale of cars and commercial vehicles in Europe and, at that time, also in Africa, as well integrate the product range manufactured in the two countries. However, it was a further decade before there was any effective European business structure and this was characterised by intensive processes of restructuring and an expansion of capacity in Mainland Europe (Tolliday, 2003:154). One consequence was a cut in the British share of assembly capacity, with the German share remaining constant. One significant factor in this weakening of what was traditionally Ford's core European operation was continuing industrial relations problems at its British plants. As such, this transfer of capacity can also be seen as a deliberate management strategy both

233 <http://media.ford.com/news/fordbeginstransitconnectproductionatitsnewplantincraiovaromania.htm> accessed on 31 May 2010.

to discipline and to avoid British employees and their unions, at least in the area of large-scale vehicle assembly.

> Faced with a crisis of employment relations in the United Kingdom, Ford's ability to manage its spatial organization now permitted the firm to threaten relocation away from the trouble spots (Bordenave, 1998: 216).

In 1998 the upgrading of the German production plants culminated in the relocation of the European headquarters from Brentwood, Essex, to Cologne-Niehl. As we discuss below, this transfer also had a number of implications for the European level of industrial relations at Ford.

10.1.3 Distribution of resources, power, culture and knowledge

Ford of Europe's headquarters in Cologne currently deals with fifty-one markets as well as the Ford's integrated European production system with plants in Belgium, Germany, France, UK, Romania, Russia, Spain, Sweden and Turkey.[234] Figure 15 sets out the distribution and size of production facilities.

Figure 15: Distribution of plants in Ford of Europe, 2008.

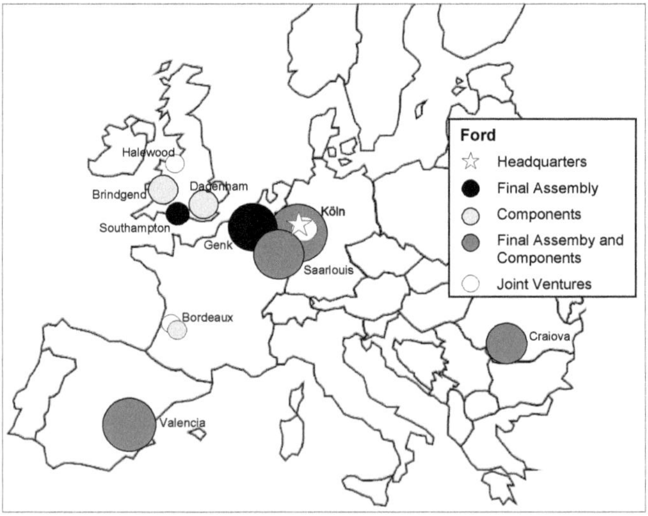

Source: authors' compilation

234 The following calculations relate to those operations within the scope of the Ford EWC. The plants in Russia and Turkey are, therefore, not included. Volvo's plants in Sweden and Belgium are also excluded as the Volvo Car Corporation has its own EWC.

Despite the increased emphasis placed on Germany as the country with the largest workforce and now the site of the European headquarters, the distribution of material and human resources in Ford of Europe is comparatively decentralised. Germany, which has the largest national workforce and which is defined as the European home country for this study, accounts for some 48 per cent of all employees in operations represented on the EWC. This is similar to other decentralised companies such as GM. Only Toyota, with 27 per cent, has fewer employees proportionally in its European home country.[235] The pattern of distribution in terms of European production volumes at Ford is even more decentralised: 37 per cent of overall production is accounted for by Ford plants in Germany.[236] Together with GME and Toyota, this is the lowest value in our sample (see for example, Renault, 47 per cent: PSA, 54 per cent: VW, 56 per cent: Daimler, 83 per cent). In addition the German plants, Cologne and Saarlouis, account for just two of the total of ten European plants, and only two of the five final assembly plants.[237] Overall the distribution of resources of Ford in Europe can be characterised as 'somewhat decentralised'.

Table 9: Global and European capacity and resources of Ford Motor Company (2008)

	Employees	**Plants**	**Production**
World	179,000	88	5,407,000
EU	48,300	10	2,142,498
EU home country (Germany)	23,200	2	789,642
'Real' home country (USA)	87,000	28	1,602,000
Largest plant	17,000		400,000
Share EU/world	27%	9%	40%
Share EU home country/EU	48%	20%	37%
Share EU home country/world	13%	2%	15%
Share 'real' home country/world	49%	32%	30%
Share largest plant/EU	35%	–	20%

Source: authors compiled from Ford Motor Company Annual Report (2008) and OICA (2008).

235 In relation to global employment, the share is 13 per cent.

236 In relation to global production the share is 15 per cent.

237 The position at the two traditional centres of Germany and the UK diverge markedly. Following the separation of the parts operation, manufacturing in Germany is concentrated at two main sites, with five smaller operations in the UK. Due to the serious financial situation in the late-1990s, there was a large cut in assembly capacity and employment in the UK, where no volume models are produced. The only final assembly is the Transit van at Southampton. Engines are manufactured at Dagenham and Bridgend, and transmissions at Halewood (GFT).

As with most of the other manufacturers in our study, the distribution of power between Ford's European headquarters and other European plants can also be characterised as 'somewhat centralised'. However, the influence of the European corporate centre is limited by the fact that the true home country of the company is located outside Europe and important decisions are taken at the headquarters of the parent company in Dearborn, Michigan. While decisions on the allocation of production to European plants or on individual models, and any associated investments, are taken by the European headquarters, the agreement of the headquarters in Dearborn is required on central and more strategic matters.

> So if we are planning to invest in a new product that also includes investment in the manufacturing process and in manufacturing equipment as well. These are open subjects to approval at the US level. [...] But the detail work in terms of 'we gonna build the new Focus in Germany', or 'we gonna build in Germany and Spain', or 'we gonna build in Germany and Spain and somewhere else' – much of that detail work is done and decided at the European level (FM01).

While strategic decisions are made in the European headquarters, plants essentially implement these within the framework of a single global production system (FM03). All long-term decisions, such as staff assessment, new employment contracts or how to respond to economic crises, are always taken with the agreement of the European headquarters. Subsidiaries must also obtain the agreement of European headquarters when hiring local managers. Although skilled workers can be hired independently by plants, any positions above middle management, and certainly plant managers, have to approved by European headquarters. However, proposals are usually accepted (FM03).

Overall the information gathered from our interviews indicates that strategic decisions are overwhelmingly taken at the level of European headquarters, but in many cases these require final approval by US corporate headquarters. Individual plants have a limited degree of autonomy from the European centre, principally on operational matters. As such the distribution of power tends towards what can be designated as 'somewhat centralised'.

The problem of a 'dual home country' makes it more difficult to assess the degree of centralism of the company in terms of its culture. Many phenomena, such as a single vehicle brand, uniform functional designations and levels of hierarchy, and standardised management training, would not suggest that the degree of centralisation in this area is below-average.

In contrast, the European home country, Germany, appears to have only slight cultural influence. One reason could be that European top management mainly originates in the USA and UK. However, there is a high degree of turnover in this group, and they are usually moved onto other roles within the Ford group after a few years (FE01). In contrast, management within manufacturing plants is much more stable and is usually drawn from the host country (FM01). Management training varies in terms of focus, depending on whether it is for regional or senior group-level management. In both cases, candidates go through standardised training and are given the option of undertaking regional or local training measures abroad. For example, local managers are assigned to other locations to gain experience with the most up-to-date technologies. Management development is standardised throughout Europe. In addition, top management has a number of programmes for leadership development, some of which take place at global level and some at European. Several programmes have also been delivered in cooperation with other brands within the group, as was the case with a management development programme taken over from Volvo, which was seen as being an exemplar within the group (FM01).

English is the corporate language, especially at management level but also in R&D teams. There are also standardised symbols and departmental designations as well as identical terms for senior group-level positions in a clear sign of a corporate culture marked by the approach of the US as the country-of-origin. The most recent programme for corporate integration, 'One Ford', emphasises the centrality of a global corporate culture, even if it is much less formalised and explicit in comparison to Toyota. One management representative described the Ford corporate culture in the following terms.

> There is a strong – Ford has been around for one hundred years – corporate culture. It is easier to say about it than to define what it is. I think it's a mixture of results from things like the size – Ford is a global big company, it's got pretty well defined processes and structures and worries about these things quite a lot, it's American owned. So I think that obviously has an influence in terms of the company culture because that's inevitable. Partly because of the ownership of the company – the Ford family still owns the controlling stake in the business. I think that has an influence on how we think and how we do things. (FM01)

Overall, therefore, Ford can be characterised as having a 'somewhat centralised' corporate culture – not from a European home country standpoint but from its American parent – and a single European staffing policy, albeit one adapted to national employment relations arrangements.

Ford's R&D capacities are concentrated at two large sites: Cologne-Merkenich, not far from the European headquarters, and Dunton, Essex, only a few miles from the British Ford headquarters (and former European headquarters). Both development centres have existed since the 1960s and in addition to new product development also have design centres, test tracks, and laboratories. The John Andrews Center at Merkenich also has the only wind tunnel in the company outside of the United States. Although the company emphasises the equivalence of the two sites, the shift of the company headquarters to Cologne is likely to bolster the position of the Merkenich development centre over the longer term as its proximity will simplify integrating strategic planning and product development.

Both sites are responsible for developing front-wheel drive small and mid-sized vehicles. After a long period in which the two centres operated relatively independently of each other, and at times carried out parallel work in developing components, the current restructuring programme aims to improve integration between

European development activities. For example, Dunton now concentrates on powertrain development and European commercial vehicles with other development work at Merkenich.

The restructuring of research activities is not limited to Europe. One element in the 'One Ford' programme has been the pursuit of global integration based on a division of labour between R&D sites in order to use specific regional competencies to develop products for other markets. For example, there were plans that responsibility for developing small and compact cars in Cologne should be used for the American market, where there is a growing demand for vehicles in this segment.

The significance of the European business to Ford can be measured by the fact that a research centre was located in Aachen in 1994. This centre is one of two facilities in the entire group that work on basic vehicle research. It employs some 250 highly qualified engineers and researchers who work on new technologies and cooperate with the two development centres. There is also an 80 kilometre long proving ground for testing vehicles that has existed since 1964 and is located in Lommel (Belgium).

Overall the distribution of European R&D capacities at Ford can be seen as decentralised, since, despite the rising significance of the German sites, there are two approximately equally strong development centres as well as a significant research centre. This distinguishes Ford of Europe from all other companies in our study in which there is one, more or less, dominant development centre for the whole of Europe.

10.1.4 Coordination of the company

The coordination of operations in Ford of Europe can be denoted as 'somewhat strong'. Individual plants are coordinated through standardised procedures as well as control and governance mechanisms that are integrated into the overall structure by the European headquarters. Each plant produces in line with a central plan produced by Ford of Europe and developed in consultation with individual plants. Models and production volumes are allocated centrally by European headquarters, often with the final decision preceded by local negotiations that may include workforce concessions as a precondition for employment and investment commitments.[238] Ford operates a platform strategy that provides for variations in body types from a standard model. Each main model has a so-called 'lead plant' that accounts for the main capacity for the vehicle: this is supplemented by 'switch plants'

238 See, for example, the agreement on retaining operations at Cologne, which provided production and employment guarantees until 2011 in return for employee concessions. The most problematic agreement was concluded for Valencia in 2006, when the EWC was not informed. There still appears to be some uncertainty as to the exact substance and scale of the concessions agreed.

that can flexibly produce several models.[239] Ford does not engage in parallel production, unlike the GM Delta platform. In fact, Ford has tended to move towards single sourcing so that individual models are increasingly manufactured at one site (FE05). The aim is to obtain cost benefits from greater specialisation. This also means that there is less open competition between plants although this cannot be entirely ignored. For example, there is a potential conflict in terms of the distribution of additional production capacity between lead plants and switch plants. The Spanish switch plant is in a difficult position as it has to fight harder than lead plants to win output allocations. Overall each plant produces vehicles for the entire European market. Based on the high degree of product specialisation, plants do not usually compete directly. However, competitive pressures are generated via an efficiency metric in the form of the global Ford Production Index.

In order to improve communication between European plants there is a formal meeting of all European plant managers every quarter. The main function of these meetings, which are usually held at the headquarters in Cologne but also occasionally at other European plants, is to exchange information and transfer ideas on best practices. The consolidation of personal networks is also a significant factor. These informal contacts are often seen as a decisive factor by HR management as they promote the transfer of knowledge between sites both at top and middle management level (FM01). As far as the frequency of formal meetings is concerned Ford is probably in an intermediate position compared with other companies in our study, but with a marked gap with the highly integrated VW group where there are weekly meetings of managers of the German plants. As well as horizontally networked forms of communication between plant managers and sites there are also markedly *vertical* structures for disseminating information from the corporate centre to functional areas or national managements.

> I would say in terms of company communication it is more traditional top down communication mostly in the sense that we work very hard to cascade information about the company, to share information about the company whether in electronic form or printed form or verbal (FM01).

Since Ford redefined its core business[240] and set about divesting other activities beginning in the mid-1990s, a process completed with the sale of Visteon and the hiving off of transmission manufacture to the Getrag Ford Transmissions joint venture in 2000, the complexity of internal supply relationships has been reduced but with a corresponding increase in the need for coordination between final

239 The lead plant for the Fiesta (B platform) is the plant at Cologne; the lead plant for the Focus (C platform) is Saarlouis. Valencia has served as a switch plant for both models over the past decade. Since 2009, the Focus has been assembled exclusively in Saarlouis. In return, the C-Max (C platform) was transferred to Valencia.

240 'Ford defined its core businesses as designing, engineering, building, distributing vehicles and main engines. [...] We think we can best buy components from other people' (FM01).

assembly operations and suppliers. Obtaining components is no longer basically a local matter but is regulated through the purchasing departments at European or global level (FE06).

Overall Ford of Europe would appear to be a comparatively strongly coordinated company. Coordination is not left exclusively to the corporate headquarters but also includes business functions and local operations either through tried and tested processes or formalised procedures. There is a regular institutionalised exchange of information and communication, not only for central management but also including plant management across Europe. The form of communication depends on the substance of the information: it can be both vertical through Ford of Europe headquarters as well as multilateral and networked through formal and informal channels at a horizontal level. In connection with the finding of a somewhat decentralised distribution of resources this suggests that Ford of Europe could be classified as a *transnational* organisation (see Chapter 3.1).

10.2 The European Ford Works Council

10.2.1 Emergence of the EWC

The European Ford Works Council was constituted on 16 September 1996 through an agreement between European Ford management and the central works council of the German subsidiary (then Ford-Werke AG, now Ford-Werke GmbH) and employee representatives from other European plants. The agreement was signed in the European Parliament building in Brussels. The voluntary agreement was concluded under Article 13 of the Directive shortly before it came into force on 22 September 1996, and the agreement was revised on 1 December 2008. The revision included the integration of a previously unpublished 'Memorandum of Understanding', negotiated on 9 October 2000, which confirmed the exclusive negotiating mandate of the forum.[241] The EWC's structure is based on the German transposing legislation, under which the body consists solely of employee representatives. The chair is usually a German works council member, with the role of deputy taken by a British employee representative.

A major influence on the formation of the EWC at Ford of Europe was exercised by Wilfried Kuckelkorn, then chair of the central works council and later EWC. He took the initiative to establish a European employee representation body and pursued this for many years in the teeth of opposition from British unions that had difficulty with the idea that workplace representatives rather than full-time officials should sit on the body. The German side was able to form an alliance with Spanish, Belgium and French unions, and the British side finally conceded. Kuckelkorn was

241 'Agreement on the Ford European Works Council and on the Provision of Information and Consultation within the European Operations of Ford Motor Company' (01.12.2008): Art. 4 'Charter of the FEWC and the Decentralized Information and Consultation Procedure'.

a noted proponent of the European project. In addition to being a member of the works council he was also for many years an MEP. His ideal of a European body for employee representation not dominated by national interests was that the it should be located outside of the home country, such as in Brussels. However, the fact that the EWC was based at the German home plant was fortunate in that, sometime later, the European corporate centre was moved to Cologne and the EWC was able to gain from the professionalism of representatives used to working within German institutions of codetermination. At the same time, the pragmatism and experience of the predominantly British management team combined with the cooperative style of resolving conflicts that characterised the German system, as well as formal and informal contacts with German employee representatives, was viewed as having helped build a foundation for future cooperation within the framework of the EWC (FM01).

10.2.2 Distribution of resources, power, culture, and knowledge in the EWC

The Ford EWC is distinguished from all the other bodies in this study in two respects: it is relatively small and is characterised by relatively homogeneous interests in that only employees from manufacturing and development plants are directly represented, not those in financial services and distribution and sales companies.[242] Moreover, membership of the EWC confined to the European plants of the core Ford brand. Volvo, owned by Ford until its sale in summer 2010 but managed directly from the US rather than Europe, had its own EWC. Jaguar and Landrover, since acquired by Tata Motors, also reported to the US and were not included in the EWC.[243] The EWC currently has eighteen members[244] representing employees of the six EU countries with production facilities. Five each are from Germany and the UK, three from Belgium, two each from Spain and Romania, and one from France, making the Ford EWC significantly smaller than the other cases in this study.

242 However, if they wish the EWC can act on their behalf.

243 Ford Press Release, 2 June 2008: 'Ford Motor Company Completes the Sale of Jaguar Land Rover to Tata Motors', <http://media.ford.com/article_display.cfm?article_id=28358> accessed on 18 March 2010.

244 In early-2010 a Russian employee representative from the Saint Petersburg plant was included as an observer. However, the Turkish joint venture has not yet been integrated into the work of the EWC.

Figure 16: Distribution of seats on the Ford EWC, 2009.

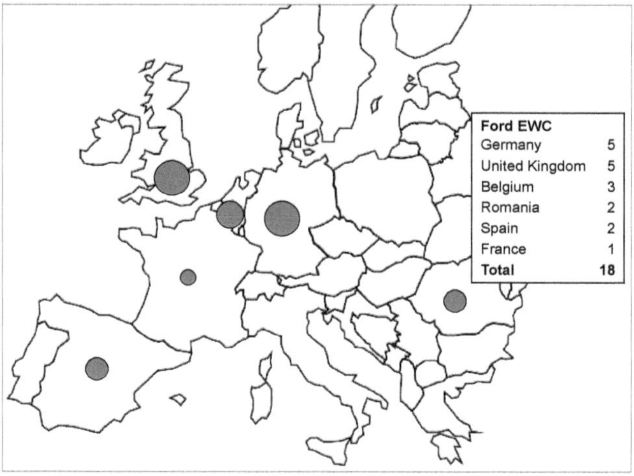

Source: author's compilation.[245]

The distribution of seats was originally determined by the number of employees in each country and has changed several times. Portugal lost its seat in 2000 following the sale of a plant. France also lost two seats when Visteon was divested, but retained one other seat after the sale of the automatic transmission plant in Bordeaux as the French EWC member has been delegated from the GFT joint venture.[246] The start of manufacture in Eastern Europe led to the inclusion of Romania in 2008. However, the distribution of seats does not always precisely match the current distribution of employment. For example, in order not to endanger the sensitive balance between German and British representatives the UK retained its five seats despite plant closures and a loss of several thousand jobs.

> Initially, there were precise criteria, which were, of course, dependent on workforce numbers [...] This has now changed very evidently. Otherwise Great Britain would perhaps have just three seats (FE01).

Measured in terms of the home country share of employment, the EWC would appear to be 'somewhat decentralised', with five of the eighteen seats reserved for German representatives. The EWC representativeness index[247] of 0.58 also suggests

245 See EWC agreement, 1 December 2008: Article 5.

246 Ford Press Release, 2 February 2009. 'Ford Confirms its Intention to Sell its Bordeaux Automatic Transmission Plant', <http://media.ford.com/news/fordconfirmsitsintentiontosellitsbordeauxautomatictransmissionplant.rtf> accessed on 18 March 2010.

247 On this the method of calculating this, see Chapter 3.3.1.

that the home country is markedly underrepresented. Were the seats in the body allocated in proportion to employment, the German sites would have four additional seats. At 0.44, this index is only lower in the case of GM and Daimler.

As with almost all the EWCs in our study, the EWC at Ford has a presidium, known as the select committee. Its tasks include preparing for EWC meetings and conducting negotiations with Ford management on behalf of EWC members (on the negotiating mandate, see below). Initially the select committee comprised three workplace employee representatives but since the revision of the agreement in 2008 it has had four members elected by the EWC. While Germany and the UK each have a permanent seat, and with this a right to include their own external experts in negotiations, the other two seats (before 2008 one), and associated advisory positions, are divided between Belgium, France, Romania and Spain.[248] Because strict application of this principle of rotation would lead to a long wait between having seats, it was abolished in early 2010. Since then all countries represented, with the exceptions of France and Russia, have a permanent seat on the select committee. This is meant to ensure that all countries with large plants can be integrated into the work of the EWC's governing body on an ongoing basis. However, as a concession to management the frequency of meetings was reduced.

The EWC, select committee and secretariat are all based in Cologne. Because of rivalry between the German and British plants this was not initially seen as a permanent solution. However, it has proved beneficial, not only because of the proximity of the EWC secretariat to Ford's European headquarters but also because of the resources available to employee representatives in Cologne. For example, EWC work is often aided by the fact that the EWC secretary, whose office is financed by the European headquarters, can also make use of additional resources (time off, equipment and resources) that are provided by the German Works Constitution Act.

> Based on our circumstances in Germany, German codetermination, we have far more access to extra resources to support and help. In particular, if it's a matter of preparing or carrying out large meetings of the EWC then the secretariat can ask one or more colleagues for support. I think these options are not available in this way in other countries (FE01).

Ford's European headquarters covers the costs for organising and implementing EWC and select committee meetings including a full time position in the secretariat and travel costs for any experts involved. The national subsidiaries cover the travel and accommodation costs of EWC meetings.[249]

The combining of the positions of EWC chair and full time EWC secretary at Cologne, and with this the option to have easy access for discussions with the HR head of Ford of Europe means that employee representatives in Cologne have a

248 See the EWC agreement (1 December 2008): Article 5.

249 EWC Agreement, 1 December 2008: Article 8.

structural advantage within the body. In addition the EWC chair is also the chair of the local works council in Ford as well as the central works council for Germany's Ford plants. Moreover, he is also the deputy chair of the supervisory board of Ford-Werke GmbH. As a consequence, he is undoubtedly the most influential of all employee representatives at Ford of Europe. In this context, one significant issue is the extent to which individual EWC members have influence, (1) over the topics to be dealt with in the EWC, and (2) the decisions made by that body.

(1) The list of topics for the EWC agenda and the select committee comprises current issues put on it by the EWC chair as well as other proposals made by EWC members. All EWC members have scope to bring up topics at any time. The secretariat obtains proposals from members ahead of the meeting.

> You know, the full EWC agrees the agenda. [...] All the countries have an input in it. Our secretary sends emails to all EWC members asking, what do you want to be placed on the agenda, this is what are thinking of placing there, do you want to add anything. It is done openly by all (FE03).

However the final choice rests with the secretary and the chair. Both are alive to the fact the EWC should not become preoccupied with national issues, which could hinder its work. As a consequence topics are rejected if is clear that they should be dealt with by local or national employee and employer representatives. 'Of course if local problems are related to policy of the group as a whole these are dealt with within the body' (FE09).

(2) Decisions in the EWC are taken by consensus, which can also lead to very protracted discussions. All EWC members have the same opportunity to represent the standpoint of their country or plant and participate in discussions. Formal voting, in which one country could be outvoted by others, is avoided.

> I think that's an important point to reach a consensus and also that this needs to be unanimous. I think it's a very important point that everybody can see their own contribution reflected in the procedure. Otherwise things wouldn't function at all (FE01).

Overall, the EWC chair and the secretariat attempt to include the opinions of all EWC members in compiling the agenda for meetings. This discursive procedure also applies to both submitting topics for EWC meetings as well as determining the agenda of the select committee. Further evidence for the equal status of EWC members can be seen in the consensual approach to making decisions in the full EWC. Situations are avoided in which ballots might produce losers. This hesitancy can also be seen in the distribution of seats, where German plants are underrepresented.

The dominance of the German representatives, which is a product of the multiple offices held by the EWC chair and the central interface represented by the secretariat in relation to the European corporate headquarters, only seems to be a latent one. Moreover, it is said that they typically do not take advantage of their position. For this reason the Ford EWC can be categorised as 'somewhat decentralised' in terms of the distribution of power.

The EWC also exhibits a number of decentralised aspects in terms of its own culture. In contrast to the French automotive companies, the number of seats for each country does not reflect local union pluralism. The decisive criterion for the allocation of seats is the number of employees in each country, with no account taken of the special circumstances of national structures of employee representation. National trade unions determine the selection criteria and processes for representatives. For example, whereas French unions agreed that the secretary of the works council of the transmission plant in Bordeaux should attend the EWC for his entire period of office, Spanish representatives have a rotation procedure. The Spanish seat on the select committee is alternately held for a period of two years by the UGT and the CC.OO, the two largest unions at the Valencia plant (FE07).

The way in which the EWC deals with national languages is also clearly decentralised. Although English, the language of the parent company, is used as a working language on many issues within the EWC, good English is not a precondition for membership. Attempts to hold meetings exclusively in English have not proved successful, and this even led to problems with communication within the select committee (FE02). For this reason EWC members and European management agreed to use simultaneous interpreters. Moreover, all relevant written documentation, such as discussion dossiers, minutes and agreements are translated into each of the seven languages. One manager from Ford of Europe described the situation in the following terms.

> It's a bit like Brussels, we don't have a meeting language at EWC. We don't say that everybody should speak English. The only rule is you speak whatever you feel most comfortable with. If you are Belgian, you can speak Flemish, if you are Spanish, you can speak Spanish and then it's our job to provide the interpreters to translate so that you can hear and contribute (FM01).

As such the cultural dimension of the Ford EWC can be characterised as comparatively decentralised.

One issue of central importance for the work of any EWC is access to information and the distribution of knowledge within the forum. Ford EWC members receive information on any proposed changes of cross-border relevance in a number of ways – both through local plant management and the EWC chair in Cologne who, because of his position in connection on the works council, has privileged access to the most up-to-date information.

National employee representatives exchange and cross-check information mainly by sending it to the EWC secretariat. Since direct exchange is often not possible due to language barriers, the secretariat has the task of accumulating the information, compiling it and ensuring that it is forwarded to EWC members as swiftly as possible. Prior to EWC and select committee meetings, the secretariat, for example, compiles and assesses information for the issues on the agenda and sends this to all members.

> Descriptions of what's happening in the group, what issues there are, what direction the strategy of the company is heading in, what effects might this have. [...] They [the EWC members] get everything in writing or in electronic form beforehand, and can make a start while they're still at home. There are numbers that we work up for them, and contexts, that no one will probably look at before [...] Often they do not have the administrative support to pull things together and put them in a form so that everyone can understand (FE01).

Finally, all EWC members receive minutes of select committee meetings, which is intended to ensure that members in the inner circle are not privileged in terms of access to information.

Overall the secretariat's active role in distributing and compiling information seems to offset to some degree the gap between the knowledge of ordinary EWC members and the EWC centre that is a product of the latter's access to the corporate hierarchy. The EWC centre makes conscious effort to ensure that there is an intensive flow of information to avoid a monopoly of knowledge at the corporate headquarters. This suggests that the distribution of knowledge should be designated as 'somewhat decentralised'.

10.2.3 Coordination of EWC activities

In order to assess the strength or intensity of the coordination of activity within the EWC we examine the special features of EWC and select committee meetings and communication and interaction between official meetings.

Usually there are two internal EWC meetings and, since the most recent change in the constitution, two meetings of the select committee each year. Before that there were four select committee meetings. The first EWC meeting, usually in the spring, takes place before the EWC meeting with management. In this case the internal meeting mainly has a preparatory function: EWC members submit country reports, cross check and bring themselves up-to-date in terms of information, and develop a joint position for the meeting with management on the following day. The EWC management meeting itself follows a standardised procedure of information and consultation in line with the agenda previously agreed between the parties. In contrast, the second meeting in the autumn is purely an internal meeting and is not followed by a meeting with management. Meetings always take place in Cologne and are prepared by the EWC chair in collaboration with the secretariat. Events have only taken place outside Cologne in the context of two training sessions that were held in Brussels.

There have been frequent extraordinary meetings over the history of the EWC, both of the plenary session (internally and with management) as well as of the select committee. Figure 17 sets out the number of annual meetings of both bodies and illustrates that the frequency of meetings is closely related to restructuring measures implemented over the past decade. For example, during the separation of Visteon in 1999–2000 there were twice as many EWC meetings as planned and almost two and a half times more select committee meetings.

Figure 17: Meetings of the Ford EWC and Select Committee, 1996–2009.

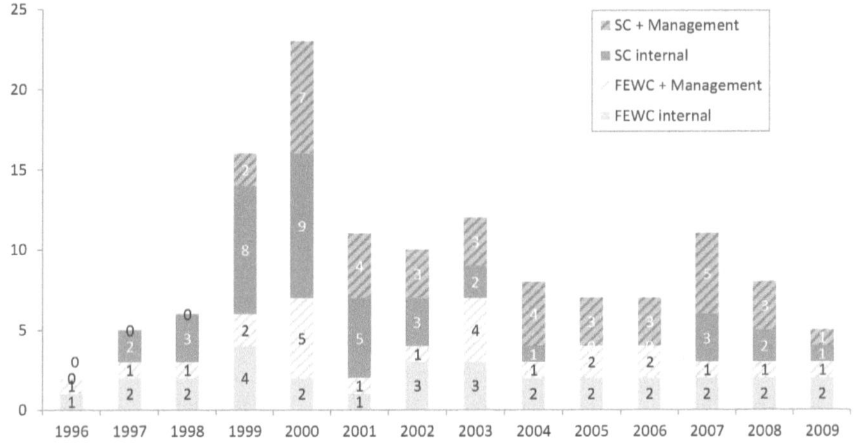

Source: Ford EWC.

In principle any EWC member can call for an extraordinary meeting of the EWC or select committee. However, in the final analysis, the EWC chair and his deputy determine whether the topic can be dealt with in the context of a routine meeting or whether an extraordinary meeting is needed (FE03).

There are no working parties or groups within the EWC dealing with particular topics, as with some other EWCs. However, once the select committee has become engaged in discussions and negotiations with management, and depending on the topic, specialist expert employee representatives from any affected operations can be brought into the negotiations, even if the country concerned is not formally represented on the select committee.

> If a topic is to be given special treatment and there are meetings of the select committee, additional colleagues are invited from this area. If they are not members of the select committee, then they come along as 'extras'. It can happen that a lot of meetings take place in small special groups to work on a topic. This happens, but there aren't standing committees as we have with the [German] central works council (FE02).

For example, representatives of the development operations played a major role in preparations for the position of the EWC in negotiations over the Dunton-Merkenich realignment project. This procedure was seen as effective by the head of the EWC and also supported by management.

> Management does not have a problem with this as, if there is a meeting with the head of development for Ford of Europe, he'd rather discuss with someone who knows what he's talking about, than with someone who has to keep asking (FE02).

The secretariat in Cologne plays a central role both in substantive preparations for EWC and select committee meetings as well as for ensuring that the outcomes are recorded. They control the entire administrative and substantive work of the EWC. As a rule, minutes and the outcomes of internal meetings are made available rapidly as the secretariat 'organises informal translations between meetings' (FE04). The central role of the secretariat in maintaining communication within the Ford EWC is due solely to language barriers. Because of his highly-developed foreign language skills, the secretary can communicate with virtually all EWC members in their own national language, whereas direct communication between members can be difficult. As a rule, EWC members contact the secretariat if they want to distribute information or contact EWC members from other countries. As such, the secretary has a mediating role between the EWC chair and EWC members.

> We all work with the secretary who provides us with information from other countries because of language barriers. He translates written material, and will also be called when needed between EWC meetings, and will call the corresponding member in the other countries and distributes information by e-mail (FE04).

> We can do it directly or we can contact the secretary and he distributes it among the rest. He is the go-between, he is the secretary. Sometimes when we have concerns we ask him to speak to Dieter [the EWC Chair] (FE03).

The frequency of contact between the secretary and individual EWC meetings does not follow any pre-given pattern. Rather it depends on the specific situation at individual plants and the problems that are seen as relevant for the EWC, as which the secretary reports.

> If people have problems they'll mail or, if something has happened, they'll make a report. It's very variable. There are some colleagues that I talk with twice a week. And there are some I'll talk with perhaps once every three months. [...] It depends on the individual, and their positions, and their problems [...] When they get in touch, or when I get in touch, depends very much on the situation.

Aside from language barriers, national differences in employee representation structures also make it difficult to sustain links between EWC members. As is the case with other EWCs, continuity of relationships between EWC members can be interrupted by varying electoral cycles in different countries. The appointment of new representatives into the EWC is not synchronised and this makes it difficult to maintain existing contacts.

> I stayed on the EWC for four years, and another colleague did this before me. In England there is a change because they have elected new members. The same applies for

Germany. Each country elects its representatives in line with their own procedures. In our case we elect the representative for the EWC every two years (FE04).

This means that horizontal links between EWC members remain weak. We only have indications of regular direct contacts for representatives of the plants at Saarlouis, Genk and Bordeaux as well as between Cologne and some British plants. This suggests that in addition to a common language, spatial proximity and mutual understanding of national employee representation cultures is a significant factor in establishing networks between EWC members.

Despite these limitations, the Ford EWC is one of the most strongly coordinated bodies in our sample.

10.2.4 Critical events and EWC outputs

The Ford EWC could be said to have been very successful, measured against the yardstick of the sheer number of agreements concluded. In all, eleven agreements have been concluded with Ford of Europe management, along with a number of official declarations issued unilaterally by the EWC. Although each of these agreements has not always involved entirely new negotiating material, as the total includes the original and revised installation agreement as well as two freshly negotiated supplementary agreements, there is a notably high level of negotiating activity. The conclusion of the pioneering agreement on the separation of the parts division not only meant that the Ford EWC was in the vanguard in quantitative terms but also substantively. The 'Agreement Governing the Separation of the Ford Visteon Organisation', signed on 25 January 2000, was the first agreement concluded by an EWC in the car industry. That is, within four years of the transposition of the Directive, the Ford EWC, as a de facto negotiating partner, had developed attributes that went considerably beyond both the spirit of the installation agreement and the EWC Directive itself.

Initially the picture was very different, however. In the first three years after its constitution, the Ford EWC functioned purely as an information body, and moreover one that was not seen as being especially important either by its own members or by management. The opportunity to enter into substantive negotiations with European management arose because of the planned divestment of the components division into a new company, Visteon. Globally this involved 78,000 employees: 52,000 of these were in the USA and 19,800 in Europe, of which 4,000 were in German plants (Klebe and Roth, 2000: 752).

Following the creeping implementation of the process of separation from 1997, the topic was raised a number of times at EWC meetings (FE07) and employee representatives succeeded in developing a common strategic position once the separation plans had been officially announced. This was laid out in an internal communiqué signed by all EWC members entitled 'Declaration of Mutual Solidarity', on 10 May 1999. This document also formally transferred the negotiating mandate for dealing with the European-wide separation of Ford's parts operation to the EWC.

Ford European management had also indicated its willingness to come to a single European solution with the EWC, given the highly complex prospect of parallel national negotiations. The advantages of this strategy were summed up by one manager as follows.

> Issues affected a number of countries and there was just no way we would progress them by negotiating nationally and parallel. It would just because you do this sequentially, well who goes first. Nobody wants to go first or last. If you are trying to do it in parallel, you just end with three of four different agreements. Where does that take us? (FM01).

Based on the scale of the restructuring, the EWC chair initially aimed for a single solution for the American and European plants – also gaining from the negotiating power of the US American car workers union UAW. In order to agree a common procedure in the group as a whole, in July 1999 a meeting of the Ford EWC took place between employee representatives from all Visteon plants affected by the divestment and Ron Gattlefinger, then vice president and now president of the UAW. This meeting was able to establish common strategic aims as well as a commitment to inform each side about the progress of negotiations. However, since Ford management categorically refused to negotiate on a global solution – partly because of the different legal provisions in the USA and Europe (Hebauf, 2000) – employee representatives agreed that the UAW should seek to achieve a model solution during its collective bargaining round with the company (Klebe and Roth, 2000: 752). In autumn 1999 the UAW did in fact succeed in concluding a collective agreement with US American Ford management that guaranteed a complete preservation of terms and conditions for the whole workforce, with employees transferred to Visteon continuing to be formally Ford employees (Klebe and Roth, 2000: 752). However, this agreement only applied to hourly-paid workers and not white-collar staff, which were not represented by the UAW.

Finally in December 1999, and after protracted negotiations, a different solution was reached for Europe. In contrast to the USA, this transferred all employees, hourly-paid and salaried, into the new company. However, there was an unlimited guarantee to preserve terms and conditions such as pay, benefits and pension rights.[250] All collective agreements would continue to apply and Visteon would also establish its own independent EWC. The economic survival of the divested part of the company was to be assured through a parts supply guarantee for two product cycles (nine to ten years).[251] In addition, it was agreed that the continued

250 For a detailed description of the outcome, see Klebe and Roth, 2000: 752f; on the negotiating strategy, see Hebauf, 2000.

251 The agreement contained detailed sourcing provisions, broken down into specific numbers of component batches for individual plants. Ford committed itself initially to purchase on a cost covering basis. However, over the longer term, Visteon was to produce at prevailing market prices.

formal employment of divested employees at Ford would represent the baseline for any future divestments and joint ventures, and would only be departed from with the mutual agreement of European management and the EWC. As such, the agreement looked beyond the Visteon case in that it indicated the path for future negotiations. The formal agreement was concluded on 25 January 2000 and signed by group management, the European management of Visteon and the Ford EWC and employee representatives of European Visteon plants. It was subsequently adapted to national legal conditions and therefore became enforceable in Germany, the UK, France, Belgium, Portugal and Spain (Rehfeldt, 2004: 8). A joint working group of EWC members and management was established to monitor compliance. Once it was established that it was possible to achieve negotiated solutions for such separations could be applied throughout Ford of Europe, management subsequently stated that it would also be willing to engage in talks over the proposed divestment of transmission manufacture (Ford of Europe/FEWC, 2006: 15). In October 2000 negotiations on the method for establishing the Getrag joint venture were successfully concluded. In this case, the EWC was able to achieve its aim of avoiding a formal transfer of undertaking, as had happened with the Visteon negotiations. The 'agreement governing the transfer of the Ford manual transmission activities into a joint venture' established that all employees affected by the divestment would continue to have a contract of employment with Ford.[252] In addition Ford of Europe also committed itself to undertake investments in new technologies in the GFT plants as well as to a long-term purchase agreement of GFT transmissions. The GFT agreement affected 3,800 employees in Bordeaux and Halewood and 1,850 in Cologne (Klebe and Roth, 2000: 753).

Two further agreements were concluded between the Ford EWC and Ford of Europe in subsequent years: one of these, on 7 June 2002 was an additional agreement for GFT and there was a further agreement for Visteon on 28 April 2003. In both cases the topic was a new provision on sourcing commitments, although under very different conditions. Whereas the joint venture with Getrag was successful and the issue was simply one of adapting the agreement to take account of the integration of Volvo's transmission manufacturing operations, the new provisions at Visteon were agreed under less auspicious circumstances. A new agreement was necessary as it hasd become evident that Ford's original commitments for a certain level of purchasing could not be sustained in practice.[253] An increase in the volume of orders to independent suppliers was justified by the fact that Visteon was unable to deliver the agreed phased price cuts. The new agreement released Ford from these quite onerous commitments and all purchasing agreements were made subject to competitive pricing (FE06). At the same time, an efficiency plan

252 That is, the standard provision for future separations envisaged in the Visteon agreement.

253 Breaches of the detailed purchase plans were reported to the EWC secretariat. The rising number of such reports meant that the EWC had to take urgent action.

was developed for each Visteon plant in order to raise its prospects for winning orders. As such the new agreement was subject to the overall cost-cutting strategy developed by management for loss-making Visteon plants. The protective shield for Visteon employees in the original agreement therefore became largely ineffective.

> The agreement, called Plan for Growth, contained a list of products in various plants, either to be expanded or eliminated, depending on the assessment of Ford and Visteon managers for future market share gains. In Germany, the agreements included redundancies, the elimination of over-tariff payments for any future workers, a wide range of outsourcing measures to bring workers into plants under cheaper collective agreements, and the creation of a 'transfer corporation' to help redundant workers find new jobs (Greer and Hauptmeier, 2007: 8).

Finally, Visteon proved to be economically unsuccessful. The limited scope for cost reductions that followed from the commitments on terms and conditions paired with the difficulties in acquiring non-Ford orders forced Visteon to undertake further adjustments within a short period. This led to a cost-cutting programme culminating in further outsourcing, redundancies, and a serious deterioration in terms and conditions for newly-hired workers.[254]

A further agreement on a divestment project in the customs operations area, which affected comparatively few employees, was concluded on 2 December 2002. In this 'agreement governing the transfer of the European Ford customs operations to Vastera' it was established that in the event of the economic failure of the transaction all transferred workers would be taken back by Ford.

Finally, there are three other European agreements in which, in a similar way, the consequences of reorganisation programmes have been regulated for employees on a cross-country basis. The context was the reorganisation of product development across brands to avoid parallel operations. The first agreement 'the framework agreement on the introduction and implementation of the international operations synergies project' was concluded on 16 November 2004 in which EWC and European management agreed that there would be no job cuts as a consequence of the IOS project. Any employees who were no longer required were to be trained for new tasks and any capital released was to be made available for developing new products. Two further agreements provided for a broadly similar outcome: the 'Framework Agreement on the Dunton Merkenich Realignment Project' (18 January 2005), which regulated the consequences of the new allocation of tasks between the two European development centres, and the 2008 agreement on the global product development strategy.

In a further agreement, signed on 4 December 2003, the Ford EWC and the management of Ford of Europe agreed to anchor the fundamental rights of employees

254 In the UK this culminated in the closure of all Visteon plants. In Germany, an agreement was concluded to rationalise the business, with major concessions for employees. A number of plants were also sold.

and duties of the company at all European plants. A similar European wide code of conduct had been agreed at GME one year before. In addition to ILO core labour standards, the company also agreed to engage in constructive cooperation with employee representatives at national and European level. Moreover, Ford acknowledged its duties in terms of employee training, health and safety, and environmental protection (Ford of Europe/FEWC, 2006: 16). Suppliers would also be supported in coming to similar provisions. Compliance with the principles was to be checked at the annual EWC management meetings. There were also efforts to extend the substance of the agreement to the entire Ford group.

The de facto negotiating mandate acquired by the Ford EWC following the precedent set during the separation of Visteon was subsequently formalised in the 'Memorandum of Understanding' agreed on 9 October 2000, which provided for the right of the EWC to negotiate with Ford of Europe in the case of cross-border problems. However, this expressly presupposed the willingness of management to negotiate on any given issue. If agreement is reached that negotiations should take place, the procedure is as follows (Ford of Europe/Ford European Works Council, 2006: 12).

1. National bodies for employee representation authorise the EWC to begin negotiations with management by temporarily transferring negotiating authority to the forum.
2. The Select Committee leads negotiations on behalf of EWC members, and keeps them up-to-date with the state of negotiations.
3. If there is agreement within the EWC as to the outcome concluded with management, EWC members will show this through signing the European agreement. Local representatives are then bound by this agreement.
4. In order to implement the agreement, national enforceable provisions are then concluded at national level on the basis of the European agreement and in line with local legislation.

The 'negotiating mechanism' set out in the 'Memorandum of Understanding' was incorporated into the main agreement when the EWC installation agreement was revised in 2008. The substantive scope of the EWC was also extended. In addition business and economic issues,[255] the EWC's remit was widened to include health and safety, and training – provided management had indicated its willingness for these to be regulated through a European-level agreement.[256] As a consequence, the new agreement not only goes some way beyond the EWC Directive's subsidiary

255 The previous agreement basically encompassed the economic situation and employment, changes in work or corporate organisation, together with mergers, divestments and plant closures, and collective redundancies.

256 In relation to the original EWC agreement, the following additional issue were included: health and safety at work, environmental protection, training and development, and discrimination and equal opportunities.

requirements by providing for a negotiating mandate (even if offset by a potential management veto in individual cases), but also because of the substantive issues it can negotiate on. Overall, the outputs of the EWC can be ranked as high.

Assessment by employee and management representatives

For the most part, the Ford EWC is seen as significant representative body, both by the EWC members and management representatives interviewed. Each indicated that they had gained from cooperation in the forum. Since its inception, the EWC has become an established element in employment relations at the company.

All EWC members interviewed confirmed that the forum had become a significant, and possibly the most important, source of information on issues related to Ford's corporate strategy, making it more difficult for the company to pit plants against other. Several employee representatives also stressed the role of the EWC as a platform for building cross-border contacts. With the exception of the Spanish representative, who sometimes returned home from meetings in a state of frustration (FM06), EWC members generally seemed very satisfied with the way that the forum had operated.

> I think that it would never occur to the colleagues to say 'Let's break it up, we don't need it any more'. Mainly because, of course, we can take a great deal of information back to our own internal meetings (FE01).

> I just think it makes us stronger, it made the company not playing one against the other. You can see the benefits because if they were propping up Britain or France it would have an effect on the rest of Ford European workers because we are so interlinked. So you needed to have a united front to stop the company from pitting them off and having a chance of making decisions and asking the company to give them information about new models, about health and safety and other relevant issues [...] Yes, [...] I think we are a stronger unit, a united body, and I think it is a good working relationship we got there and I believe it is one of the best EWC anyway (FE03).

While all the employee representatives interviewed confirmed that the forum was effective as a platform for information and consultation, its practical influence on management was judged to be meagre or even insufficient by some EWC members. The Spanish representatives insisted that it was an information body – like all other EWCs they had encountered (FE07); and a French representative took a rather resigned position in view of the sale of the automatic transmission plant in Bordeaux.

> Negotiations yes, but the EWC has more a representative character for European management. It's there to exchange information [...] The EWC does not have enough influence. But that is the same in France. In the French *comité d'entreprise*, one can have a discussion, one can offer an opinion, but one does not have the right to decide, there is no right of veto. There's a lot of talk, but then management decides what it wants (FE04).

Irrespective of how the negotiating power of the EWC is judged, one important and undisputed outcome of its existence and operation is the significant improvement in mutual understanding between employee representatives at different European plants. Both trust and mutual dependence have grown.

> [Mutual understanding of employee representatives] Yes, definitely, we didn't before because we didn't have the EWC. You do now because when you have the meeting you can hear their reports and all reports are similar to the same issues what we have in the UK, it's just the rules and regulations are different in Europe than we have in the UK. We do understand it a lot more than we did because it was always them and us, which is ridiculous (FE03).

> [...] the invention, as it were, of this instrument of European agreement led – I think – to a great deal of change. Firstly, there was the initial phase [...] which we have now definitively got through. People began to learn from each other, to trust each other, and to see that work in the European Works Council can provide some valuable services. Of course, this context leads to quite different types of dependence than before. If you have become a partner through the EWC agreement, then compliance depends on everyone (FE02).

The EWC was also acknowledged by management for its professional way of working. This applied both for exchange with European management, which, despite a number of challenging and conflictual issues, was, it was said, always characterised by a matter-of-fact approach and for the internal process through which employee representatives agreed between themselves. The EWC succeeded in organising an effective and democratic-discursive decision-making style that, in turn, facilitated reaching agreement with management.

> We seem to have almost got the best of everything, really. You know, I think the German team has brought the structure and the discipline of German employee relations to the table. But being able to combine that with everybody feeling that they are represented (FM01).

> They spend a lot of time and they are professional I think behind the scene to have pre-meetings, getting aligned, agreeing on position and then sticking to that position. And if they need more discussion, they will have their discussion and get back together again. I think that's certainly important for them to be successful. But it helps the committee [employee and management representatives] to be successful, too. To that extent I think the European – the fact that it is not totally dominated by Germany – it is probably a good thing. Because it makes everybody feel that it is a fair representation of everybody's interests (FM01).

Management values cooperation with the EWC in the context of European information and consultation. Dialogue with employee representatives, it was said, was marked by trust and openness.

> It's pretty much a transparent process. We tell them pretty much – as much as we know. And again I think that has helped us to build a good relationship because the both sides are recognized (FM01).

> I think the strengths are that from values that support effective, ongoing relationships and partnership between senior union representatives and the European management team (FM04).

The European level of representation was seen to offer management access to resolve international issues as well as an instrument for building understanding with European employee representatives. The EWC was accepted and valued, as long as the prevailing balance between issues to be agreed at national level and those at European level was not shifted.

> I think the second [strength of the EFB] is that it provides the vehicle to efficiency and consistently consulting each agreement on some strategic business change initiatives that impact more than one country. [...] I think in summary we feel we've got a good balance [between national and European level], whereby we don't see the European Works Council as a hindrance [...] in any way. But I think we would if the expectation was that local matters affecting one plant or one country would frequently escalate to the European Works Council (FM04).

Up until the recent revision of the EWC agreement and despite these negotiated agreements, the Ford EWC was seen by European management primarily as an information and consultation body, which would only act beyond this under certain circumstances. Moreover, in the pragmatic assessment of one European-level manager, it was not impossible that management might be willing to negotiate European solutions to deal with future challenges.

> We weren't formally saying that we now recognize the EWC as a negotiating body because we don't. The charter is still: its there for information and consultation.[257] But on those occasions we mutually agreed that the best way for both sides was to reach an agreement at the European level. [...] We certainly did not formally change the European Works Council. It's not a negotiating body, it has no negotiation rights. But I guess in the future by mutual agreement we might do something as well (FM01).

10.3 Provisional assessment

Ford of Europe overwhelmingly exhibits the features of a *transnational* organisation. Of these, the most notable is a decentralised distribution of resources, expressed in particular in capacities in the fields of production, R&D, and to a lesser degree, the cultural autonomy of local operations. In contrast, the distribution of power,

257 This was stated at the time when interviews were conducted in the summer of 2007. In late-2008, the negotiating option was officially incorporated in the agreement.

expressed in the relatively low degree of autonomy of the affiliates, could be designated as 'somewhat centralised'. Strategic decisions are reserved for the European headquarters or, in many cases, require confirmation by the US parent. Strong coordination of the integrated European production system by the European headquarters in Cologne includes, amongst other things, a high level of specialisation between plants and the almost complete absence of parallel production. Instead, Ford in Europe uses a system of lead plants backed up by the highly flexible switch plant in Valencia.

These corporate structures are matched by a strongly coordinated EWC that is also decentralised in terms of the distribution of resources, and, as such, can also be designated as *transnational* in accordance with our definition.

Although the regulatory need on the employee side, which is a product of inter-plant competition caused by the parallel production of identical or substitutable models, is less marked at Ford as compared with GM or Renault, the Ford EWC is, nonetheless, both comparatively active and effective. Because the EWC is a fairly transparent and homogeneous forum, and has access to but is not dominated by a highly professional leadership, it has been able to develop a notably high level of capacity to take action compared with the other EWCs in this study and to establish itself as a recognised partner by management in the regulation of European employment relations. Its relationship to management is characterised by mutual recognition and pragmatic cooperation. With the incorporation of a negotiating mandate into the governing agreement in 2008, the EWC acquired powers that evidently exceed those envisaged by the EWC Directive. The home-country effect is twofold in this area. The fact that the EWC secretariat is located at the (new) European headquarters in Cologne means that the EWC gains from the resources and procedures provided to workplace employee representatives under the German Works Constitution Act, which governs the operation of works councils. Secondly, the fact that the main headquarters for the entire group is located outside Europe favours the establishment of common positions and the generating of solidarity within the forum.

The key event in the history of the EWC was the separation of Visteon in 2000. This offered the EWC a unique opportunity to position itself as a negotiating partner for European-level management, although at this time it was still formally purely an information and consultation body. The fact that it was possible to arrive at a genuinely European solution was due to a number of favourable incidental circumstances. Firstly, the fact that the separation created a single issue for management raised its willingness to engage in a cross-border process; and secondly, for the employee side, it represented a situation in which all European plants with component manufacture were equally affected, a situation which created a high degree of homogeneity of interests as well as the realisation that parallel negotiations for individual plants would probably not have yielded a better outcome. Finally, cooperation between the EWC and UAW encouraged management to look for a negotiated solution.

In addition, the Visteon case also offered scope for a single European framework provision, since this entailed a very different situation to plant closures or the allocation of production to particular sites in which inter-plant competition can play a major role. The divestment of the internal supplier division did not raise any such issues for the final assembly plants represented on the EWC. At most, competition might be expected between the individual Visteon plants, although this was also unlikely, given their high degree of specialisation. Rather, the simultaneity of the collective transfer of sub-divisions of plants under broadly identical conditions created a situation in which competitive conditions would be held constant. Under these circumstances, the operating maxim for the EWC was to 'obtain the most possible for the workforce' (FE05). Since management was keen to complete the project as quickly as possible, and the trade union benchmark of the retention of employees at Ford was already known (and had been agreed shortly before in the UAW agreement concluded in the United States), the parties were able to agree on a European solution.

What is noteworthy is that the agreements at Ford (unlike GM) were concluded without any preceding protest actions. This is certainly in part attributable to the pragmatic stance adopted by Ford management, but also a predisposition on the part of the German Ford works council as well as the EWC to refrain from public conflict. 'In our experience, we have done better with our cooperative approach' (FE02). One other factor is that the EWC had also previously not participated in symbolic solidarity actions organised by the European Metalworkers' Federation (EMF), although there is contact with IG Metall and the EMF through the presence of trade union experts at EWC meetings.

Finally, the nature of the agreements is noticeable for the fact that they predominantly deal with issues raised by divestment. There is no discussion, let alone negotiation, on the allocation of production between plants, as practised at GM for the Delta platform. 'Of course, we had to make sure that everyone could live' (FE04). As a consequence, the EWC chair, in particular, sought direct discussions, which proved successful, with European management for as fair a distribution of production volumes as possible. However, the EWC expressly did not pursue a strategy of pain-sharing, given that the low plant utilisation rates that this implies would not have offered a long-term solution. One consequence would have been that a plant would have had to close anyway, as eventually happened at GM in Antwerp. 'This would have been too much for the EWC. [...] You could say that we were lucky that the English accepted the end of final assembly at Dagenham in 2000. Employees were more concerned to get their redundancy pay than organise protests. This closure cut most of the overcapacity' (FE06).

In addition to effective coordination, the success of the EWC is also possibly one result of the fact that the forum has restricted itself to the 'feasible'. On the other hand, this means that it is unlikely that the negotiating mandate will be extended in the future to embrace influencing decisions over the allocation of models and production volumes, as has been practised in the past at GM.

Chapter 11: General Motors

11.1 The General Motors group (GM)

11.1.1 History and characteristics

From the outset General Motors (GM), established in 1908, adopted a different strategy to that pursued by Ford. For Ford, the main concern was to pursue a high level of product standardisation, expressed in the production of the Model T, also introduced in 1908, and encapsulated in the phrase: 'Any customer can have a car painted any color that he wants so long as it is black' (Ford, 1922: 57). In contrast, General Motors' strategy, subsequently referred to as Sloanism, took a radically different direction. Alfred P. Sloan, president of General Motor from 1923 to 1937, adopted an approach based on continuous product improvement and annual model changes, combined with creating a wide range of cars tailored to different customer groups: 'A car for every purse and purpose' (Sloan, 1963: 438).

The fundamental corporate philosophy was expressed in the structure of the company. Firstly, this entailed the integration of a large number of different marques under the General Motors umbrella; secondly, it involved the early adoption of a targeted strategy of internationalising production operations, including outside North America; and thirdly, it required the development of a matrix structure, with lines of responsibility both by brand and by region. GM was extremely successful in this strategy throughout the twentieth century. From the 1930s up until 2007, GM was largest vehicle manufacturer in the world,[258] with around a dozen different marques and corresponding companies, often with highly regionally-specific production and sales: Buick, Cadillac, Chevrolet, Corvette, GMC, Pontiac, Saturn (all USA); Opel (Germany and Europe); Vauxhall (UK); GM Daewoo (South Korea); Holden (Australia); Hummer (USA and South Africa); and Saab (Sweden). At the start of the 21st century, the GM group had plants in thirty-three countries and national sales and marketing operations in over 200.

Meeting the diverse requirements of a highly differentiated range of products, in terms of marques and vehicle types, at reasonably competitive prices, necessitated the creation of a complex corporate organisation down by level of hierarchy, product division and sales area. This applied in particular to the structuring of company in terms of brands, sales areas, and product groups.

In 1911, only three years after its founding, GM began to market cars and small commercial vehicles in Europe. Manufacturing facilities were opened in Europe during the 1920s (1923 in Denmark; 1925 in Belgium). In addition to building new

258 In 2007, GM produced 9.35 million units produced, the largest in the world in terms of volume. See <http://oica.net/category/production-statistics/2007-statistics> accessed 18 November 2009.

plants, the company's internationalisation strategy also included acquiring other companies: Vauxhall in the UK was bought in 1925, and Opel in Germany in 1929. After the Second World War, GM expanded rapidly in Europe, both by opening new plants as well as acquiring and integrating existing capacity. In 1963 production was begun at Ellesmere Port; in 1967 the Antwerp plant was opened; in 1982 production was started at the new Zaragoza plant, the largest new GM plant outside the US. In the same year, production began at a new engine plant in Aspern (Austria). In 1989, GM bought a 50 per cent stake in Saab and expanded its assembly capacity in Turkey. In 1992 a new plant was opened in Eisenach in the East German region of Thuringia, formerly part of the German Democratic Republic. In 1998, the Gliwice (Poland) plant was opened and the Opel corporate centre in Rüsselsheim was also extensively restructured. In 2000, GM acquired the remaining shares in Saab, and in 2006 the foundation stone for a completely new plant was laid in St. Petersburg, with the plant brought into operation two years later.

Figure 18: GM operations in Europe.

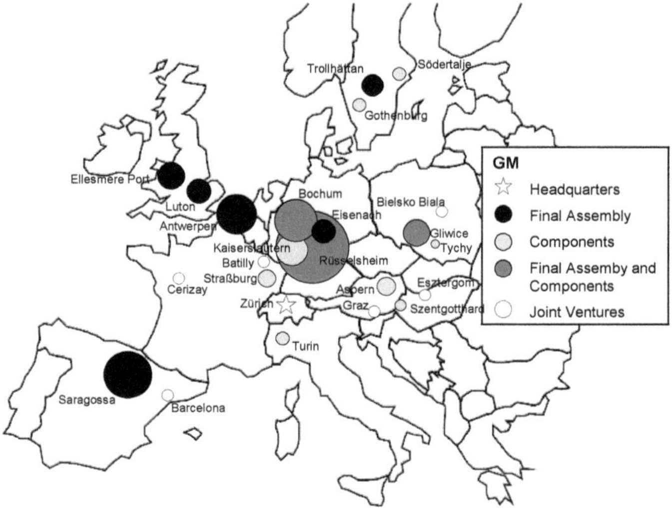

Source: authors, compiled from *GM in Europe. Facts & Figures 2008*; circles are proportionate to employment at each site.

In 2008, GM Europe (GME) had ten full assembly plants as well as transmission and other component plants[259] in eleven countries in Europe, including Russian,

259 For an overview of joint ventures, R&D and sales and marketing activities, see 'GM in Europe. Facts & Figures', published annually.

employing 54,000 workers and producing 1.6 million vehicles. GM has three marques in Europe: Opel/Vauxhall, Saab[260] and Chevrolet (of which some 1,200 were sold in 2008). GM's European manufacturing plants (excluding joint ventures) represent around one-third of its worldwide total. As already noted, GM expanded in Europe from the 1990s with its own assembly and manufacturing operations, principally in Central and Eastern Europe (St. Petersburg in Russia; Gliwice and Warsaw in Poland; plants in Turkey and Hungary).

As with Ford and Chrysler, GM ran into a crisis in the late-1980s that intensified in the 1990s. In Europe, GM was able to sustain or increase production and employment in absolute terms in the 1990s following the implosion of the Eastern bloc. However, profits fell both in Europe and for the group as a whole, and Opel's market share dropped markedly in Germany and Europe from the 1990s from around 20 per cent to 10 per cent. This prompted repeated adjustment and restructuring programmes involving reconfiguring European ownership and management structures (conversion of Adam Opel AG into a GmbH, strengthening of the European headquarters and relocation to Zurich), a policy of divestment and joint ventures (Delphi group, Fiat Powertrain), as well as constructing new manufacturing facilities in Central and Eastern Europe. As a consequence, the development of the EWC at GME – in particular since the late-1990s – needs to be seen in the context of a persistent crisis afflicting the group as a whole and its European operations. No other company in our study has suffered such a fall in sales and output since the 1990s or been subject to such subsequent pressures from rationalisation and workforce reductions.

11.1.2 Distribution of resources, power, culture and knowledge

Compared with other automotive companies in Europe, the corporate structure of GME is comparatively decentralised, in line with the tradition of the group as a whole. For example, there were separate European coordination centres for each of the three marques: Opel (Rüsselsheim), Vauxhall (Luton) and Saab (Trollhättan). In addition, there was a separate sales organisation for Cadillac, Corvette and Hummer based in the Netherlands. Finally, up until 2010, the main GME headquarters was in Zurich.[261] This itself is illustrative of the high degree of horizontal and vertical differentiation of the company and gives some indication of the effort needed to coordinate plants and brands.

260 Saab was sold to Spyker Cars N.V. in 2010.

261 In 2009, there was a separation between European coordination for Opel, which was moved to Rüsselsheim, and Chevrolet, which is concentrated in Glattbruck near Zurich.

Table 10: Distribution of employees, plants and production, General Motors/GM Europe (2008)

	Employees	Plants	Production
World	235,000	45*	8,282,803
EU	53,742	16	1,643,717
EU home country (Germany)	25,103	4	614,491
'Real' home country (USA)	91,000	28*	2,356,576
Largest plant	15,000	–	–
Share EU/world	23%		20%
Share EU home country (Germany)/ EU	47%	25%	37%
Share EU home country (Germany)/ world	11%		7%
Share EU 'real' home country/world	39%		28%
Share largest plant/EU	28%	–	–

Source: compiled by the authors on the basis of GM Annual Report 2008 and OICA (2008).

* final assembly only

As far as the distribution of resources is concerned, in 2008 GME manufactured in eleven countries (including Russia), with some 54,000 employees. Employment in direct vehicle production was concentrated in five countries: Germany, Spain, UK, Poland and Belgium. Of these, Germany, with 25,000 employees (including administration and R&D) accounted for just under a half (47 per cent) of all European employees. Production workers in Germany are spread across four plants: Bochum, Eisenach, Kaiserslautern and Rüsselsheim), each of which is comparable in scale with other European plants.

In 2008, GM sold just over 2 million vehicles (2,039,360) in Europe, of which only 72 per cent were produced in GM plants in Europe, compared with some 90 per cent in 2006.[262] GM's production arrangements in Europe are characterised by a high level of parallel production, with the same model assembled at several plants. This applies in particular to the Astra (Belgium, Germany, the UK and Poland), the Zafira (Germany and Poland), and the Corsa (Germany and Spain). These three models account for the bulk of production within Europe.

262 This major change can mainly be explained by the assembly of GM Chevrolet cars in European plans that were not owned by GM (as in Poland, Russian and the Ukraine).

The pattern of resource distribution in terms of power is no less complex. In contrast to companies with their corporate headquarters in Europe (Daimler, PSA, Renault and Volkswagen), in 2008 GME was characterised by a distinctive European management structure with a European power centre in Zurich, and only limited decision-making powers at plant-level on issues such as investment and hiring. However, the relatively strong position of the Zurich centre is not due to any local concentration of manufacturing or knowledge resources but is a function of its role its the 'bridgehead' to the group's principal headquarters in Detroit, with which it is closely linked.

As far as the pattern of the distribution of culture is concerned, GME can be characterised as 'somewhat decentralised'. Individual marques cultivate and maintain their own identity. There is a fairly low level of circulation of middle managers between countries, allowing local organisational cultures to emerge that contribute to noticeable plant-specific perspectives and inter-plant tension – even within a single country (as between Bochum and Rüsselsheim in Germany). Although there is a single company language in Europe – English – neither the corporate headquarters in Detroit nor the European headquarters in Zurich place any great weight on having a uniform European corporate culture in Europe when compared with a company such as Toyota.

As far as the pattern of the distribution of knowledge is concerned, GME can be designated as 'somewhat decentralised'. In 2008, there were three R&D centres in Europe – corresponding to the three marques: Rüsselsheim (Opel), Luton (Vauxhall) and Trollhättan (Saab). At the same time, manufacturing knowledge was not concentrated exclusively at these locations. The most important centres of manufacturing output and employment in Europe are in Zaragoza and Bochum.

Overall, GME is characterised by a remarkable distribution of resources, power, culture and knowledge that can only be understood in the context of local and national constellations of interests. Whereas production and employment are heavily concentrated in Germany and in the Opel marque, there are also strategically significant plants in Belgium, Poland, Spain and the UK in terms of both employment and production (with the consequence that national governments become rapidly mobilised on occasions). In addition, since the 1990s, the GM group has made great efforts to build up a separate European management layer in Zurich. The concentration of resources in Germany needs to be seen in the context that parts production and final assembly are distributed across four locations (Bochum, Eisenach, Kaiserslautern, Rüsselsheim), each of which can mobilise a substantive influence should threats to these operations emerge (such as a loss of jobs) as each is located in a different constituent region (*Land*) with an elected administration. These specific features are also central to understanding the structural problems confronting GM globally and GME in Europe over the past decade or so. Although the bulk of production, R&D and employment resources are concentrated in Germany, this has not generated a centralised pattern of distribution in Europe, in contrast to almost all the other firms considered in this study.

Given the highly diffuse product range and multiplicity of plants, since the mid-1980s the company has focussed on a strategy of reducing the complexity of coordinating production by spinning off some areas of parts manufacture. For example, in the 1990s all powertrain manufacturing operations were concentrated in a specific set of plants (GM Powertrain) and an attempt was made to manufacture engines jointly with Fiat. Although the large-scale joint venture with Fiat did not prove feasible, GM continued to look for strategic alliances in the area of parts manufacture (such as cooperating with Fiat in engine manufacture in Bielsko, Poland). Overall, production and employment structure in GME are relatively highly decentralised – both in parts manufacture and vehicle assembly.[263]

The strongly Europeanised production profile of GM is also matched by a comparatively highly developed European management structure. Efforts to introduce greater uniformity in product platforms as a basis for several models and a common parts strategy for non-visible vehicle sections were defined at a fairly early stage, given the wide range and price sensitivity of GM models. The organisation of production is based on strategic centralisation, differentiated by product lines and regions, combined with functional decentralisation. The dominant corporate strategy is to maximise the use of common parts to reduce costs and widen the model range to stimulate demand. As such, GM has continued to pursue its long-standing and successful strategy of being a mass producer offering differentiated but standardised products – and as such has not acknowledged changed product and customer requirements in terms of quality, efficiency and emissions that have been evident since the 1990s (see in general Flynn, 1998: 203ff.). Whereas GM in the USA has been hard pressed by Japanese competition since the 1990s, sales in Europe suffered because of perceived problems with quality and the lack of technical innovation demanded by European customers.

11.1.3 Coordination of corporate activities

Since the onset of the crisis in the 1990s, the company has centralised and tightened coordination across the whole group and also at European level. As already noted, this was accompanied by the separation and transfer of specific areas of production and functions in the value chain, and in particular the divestment of Delphi and its establishment as an independent parts supplier, together with strategic cooperation with Fiat and Daewoo. A further wave of group-level restructuring was undertaken from the early-1990s with the introduction of regional management centres for North America, Asia, Latin America and Europe. The establishment of a European group headquarters in Zurich in 1986, which entailed relocating the overall coordination of all of GM's activities from Rüsselsheim to Zurich, was one expression of this. From the 1990s, strategic group level management and control

263 On component manufacture in plants that do not belong to GM, see 'GM in Europe. Facts and Figures 2009'.

was increasingly concentrated in Detroit, limited the scope for genuine autonomy on the part of the new regional management centres over product lines and investment. In essence, they became offices for regionally executing and monitoring plans set in Detroit.

In view of the range of brands and the existence of parallel production in two or three European plants, GME has a particularly high level of need for European-level coordination. One central instrument for this is the systematic organisation of internal inter-plant competition, organised in the form of bids by plants to obtain allocations of new models. Tenders are awarded on the basis of plant-based performance indicators intended to reflect the capability of a location (such as vehicles produced per employee, defects per vehicle, average weekly working hours, absence rates etc.). These production-based benchmarks then serve as the criteria for strategic decisions as well as for coordinating ongoing operations. This benchmarking system also enables a high degree of formalisation and control.

The comparatively strong and effective coordination at European level through inter-plant competition and benchmarking is taken very seriously by all actors – not least because performance indicators are decisive when production volumes are allocated to plants. Strong coordination is underlined by monthly meetings of heads of department (production, purchasing, sales). As such, the formal matrix structure of regional and functional responsibilities, which was developed for GME at European level, is 'lived' in practice through the substantive processes of coordination.

Taken together, the corporate profile of GME exhibits a number of special features that are of considerable significance for understanding how the GM EWC operates. One might even say – as we hope to show below – that the degree of organisational fit between the company structure and the EWC structure is especially marked. GM in Europe has a wide range of marques and models. The company has a relatively high number of production facilities distributed across a fairly large number of countries and locations. This high level of internal differentiation is further enhanced by a strategy of spinning off parts manufacture. Given the fact that the largest volume models are manufactured in parallel at several locations, there is a high need for internal alignment and coordination.

Although the GM European headquarters in Zurich is available to undertake these complex tasks as a governing centre, it is geographically distant both from the actual production facilities and from the real power structures. Strategic decisions and power flow from Detroit; research and development capabilities are located in Rüsselsheim; and operational power embodied in the production process is distributed across a number of countries and plants. GME's coordination centre in Zurich, entrusted with the role of coordinating an extremely complex and decentralised production structure in Europe, is formally and substantively very weak when compared with all other companies in this study, and notably lacks the lacks the loyalty and organisational weight of a powerful manufacturing operation.

11.2 The EWC at GM

11.2.1 Origins of the EWC

The EWC at General Motors Europe was constituted on 16 September 1996 with the formal title of European Economic Forum (EEF), six days before the expiry of the deadline provided for in the 1994 EWC Directive before which forums could be established on a voluntary basis outside the statutory procedure ('Article 13 agreements'): we use the terms EWC and EEF synonymously here. The initiative to establish the EWC came from European employee representatives who had called on GME management to begin immediate talks on setting up an EWC at a meeting organised by the European Metalworkers' Federation (EMF) in 1992 (Eller-Braatz and Klebe, 1998: 445f.; Rott, 2006: 51ff.). However, GME management had refused this request as long as it was not legally required to do so.

The EWC was established under Belgian law: as with the 'French model' this provides for a joint body of employee representatives and management and is chaired by a management representative. The choice of jurisdiction was a deliberate one on the part of the employee representatives.

> We wanted to do this Belgium as the law in individual terms is more favourable than in Germany. For example, under Belgian law it's possible to strike over a plant closure – but not in Germany. That is, we adopted a conscious legal strategic choice during negotiations. We were clear that we wanted Belgian law, but actually argued for German. Then they said, you're Germany, and German codetermination, that's terrible, and they had all these prejudices. And then they put a tick by Belgian law and only noticed later they had messed up (GME01).

Article 9 of the installation agreement listed the following areas for consideration by the EEF: GME's economic and financial situation; production and sales trends; investments; employment situation and trends; plant level productivity and cost trends; planned relocations of production and service areas; introduction of new production technologies; and the introduction of new forms of work organisation. The EEF can intervene on these issues if workers in at least two countries are affected. Under Article 9:2, the forum may not deal with nationally or locally negotiated terms.

11.2.2 Distribution of resources, power, culture and knowledge in the EWC

Under Article 4 of the installation agreement, the EEF has thirty members. At the time of our research, there were, however, only twenty-nine members as one seat was vacant due to the closure of the Azambuja (Portugal) plant.[264] This seat was

264 One member of the employee side from the UK was appointed as 'Chief Officer for Diversity' and switched to the management side.

scheduled to be allocated to a representative from Poland, according to the EEF chair, in order to reflect the increased significance of Central and Eastern Europe. Overall there were six representatives from Germany, four from the UK, three each from Spain and Belgium, two each from France and Austria, and one representative each from Poland, Hungary and the Netherlands.

Following the renegotiation of the EEWF agreement, which took affect from 1 October 2010, additional places were provided for the sales organisations in the Nordic Cluster (Denmark, Ireland, Norway and Finland) and the South East Cluster (Greece and Ireland). The distribution of seats, based on an application of the formula under which the German plants gave up eight seats,[265] was deliberately chosen to allow all EU countries in which there was a GM production operation to be represented on the EEF. 'This was deliberate as we said that we cannot dominate it if we want to deal with each other on equal terms' (GME01). The issue also turned on 'distributed mandates as widely as possible so that information can be spread to all corners of Europe and not just within a small circle' (GME12). The period of office for EEF members is four years.

Figure 19: Distribution of seats on GM EWC, 2008

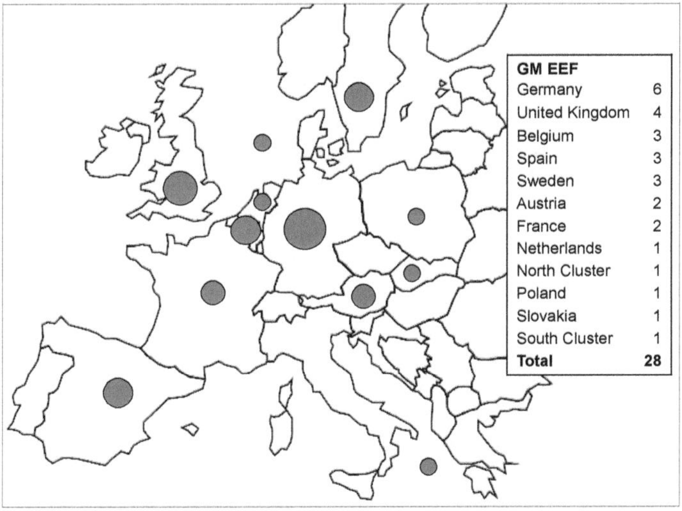

Source: authors' calculation

Employee representatives from Poland and Hungary were admitted as full voting members in 2000, five years before EU enlargement (and hence before the EWC Directive formally applied in Poland) (Kotthoff, 2006b: 7). The EEF chair comes from

265 Under a strict application of the formula, Germany would have 14 seats in all.

the largest location, measured in terms of employees (Rüsselsheim). In general, care has been taken to ensure that countries with several influential trade unions at GME operations can send as many representatives as possible. As with some other EWCs, this principle of pluralist representation has led to a non-proportional composition in terms of employment numbers at plants and nationally.[266]

The location of the EEF chair is also that of the EEF secretary, typically an individual with a social research background,[267] whose task is to support the EEF organisationally and maintain contact with the members of the EEF between meetings. The steering committee, which carries out the work of the forum between plenary meetings, consists of one representative each from Sweden, Spain, Belgium, the UK, Germany (Kaiserslautern), together with the chair of the EEF. As such, the steering committee includes all EU countries with a production facility, aside from Poland – and there is an intention to expand the committee to include a Polish member in the future (GME01).

The choice of representatives from the German plants was not without controversy as the member did not come from Bochum, the second largest in employment terms and largest in terms of vehicle production, but the smaller component plant in Kaiserslautern. This led to representatives from Bochum feeling marginalised, especially as their representative lost in a vote against the Kaiserslautern candidate. Moreover, there is no provision for a rotation of mandates to the steering committee: 'And elections are not held like those for works councils – that is, every four years, [...] but when someone drops out' (GME02: 11).

The distribution of seats in the EEF and steering committee can be characterised as decentralised. The EU home country (Germany) has 21 per cent of the seats. This is a much lower value than other EWCs in our sample, standing just ahead of Toyota (17 per cent) and behind Ford (28 per cent). In addition, the German employee representatives relinquished seats in order to include representatives from all countries, operations and to accommodate union pluralism in information, consultation and decision-making processes. The EWC representativeness index[268] is 0.44, the third lowest after Honda (0.29) and Daimler (0.44). Inequality in the distribution of seats to the advantage of non-German representatives is also fairly marked. The EWCs at Ford (0.58), VW (0.53) and Toyota (0.63) have higher values.

GME covers the costs of approved meetings, together with expenses for time-off and travel. The company also finances language training for members of the EEF: for example, one-week courses were held in 2006 and 2007. EEF meetings are held in English with simultaneous interpretation into Polish, Hungarian, Spanish,

266 For the Spanish delegates, care was taken to ensure that the three major unions (UGT, CC.OO and CGT) each had a representative on the forum (GME04). In the case of France, it was also ensured that the two largest unions were represented.

267 A number of full-time functions in employee representation in larger companies in Germany are frequently exercised by graduates in social science or industrial relations, often with a research background in the industry in which they work.

268 On the calculation of the index, see Chapter 3.3.1.

Portuguese, German, French and Italian. Minutes are made available in all these languages. Costs of interpretation and translation are borne by the company.[269]

The EFF can also drawn on external experts for advice to prepare their own resolutions and evaluate management proposals. This not only entails trade union advisers from the EMF and IG Metall but also consulting firms engaged by the company on application from the EWC.

> If we ask for [experts], then we get them. In the case of the Azambuja plant and Delta Management Engineers – these were globally operating consultants, very professional people who mainly advise the capital side [...]. We got them and they're not cheap. They had to pay for that for us, and that was that and there was no discussion (GME01).

The chair occupies a very strong position within the EEF position for several reasons. As chair of the Rüsselsheim works council, and the central and group works councils in Germany at the time of our research, this individual represented around half of all the company's employees in Europe. As a member of all these bodies and membership of the Opel supervisory board, the chair had early access to comprehensive information with extensive scope for influence. In addition, he was provided with high quality resources in terms of staff and equipment, and had very good links to IG Metall, the largest metalworkers' trade union in Europe.

The EWC secretary is located in Rüsselsheim along with the EEF chair. This individual is not only responsible for administering the body but also acts as a gatekeeper between the EEF and steering committee and the wider EEF membership. A very large proportion of the communication with and between EWC members runs through him. 'Information comes from [the secretary] and is distributed throughout Europe' (GME07). 'Virtually all communication is centralised here at the [chair's and secretary's office] because all of that runs through them' (GME05).

There is usually direct communication between members of the steering committee. According to EEF members, the agenda for meetings is determined by the chair together with the secretary and GME HR manager. This can be expanded by members of the steering committee or EEF.

> Well, I have got no doubts in theory, everyone knows what is going on, Klaus Franz is well-informed because of his position, because of the laws you have here in Germany, the ability to know things. And the HRM guy and he get together and decide what should be on the agenda, and then we get the opportunity to put items on the agenda as well (GME08).

There were a number of differing views about the way in which strategies were determined within the EEF. Whereas some EWC members saw the development of strategy as a discursive process that involved the whole EEF, others considered that

269 The EMF has established its own blog for GME that is maintained by the EEF secretary and also serves as a basis for an intensive network of communication.

the EEF centre exercised disproportionate influence. 'That is decided in Rüsselsheim, that takes place exclusively in Rüsselsheim' (GME03).

Overall, the distribution of power within the GM EWC can be characterised as 'somewhat centralised'. Some steps taken by the company have mitigated this to some degree. For example, moving the European HQ from Rüsselsheim to Zurich created a situation in which no plant was privileged, with all plants having a similar degree of access to the European centre. GME's integrated European management structure also facilitated interaction at the same level – that is, European – as the EWC and brought about a *perception* that all plants were equal in relation to Zurich, However, the EWC's structures (such as a strong chair anchored in German codetermination and the sheer scale of Rüsselsheim) continue to promote a somewhat centralised structure of power and influence.[270]

The main competences of the steering committee are to prepare for meetings and manage ongoing EWC business. The steering committee is the first point of contact for management at European level and discussions with European management usually take place between the steering committee and European group headquarters (GME01). Those members of the steering committee that we interviewed noted that decisions are taken democratically, but as yet there has been no need for a formal ballot.

> We have never had a formal vote; in fact, there has never been a ballot. We have just tried to discuss matters for as long as possible (GME01).

> Resolutions are usually reached in the EEF with 100 per cent consensus. That is important too. At that level you can't just leave yourself open and say that we've had a ballot for or against. You have to find a solution that includes everyone, and that it was we did when we made our solidarity commitments (GME03)

Despite differing union traditions, there is a high level of agreement about negotiating strategies and outcomes. The inclusion of all production locations (with the exception of Gliwice) in the steering committee ensures a relatively equal participation by all locations and countries within the EEF.

> It is very rarely that we get to the vote; we talk through things, we get some form of consensus, the chair is very good, very effective. It is unusual to have major disagreements in the group. Obviously, when the Delta bidding process was going on, that was awful, but it was successful, no plant closures. It is very rarely that we get to a formal vote. In fact, I think, every now and then we agree to have mass meetings or days of action and everybody would agree to it. I am not sure how democratic it would be if we took a vote it wouldn't bind us in the UK anyway (GME08).

---

270 The resource provisions also support this relative centralism. The time spent by the chair and their deputy for EEF activities accounts for 50–80 per cent of their working time, depending on need (Kotthoff, 2006a: 32). This represents a major diffference to other EWCs, in which the amount of time spent on European matters is considerably lower.

As far as the culture of the EEF is concerned, no one country tradition is dominant. However, this was not always the case, as the EEF chair Klaus Franz set out in a newspaper interview:

> The German model of codetermination offers a number of advantages, especially as far as the long-term nature and depth of information is concerned. In the late-1990s, we made the mistake of formally overwhelming employee representatives from other countries with this and concentrated the then plant security agreement [*Standortvertrag*] on Germany. [...] This threw up unnecessary barriers between EWC members and the German colleagues came over as know-alls.[271]

Nonetheless, representatives from other operations still continue to perceive a 'German codetermination advantage', mainly through the strength of IG Metall within the EEF.

> One should not underestimate the advantage that Germany has when it comes to one plant, one trade union – that really counts. That can make it really difficult for other plants (GME03).

IG Metall exercises a relatively strong influence over the EEF. Traditionally, it appoints the EMF coordinator that supports the EWC and, as such, attends every meeting. In other countries, pluralistic union structures are drawn into the EEF. For example, there is one representative for each of the main unions at the company's operations in Belgium and Spain. The three GME marques – Opel, Vauxhall and Saab – also contribute to the more decentralised culture within the EEF. Overall, there is high degree of differentiation of EEF members by brand, country and political-confessional union.

The EEF operates in English, which is spoken by all the members of the steering committee – a fact of considerable significance for communication between members. According to one EEF member, around 80 per cent of communication takes place in English (GME04).

There are some indicators that point to a common culture, in terms of expectations, behavioural norms and other cultural elements. As far as the culture of cooperation within the EWC is concerned, the chair of the forum summarised the rules for close cooperation with the members of steering committee in the following terms in an interview:

> We have an established set of principles. In short these are: openness, honesty and transparency, and persuasive and authentic communication. We have to keep to these principles in order to be able to find a cultural common ground. This creates trust between the EWC members, but requires hard work and took between five and eight years.[272]

---

271 ' "Unsere Strategie hat sich ausgezahlt": Opel-Betriebsrat Franz über die Zusammenarbeit in der Europäischen Arbeitnehmervertretung von General Motors', *Frankfurter Rundschau*, 30 March 2005, p. 10.

272 *Frankfurter Rundschau*, ibid.

These principles, which can be seen as the foundation for internal coordination and which subsequently were also expressed in the EEF's strategy, were also shared by other EEF members.

> Cooperation, collaboration – for us that means at the moment that we exchange with each others, build trust, talk with each other, cut through boundaries, and get to know each other. [...] The second step is that we try to develop some common ground, such as that a collective regulation should not be undercut be a statutory provision. That is, to set certain standards that will certainly be had to deal with in practice as each plant as its own agreed regulations and legal provisions. But it is also important that at some stage we find some common ground (GME13).

As already noted, the members of Opel's supervisory board have the advantage that they get early access to important company information when compared with non-German employee representatives. The same applied for EEF members who are on works councils at German plants. The institutional rights granted by German law on works councils[273] means that the level of information, but also skill, is very high for these German EEF members. In this respect, there is a certain structural asymmetry in the distribution of knowledge – as applies in other companies in this study. There are a number of different views about the distribution of information within the EEF on the forum's strategies. While one group emphasises the rapid and comprehensive information by the steering committee and EEF secretary, other EEF members thought that were shortcomings in this area in terms of forwarding information from the steering committee: 'There are minutes, but they are not sent here. If so, then we only get this information after a delay' (GME03).

The creation of the EEF economic committee in 2005 lead to a more decentralised distribution of knowledge within the EEF about management planning.

11.2.3 Coordination of EWC activities

The EEF is strongly networked both vertically and horizontally and relatively strongly coordinated in terms of internal processes: there are also close inter-organisational relationships between the EEF and EMF. The large number of agreements it has concluded also means that there is intensive contact with management. At the intra-organisational level there is a close network of relationships between the EEF and the Delta Working Group (see below), the economic committee, and the manufacturing committee (see below). In the vertical dimension, the EEF is also strongly integrated in the national interest representation bodies and national trade unions.

273 The Works Constitution Act (*Betriebsverfassungsgesetz*).

The EEF relationship network has grown up historically and is in large measure an outcome of the actors' strategies. Following an internal crisis over a plant retention agreement ('Site Pact II')[274] in which German plants were able to obtain guarantees about maintaining operations but at the expense of other GM plants in Europe, cooperation within the EEF sank to a low point (GME01). This situation only began to change once the former EEF chair, Rudi Müller, retired and was replaced by Klaus Franz, who emphasised the need to rebuild trust within the EEF.

> This European Form was very much expanded and intensified by Klaus Franz. It was not taken as seriously before that (GME11).

Under Article 7 of the installation agreement, the EEF meets once a year. The manufacturing committee and the steering committee also meet once a year. Conflicts over plant closures led to a number of extraordinary meetings of both the EEF and steering committee. However, not all meetings requested have been granted by management. The costs for these meetings were then borne either by the EMF or national trade unions. EEF extraordinary meetings are usually initiated by the steering committee, but every EEF member may request a meeting.

The EEF chair and deputy telephone each other almost daily, with members of the steering committee kept up-to-date mainly by e-mail.

> If there is something going on, if there is an issue we have our telephone numbers and we have the E-mail addresses. And [the secretary] informs us on a regular basis because he makes it his business and we have the GM blog. Fairly often we communicate via [the secretary] and Klaus and the Vice-chair, if there is a need and an issue going on. And every now and then one of the others asks for some information or we'll ask them what is going on, is that true, the rumour? It is easier now we have made the contacts. Years ago, you heard the rumours: is it the truth? And now you can pick up the phone. [...] if we got a question, we send them an E-mail. They always answer and we do the same (GME08).

The communication structure within the steering committee can be characterised as decentralised and networked, but with radial communication by the wider EEF membership. EEF members are mainly kept informed by the EEF secretary.

The EEF has three working groups. The economic committee was established in an agreement with management in 2005 and ensures that all EEF members are provided with extensive information. In terms of its powers and scope, it is comparable with economic committees constituted under the German

274 For an outline, see Schulten et. al (2002) <http://www.eurofound.europa.eu/areas/industrialrelations/pecs/pdf/french/pecs_adam_opel_ag.pdf> accessed 30 April 2012.

Works Constitution Act[275] and receives information mainly on GME's business situation.[276]

> We achieved an amendment to the European Directive with General Motors on a voluntary basis, an agreement, a voluntary agreement, a so-called European Economy Committee. [...] The topics for this economic committee are defined. It's clear defined, information and consultation have to take place at a time before management has made a decision, and the ideas, opinions, calculations of employee representatives have to be included in this decision – that's good stuff (GME01).

The second body in addition to the steering committee is the manufacturing committee, in which employee representatives from production operations meet annually to discuss their specific concerns. The third forum is the Delta Working Group, in which employee representatives from the five plants assembling vehicles based on the Delta platform (Astra and Zafira) meet (see also the next section).

11.2.4 Critical events in the history of the EWC and its representative effectiveness

There is a large research literature on the history of the GME EWC, with a wide range of assessments of the EEF's role. Whereas the adversarial relationship between management and employee representatives and the wide scale of pan-European actions that it has organised have led some researchers to view the EEF as the most advanced example of an real negotiating body with a new quality of employee countervailing power at European level (Kotthoff, 2006b; Greer and Hauptmeier, 2007), others have arrived at a more sober assessment of the structures and development of the EEF and located this in the context of the particular economic and organisational features of GME (Eller-Braatz and Klebe, 1998; Hertwig et al., 2008; Pries, 2004; Rott, 2006).

The EEF developed in a context in which national strategies of employee representation had failed and in the circumstances of the stringent rationalisation and restructuring pursued by European GM management from the late-1990s. This course can best be denoted as a 'path-dependent learning curve' for both the EEF and GME management.

275 The German Works Constitution Act (Section 106) provides for the establishment of an 'economic committee' in companies by works councils for information and consultation on the business situation of the company and the implications for staff planning. Information should cover: economic and financial state of the business; production and investment; rationalisation; operating methods; cuts or closures, transfer or relocation of operations; mergers or divestitures; other 'circumstances and projects that may materially affect the interests of employees'.

276 In the EWC literature there has been no previous instance in which the information on which the EWC can operate has been extensively regulated on a voluntary basis.

Although the installation agreement requires EEF members not only to represent employees from their own operation but all employees in the country in which the operation is located, it seemed almost impossible to establish pluri-local solidarity during the initial years of the EEF's existence, when questions of allocating production capacity fed mistrust and mutual estrangement. For example, the German 'Site Pact II' in 1998 was negotiated without informing or involving other EEF members. However, the positive outcome of this agreement for the German plants (Kaiserslautern and Bochum) came at the expense of other European plants, in particular Luton (Kotthoff, 2006b: 14). Reflecting on this development in his study of EWCs in the car industry, Hancké (2000) concluded that EWCs – and notably at GM – are captured and used by national unions to secure their own local interests, despite the nominal organisational function of EWCs to mediate between national employee representatives.

This interpretation seems entirely appropriate for the period prior up to the turn of the century. In the case of GME, the behaviour of employee representatives enabled GME management to exploit the lack of agreement between plants to extract concessions on labour and personnel costs from employee representatives at all plants.[277] For the employee side, however, this led to what were at times painful learning processes following the establishment of the EEF in 1996, in which it passed through various stages of growing awareness of the need for greater cross-national coordination.

Internal inter-plant competition intensified in 1997 with the attempt by GM management to implement the results of the so-called 'Template Study'. This implemented a benchmarking and rationalisation process in the company's European plants in line with a set of criteria initially tried out at the joint GM/ Toyota NUMMI plant in Fremont, California. This study then formed the backdrop to agreements to secure and retain production operations concluded in 1998 in Germany and Belgium. Furthermore, in 1998 many European plants were reconfigured from two- to single-line operation to cut overcapacity.

The conflict over implementing the Template Study showed local and national employee representatives at GME that local and national agreements to secure plants could be at the expense of other sites and trigger a 'race to the bottom'. This conflict with management was also one of the first occasions on which the EEF became active. The EEF was not informed about the implementation of the Template Study and immediately feared a massive loss of jobs. Management also rejected a request for a joint meeting of the EEF. This prompted an internal meeting of the EEF at which it obtained information about how far the study had been implemented at

277 Zagelmeyer (2001) refers in this connection to 'regime competition', in which employment relations continue to be regulated at national level although they are embedded horizontally and vertically in international corporate structures and hence management, which is organised and acts cross-nationally, is in an immediately advantageous position (see too Banyuls, 2008).

individual plants. Management's behaviour towards the European plants and EEF was severely criticised by the EEF employee side, and a common position towards management was worked out (see Eller-Braatz and Klebe, 1998: 445f.). However, it did not prove possible to induce management to enter into European negotiations.

One important element in activating the EEF was the strengthening of the European coordination office in Zurich in relation to the Opel headquarters in Rüsselsheim during the 1990s. This cut the direct access enjoyed by employee representatives at Rüsselsheim and the direct personal exchange between important employee representatives and the European corporate centre, making it more difficult to pursue national or plant-based strategies, even for large plants such as Rüsselsheim and Bochum.

As well as the installation agreement and its revision, by the reference year for this study (2008) a total of eight European framework agreements had been concluded by the EEF and GME management. The first was agreed on 6 July 2000 and was preceded by pan-European protest actions organised by EEF members. The context for this were rumours of a planned joint venture between GME and Fiat, the aim of which was to separate off the production of engines and transmissions.[278] Employee representatives from General Motors Europe and the European trade unions feared that the joint venture would lead to the lost of some 15,000 jobs in Europe and a further 15,000 in Brazil.

The EEF was neither informed nor consulted about the decision beforehand. The members of the EEF saw this as a breach of their rights under the EWC Directive, and responded with a wave of actions across Europe. There were also spontaneous ('wildcat') strikes at Bochum and Kaiserslautern, which would have been hardest hit by the proposal. GME management was visibly shaken by the force of the reaction and sanctioned negotiations with the EEF with the aim of concluding an agreement. Amongst other things, the subsequent framework agreement stipulated that transferred employees should not suffer a detriment, that employees in the joint venture would continue to be represented by the EEF, and in the event that the venture failed they would have the right to return to their previous jobs.[279]

This framework agreement was one of the first substantive agreements negotiated and signed by an EWC, a European Trade Union Federation (the EMF) and central management. It was the result of intensive communication between employee representatives at European level and coordinated protest actions at plants in Europe. Although activities were organised locally, they were coordinated by the EWC and presented in public as European actions. As well as exercising the tasks

---

278 The planned synergy effects were to produce savings of US $ 1.2 billion after the third year and US $2 billion from the third year. For detailes see <http://www.eurofound.europa.eu/de/observatories/eurwork/articles/other-business/general-motors-and-fiat-spa-form-alliance> accessed 30 April 2012.

279 It was also agreed that employees would be treated as if they had continued to work for their previous employer. The agreement was to be implemented at national level.

of information, communication and coordination, the massive protests and public awareness also meant that this was the first time that the EWC took on the role of leading negotiations with GME management.

This agreement was of immense importance for the subsequent development of the EEF as it showed members that it was possible to achieve movement at European level.

> This was the breakthrough in a substantively excellent agreement, which was not achieved at any other company up to that date. We also noted the strength we can muster as a negotiating partner as the agreement is legally binding – and we took to care to make sure of that (GME01).

The following four agreements were concerned with restructuring initiatives taken by GME management. In December 2000, GME management publicly announced that the Vauxhall plant in Luton was to be closed. The EEF itself was only informed immediately beforehand. While the British trade unions responded with immediate strike action, the EEF organised a European Day of Action in close cooperation with the EMF in parallel with negotiations with GME management in which 40,000 employees participated. The Day of Action was notably successful because management had sought to implement its closure plans without any prior consultation either at local level with trade unions at Luton or at European level. In this case, corporate management, whose initial position was not to negotiate a new framework agreement, was again surprised by the scale of the protest actions – in particular because employees in plants that might have gained from Luton's closure also took part.

> In the dispute over the closure of the Luton plant we brought the whole of Europe to a standstill for several hours all on the same day and organised from here in Germany, or from Zurich where we were conducting negotiations. We hade teleconferences with all the plants in Europe via dedicated lines and spoke with those on strike – that is, we planned it like a military campaign and it worked very well. This was a breakthrough and the English noted that although Rüsselsheim would have benefited from the closure of the Vectra plant and got a higher level of utilisation, that despite this a strike was called so that others would have an alternative, a perspective. Yes and that was for them – for all of us – it represented a breakthrough: they understood, they learnt. And from then on we've built up the EEF very systematically, and put a lot of work into building relationships (GME01).

For the EEF's members, the strategy of focussing on European-wide cooperation to achieve negotiated and socially-responsible solutions, that took into account the interests of all European plants, and an and an assertive public campaign was seen as a success. Through this the perception grew both within GM and externally that the EWC could be an important and effective forum of interest regulation.

> I think that the closure of the Luton plant was an important moment in the history of the EEF as the attention of the workforce was focused on the question as to what role the EWC should play (GME08).

Finally, GME management conceded negotiations with the EEF over a new framework agreement. The second framework agreement, signed on 5 March 2001, for the first time included firm commitments for the two English plants at Luton and Ellesmere Port in an agreement negotiated at European level.[280] National representatives were responsible for ensuring that the agreement would be legally binding for both individual employees and the negotiating parties (Article 7 of the framework agreement).

Just six months later, European employee representatives were confronted by 'Project Olympia', which envisaged a series of restructuring exercises, mainly at the Antwerp and Bochum plants that produced the Astra, and at Eisenach and Zaragoza that produced the Corsa. The aim was to cut output by 350,000 units a year and obtain annual savings of €2 billion. This was to be achieved by cutting some 1,600 jobs on top of natural wastage (GM Press Release, 16 October 2001). Three objectives were formulated at an extraordinary meeting of the EEF held on 20 August 2001: (1) no production sites to be closed, (2) restructuring to take place without compulsory redundancies, and (3) measures in the Olympia plan to be negotiated with the trade unions (Broughton, 2001). In the subsequent – and third – agreement concluded between the EEF and GME management it was agreed that no plant would be closed and that the reduction in the workforce would be dealt with in a socially-responsible way (with no compulsory redundancies, early retirement, transfers to other GM locations etc.).

In 2002, GME management and the EEF signed a document entitled 'Principles of Social Responsibility'. As well as a general statement of support for human rights by GME, this document also included principles of equal opportunities, non-discrimination, equal pay, no child or forced labour, the promotion of health and safety at work, freedom of association and the right to conclude collective agreements. The legal status of the agreement is unclear, however: control over compliance rests with an internal 'Control Audits Group'.

The situation was immeasurably exacerbated in the summer of 2004 by GME management's announcement that it would close a plant in Europe – without informing the EEF. Cost comparisons had been carried out in the two competing plants of Trollhättan, in Sweden, and Rüsselsheim. In September 2004, the EMF called an emergency meeting and shortly after the GM European Trade Union Coordination Group (GMTUCG) was constituted to support the EEF. A European Day of Action was agreed at the group's second meeting, held on 19 October 2004, in which more than 50,000 employees were subsequently involved (Harper, 2004). The 'Copenhagen Declaration', agreed by the heads of the German and Swedish unions (IG Metall, Svenska Metall, SIF and CF) and the EMF, set out the EEF's five

280 It was agreed that Luton would have an annual volume of 84,000 units of the X-83 Vivaro van in a joint venture with Renault, and 18,000 units of the Frontera; for Ellesmere Port it was agreed that 180,000 units would be produced on the Epsilon platform.

key demands for negotiations with management. These were: no plant closures, no compulsory redundancies, a long-term sustainable sales campaign, a future perspective for Opel, Vauxhall and Saab, and compliance with collective agreements (Dribbusch, 2004). Following a phase of conflict, involving several plants and during which production was halted at Bochum for six days, there was agreement on a fourth European framework agreement, concluded on 8 December 2004. As a quid pro quo for not closing a plant and lifting the threat of compulsory redundancies, agreement was reached on measures to cut costs by €500 million and reduce the workforce through voluntary redundancy, early retirement and the transfer of 12,000 jobs to joint ventures.[281] In addition, criteria were agreed for future volume allocations and plant appraisals. These were financial efficiency, competitiveness, production strategy, sales and marketing strategy, the employment situation, and severance costs. For the EMF, inclusion of these final two criteria represented a 'real innovation in a European framework agreement' (EMF, 2005: 20). In contrast, employee representatives at Bochum criticised the agreement because, in their view, it provided for an insufficient allocation of production capacity.

Following the announcement of the closure of three Western European plants in 2005 by the chair of GME, Carl Peter Forster, combined with a request to plants (and their employee representatives) to bid for future production, the EEF and GMTUCG (see above) set up the 'Delta Group' consisting of employee representatives and trade union members from Antwerp, Bochum, Ellesmere Port, Gliwice and Trollhättan.[282] The members signed a 'European Solidarity Pledge' in which they committed themselves to mutual information, joint negotiations with management, and a monitoring procedure for production figures for all plants (Telljohann and Tapia, 2006).

Following the winning of the EEF's right to be consulted in 2000 as a result of the conflict over the joint venture with Fiat and the prevention, for the first time, of a plant closure at Luton in 2001, the establishment of the Delta group marked a further important step in the development of the EEF. In December 2005 employee representatives from Delta plants met for the first time, together with the GMTUCG, to work out a strategy on how to deal with inter-plant competition within the group.[283] This was significant as GME management based its decision on site selection for the production of new models much more on competition between plants that wanted to be considered than other vehicle producers – an approach dubbed

281 Of these, 9,500 were in Germany (5,000 in Rüsselsheim, c. 4,000 in Bochum, and several hundred in Kaiserslautern) (Dribbusch, 2004).

282 The chairs are Rudi Kennes (deputy chair of the EEF) and Jürgen Ratayczak (EMF coordinator for GME).

283 Financing the Delta group soon emerged as a major problem for those involved as the company was not willing to pay and neither the EMF nor national trade unions were able to take on the costs. As a result, a project application (GMEECO) was submitted to the European Commission within the budget line for Social Dialogue. This then took on the costs of the working group.

'beauty contests' by EEF members, and one which inevitably culminated in mutual underbidding by plants on labour costs and working conditions.

GME management initially refused to negotiate with the Delta group. It was only after protracted and intensive employee protests at the plants concerned that the company changed its mind and negotiated a framework agreement on future production allocations for vehicles using the Delta platform.

While up until 2005 the EEF had been relatively successful in mitigating and spreading the social consequences of GM's restructuring with its 'pain-sharing' strategy, from 2006 it began to be faced by the problem that all plants were now so implicated in the pan-European contraction of the business that simply continuing to press for the principle of 'equitable' burden sharing no longer seemed feasible. In June 2006 GME management announced the closure of the Azambuja plant, which had some 1,100 employees. Following this, the EEF and GMTUCG – once more – decided on a series of pan-European actions. On this occasion, the actions did not take the form of centrally planned and simultaneous protests but ran over a period of almost four weeks and affected all European plants – albeit with less public visibility. In view of the unexpected intensity of these protests, management eventually stated that it was prepared to negotiate on a socially-responsible closure of the plant, but not the closure as such. The upshot was the achievement of a severance package that was seen as extremely generous, and which provided for comparatively high severance payments and early retirement provisions.

In 2008, two European framework agreements were concluded between GME management and the EEF, one covered outsourcing and spin-offs and the other volume allocations for the new Delta platform. What was innovative in the outsourcing agreement was that specific provisions were agreed on information and consultation. This included a stipulation that the information and subsequent consultation process had to take place at European level for outsourcing or spin-offs affecting at least two European countries represented on the EEF – a provision already implicit in the EWC Directive. However, the fact that GME management had repeatedly sought to carry out restructuring *without* involving the EEF meant that this clause signalled an acknowledgement by management of this obligation. In the event of a transfer of employees, the content of the employment contract and its previous provisions and conditions were to be maintained for five years (as with the first framework agreement concluded on the joint venture with Fiat). The contract with the sub-contractor or new employer was to include a clause stating that employers would be able to return to GME within five years should the outsourcing contract end.

In the simultaneously published agreement on volume allocation for Delta platform production, future volume allocations for Delta sites were agreed together with the 'necessary and required investments' at Bochum, Ellesmere Port, Gliwice, and Trollhättan. The agreement can be seen as innovative in that it provided for an intervention in the allocation of production volumes – an issue previously solely within management's prerogative. Any necessary adjustments in headcount were to be implemented in a socially-responsible way, with the aim of avoiding compulsory redundancies. The agreement also included a commitment to manufacture a new generation SUV at Antwerp.

Although both these 2008 agreements involved successful provisions on procedural minimum standards for company restructuring, they did not solve the underlying problem of stagnating volume in Europe and a further contraction in the GME workforce in Western Europe. In 2006, Opel had succeeded in gaining some ground in terms of quality rankings due to new models, and there was some rise in output, but these were not enough to offset serious profitability problems in Europe, especially in the context of the turbulence surrounding the GM parent company in the US that culminated in the company's insolvency under Chapter 11 of the US Bankruptcy Code in 2009. Following the reacquisition by the 'new' GM of Opel and GME shares from the trustees, the new GME management's announcement that the Antwerp plant would be closed met with only symbolic protests from the EEF.

Although the EEF's activities were not always crowned with success, the restructuring agreements it was able to negotiate were seen as highly significant by EWC members that we interviewed.

> I think it has a relevance, because [...] when we reached the framework on outsourcing, when we reached the framework for the Delta, that was because of the EEF, the subcommittees that we had set up. And we go back into the plants on that occasion – that is a decision reached in Europe, signed in Europe and local managers, whether you like it or not (GME08).

For some non-German EEF members, the added-value offered by the body lay in the quality of the information provided by management to the EEF and economic committee, which was both better and more topical than that provided by local management.

From the standpoint of the employee representatives that we interviewed, employees also saw the EEF as an important institution.

> They realise increasingly that we adopted the right course and acted at a European level although it was amazingly difficult. 'Why aren't you here, they care more about them than about us' – the contradiction is clear. There is no question, but at every works meeting at every plant there is always a fixed item on the agenda 'Report from the European Works Council' (GME01).

This was also confirmed by non-German EEF members.

> It's important, what we can take from here and there is good acceptance by the workforce. They can also see that I come back with other important things from the EEF, and then they respect what I'm doing here (GME07).

> The people gradually realised that this is important [...]. You have to have the information [...] Initially it was difficult (GME11).

For management, and despite the frequent negotiations and agreements between the EEF and the company, the EEF remained purely an information and consultation body. 'The EEF is a consultative forum and no more' (GMM01). In their view, the adoption of framework agreements was not be seen an expression of the EEF's negotiating power but rather a means for showing how the company implemented its strategies across Europe.

For EEF members, the question as why European management negotiated with the EEF was seen differently. They stressed that pan-European coordination was able to exert the pressure needed to force management to negotiate and make concessions to employees.

> Yes, it's quite a straightforward thing: they know that if they come to an agreement with us, they'll have peace throughout Europe. They can also use the other strategy they've tried – ask here, ask there, what did they have to say about that. The Swedes say stop, yes, we won't do anything before we've got a European Framework agreement, we'll just block it [...] In Kaiserslautern we can switch off all of Europe within 1.5 days, and they know that GME01).

11.3 Provisional assessment

The European Works Council at GME certainly represents one of most researched bodies of this type, and has been the subject of a large number of studies. Some authors see it as the most developed example of European representative body both in terms of its operations and capacity to prevail in relation to the company. Our work suggests a more nuanced perspective.

The GME EEF succeeded in including all the group's important locations in Europe. Its strong coordination and capacity was evident, amongst other things, in the large number of internal bodies, the frequency and intensity of meetings, and, in particular, the number of framework agreements concluded with European management. In virtually no other European group did an EWC coordinate and organise a comparable range of activities by employees and their local and national representatives. Our interviews and other studies suggest that the GME EEF developed a strong collective identity and set of common values compared with other companies. However, the decisions to close manufacturing operations in Portugal (2006) and Belgium (2009), as well as the insolvency of the parent company in 2009 illustrate the structural limits to interest regulation by the EWC.

In the light of the conceptual framework used in this study, it is possible to elaborate a broader interpretation of the GM EWC case. At first glance, there is a clear organisational fit between the structure of the group and its EWC. Based on our typology, a transnational company with decentralised resources and strong coordination is mirrored by a (transnational) European Works Council that has adapted to these characteristics. The specific historical constellation of a formerly strong British constituent in the group, a significant accumulation of resources and power in Rüsselsheim, and a European headquarters that is delinked from both of these in Zurich, with distinctive production operations in Bochum and Spain, together with a very self-confident Swedish subsidiary (Saab) explain why both GME and the EWC is characterised by relatively decentralised patterns of distribution along a number of dimensions. At the same time, the EEF chair, and his strong position within the German institutional system of codetermination, as well as the high level of trust and commitment built up over many years of joint activity, enabled EWC activities to be effectively coordinated. It should be emphasised in this context that leading employee representatives both at individual plants as well as in the European leadership demonstrated more continuity than their negotiating counterparts on the management side. Not least the crisis that hit the parent company in the US led to a high turnover of European managers.

The GM case also reveals the significance of distinguishing the need for regulation, the level of activity, and regulatory outputs when analysing and understanding EWCs. The GME EWC was particularly active because management came forward with an unceasing wave of restructuring measures during the first decade of the new century. This was responded to with a very high level of activity on the part of the EWC – based initially on only average levels of resources, measured in terms of operational capacity, power centres and recognition by management. Set against the challenges, and also in comparison to other companies, there were a noteworthy number of procedural and substantive stipulations in the European framework agreements. This not only mirrored the fact that the EWC was especially active but was also an expression of the low trust relationships between management and employee representatives and the overarching logic of a zero-sum game in terms of their interests. In addition, the GME EEF also attracted such a high level of attention as it was much more in the public eye than in other instances considered here, such as Ford. For employee representatives, this might have been seen as the only opportunity to build a degree of counterpower to the company. However, such a strategy does not necessarily reflect strength but possibly also the weakness of the organisation's negotiating position.

Compared with all the other automotive companies in our study, the need for regulation at European level was probably the greatest at GME in the period after the establishment of the EWC in 1996. This is related to the crisis and contraction both of the group as a whole and GME as well the fact that it was not possible to embed and consolidate recognition of the EWC as a body for information and consultation that had to be taken seriously, not least because of the high turnover of managers. Compared with the other EWCs looked at in this study, the high level of public activity and conflict at GME should, therefore, be seen as an expression of the lack of recognition of the forum by management. Although the number of European agreements concluded at GME is comparatively high, they were not able to prevent plant closures or a massive rundown in the workforce. Considering the difficult initial conditions and context of persistent crisis at the company and the low value placed on the EWC by management, its representational effectiveness was relatively high. However, when looked at in terms of the degree to which employee interests in sustainable employment and responsible participation were taken account of by management, compared with other EWCs the GME EEF can scarcely be said to have secured a positive future.

Chapter 12: Summary and prospects – EWCs as transnational European institutions?

The main aim of this study was to examine the structures and patterns of action of European Works Councils (EWC), drawing on a number of different theoretical and research traditions. Specifically, we brought together perspectives from industrial sociology, which have largely dominated the field, with approaches from organisational studies and transnationalisation research. One major strand, especially in the German literature and drawing on national research into works councils, has been to assess EWCs against the benchmark of German works councils in terms of their capacity to develop comparable functions and ways of working. For studies in the traditions of trade union research, the key research questions have been, firstly, the significance of EWC influence on unions' organising and mobilising capacity and, secondly and conversely, whether unions for their part might be able to use EWCs as arenas of influence. Management studies have dealt with EWCs either as an additional bureaucratic hurdle or, alternatively, as an interesting new instrument for European-level workforce communication. Our own prime focus has been to understand the organisational structures and operational methods of these new European institutions and analyse how they are embedded in a highly complex and multi-level environment.

From the standpoint of organisational studies, our approach differs from previous approaches to EWC research in that we see EWCs as European non-profit organisations acting within and in relation to for-profit organisations (commercial undertakings). Although such businesses operate across Europe (otherwise there would be no EWCs), unlike the new legal form of the *Societas Europeae* they are anchored in national legal and institutional frameworks. In contrast, EWCs are based in the first instance on European law (see Kotthoff, 2006a: 11). It is only in a second step that they are adapted to a specific national setting through a mixture of private (company agreement) and public law (transposing legislation). As collective actors, EWCs are focussed at the level of the European-scale company as a corporate actor. As such, they are simultaneously tied to national *and* European institutions.

As well as conceiving of EWCs as non-profit organisations, we also viewed them as (potential) 'platforms of inter- and intra-organisational interest regulation' that operate in relation to locally distributed operations and employees in their companies and that, as a result, are embedded in multi-dimensional and multi-level structures. The notion of a 'platform of inter- and intra-organisational interest regulation' is intended to underline the fact that within the inter-organisational negotiating process EWCs assume interest representation functions in relation to European management. However, they are also simultaneously engaged in interest regulation in intra-organisational processes of negotiation between their own members, as representatives of particular local and national interests and strategies, and aim to aggregate these interests and strategies in a way that renders them sufficiently homogeneous to make them amenable for negotiation. In essence, both functional aspects – inter- and intra-organisational negotiation – are intrinsic to the operation of EWCs. The relationship between these and their weight within the operation of any given EWC will depend on its governance structure (mixed forum meetings, as with Honda, or sequential with an employee meeting followed by an information and negotiating meeting with management) and the strategies of the actors. As a consequence, EWCs can either be primarily intra-organisational or inter-organisational negotiating platforms.

In looking at companies and EWCs as cross-border organisations, we drew principally on Bartlett and Ghoshal's (1989) typology of four ideal-types of cross-border enterprise. Organisations are characterised depending on how their resources are distributed and the strength of cross-border coordination. We operationalised the pattern of distribution (of material and human resources, power, culture and knowledge) and the intensity of coordination into empirically deployable sub-categories and characteristics, both for EWCs and, at European level, for the companies in which they are constituted. We were also able to control for possible variance in EWC and corporate structures by branch through limiting our research to the automotive industry. As such the study does not aim to provide an explanatory framework that can be applied to the whole economy but does offer a potentially fruitful approach to understanding a number of developments in the automotive industry.

In summarising and theorising our results, we begin by comparing the structures and processes of EWCs in order to categorise them as focal, global, multinational or transnational organisations (Chapter 12.1). We then place them in their company context and pursue the issue of *organisational fit* (in Chapter 12.2), with the aim of ascertaining the relationship between EWC and company structures. In a further step (Chapter 12.3) we then evaluate the significance of the institutional influences of the home country of the companies concerned. The eight vehicle manufacturers were deliberately chosen so that two companies each had their primary country-of-origin and headquarters in France, Germany, the US and Japan. As well as the national effects observable in each case, this also allowed us to consider any effects related to whether a group had its corporate headquarters within or outside the EU (in our sample, there was a four to four breakdown). We then consider the extent to which EWCs' historical development and experience of critical events might serve to explain their structures (Chapter 12.4). Finally, we undertake a comparative assessment of the influence of actors and actors' strategies in order to draw together structure and agency perspectives (Chapter 12.5). Following on from this consideration of EWC structures, in a concluding section we turn to the issue of explaining the representative effectiveness and outputs of EWCs (Chapter 12.6). Here we are able to offer a number of both interesting, and in some respects, surprising results, presented comparatively, as well as identifying desiderata for future EWC research.

12.1 Organisational pattern and types of EWC

Looked at in relation to the distributive pattern and strength of coordination of EWCs, our strategy of using a comparatively simple four-field matrix (of centralised and decentralised structures of distribution; weak and strong coordination) has proved sustainable. Overall, there was an even distribution of strongly and weakly coordinated EWCs in the sample of eight companies. At the level of EWCs, Daimler, Honda, PSA and Toyota were found to have weak coordination of cross-border activities when compared with the other companies. The EWC at PSA emerged as very weakly coordinated. In contrast, at Renault the coordination of cross-border EWC activities could be categorised as a 'somewhat strong', and for Ford, General Motors and Volkswagen very strong. Inasmuch as we were able to discern changes in the pattern of coordination over time, cooperation and information exchange appeared to have become progressively more intensive. This suggests a general trend for EWCs in this study to move towards becoming global and transnational organisations. We also noted that the strengthening of EWC's coordination activities mostly takes place in a punctuated fashion, when major changes on the corporate side are imminent or have been announced. At the same time, there is a high degree of variance between EWCs in terms of the strength of coordination of their activities as well the degree of centralisation of resources. Even in a relatively concentrated branch with a comparatively small number of significant producers in Europe, there is considerable variation in the arrangements of each EWC.

As far as the patterns of distribution within the EWCs are concerned, power, knowledge and culture tend to be largely centralised. As a rule, employee representatives at the company's home country or corporate headquarters have much greater scope to influence the activities and strategies of the EWC than their foreign colleagues. At the same time, human and material resources (number of representatives by country and plant, equipment) tend to be decentralised. Power exhibited a centralised distribution throughout. Only in the cases of Ford and GM could the overall structure of distribution be characterised as 'somewhat decentralised'. The EWCs at Daimler and PSA were at the extreme opposite, with a high degree of centralisation. The EWCs at Honda, Renault, Toyota and Volkswagen were characterised as 'somewhat centralised'.

As far as change is concerned, we observed a number of developments. While in some cases (Daimler, PSA) no major changes had taken place since the inception of EWC activity, the EWCs at Toyota, Renault and Volkswagen had moved towards either decentralisation or a greater role for all or at least some European operations. As far as the pattern of distribution of material and human resources were concerned, this shift to decentralisation was evidenced in a greater (and in relation to their share of employment, over-proportional) inclusion of smaller and 'peripheral' operations or even operations outside the EU (Argentina in the case of Renault, Russia in the case of Volkswagen). In the case of GM, in terms of the distribution of EWC resources (and particularly power), there has been a certain ebb and flow from 'somewhat centralised' (up until the late-1990s) to 'somewhat decentralised' and then '(wholly) decentralised (up until 2007), and back to 'somewhat decentralised' (since the crisis of the GM parent in the US). Since the mid-1990s, the Ford EWC has moved towards greater decentralisation in the distribution of resources.

Half the EWCs in this study were characterised as focal organisations – that is, a centralised structure of distribution and weak coordination. Two EWCs were characterised as global and two as transnational organisations. Six of the eight EWCs accordingly exhibit either a centralised or somewhat centralised pattern of distribution (global and focal types) and only two EWCs were either 'strongly decentralised' (Ford) or 'somewhat decentralised' (GM). Only half the cases exhibited strong coordination of EWC activities (see Figure XX).

Figure 20: Structures of distribution and patterns of coordination in companies and EWCs

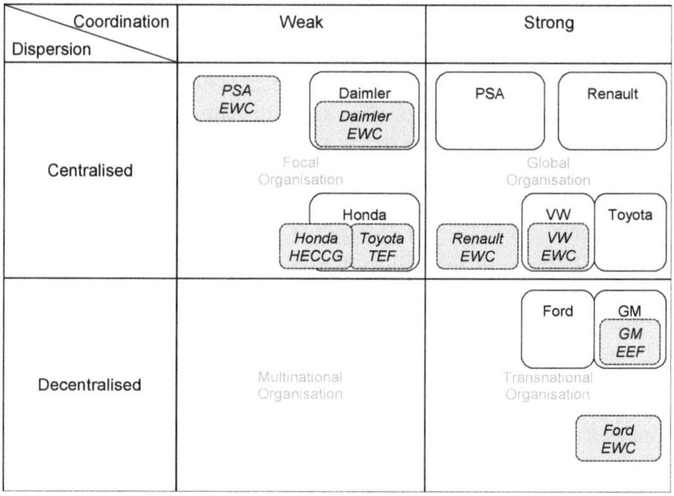

Source: author's compilation

Interestingly, none of the EWCs can be assigned to the category of multinational organisation – that is, a decentralised distribution of resources with weak coordination. The only candidates might be Daimler and Honda, based on their high degree of divisionalisation compared with other companies in the sample. This finding certainly has a great deal to do with the specific context of vehicle manufacture, with its high degree of operational integration. More decentralised corporate structures, with the likelihood of correspondingly decentralised and weakly coordinated EWCs, might be found in other industries, such as food or textiles. Our findings would suggest that weakly coordinated and strongly decentralised EWCs would be most likely to occur where there is little need for cross-border regulation, where cross-border corporate alliances have emerged at European level, possibly as a result of acquisitions or joint ventures, and where there is, as a consequence, little common history, or where a group consists of a number of independent divisions (that is, the multinational type). Such configurations are now much less likely to be found in vehicle manufacture.

In view of the fact that most EWCs considered in this study were constituted between 1994 and 1996, and that this in itself required a sufficiently high level of cross-border cooperation to surmount a range of obstacles, then EWCs in most of these companies have emerged as well-established and independent organisational structures with corresponding resources and mechanisms for cooperation. Despite shortcomings in the effectiveness of cooperation evident in some cases (PSA, Toyota and Honda), these are noteworthy results. They run counter to some previous assessments, under which EWCs were viewed either as incapable of constituting independent and viable forums or simply as the extended arm of employee representation arrangements at the home country. It is undoubtedly true that vehicle manufacture – with chemicals, mechanical engineering and electrical engineering – represent areas within the EU in which EWC activity is particularly prevalent. One issue for further discussion would, therefore, be whether the EWCs considered here represent, and will remain, enclaves or whether they offer exemplars of European-level representation that might be adopted in other branches and companies.

12.2 Organisational fit between EWCs and companies

Understanding EWCs as non-profit organisations located within for-profit organisations allows a systematic comparison to be made between the structures of each of these organisations using the same approach. Our initial assumption was that there would be a systematic link between the characteristics of the organisation of a company and that of its corresponding EWC. This was consistent with our judgement that EWC research has tended to underemphasise the structural preconditions and exigencies to which such bodies are subject, with the consequence that their potential has often been judged from a more voluntaristic standpoint. For example, categories are created that rest on implicitly normative foundations (such as the level of open conflict or mass action) or are directed solely at the level of activity exhibited by EWC leadership groups (such as a scale ranging from 'barely active' to 'highly active': see Chapter 2).

In all the eight cases studies considered here, it has been possible to establish a very close association between the form of internationalisation of the company and that of its EWC. Of the eight companies, four – that is, half – exhibit a direct match between the form of internationalisation of the company and the form of internationalisation of the EWC: Daimler, Honda, General Motors and Volkswagen. In the case of Daimler, for example, the lack of parallel production within Europe and the very diversified divisional structure within the regulatory scope of the EWC (ranging from commercial vehicles to cars and the sales organisation), as well as the comparatively low structural similarity between locations, evidently generated only a a weak need for regulation at European level. The fact that the company is highly centralised in Europe, with Stuttgart as the clear centre of resources, power, knowledge and culture, and that a strong works council structure at corporate level in Germany exists alongside this highly centralised yet weakly coordinated European-level corporate structure, makes it likely that a centralised but weakly coordinated EWC will emerge at European level. This also indicates that it is inappropriate to judge or classify the level and standard of activity and output of an EWC in isolation from its corporate environment and the challenges it faces that require regulation.

In contrast to Daimler, precisely the opposite considerations apply in the case of General Motors, where there is a relatively decentralised and dispersed company in terms of employees, production volumes and R&D capacities in Europe, with a high level of coordination based on multiple instances of parallel production and marked European management structures. As a consequence, General Motors can be characterised as a transnational undertaking. While the EWC at General Motors was initially somewhat weakly coordinated, a context that called for more regulation led to the emergence of an increasingly strongly coordinated yet also relatively decentralised organisational structure.

In the case of the other four companies in which the organisational fit is less than complete, there are, nonetheless, systematic parallels between company structures and those of the corresponding EWC. In the case of PSA, this relates to a similarly high degree of centralisation of resources with weak coordination for the EWC and somewhat strong coordination for the company. There is a similar gap between the characteristic features within the organisational matrix at Toyota: strong company coordination and somewhat weak coordination of the EWC is combined with a more centralised overall distribution of resources in both cases (the distribution of material resources is decentralised, but the centralised structure of knowledge, power and culture generates a somewhat centralised structure overall). In the case of Renault, company and EWC structures are in the same quadrant – as global organisations. This also applies to Ford, although in this case the company and EWC structures are both strongly coordinated and differ only slightly in terms of the degree of decentralisation.

Comparison of the case studies yields a number of interesting and unexpected findings. Firstly, detailed comparison of patterns of distribution and coordination indicates that the organisational fit between the type of company and the type of EWC is more marked for distribution than for coordination. For example, there are generally marked parallels between the number of employees in a country and the number of EWC seats; the distribution of power also often resembles that of the company. It would be reasonable to suppose that the pattern of distribution – as a contextual condition – initially provides the 'objective context' for strategies that are likely to emerge and the pattern of coordination is then highly dependent on this.

Moreover, the pattern of distribution of resources of EWCs is more decentralised than that of the companies. One important factor behind this is that a strict principle of proportionality between national employment levels and EWC seats is usually departed from in order to promote greater inclusion of employee representatives from foreign operations.

And thirdly, in some cases, the distribution of power within EWCs is more centralised than in the corresponding companies when the opposite might have been expected – since foreign subsidiaries are usually managed by the headquarters whereas EWC members are delegated on the basis of equal participation by national operations. One explanation for this is that in some cases a strong institutional influence is exercised by a few EWC members or chairs that they acquire by virtue of national legislation on employee representation and, in particular in Germany, codetermination. For example, it was repeatedly emphasised in interviews that the 'direct line' between EWC chairs and (European) group-level management meant that they were sometimes better informed about strategic developments than many local managers. One further explanation is that although the EWC chair and presidium conduct the 'business' of the EWC (and are elected to do so), in contrast to corporate headquarters they do not have or claim any rights of direction and control over EWC members. The form of power exercised within the EWC and the company is, therefore, fundamentally different.

These systematic associations between the types of internationalisation of companies and their corresponding EWCs – detailed in the case studies – represent one important outcome of our research. One task for future EWC research would be to explore and register these structural associations between patterns of resource distribution and coordination in European-scale companies and their related EWCs. The notion of organisational fit allows the framework of action in which EWC activities take place to be determined more precisely.

One important issue is that of the mechanisms that operate on the various dimensions and that bring about the adaptation of an EWC to its company. The various dimensions of analysis employed here might offer some help in this respect. As far as the distribution of resources in companies is concerned (employees by operation, operations by country, production volumes by plant) and in EWCs (members by country, resources for EWC activities), there is often a fairly direct association as the distribution of EWC members is aligned with the national workforce distribution in countries in which the company operates. However, there is some divergence from direct proportionality in nearly all the cases considered here. The central actors in an EWC often regard it as important to ensure that all countries are included in the EWC or to take account of national trade union features, such as union pluralism. Although there is a comparatively close fit between the distribution of employees and the distribution of EWC seats in many of the EWCs in our sample – as at PSA, Renault and Ford (see also the EWC representative index and Figure 25) – the strict application of the formula may be 'breached' in practice in order to integrate all operations and functional areas (VW, GM, Daimler, Toyota) or to ensure the operational capability of the EWC (VW, Ford).

As far as the issue of the distribution of power is concerned, in terms of organisational fit the power centre of an EWC is usually co-located at the power centre of the company, also simultaneously the European headquarters. Although this might appear to be a rational and functional construction, as direct access and proximity to the decision-making centre holds out the prospect of more influence for the EWC, it is not usually the product of a conscious decision. In reality, the question of where the EWC centre should be located is never posed as it is a (path dependent) product of existing structures of interest regulation. In the cases of Daimler or VW, for example, no one would consider locating the EWC centre anywhere other than at the corporate centre. In other cases, the company made a unilateral decision about where the EWC centre would be (Toyota, Honda). At the level of the EWC, power is not characterised by hierarchy. In a very small number of cases, decisions might be made by formal ballot: however, in line with the non-profit logic of a collective actor that does not enforce decisions through instruction, most EWCs engage in discussions until they reach agreement. Finally, it is important for both an EWC chair and the steering committee to be elected to conduct the EWC's business, structure decisions, propose topics etc. and, as a consequence, pre-form certain decisions. This entails delegated power that must on occasions necessarily be exercised, given that many EWC members – as the case-studies showed, precisely those from non-home country operations – seem to be relatively passive and bring few issues to the EWC.

As far as the influence of culture on organisational fit is concerned, the case studies initially indicated that the influence of the company and industrial relations culture had a varying influence on the EWC. For example, the particular culture of codetermination at Volkswagen has had a major impact on EWC structures and processes. There was also an evident home-country effect on management style and employment regulation for all eight case studies. For the two companies whose home country was France (PSA and Renault), this relates to a culture of conflict and in some respects mistrust between (trade union) employee representatives and management that is regarded as normal. For the two companies with Japan as their country-of-origin, the culture of enterprise-focused harmonious employment relations has also imprinted itself on the culture of the EWC. For the US American businesses (Ford and GM), management's pragmatic business approach tends to shape its dealings with the EWC; and for the two companies with German roots (Daimler and Volkswagen), the German culture of workplace and company-focused employee participation and a tradition of 'cooperative conflict resolution' also leads to a close organisational fit between type of company and type of EWC. Nevertheless, we also noted that over time some degree of cultural change had taken place through interaction and communication between members in the EWC. In this sense, some EWCs have 'emancipated' themselves to a considerable extent from the culture of their organisation and begun to construct their own identity as collective actors at European level (see too Telljohan, 2009; Whittall et al., 2007).

The impact of the culture of employment relations and regulation in the home country on the culture of the EWC led in several of our cases to evident tensions and even conflicts. For example, the Japanese enterprise-based syndicalist and harmonious forms of cooperation that determine the culture of Toyota management in Europe is only compatible to a very limited degree with the more conflict-oriented approach to interest representation of Belgian trade unionists and is also hard to accommodate to the expectations and traditions of German EWC members who have been socialised as works council members in a culture that embraces both cooperation and conflict.

As far as the dimension of knowledge is concerned, the case studies indicated no strong association between the characteristics of EWCs and their corresponding companies. The fact that the substance of knowledge at the level of for-profit organisations is very different from that relevant for non-profit EWCs means that there is scarcely any association in this area. Rather, access to strategic knowledge (in the form of company data and performance indicators, management strategies, plans) represents a power resource for an EWC.

Finally, as far as the dimension of coordination is concerned, there are overlaps between the features of companies and EWCs. This can be explained principally by the fact that – as already supposed at the outset of this study based on existing research and theoretical reflection – the need for coordination at the level of the EWC is almost directly correlated with the strength of coordination at European company level. This can be seen primarily in aspects of integrated cross-plant manufacture, parallel production and competitive tendering within companies as well as the issue of pan-European corporate restructuring (in particular in the cases of spinning out business divisions). As far as inter-plant competition etc. is concerned, strong coordination generates a comparably high need for regulation on the part of the EWC, which strong EWC coordination is able to achieve.

12.3 Institutional and home-country effects

The systematic selection of case-study companies allowed us to obtain a very accurate assessment of the effects that the home country and locally prevalent institutional regulations have on interest regulation, employee participation and trade union activities (as noted in the preceding section). For all the home countries considered here – Germany, France, Japan, US – there are material influences on EWC structures and modes of operation that are explicable by a home-country effect. For Volkswagen and Daimler, this is the German codetermination system and the rights that this affords to information, consultation and codetermination at national and group level. Although EWC work is taken seriously in both companies, its strength and dynamism derives to a considerable degree from the German model of employment regulation in Germany.

For those groups with their corporate headquarters outside Europe, the situation is complicated by the fact that in some instances the European (regional) headquarters also has a marked influence on the mode of EWC operation, but in other cases the effect of the European headquarters is comparatively muted. This is expressed, for example, in the centralised structure of distribution of material and human resources, power, knowledge and culture in the EWCs at Volkswagen and Daimler. As with many other cases, the pressure on German employee representatives to develop the EWC into a forceful actor is not as marked as in companies with their ultimate headquarters outside Germany. Access to information and the construction of veto positions can be regarded as largely secured for the German HQ (that is for Volkswagen and Daimler) without any need for vigorous EWC activity. European-level activity within Daimler is correspondingly extremely low. In contrast, within the Volkswagen group there has been a growing culture of international cooperation on the employee side over several decades that additionally indicates a certain organisational fit with the worldwide and, since the 1950s, highly internationalised structures of the group. This German home-country effect (strong support of the EWC scope for information and consultation through the German codetermination system) also applies in the European context with some reservations for the two US-based companies, Ford and GM, as their European coordination centres are also now based in Germany (Cologne and Rüsselsheim).

In the case of the two EWCs with their country-of-origin in France (PSA and Renault), there are also some common features that are attributable to the institutional setting. This includes the culture of joint meetings between management and employee representatives promoted by the *comités d'entreprise.* Whereas in the German employment culture, works councils are the most important body for interest representation for employees in relation to company management, the modus operandi of the EWCs at PSA and Renault are heavily influenced by the fact that trade unions are the key bearers of interest representation. This leads to the somewhat paradoxical situation that in France it is trade unions who keep watch to ensure that EWCs do not stray beyond being information and consultation bodies and develop into negotiating forums (possibly endangering their own status). French union pluralism also influences the operation of the EWCs in these two companies. Because three or more major unions are usually represented in large French firms, institutions for representation (including *comités d'entreprise* and EWCs) constitute arenas for inter-trade union competition and dissent.

The trade union spectrum is also wider in France than in Spain. Whereas in Spain the main competition is between a social democratic union (UGT) and a union with communist traditions (CC.OO), and on occasions with regional union federations, in France the range extends from the left-wing CGT and its affiliates to more employer-friendly organisations, such as Force Ouvrière. In the case of PSA and Renault, this home-country effect has inflicted a significant degree of paralysis on their EWCs as all unions in France feel themselves obliged to pursue the immediate and specific interests of their – national – client groups (especially as regards competition with other unions) and it is rare to find a common denominator that can serve as a negotiating position on most central bargaining issues.

For the two groups with the headquarters in the US (Ford and GM), there are some extremely interesting effects connected with the fact that their headquarters are located outside the EU. Both groups have fairly elaborate arrangements for European-level management compared with firms with the headquarters in France and Germany. This can be seen in the existence of independent group headquarters (for GM in Zurich), the capacity to relocate European centres (as with Ford from the UK to Germany) and the scope for mechanisms for coordination at European management level. The very fact that the headquarters is not in Europe means that there is a high probability that less centralised structures at the company and EWC site will emerge (this also applies for the companies ultimately headquartered in Japan, Honda and Toyota, which we consider immediately below). One further effect of the US institutional structure of employment regulation concerns the initially tentative and, sometimes, hostile relationship of many managers towards works councils and EWCs. Over time, the management side in both groups has developed a highly pragmatic relationship to EWCs as channels of communication and addressees for restructuring programmes. In the case of Ford and GM it is possible to speak of a 'second home-country' effect (or rather effect of the EU home country). This reveals a clear difference to Toyota, where the EWC would also probably be 'more Japanese' even if the European home country were Germany.

Finally, the two companies with their ultimate headquarters in Japan also introduced a number of particular features. This primarily concerns the unitarist conception of industrial relations. At Toyota, the EWC is seen mainly as an instrument and platform to meet corporatist objectives and less as a setting for resolving differing collective interests. At the time that our research was conducted, this applied both for the management and employee sides at European level in general (although more German and British employee representatives on the EWC took more adversarial positions). At Honda, by contrast, management has used the EWC as an instrument of dialogue between group management and the workforce in its European plants within a highly communicative and conflict-averse corporate culture. The structures and processes implemented by management serve more as an element of legitimation and allow employees little scope to identify and articulate collective interests. The EWC ultimately leads to the fact that an autonomous representation of employee interests does not come about and trade unions have only minimal influence.

As with the US groups, the Japanese companies also have active and independent European centres when compared with the French and German companies. In the case of Toyota, this exercises a strong coordinating role; in the case of Honda, this is less the case due to the high degree of divisionalisation of manufacturing into cars, motor-cycles and engines. Overall, control and management from the home country – Japan – play a significant role for their European operations (as with GM). At EWC level, there were weak coordination mechanisms in both companies: this corresponds with the organisational fit hypothesis for Honda but not for Toyota. This complex situation in the case of the two groups with their home base in Japan can be explained in part by their comparatively brief history, the divisionalisation of production operations in Europe (for Honda), and in part the very involved structure of European coordination (for Toyota) and a defensive stance towards independent employee representation. Moreover, the very positive sales trend in Europe for both groups over a long period led to the perception that there was little regulatory need. Compared with the other vehicle manufacturers in our study, production has risen in recent years at Honda and Toyota (see Figures in the Appendix).

12.4 Developments and critical events

The specific structures of EWCs' modes of cooperation cannot be explained solely by organisational fit and home-country effects. In all the cases considered in our research, critical – and often contingent – events have played a significant role in the trajectory of companies and EWCs. This is particularly evident in the case of some companies, less so in others. In some instances these events, which have made a deep impact on the 'organisational memory' of the company, lie many years in the past. At Toyota, for example, the large-scale conflicts during the reconstruction phase of the company in the immediate post-war period created the foundation for the non-adversarial structure of collective employment relations, not only at the Japanese parent company but also for plants established subsequently in Europe. As a consequence, there have been initiatives to reconfigure national traditions of employment relations by means of Toyota-specific representational arrangements in some European operations, as with the main plant at Burnaston, in England, where a consultation forum (the Toyota Members Advisory Board, TMAB) was established consisting of elected employee representatives and management on Japanese lines. Even the extreme conflict-averse employee-management interaction in the EWC is understandable in the context of this organisational experience. However, for Toyota the establishment of its production facilities in Britain in the 1990s was key event. During the initial years of production, Toyota management, most of which were Japanese expatriates, had difficulty in responding appropriately to the British culture of employment regulation and conflict resolution. A simple transfer of the Toyota production system, with its associated principles of life-long employment, internal promotion, flat hierarchies and a 'family' work atmosphere, collided with a quite different employment culture in Britain. As a consequence, there were repeated disputes and a high rate of absenteeism and employee turnover (Pardi, 2005 and 2006). It also took some time to arrive at a 'production consensus' with the workforce at the plant in France.

These developments meant that for Toyota management, the EWC took on a very central function in constructing a paternalistic-familial corporate culture with employee representatives. The operation and approach of the Toyota EWC cannot be understood without considering the influences of the Japanese production and employment culture and the experiences of workplace conflict in Britain and France. Whereas EWCs at other companies, such as Ford, GM and Volkswagen, established and strengthened themselves as independent bodies mainly via major restructuring exercises or announcements of plant closures that served as critical events, in the case of Toyota this was more the outcome of experiencing a cultural 'mismatch' between management and employees (and their trade unions) – which was of existential significance both for European management and employees in Britain and France – in relation to their prevailing understanding of industrial relations and employment regulation. Similarly, the more averse stance of Honda towards independent collective representation is also, in part, due to its previous negative experiences with Belgian unions in the 1960s and with US trade unions.

The operation of the Ford EWC was crucially influenced by the move of the European headquarters from the UK to Germany. Ford's British plants had a tradition of conflictual workplace industrial relations and a strong trade union presence. However, the fact that most union representatives were lay trade union officials with a marked workplace focus also led them to argue for a greater degree of influence within the EWC for the formal, and more professionalised, trade union apparatus, which was also one factor leading to the relative lateness in the establishment of the Ford EWC. In this respect, the transfer of the European headquarters to Cologne represented a critical event. Ford's European management in Germany encountered a fundamentally different workplace tradition of cooperative conflict resolution and codetermination. The move to Cologne considerably improved communication and trust between European management and the chair of the German works council, a robust representative who was also head of the EWC. One further key event in the development of the EWC's operations was the process of spinning off important areas of component manufacture in the late-1990s and the establishment of a new company, Visteon. It was precisely this conflict over the restructuring of the company, and related issues of employment security, wages and working conditions, that enabled the EWC to secure a sustained influence at European level and laid the basic pattern for the subsequent cooperative strategy of conflict resolution. These issues, that affected all Ford's operations in Europe, gave the Ford EWC broad recognition both from the employee and management side.

In the Volkswagen group, the introduction of teamworking across the company and new forms of working time flexibility met with strong resistance in a number of countries during the 1990s, in particular in Spain. The employment culture of VW employees at Pamplona and at SEAT in Barcelona initially led to serious conflicts that management could not have envisaged. One major development was the integration of SEAT, acquired in 1986, into the VW group, not least the new marque had been put in a competitive position with VW's German plants from the outset. Although the German delegates on the VW EWC were not really dependent on the European body to defend their local interests, conflicts and problems at European level made it clear to both management and employee representatives in the 1990s that any Europeanisation of production strategies and personnel policies would not be feasible without a European level of interest regulation.

Finally, for GM there were a number of events of significance for understanding the dynamics of EWC development at the company. These have included the employment security agreement in Germany negotiated by the works council in the late-1990s, which was seen as a purely national arrangement by GM workers in other European countries and in some respects as an affront or act of selfishness intended to force the burden of adjustment onto other workforces. The limits of such a national strategy of interest regulation became evident in 2000 in the case of GM Europe, as with Ford and Visteon, with the spinning off of component manufacture and the joint venture with Fiat.

Since that point, the development of GM in Europe has been characterised by continuous cuts in output and employment, and with this a significant need for interest regulation. One major factor in shaping the identity of the EWC was the conflict over the announcement to close the Vauxhall plant in Luton in 2001. In order to prevent this, the EWC organised a pan-European Day of Action. The large-scale response to the proposed closure was unexpected both by employees and management. Around 40,000 workers across Europe participated in the associated actions.

This was an important experience at European level for local active employee representatives that had a major impact on the subsequent work of the EWC. It will be some time before it is possible to assess the short and medium term disruption to the work of the EWC caused by the (short-lived) bankruptcy of GM in the US, and the failed disposal of GM Europe and its management by trustees.

Compared with the foregoing, there is no comparable critical event in the development of the EWC at Daimler that helps understand its evolution. This is partly because the truly relevant breaks of continuity, such as cooperation with and subsequent separation from Chrysler, were enacted at global rather than European level and, as a consequence, were dealt with by the World Employee Committee – and also had only minor (or event positive) implications for European employment. For Renault and PSA, the conflicts over the plant closures at Ryton and Vilvoorde were critical events that are central in understanding the constitution of the EWC type in terms of the hypothesis of path-dependency.

Finally, our findings strongly indicate that a synchronic perspective on organisational fit and home-country contexts is not sufficient to understand the specificities of the structure and operations of EWCs. A diachronic perspective that takes into account the historical development and, in particular, critical events is no less important.

12.5 Actors' strategies and the significance of individuals

Similar considerations to the above apply in the case of specific actors, both collective and individual. In the final analysis, EWCs are not composed of formal structures and assemblages of resources but networks of individuals, interpersonal relationships and – often strong – personalities who structure and undertake the forum's work. The significance of such personalities can also be seen in the case studies. Even in the case of the comparatively weakly coordinated EWC at Toyota, the external adviser plays a crucial role in determining how the forum operates as one of the few people who have worked with the EWC from its inception and who is integrated into all its activities and decision-making processes. In the case of the Daimler and VW EWCs, the chairs of their group works councils have played a significant role. In turn, Klaus Franz, the chair of the GM group works council in Germany and of the EWC, exercised a key role. The significance of these individuals has been highlighted in the relevant chapters, which have pointed to their biographies and values.

However, it is not only – or even primarily – individuals that are decisive. Rather, it is the interplay of different actors strategies and particular actors or groups of actors. For example, employee representatives at Ford Valencia (Spain) developed a local strategy that was strongly focused on local interests and based more on cooperation with local management that European employee cooperation. In contrast, at VW the constellation was very different in the case of the relationship of SEAT employee representatives from Barcelona within the VW EWC, where the dominant factor was individual relationships based on trust between employee representatives in Barcelona and Germany that allowed agreements to be concluded on both local and joint strategies.

This level of actor strategies has been especially important for both the French-based groups and EWCs, as in these cases, and depending on the respective strenghts of the trade unions involved, very complex and often intransparent relationships and strategies have emerged. This became very clear in the well-documented case of the closure of Renault's Vilvoorde plant (Rehfeldt, 1998), where the lines of cleavage ran not only between EWC and management but also within the EWC. In particular, Belgian representatives did not want to negotiate at European level. There were also differences amongst French employee representatives on how to deal strategically with transfers of production – despite agreement on rejecting the closure of Vilvoorde. While the CGT insisted on a strategy of 'produisons français' and the use of channels of French interest representation, the CFDT wanted to include EWC members.

It is possible to discern distinctive and typical workplace and company-related cultures of employment regulation in different companies. Whereas Ford is dominated by a strategy of robust but cooperative representation, but with a latent capacity to engage in conflict, the GM group and its EWC have more of a 'tit for tat' strategy based on a comparatively low level of trust between management and employee representatives. VW and Daimler are heavily influenced by the German codetermination culture of co-management.

At Toyota, management initially adopted a very restrictive stance towards the EWC, expressed, for example, in the fact that they occupied the majority of the seats in the forum. Over time, this position was relaxed, not least due to the experience that EWCs in general, and the TEF in particular, turned out to be institutions that did not have to be feared. In practice, it emerged that the important Belgian trade unions (and in particular the liberal one) pursued a similar approach to interest regulation as management: in addition, the EWC could be held to the company line through the external adviser and EWC secretary, who was both close to management culturally but also structurally weak.

Honda has remained the only company in our sample that – over some fifteen years – has retained its defensive stance towards an EWC, nourished by an ideology of harmonious workplace employment relations in which contrary interests are either declared to be unimportant or even denied, given the convergent interests of management and 'associates', and which are expressed in an almost systematic 'EWC avoidance strategy'. Honda has established procedures for informing employee representatives at local level that are understood as European-level meetings, and therefore complies with the formal requirements of the EWC Directive. However, the structures and processes that have been installed have hindered the emergence of independent collective employee representation at supra-local level. European information meetings are unequivocally dominated by management representatives. Not all employee representatives are elected by employees but appointed by their managers. There are also indications that 'awkward' participants soon depart from the forum. Some German works council members have simply refused to take part in the information meetings. It is only recently, under the impression of the crisis, that some movement has been seen in meetings, as employee representatives now have an increased need for information and responses to questions about future developments.

12.6 Regulatory effectiveness and outputs

As already discussed in Chapter 3.3.2, we distinguish here between an EWC's level of activity and its outputs in terms of interest representation, with the aim of arriving at a more nuanced assessment of the regulatory and representative capability of EWCs – given that the level of activity of an EWC, measured in terms of the number of extraordinary meetings or formal agreements, can diverge from its success in negotiation or the work of interest representation. Moreover, representative effectiveness also ultimately depends on the actual problems and challenges that confront an EWC. We began with the assumption that, for example, there might not be a sufficient need for regulation in a prospering company to activate a formally existing EWC and transform it into an effective operational body.

A number of findings in this study confirm and illustrate this assessment. For example, the EWC at Daimler was comparatively inactive for more than a decade after it was established. This can hardly be explained in terms of any fundamental weakness of employee representatives in the home country but is rather a function of the fact that strongly divisionalised company structures and extremely stable production and employment arrangements meant that very few issues and occasions arose that called for regulation. Similarly, at Toyota and Honda there was no major challenge up until 2008 in the shape of programmes for restructuring or reducing headcounts that called for regulatory activity.

While a large number of publications (Carley, 2002; Greer and Hauptmeier, 2008; Kotthoff, 2006) have used the criterion of the number of agreements concluded as a benchmark for the effectiveness of EWCs, we have argued that the absence of formal agreements between management and the EWC might be due to the fact that there is little requirement for regulation at a company. An EWC that is perceived as 'weak' from the outside – for example, in terms of the number of agreements or publicly visible actions – can, therefore, only be judged for regulatory effectiveness in the context of its specific circumstances (level of Europeanisation of corporate structures and strategies and the need for regulation). Conversely, a high level of public activity by an EWC might be the product of conflicts at a company or developments prompted by an economic crisis and is not necessarily an indicator of a high level of regulatory efficacy. This applies, for example, to the EWC at GM, which was seen as the epitome of a strong and effective negotiating European body by some authors (see in particular Greer and Hauptmeier, 2008; Kotthoff, 2006b). From a comparative perspective, it is also important to emphasise that there was a considerable need for regulation at GM, based on its protracted crisis, that the form of highly visible protest chosen by the EWC reflected its generally weak negotiating position, and that the negotiated output frequently consisted in measures to slow down the process of adjustment, at least for a period, and share the impact more equally over the whole workforce.

Finally, as far as representative effectiveness is concerned, it should be remembered that EWCs, especially in large companies, are not the only institution for interest regulation. Space for the EWC to emerge as an independent actor is also restricted where independent (cross-border) institutions emerged prior to 1994. Analysis of the level of activity and outputs should, therefore, take into account the role and function of the EWC in the overall matrix of internal institutions of interest regulation. Seen from this standpoint, for example, the VW EWC would not appear to be a deficient and weak representative forum but rather an important European platform for activities and an additional source of power for the (any strong) employee representation within the VW group, able – if needed – to assume important coordination functions and mobilise the solidarity needed for joint employee action.

All the individual and collective actors at the level of EWCs have additional and alternative roles and fields of activity. As a rule, they are integrated into workplace and national representative arrangements as works council members, shop stewards, and trade union members. The European level represents an additional and resource-intensive arena of regulation – a consideration that also applies to management. As a consequence, the level of activity depends very much on the perceived need for regulation, which for its part is a function of the capacity of relevant interest groups to articulate their concerns.

This study argued that in some cases there may be an organisational fit between EWC structures and corporate structures.[284] For the most part, this assumption was confirmed for the eight automotive companies as far as regulatory effectiveness was concerned. However, it was also evident that there was no automatic link between company coordination and EWC coordination. The case of PSA, for example, showed that the level of activity of an EWC depended both very much on the *perceived* need for regulation on the part of EWC members (or a dominant influential coalition within the EWC) and an EWC's organisational capacity and resources, as well as on individuals able and willing to set matters in motion.

There was a stronger need for regulation in the (somewhat) strongly coordinated cases of Ford, GM, Renault, VW, Toyota and PSA (global or transnational groups). In the cases of Ford, GM, Renault and VW, this led – at least for some periods – to a corresponding activation of the EWC. In contrast, at Toyota attempts by some EWC contingents to do so foundered on the resistance of a coalition of EWC members at the Brussels headquarters that were generally more positively-inclined to management, European HRM, and the influential external adviser. In the case of Daimler and Honda, which we characterised as (somewhat) weakly coordinated, the need for regulation was also perceived as comparatively weak: but also here – and especially at Honda – a higher need for regulation cannot be expected to automatically

284 Compare the Introduction to the English Edition, in this volume.

lead to a higher level of activity. It is primarily the culture of the company and the structural shortcomings of the EWC that obstruct such a development.

Overall, the EWCs analysed here are far removed from institutions of 'codetermination' in the German sense of formalised and extensive rights to information, consultation and – critically – scope to block or veto management decisions on some issues. However, in some instances EWCs, through their interplay with other group-wide structures and institutions of interest regulation, might enable some, originally national, rights to be extended to the European level – albeit possibly limited both in time and geographical application. Although the effectiveness of interest representation is influenced by many factors, a comparison of the cases in our sample suggests that this depends to some degree on the type of EWC. For instance, transnational (Ford, GM) and global (VW, less so Renault) EWCs demonstrate a high level of representative effectiveness and scope for influence that goes beyond the information and consultation rights provided for in the Directive. By contrast, focal EWCs (PSA, Honda, Daimler, Toyota) seem to exhibit scarcely any European added-value. One major reason for this almost certainly lies in coordination weaknesses, which hamper ongoing interest representation and rapid responses to imminent regulatory needs. Transnational and global 'codetermination' in some respects requires the existence of a functioning network of communication and cooperation based on mutual trust and confidence. Both transnational and global EWCs obtain their representative strength, however, through their anchoring in institutions (in all our cases German) of workplace and company-level codetermination, and through a strategic and skilful linking of different levels and institutions of representation (supervisory board, central and group works council, EWC). As such, cross-border 'transnational codetermination' does not emerge solely through the activity of a network in the vacuum of cross-border coordination but is rather rooted to a great extent in existing local and national institutions and networks of relationships of interest regulation within companies and groups.

We consider that our conceptual borrowings from organisational studies have proved useful in addressing our research questions. Characterising EWCs as non-profit organisations and collective actors that have to develop their aims, modus operandi, structure and resources in the context of and in relation to a for-profit organisation has allowed us to take more systematic account of the complex multi-level relationships between local operations, countries and the EU within the intra- and inter-organisational dynamics of interaction. By differentiating four forms of internationalisation (global, focal, multinational, transnational) it was possible to locate both companies and their EWCs more precisely in terms of their organisational pattern. As such, it enabled a more systematic exploration and testing of the hypothesis of organisational fit.

The results of the study show that it is worthwhile distinguishing the dimensions of resources, power, culture and knowledge in analytical terms in order to explain and understand EWCs and their representational effectiveness. In fact, such a distinction is a prerequisite for being able to ascertain that, as far as causal relationships between the internationalisation of companies and EWCs are concerned, material and personnel resources and power are of considerable significance and culture and knowledge seem to play a more minor role.

One task for future research might be to conceptualise and empirically explore these four analytical dimensions, in particular knowledge and culture. There is also still a need for more investigation of the transferability of our research design and results to other industries, and for a closer relationship between industrial relations research and the findings of organisational studies and transnationalisation research.

Appendix

Figure 21: Home Country Share: Employment, Production Sites and Production (2008)

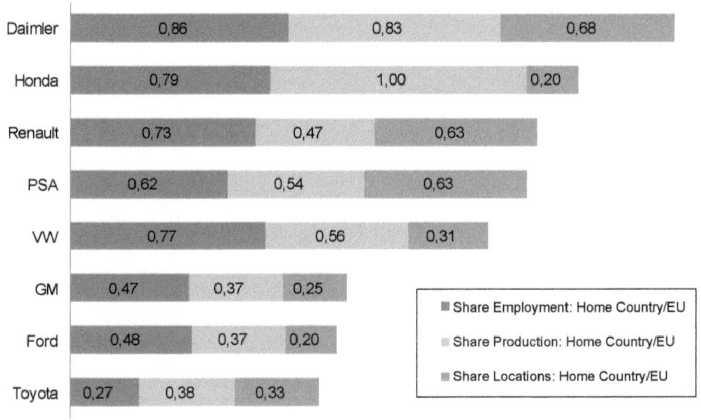

Source: calculated by the authors from company data

Figure 22: Car Production Europe 1998–2008

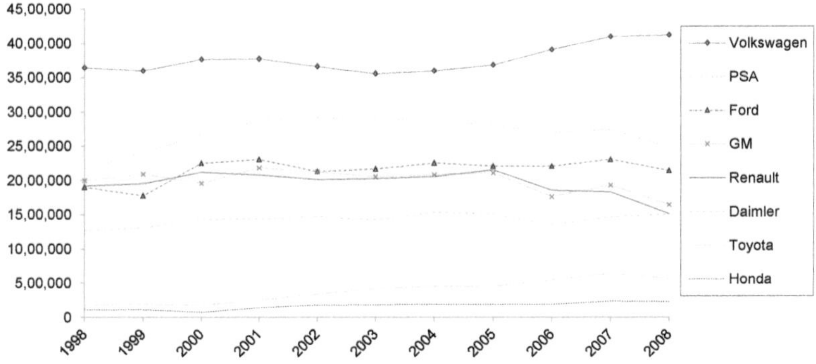

Source: OICA, several years

Figure 23: Index Car Production Europe 1998–2008 (1998=100)

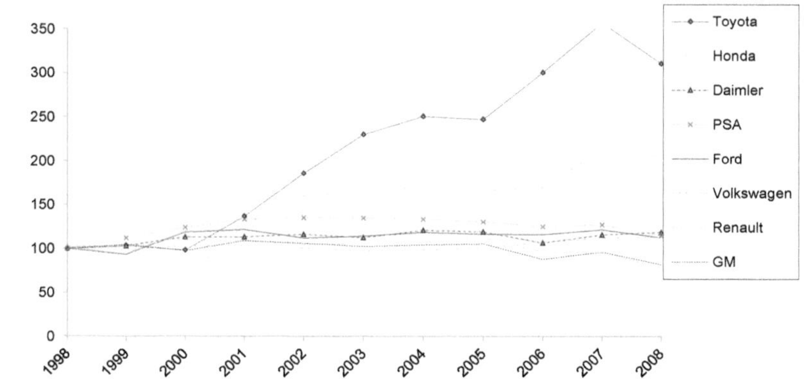

Source: OICA, several years

Figure 24: Share of Home Country Representation at EWC and S.C.

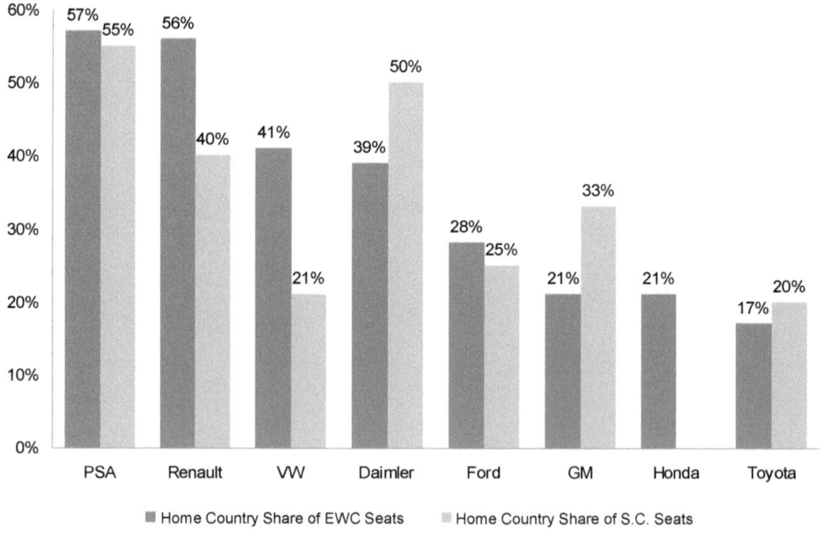

Source: calculation by the authors according to interviews and EWC agreements

*Figure 25: EWC-Index of Representativity**

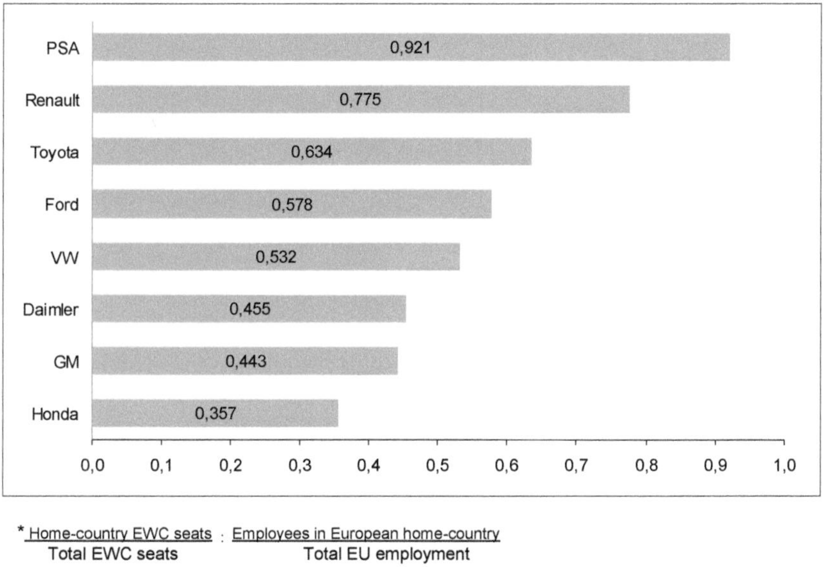

Source: calculation by the authors according to interviews and EWC agreement

Table 11: Dispersion of Employment, Production Sites and Production (2008/2009)

	Ford	General Motors	Volkswagen	Daimler	Renault	PSA	Toyota	Honda
Employment								
World	179.000	235.000	337.789	273.216	129.068	207.800	316.121	181.876
EU	48.300	53.742	230.000	194.233	83.768	182.200	17.792	7.200
EU Home Country	23.200 (DE)	25.103 (DE)	178.000	167.753	60.791	113.700	4.835 (GB)	3.000 (GB)
Home Country	87.000 (US)	91.000 (US)	178.000	167.753	60.791	113.700	65.800 (JP)	60.000 (JP)
Largest EU-Site	17.000	15.000	43.500	28.804	5.071	14.300	4.140	2.500
Share EU / World	27%	23%	68%	71%	65%	88%	6%	4%
Share EU Home Country / EU	48%	47%	77%	86%	73%	62%	27%	79%
Share EU Home Country / World	13%	11%	53%	61%	47%	55%	2%	3%
Share Home Country / World	49%	39%	–	–	–	–	21%	33%
Share Largest Site / EU	35%	28%	19%	15%	6%	8%	23%	79%
Production Sites								
World	88	–	50	72	35	31	75	39
EU	10	16	36	22	19	19	6	5
EU Home Country	2	4	11	15	12	12	2	1
Home Country	28	-	-	-	-	-	15	5
Share EU / World	9%	-	72%	31%	54%	61%	7%	13%
Share EU Home Country / EU	20%	25%	31%	68%	63%	63%	33%	20%
Share EU Home Country / World	2%	–	22%	21 %	34%	39%	3%	3%
Share Home Country / World	32%	–	–	–	–	–	20%	13%

Table 11: (continued)

	Ford	General Motors	Volkswagen	Daimler	Renault	PSA	Toyota	Honda
Production								
World	5.407.000	8.282.803	6.437.414	2.174.299	2.417.351	3.325.407	9.237.780	3.912.700
EU	2.142.498	1.643.717	4.124.820	1.505.505	1.510.977	2.477.812	561.686	230.423
EU Home Country	789.642	614.491	2.326.481	1.244.334	716.979	1.348.866	213.400	230.423
Home Country	1.602.011	2.356.576	2.326.481	1.244.334	716.979	1.348.866	4.911.861	1.264.381
Share EU / World	40%	20%	64%	69%	63%	75%	6%	6%
Share EU Home Country / EU	37%	37 %	56%	83%	47%	54%	38%	100%
Share EU Home Country / World	15%	7 %	36%	57%	30%	41%	2%	6%
Share Home Country / World	30%	28 %	–	–	–	–	53%	32%

References

Ackermann, R. (2003). 'Die Pfadabhängigkeitstheorie als Erklärungsansatz unternehmerischer Entwicklungsprozesse'. In Schreyögg, G. and Sydow, J. (ed.), *Managementforschung*, pp. 225–255 Wiesbaden.

Addison, J. T. and Belfield, C. R. (2002). 'What Do We Know about the New European Works Councils? Some Preliminary Evidence from Britain', *Scottish Journal of Political Economy*, 49 (4), 418–444.

Adelt, B., Sander, L. and Stadler, R. (2008). *Controlling im Volkswagen Konzern*. Wolfsburg.

Aldrich, H. (1979). *Organizations and Environments*. Englewood Cliffs.

Ando, K. (2005). *Japanese Multinationals in Europe. A Comparison of the Automobile andPharmaceutical Industries*. Cheltenham.

Araki, T. (2005). 'Corporate Governance Reforms, Labour Law Developments, and the Future of Japan's Practice-Dependent Stakeholder Model', *Japan Labour Review*, 2:1, 27–53.

Banyuls, J., Haipeter, T. and Neumann, L. (2008). 'European Works Council at General Motors Europe: Bargaining Efficiency in Regime Competition?', *Industrial Relations Journal*, 39 (6), 532–547.

Bartlett, C. and Ghoshal, S. (1989). *Managing Across Borders: The Transnational Solution*. London.

Baerlett, C., Ghoshal, S., and Beamish, P. (2008). *Transnational Management*. International Edition. Boston: McGraw-Hill.

Bartmann, M. (2005). 'Facing Tough Decisions: Wenn es ernst wird im Eurobetriebsrat: Standortkonkurrenzen bei GM Europe', *Die Mitbestimmung*, 51 (8), 32–36.

Bartmann, M. and Blum-Geenen, S. (2007). 'Wie die europäische Arbeitnehmervertretung bei GM Europe im jüngsten Standortwettbewerb punkten konnte', *Die Mitbestimmung*, International Edition 2007, 1–5.

Bartmann, M. and Dehnen, V. (2009). 'Cooperation versus Competition: Union and Works Council Strategies in the Delta Site-Selection Process at General Motors Europe', in Hertwig, M., Pries, L. and Rampeltshammer, L. (eds), *European Works Councils in Complementary Perspectives*, pp. 301–328, Brussels.

Bercusson, B. *(1992)*. 'Maastricht: A Fundamental Change in European Labour Law', *Industrial Relations Journal*, 23(3), 117–190.

Bercusson, B. and Dickens, L. (1996). *Equal Opportunities and Collective Bargaining in Europe*. Dublin.

Beyer, J. (2005). 'Pfadabhängigkeit ist nicht gleich Pfadanhängigkeit! Wider den impliziten Konservatismus eines gängigen Konzepts', *Zeitschrift für Soziologie,* 34 (1), 5–21.

Beyer, J. (2010). 'The Same or Not the Same – On the Variety of Mechanisms of Path Dependence', *International Journal of Social Sciences,* 5:1 2010. 1–11.

Bicknell, H. (2007). 'Ethno-, Poly- and Eurocentric European Works Councils'. In Whittall, M., Knudsen, H. and Huijgen, F. (eds), *Towards a European Labour Identity: The Case of the European Works Council,* pp. 111–13, London.

Blanke, T. (1999). 'Recht und Praxis der Europäischen Betriebsräte«, in: Kritische Justiz, Jg. 32, H. 4, PP. 497–526.

Bordenave, G. (1998). 'Globalization at the Heart of Organizational Change: Crisis and Recovery at the Ford Motor Company'. In Freyssenet, M., Mair, A., Shimizu, K. and Volpato, G. (eds), *One Best Way? Trajectories and Industrial Models of the World's Automobile Producers, the International GERPISA Programme 'Emergence of New Industrial Models',* pp. 211–241, New York.

Borghoff, T. (2005). *Evolutionary Theory of the Globalisation of Firms.* Wiesbaden.

Bosch, A., Ellguth, P., Schmidt, R. and Trinczek, R. (1999). *Betriebliches Interessenhandeln: Zur politischen Kultur der Austauschbeziehungen zwischen Management und Betriebsrat in der westdeutschen Industrie.* Opladen.

Boyer, R., Charron, E., Jürgens, U. and Tolliday, S. (1998). *Between Imitation and Innovation. The Transfer and Hybridization of Productive Models in the International Automobile Industry.* New York.

Boyer, R. and Freyssenet, M. (1999). 'Rewriting the Future. Profit Strategies, Forms of Internationalisation and New Spaces in the Automobile Industry' In Eckardt, A., Köhler, H.-D. and Pries, L. (eds), *Global Players in lokalen Bindungen. Unternehmensglobalisierung in soziologischer Perspektive,* pp. 81–97, Berlin.

— (2002). *Produktionsmodelle. Eine Typologie am Beispiel der Automobilindustrie.* Berlin.

Brown, R. K. *(1992). Understanding Industrial Organizations. Theoretical Perspectives in Industrial Sociology.* London/New York.

Bruggemann, F. (1997). 'The Renault Ruling Examined', *European Works Councils Bulletin,* Vol. 12, 15–16.

Bruyninckx, H. (1997). 'The Closure of Renault-Vilvoorde', *European Industrial Relations Observatory on-line,* Vol. 3, 1–3.

Bueggel, A. (2002). Comparative Tables on EWC Legal Proceedings (Court and Out-of-Court/ Extrajudical) in the EU Member States, <www.emf-fem.org/ content/ download /17654/184737/ version/2/file/English.pdf> accessed 30 April 2010.

Buschak, W. (1997). 'Stand der Umsetzung der EBR Richtlinie in nationales Recht'. In Deppe, J., Hoffmann, R. and Stützel, W. (eds), *Europäische Betriebsräte. Wege in ein soziales Europa,* pp. 92–114, Frankfurt am Main/New York.

Cantwell, J. A. and Piscitello, L. (1999), 'The Emergence of Corporate International Networks for the Accumulation of Dispersed Technological Capabilities', *Management International Review*, Vol. 39, 123–147.

Canzler, W. and Schmidt, G. *(eds)* (2003). *Das zweite Jahrhundert des Automobils. Technische Innovationen, ökonomische Dynamik und kulturelle Aspekte.* Berlin.

Carley, M. (2001). *Bargaining at European Level? Joint Texts Negotiated by European Works Councils.* Brussels.

— (2002), 'European-Level Bargaining in Action? Joint Texts Negotiated by European Works Councils', *Transfer*, 8 (4), 646–653.

Carley, M. and Hall, M. (1996). 'Comparative Analysis of Agreements. Review of Current Agreements on Information and Consultation in European Multinationals' *Social Europe Supplement*, 5–59.

Carroll, W. K. and Fennema, M. (2002). 'Is There a Transnational Business Community?', *International Sociology*, 17 (3), 393–419.

Child, J. (1997). 'Strategic Choice in the Analysis of Action, Structure, Organizations and Environment: Retrospect and Prospect', *Organization Studies*, 18(1), 43–76.

Crouch, C. (1993). *Industrial Relations and the European State Traditions.* Oxford.

Crozier, M. and Friedberg, E. (1977). *Die Zwänge kollektiven Handelns. Über Macht und Organisation.* Frankfurt.

Czarniawska, B. and Joerges, B. (1996). 'Travels of Ideas'. In Czarniawska, B. and Sevon, G. (eds), *Translating Organizational Change*, pp. 13–48, Berlin.

Daimler (2008). *Geschäftsbericht: Innovationen für nachhaltige Mobilität.* Stuttgart.

Danis, J.-J. and Hoffmann, R. (1995). 'From the Vredeling Directive to the European Works Councils Directive – Some Historical Remarks', *Transfer*, 1(2), 180–187.

David, P. A. (1986). 'Understanding the Economics of QWERTY: The Necessity of History'. In Parker, W. N. (ed.), *Economic History and the Modern Economist*, pp. 30–49, Oxford.

Dehnen, V. and Rampeltshammer, L. (2010). 'Transnationale Solidarität auf betrieblicher Ebene: Utopie oder Realität? Am Beispiel des Europäische Betriebsrat bei General Motors Europe'. In Gerlach, F., Greven, T., Mückenberger, U. and Schmidt, E. (eds), *Gewerkschaftliche Solidarität unter Bedingungen von Krise und globaler Konkurrenz*, Münster.

Dilger, A. (2002). Ökonomik betrieblicher Mitbestimmung: Die wirtschaftlichen Folgen von Betriebsräten. München/Mering.

DiMaggio, P. J. and Powell, W. W. (1983). 'The Iron Cage Revisited: Institutional Isomorphism and Collective Rationality in Organizational Fields', *American Sociological Review*, 48(2), 147–160.

Djelic, M.-L. and Quack, S. (2007). 'Overcoming Path Dependencies – Path Generation in Open Systems', *Theory and Society*, 36(2), 161–186.

Dombois, R. (1992). 'Volkswagen in USA'. In Dombois, R. and Doleschal, R. (eds), *Wohin läuft VW? Die Automobilproduktion in der Wirtschaftskrise.* Reinbeck.

— (2009), 'Die VW Affäre – Lehrstück zu den Risiken deutschen Co-Managements?', *Industrielle Beziehungen,* 16(3), 207–231.

Dörrenbächer, C. (2000). *Measuring Corporate Internationalisation. A Review of Measurement Concepts and Their Use.* (WZB Discussion Paper FS 00–101). Berlin.

Dorssemont, F. (2006). 'The Renault Saga (Revisited)', *European Company Law,* 3(1), 5–10.

Doz, A. J. S. and Williamson, P. (2001). *From Global to Metanational. How Companies Win in the Knowledge Economy.* Boston.

Dribbusch, H. (2004): *Agreement on restructuring and cost-cutting at GM Germany,* <http://www.eurofound.europa.eu/observatories/eurwork/articles/agreement-on-restructuring-and-cost-cutting-at-gm-germany> accessed 30 April 2010.

Dunning, J. H. (1979). 'Explaining Changing Patterns of International Production: in Defence of the Eclectic Theory', *Oxford Bulletin of Economic and Statistics,* 41(4), 269–295.

— (1995), 'The Global Economy and Regimes of National and Supranational Governance', *Business and Contemporary World,* 7(1), 124–136.

Eckardt, A., Köhler, H.-D. and Pries, L. (2000). 'Auf dem Weg zu global operierenden Konzernen? Fallstudien zu den Internationalisierungsverläufen deutscher Automobilkonzerne in den 90er Jahren' (Forschungsbericht), Erlangen.

Eller-Braatz, E. and Klebe, T. (1998). 'Benchmarking in der Automobilindustrie – Folgen für Betriebs- und Tarifpolitik am Beispiel General Motors Europe', *WSI-Mitteilungen,* 51(7), 442–450.

Emmerson, R. N. (1962). 'Power-Dependence Relations', *American Sociological Review,* 27(1), 31–41.

Eurofound (2006). *EWCs in the new Member States. Case study: Volkswagen.* Brussels, <www.eurofound.europa.eu/pubdocs/2006/656/en/1/ef06656en.pdf>.

European Metalworkers' Federation, EMF (2005). 'GME Restructuring and Framework Agreements: An Example of EMF European Company Policy', *EMF Focus N 1,* Brussels.

Ferner, A. and Hyman, R. (eds) (1999). *Changing Industrial Relations in Europe.* Oxford.

Ferner, A., Quintanilla, J. and Varul, A. (2001). 'Country-of-Origin Effects, Host Country Effects and the Management of HR in Multinationals: German Companies in Britain and Spain', *Journal of World Business,* 36(2), 117–127.

Fetzer, T. (2008). 'European Works Councils as Risk Communities: The Case of General Motors', *European Journal of Industrial Relations,* 14(3), 289–308.

Fisch, J. H. and Oesterle, M.-J. (2003). 'Exploring the Globalization of German MNCs with the Complex Spread and Diversity Measure', *Schmalenbach Business Review*, 55(1), 2–21.

Fischer, S. (1998). *Human Resource Management und Arbeitbeziehungen im Betrieb. Eine empirische Untersuchung in der Chemischen Industrie Deutschlands.* Munich/ Mering.

Fitzgerald, I. and Stirling, J. D. *(eds)* (2004). *European Works Council: Pessimism of the Intellect, Optimism of the Will?* London.

Flynn, M.S. (1998). 'The General Motors Trajectory: Strategic Shift or Tactical Drift'. In Fre Freyssenet, M., Mair, A., Shimizu, K. and Volpato, G. (eds), *One Best Way? The Trajectories and Industrial Models of World Automobile Producers*, pp. 179–210, Oxford/New York: OUP.

Ford, H. (1922) *My Life and Work*, London: Heinemann (reprinted Dodo Press).

Ford of Europe and FEWC (2006). *Sustainable Workers' Participation in Europe. Ford European Works Council – First Ten Years.*

Freyssenet, M. (1998). 'Renault, from Diversified Mass Production to Innovative Flexible Production'. In Freyssenet, M., Mair, A., Shimizu, K. and Volpato, G. (eds), *One Best Way? The Trajectories and Industrial Models of World Automobile Producers*, pp. 365–394, Oxford/New York.

— (2009a). 'PSA: The Difficulties of a Volume and Diversity Profit Strategy'. In Freyssenet, M. (ed.). *The Second Automobile Revolution. Trajectories of the World Carmakers in the 21the Century*, pp. 246–266, Basingstoke/New York.

— (2009b). 'Renault, 1992–2007: Globalisation and Strategic Uncertainties'. In Freyssenet, M. (ed.). *The Second Automobile Revolution. Trajectories of the World Carmakers in the 21the Century*, pp. 267–286, Basingstoke/New York.

— (ed.) (2009c). *The Second Automobile Revolution, Trajectories of the World Carmakers in the 21st Century.* New York.

Freyssenet, M., Mair, A., Shimizu, K. and Volpato, G. *(eds)* (1998). *One Best Way? The Trajectories and Industrial Models of World Automobile Producers.* Oxford/ New York.

Fürstenberg, F. (1958). 'Der Betriebsrat – Strukturanalyse einer Grenzinstitution', *Kölner Zeitschrift für Soziologie und Sozialpsychologie*, 10(3), 418–429.

Giddens, A. (1984). *The Constitution of Society. Outline of the Theory of Structuration.* Cambridge: Polity Press.

Gilman, M. and Marginson, P. (2002). 'Negotiating European Works Councils: Contours of Constrained Choice', *Industrial Relations Journal*, 33(1), 36–51.

Goetschy, J. (1998). 'France: Limits of Reform'. In Ferner, A. and Hyman, R. (eds), *Changing Industrial Relations in Europe*, pp. 357–394, Oxford.

Goetschy, J. and Rozenblatt, P. (1992). 'France: The Industrial Relations System at a Turning Point?', In Ferner, A. and Hyman, R. (eds), *Industrial Relations in the New Europe*, pp. 404–444, Oxford.

Goldthorpe, J. H. (1997). 'Current Issues in Comparative Macro-Sociology. A Debate on Methodological Issues', *Comparative Social Research*, 16(1), 1–26.

Gordon, M. E. and L. Turner (Eds.), *Transnational cooperation among labor unions*. Ithaca, NY: ILR Press/Cornell University Press.

Granovetter, M. (1985). 'Economic Action and Social Structure: The Problem of Embeddedness', *American Journal of Sociology*, 90(3), 481–510.

Greer, I. and Hauptmeier, M. (2007). 'Political Entrepreneurship and Co-Managers: Labour Transnationalism at Four Multinational Auto Companies', *British Journal of Industrial Relations*, 46(1), 76–97.

Haipeter, T. (2000). *Mitbestimmung bei VW. Neue Chancen für die betriebliche Interessenvertretung?* Münster.

— (2006). 'Der Europäische Betriebsrat bei General Motors – Auf dem Weg zur europäischen Mitbestimmung?', *WSI-Mitteilungen*, 59(11), 617–623.

Hall, M. (1992). 'Behind the European Works Councils Directive: The European Commission's Legislative Strategy', *British Journal of Industrial Relations*, 30(4), 547–566.

Hall, P. and Soskice, D. (eds) (2001). *Varieties of Capitalism: The Institutional Foundations of Comparative Advantage*. Oxford.

Hancké, B. (1998). *Industrial Restructuring and Industrial Relations in the European Car Industry – Instruments and Strategies for Employment*. Berlin.

— (2000). 'European Works Councils and Industrial Restructuring in the European Motor Industry', *European Journal of Industrial Relations*, 6(1), 35–59.

— (2002). *Large Firms and Institutional Change – Industrial Renewal and Economic Restructuring in France*. Oxford.

Hannan, M. and Freeman, J. (1977). 'The Population Ecology of Organizations', *American Journal of Sociology*, 82(5), H. 929–964.

Harper, B. (2004). *Day of action against GM job cuts*,<http://www.eurofound.europa.eu/observatories/eurwork/articles/day-of-action-against-gm-job-cuts> accessed 30 April 2010.

Harzing, A. W. (2000). 'An Empirical Analysis and Extension of the Bartlett and Ghoshal Typology of Multinational Companies', *Journal of International Business Studies*, 31(1), 101–119.

Hauser-Ditz, A., Hertwig, M. and Pries, L. (2008). *Betriebliche Interessenregulierung in Deutschland. Arbeitnehmervertretung zwischen demokratischer Teilhabe und ökonomischer Effizienz*. Frankfurt/New York.

Hebauf, R. (2000). 'Die Ford-Visteon-Vereinbarung', *Die Mitbestimmung*, 12/2000.

Helbig, M. (1999). 'Die Richtlinie über Europäische Betriebsräte in der Anwendung: Das Beispiel Volkswagen', *Zeitschrift für Rechtssoziologie*, Vol. 20, 244–261.

Helbig, M., Piorr, R. and Taubert, R. (2001). 'Der Europäische Betriebsrat zwischen Überregulierung und Social Dumping: Erkenntnisse aus dem Beispiel Volkswagen'. In Clermont, A., Schmeisser, W., Krimphove, D. (eds), *Strategisches Personalmanagement in Globalen Unternehmen*, pp. 653–667, Munich.

Hertwig, M., Pries, L. and Rampeltshammer, L. (2008). *European Works Councils in the Automotive Industry*. Paper presented at the 16th GERPRISA Colloquium. <http://www.ruhruni- bochum.de/soaps/download/EWCs_as_transnational_orgs_16th_GERPISA_Colloquium_in_Turin_RUB_final_4.pdf> accessed on 30 April 2010.

Ireland, P. (2000). *Defending the Rentier: Corporate Theory and the Reprivatization of the Public Company.In* Parkinson, J., Gamble A., and Kelly, G. (eds), The Political Economy of the Company, *pp.141–174,* Oxford/*Portland.*

— (2009a). 'European Works Councils as International Non-Profit-Organisations: An Organisational Research Approach to a Crucial Element of Europeanisation'. In Hertwig, M., Pries, L., and Rampeltshammer, L. (eds), *European Works Councils in Complementary Perspectives*, pp. 13–46, Brussels.

— (ed.) (2009b), *European Works Councils in Complementary Perspectives*, Brussels.

Hoffmann, A., Hall, M., Marginson, P. and Müller, T. (2002). *If the Shoe Fits: The Effects of European Works Councils on Industrial Relations at National Level in Eight US- and UK-based Multinationals*, unpublished paper, Coventry: University of Warwick.

Hoffmann, R. (1997). 'Europäische Betriebsräte – ein Baustein zur Europäisierung industrieller Beziehungen' In Deppe, J., Hoffmann, R. and Stützel, W. (eds), *Europäische Betriebsräte. Wege in ein soziales Europa*, pp. 115–131, Frankfurt/New York.

Hofstede, G. (1980). *Culture's Consequences, International Differences in Work-Related Values.* Newbury Park.

— (1980). *Culture's Consequences.* Beverly Hills.

— (1997). *Cultures and Organizations. Software of the Mind.* New York.

Hofstede, G. and Hofstede, G. J. (2005). *Culture and Organizations. Software of the Mind. Intercultural Cooperation and its Importance for Survival.* New York.

Hollingsworth, J. R. and Boyer, R. (eds) (1997). *Contemporary Capitalism. The Embeddedness of Institutions.* Cambridge.

Honda (2009). *Annual Report.*

Hürtgen, S. (2008). *Transnationales Co-Management: Betriebliche Politik in der globalen Konkurrenz.* Münster.

Hyman, R. (2004). 'Editorial' *European Journal of Industrial Relations*, 10 (2), 115–116.

Jachtenfuchs, M. (1998). *Ideen und Integration. Verfassungsideen in Deutschland, Frankreich und Großbritannien und die Entwicklung der EU.* Mannheim.

Jachtenfuchs, M. and Kohler-Koch, B. (1996). 'Regieren im dynamischen Mehrebenensystem' In Jachtenfuchs, M. and Kohler-Koch, B. (eds), *Europäische Integration*, pp. 15–44, Opladen.

Jäger, R. (1996). 'Euro-Betriebsräte und Entwicklung transnationaler Kommunikationsstrukturen-Praxis und Perspektiven', *WSI Mitteilungen*, 49(8), 483–488.

Japan Labor Bulletin (1995). 'Honda Launches First Works Council in Europe', *Japan Labor Bulletin*, 34(6) <http://www.jil.go.jp/jil/bulletin/year/1995/vol34-06/04.htm> accessed 30 May 2010.

Jürgens, U. (1998). 'The Development of Volkswagen's Industrial Model, 1967–1995'. In Freyssenet, M., Mair, A., Shimizu, K. and Volpato, G. (eds), *One Best Way? Trajectories and Industrial Models of the World's Automobile Producers*, pp. 273–310, New York.

– (2009). 'The Final Chapter of the ›VW Model‹? The VW Trajectory 1995–2005'. In Freyssenet, M. (eds), *The Second Automobile Revolution: Trajectories of the World Carmakers in the 21st Century*, pp. 225–245, New York.

Kawabe, N. (2004). 'Honda'. In Kumon, H. and Abo, T. (eds), *The Hybrid Factory in Europe. The Japanese Management and Production System Transferred*, pp. 246–249, Houndmills, Basingstoke.

Keck, E. and Sikkink, K. (1998). *Activists Beyond Borders*. Ithaca.

Keller, B. (1997). *Einführung in die Arbeitspolitik*.Vienna/Munich.

– (2001), *Europäische Arbeits- und Sozialpolitik*. Oldenbourg.

Kerckhofs, P. (2003). Europäische Betriebsräte. Fakten und Zahlen, Brüssel.

Kessler, L. (2006). *Der Boykott von Peugeot*. (FES Blickpunkt Großbritannien). London.

Kieser, A. and Walgenbach, P. (2003). *Organisation*. Stuttgart.

Klebe, T. and Roth, S. (2000). 'Die Gewerkschaften auf dem Weg zu einer internationalen Strategie? Am Beispiel der Automobilindustrie', *Arbeitsrecht im Betrieb: Zeitschrift für Betriebsratsmitglieder*, 21(12), 749–759.

Klemm, C. and Siebens, F. (2004). 'Erfolgreiche Bildung eines Europäischen Betriebsrats am Beispiel der Unternehmensgruppe der Deutschen Teleko', *Arbeitsrecht im Betrieb*, 25 (6) 355–359.

Klemm, M. and Popp, M. (2005). 'Skoda als ›Learning Community‹. Empirische Befunde zu kulturell-kommunikativen Bedingungen von Wissensaustausch im ›Tochter‹-Konzern-Verhältnis'. In Pries, L. and Hertwig, M. (eds), *Deutsche Automobilproduktion im globalen Wandel. Altindustrie im Rückwärtsgang oder Hichtech- Branche mit Zukunft?*, pp. 125–45, Berlin.

Koch, G. (1987). *Arbeitnehmer steuern mit*. Cologne.

Köhler, H.-D. (2003). 'The DaimlerChrysler Deal: A Nice Marriage or a Nightmare?'. In Freyssenet, M., Shimizu, K., Volpato, G. (eds), *Globalization or Regionalization of the European Car Industry?*, pp. 73–102, London and New York.

– (2009). 'The DaimlerChrysler Deal: A Nice Marriage or a Nightmare?'. In Freyssenet, M. (ed.), *The Second Automobile Revolution. Trajectories of the World Carmakers in the 21st Century*, pp. 309–331, London and New York.

Köhler, H.-D. and González Begega, S. (2009). 'European Works Councils in Spain'. In Hertwig, M., Pries, L. and Rampeltshammer, L. (eds), *European Works Councils in Complementary Perspectives*, pp. 187–217, Brussel.

Kotthoff, H. (1981). *Betriebsräte und betriebliche Herrschaft. Eine Typologie von Partizipationsmustern.* Frankfurt am Main.

– (2006a). *Lehrjahre des Europäischen Betriebsrats: Zehn Jahre transnationale Arbeitnehmervertretung.* Berlin.

– (2006b). 'Ten Years General Motors European Employee Forum (EEF)'. Manuscript for the Hans-Böckler-Stiftung, Düsseldorf.

Kotthoff, H. and Reindl, J. (1990). *Die soziale Welt kleiner Betriebe.* Göttingen.

Kutschker, M. and Schmid, S. (2006). *Internationales Management.* Munich/Vienna.

Lecher, W., Nagel, B., and Platzer, H.-W. (1999). *The Establishment of European Works Councils. From Information Committee to Social Actor.* Aldershot: Ashgate.

Lecher, W. and Platzer, H.-W. (2003). 'Europäische Betriebsräte'. In Schroeder, W and Weßels, B. (eds), *Die Gewerkschaften in Politik und Gesellschaft der Bundesrepublik Deutschland*, pp. 588–613, Wiesbaden.

Lecher, W., Platzer, H.-W., Rüb, S. and Weiner, K.-P. (2001). *European Works Councils: Developments, Types and Networking.* Aldershot: Ashgate.

– (2002). *European Works Councils: Negotiated Europeanisation. Between Statutory Framework and Social Dynamics.* Aldershot: Ashgate.

Liker, J. K. (2004). *The Toyota Way.* New York.

Lorber, P. (1997). 'The Renault-Case: The European Works Council Put to the Test', *The International Journal of Comparative Labour Law and Industrial Relations*, 13(2), 135–142.

Loubet, J.-L. (1998). 'Peugeot Meets Ford, Sloan and Toyota' In Freyssenet, M., Mair, A., Shimizu, K. and Volpato, G. (eds), *One Best Way? Trajectories and Industrial Models of the World's Automobile Producers*, pp. 338–364, Oxford/New York.

– (2003). 'The Cautious and Progressive Internationalization of PSA Peugeot Citroen'. In Freyssenet, M., Shimizu, K. and Volpato, G. (eds), *Globalization or Regionalization of the European Car Industry?*, pp. 170–197, Basingstoke und New York.

Luethge, D. J./Byosière, P. (2009). 'Honda: Serendipity or Strategy from 1997–2007?'. In Freyssenet, M. (ed.), *The Second Automobile Revolution. Trajectories of the World Carmakers in the 21st Century*, pp. 112–128, New York.

Macharzina, K. (2003). *Unternehmensführung. Das internationale Managementwissen.* Wiesbaden.

Mair, A. (1994). 'Honda's Global Flexifactory Network', *International Journal of Operations & Production Management*, 14(3), 6–23.

– (1998). 'The Globalization of Honda's Product-Led Flexible Mass Production System«, in: Freyssenet, M./Mair, A./Shimizu, K./Volpato, G. (Ed.), One Best Way? Trajectories and Industrial Models of the World's Automobile Producers, New York/Oxford, S. 110–138.

March, J. G. (1986). 'Bounded Rationality, Ambiguity, and the Engineering of Choice'. In Elster, J. (ed.), *Rational Choice*, pp. 142–170, Oxford.

March, J. G. and Simon, H. A. (1958). *Organizations*. New York.

Marginson, P. (1992). 'European Integration and Transnational Management-Union Relations in the Enterprise', *British Journal of Industrial Relations*, 30(4), 529–545.

– (1998), 'European Works Councils: The Role of the Negotiated Option'. In Lecher, W. and Platzer, H.-W. (ed.), *European Union – European Industrial Relations*. London: Routledge, pp. 223–233.

Marginson, P., Hall, M., Hoffmann, A. and Müller, T. (2004). 'The Impact of European Works Councils on Management Decision-Making in UK and US-Based Multinationals: A Case Study Comparison', *British Journal of Industrial Relations*, 42(2), 209–233.

Marshall, B. (ed.) (1991). *The Real World*. Boston.

Martin, A. and Ross, G. (1999). 'In the Line of Fire. The Europeanization of Labor Representation'. In Martin, A., Ross, G., Baccaro, L., Daley, A., Fraile, L., Howell, C., Locke, R., Mahon, R. and Silvia, S. (eds). *The Brave New World of European Labour. European Trade Unions at the Millenium*, pp. 312–367, New York/Oxford.

Martínez Lucio, M. (2009). 'The Regulatory Politics of European Works Councils in the United Kingdom: The Challange of Connecting'. In Hertwig, M., Pries,L. and Rampeltshammer, L. (eds), *European Works Councils in Complementary Perspectives*, pp. 127–152, Brussels.

Maurice, M. and Sorge, A. (2000). *Embedding Organizations*. Amsterdam.

Mayntz, R. (2003). 'Governance im modernen Staat'. In Benz, A. (ed.), *Governance. Eine Einführung*, pp. 71–83, Dreifachkurseinheit der FernUniversität Hagen.

Mayntz, R. /Scharpf, F. W. (1995): Der Ansatz des akteurzentrierten Institutionalismus. In: Dies. (Hg.): Gesellschaftliche Selbstregelung und politische Steuerung. Frankfurt (Main)/New York: Campus, pp. 39–72

McKelvey, B. and Aldrich, H. E. (1983). 'Populations, Natural Selection, and Applied Organizational Science', *Adminstrative Science Quarterly*, 28(1), 101–128.

McKersie, R. B. and Walton, R. E. (1992). 'A Retrospective on the Behavioral Theory of Labor Negotiations', *Journal of Organizational Behavior*, 38(13), 277–285.

Meier, A. (1997). *Das Konzept der transnationalen Organisation*. Herrsching.

Mense-Petermann, U. and Wagner, G. (eds) (2006). *Transnationale Konzerne. Ein neuer Organisationstyp?* Wiesbaden.

Mertens, V. (1994). *Europaweite Kooperation von Betriebsräten multinationaler Konzerne. Das Beispiel des Volkswagen-Konzerns.* Wiesbaden.

Meyer, J. W. and Rowan, B. (1977). 'Institutionalized Organizations: Formal Structure as Myth and Ceremony', *American Journal of Sociology,* 83(2), 340–363.

Miles, R. E. and Snow, C. C. (1984). 'Fir, Failure and the Hall of Fame', *California Management Review,* 26(3), 10–28.

Minssen, H. (2006). *Arbeits- und Industriesoziologie.* Frankfurt am Main/New York.

Morley, M. J., Gunnigle, P. and Collings, D. G. (eds) (2006). *Global Industrial Relations.* London/New York.

Müller-Jentsch, W. (1997). *Soziologie der Industriellen Beziehungen – Eine Einführung.* Frankfurt am Main/New York.

— (2007). *Strukturwandel der industriellen Beziehungen. 'Industrial Citizenship' zwischen Markt und Regulierung.* Wiesbaden.

Müller-Jentsch, W. and Seitz, B. (1997). *Betriebsrätebefragung im Maschinenbau 1996.* Arbeits- und Diskussionspapiere Lehrstuhl Mitbestimmung und Organisation, Bochum.

— (1998). 'Betriebsräte gewinnen Konturen. Ergebnisse einer Betriebsräte-Befragung im Maschinenbau', *Industrielle Beziehungen,* 5(4), 361–387.

Müller, M. and Girndt, C. (2009). 'Interview "Allein würden wir keine zwei Jahre überstehen"', *Die Mitbestimmung,* No. 2.

Müller, T. and Hoffmann, A. (2001). 'EWC Research: A Review of the Literature'. Warwick.

— (2002). 'Euro-Betriebsräte unter der Lupe. Zusammenfassender Bericht über die Forschungsliteratur', *Industrielle Beziehungen,* 9(1), 103–111.

Müller, T. and Platzer, H.-W. (2003). 'European Works Councils: A New Mode of EU Regulation and the Emergence of a European Multi-Level Structure of Workplace Industrial Relations'. In Keller, B. and Platzer, H.-W. (eds), *Industrial Relations and European Integration,* pp. 58–84, Aldershot.

Müller, T., Platzer, H.-W. and Rüb, S. (2004a). *Globale Arbeitsbeziehungen in globalen Konzernen? Zur Transnationalisierung betrieblicher und gewerkschaftlicher Politik. Eine vergleichende Fallstudie.* Wiesbaden.

— (2004b). *Grenzübergreifende Arbeitsbeziehungen in globalen Konzernen: Wege und Instrumente transnationaler Interessenvertretung.* Düsseldorf.

Münch, R. (2001). *Offene Räume. Soziale Integration diesseits und jenseits des Nationalstaats.* Frankfurt am Main.

— (2004). 'Perspektiven der sozialen Einigung Europas', *Gewerkschaftliche Monatshefte,* 55(1), 285–291.

Nagel, B. (1999). 'Euro-Betriebsräte: Struktur und Entwicklungspotentiale'. In Nutzinger, H. G. (ed.), *Perspektiven der Mitbestimmung. Historische Erfahrungen und moderne Entwicklungen vor europäischem und globalem Hintergrund*, pp. 347–360, Marburg.

Neyer, J. (1999). 'Legitimes Recht oberhalb des demokratischen Rechtsstaates? Supranationalität als Herausforderung für die Politikwissenschaft', *Politische Vierteljahresschrift*, 40(3), 390–414.

Nomura, M. and Jürgens, U. (1995). *Binnenstruktur des japanischen Produktionserfolges: Arbeitsbeziehungen und Leistungsregulierung in zwei japanischen Automobilunternehmen*. Berlin.

Nonaka, I. (1991). 'The Knowledge-Creating Company', *Harvard Business Review*, 69(6), 96–104.

Ortmann, G. (1995). *Formen der Produktion*. Opladen.

Ortmann, G., Windeler, A., Becker, A. and Schulz, H.-J. (1990). *Computer und Macht in Organisationen – Mikropolitische Analysen*. Opladen.

Osterloh, M. (1993). *Interpretative Organisations- und Mitbestimmungsforschung*. Stuttgart.

Pardi, T. (2005). 'Where Did It Go Wrong? Hybridization and Crisis of Toyota Motor Manufacturing UK, 1989–2001', *International Sociology*, 20(1), 93–118.

— (2006). 'Beyond Labour Costs: Political and Strategic Factors in the Investment Strategy of Toyota in Europe (1989–2004)'. In Pries, L. and Bosowski, C. (eds), *Europäische Automobilindustrie am Scheideweg. Harte globale Herausforderungen und weiche lokale Erfolgfaktoren*, pp. 47–60, Munich/Mering.

Pedersini, R. (2003). *Industrial Relations in the Automotive Sector*, <http://www.eurofound.europa.eu/eiro/2003/12/study/tn0312102s.htm> accessed 30 May 2010.

Perlmutter, H. V. (1969). 'The Tortuous Evolution of the Multinational Corporation', *Columbia Journal of World Business*, 4(1), 9–18.

Pierson, P. (2004). *Politics in Time: History, Institutions, and Social Analysis*. Princeton.

Platzer, H.-W. (2009). 'Approaching and Theorizing European Works Councils: Comments on the Emergence of a European Multi- Level – Structure of Employee Involvement and Participation'. In Hertwig, M., Pries, L. and Rampeltshammer, L. (eds), *European Works Councils in Complementary Perspectives*, pp. 47–69, Brussels.

Platzer, H.-W., Müller, T. (2011). *Global and European Trade Union Federations* (with Rüb, S., Oetgen, T. R., Helmer, M.) Oxford/Berne: Peter Lang.

Platzer, H.-W. and Weiner, K.-P. (1998). 'Europäische Betriebsräte – eine Konstitutionsanalyse. Zur Genese und Dynamik transnationaler Austauschbeziehungen', *Industrielle Beziehungen*, 5 (4) 388–412.

Porter, M. E. (1986). *Competition in Global Industries*. Boston.

Portes, A., Haller, W. J. and Guarnizo, L. E. (2002). 'Transnational Entrepreneurs: An Alternative Form of Immigrant Economic Adaption', *American Sociological Review*, 67(2), 278–298.

Pries, L. (1999a). *Auf dem Weg zu global operierenden Konzernen? BMW, Daimler-Benz und Volkswagen: Die Drei Großen der deutschen Automobilindustrie*. Munich/Mering.

— (1999b). 'Restrukturierung und Globalisierung der deutschen Automobilhersteller', *Industrielle Beziehungen*, 6(2), 125–150.

— (2002). 'Globalisierung und Arbeitnehmer-Interessenvertretung', *Lernchancen und Marktzwänge. Bildungsarbeit im flexiblen Kapitalismus*, 47–68.

— (2005). *Kräftefelder der Strukturierung und Regulierung von Erwerbsarbeit. Überlegungen zu einer entwicklungs- und institutionenorientierten Sozialwissenschaft der Erwerbsarbeit*. Bochum.

— (2008a). *Die Transnationalisierung der sozialen Welt*. Frankfurt.

— (2008b). 'European Works Councils as Transnational Interest Organisations?'. In Pries, L. (ed.), *Rethinking Transnationalism: The Meso-Link of Organisations*. Milton Park, N.Y.

— (2010). *Erwerbsregulierung in einer globalisierten Welt*. Wiesbaden.

Pries, L. and Bosowski, C. (2006). *Europäische Automobilindustrie am Scheideweg*. Mering.

Pries, L. and Hertwig, M. (2005). *Deutsche Autoproduktion im globalen Wandel. Altindustrie im Rückw.rtsgang oder Hightech-Branche mit Zukunft*? Berlin.

Pries, L. and Schweer, O. (2004). 'The Product Development Process as a Measuring Tool for Company Internationalisation? The Case Studies of DaimlerChrysler and Volkswagen', *International Journal of Automotive Technology and Management (IJATM)*, 4(1), 1–21.

Pries, L. and Sezgin, Z. (Ed.) (2010). *Jenseits von 'Identität oder Integration'*, Wiesbaden.

PSA (2008a). *The Group in 2008*.

— (2008b). *Memento 2008*.

Pugh, D. S. and Hickson, D. J. (eds) (1976). *Organizational Structure in its Context. The Aston Programme I*. Westmead.

Pugh, D. S., Hickson, D. J., Hinings, C. R., Macdonald, K. M., Turner, C. and Lupton, T. (1963), 'A Conceptual Scheme for Organizational Analysis', *Administrative Science Quarterly*, 8(4), 289–315.

Pugh, D. S. and Payne, R. L. (eds) (1977). *Organizational Behaviour in its Context. The Aston Programme III*. Westmead.

Rampeltshammer, L. (2008). *Globalization and Industrial Relations*. Frankfurt/New York.

Rampeltshammer, L. and Wachendorf, N. M. (2009). 'European Works Councils in Germany'. In Hertwig, M., Pries, L. and Rampeltshammer, L. (eds), *European Works Councils in Complementary Perspectives*, pp. 219–258, Brussels.

Ramsay, H. (1997). 'Fool's Gold? European Works Councils and Workplace Democracy', *Industrial Relations Journal*, 28(4), 314–323.

Rehfeldt, U. (1998). 'Der Renault-Vilvoorde Konflikt und seine Bedeutung für die europäische Gewerkschaftspolitik', *WSI-Mitteilungen*, 51(7), 450–459.

— (2004). 'European Works Councils and International Restructuring: A Perspective for European Collective Bargaining?'. In Charron, E. and Stewart, P. (eds), *Work and Employment Relations in the Automobile Industry*, pp. 183–194, Basingstoke/ Hampshire/ New York.

— (2009). 'European Works Councils in France'. In Hertwig, M., Pries, L. and Rampeltshammer, L. (eds), *European Works Councils in Complementary Perspective*, pp. 153–186, Brussels.

Renault (2008). *Renault Atlas September 2008.*

Riedl, C. (1999). *Organisatorischer Wandel durch Globalisierung. Optionen für multinationale Unternehmen*, Belrin u.a.

Riehle, W. (1996). 'Globalisierung als unternehmerischer Entwicklungsprozess'. In Steger, U. (ed.), *Globalisierung der Wirtschaft*, pp. 245–265, Berlin/Heidelberg.

Rigaux and Dorssemont, F. (1999). *European Works Councils. A Legal Analysis of the European Works Council: Towards a Revision of the Directive (EC) No 94/45?*, Antwerp.

Rivest, C. (1996). 'Voluntary European Works Councils', *European Journal of Industrial Relations*, 2(2), 235–253.

Rosenzweig, P. M. and Singh, J. V. (1991). 'Organizational Environments and the Multinational Enterprise', *Academy of Management Review*, 16(2), 340–361.

Rott, V. (2008). *Europäische Kooperation und Solidarität.* Berlin.

Rüb, S. (2001). 'Globale Konzerne – globale Arbeitsbeziehungen', *WSI Mitteilungen*, 54(4), 257–264.

Rudolf, S. and Stegemann, K. (2009). 'European Works Councils Activity in Poland'. In Hertwig, M., Pries, L. and Rampeltshammer, L. (eds), *European Works Councils in Complementary Perspectives*, pp. 101–125, Brussels.

Ruigrok, W. and van Tulder, R. (1995). *The Logic of International Restructuring.* London.

Sahlin-Andersson, K. (1996). 'Imitating by Editing Success. The Construction of Organizational Fields and Identities'. In Czarniawska, B. and GujeSevón (eds), *Translating Organizational Change*, pp. 69–92, Berlin.

Schardt, V. (2010). *Europäische Betriebsräte in der deutschen, englischen und französischen Forschung. Eine Literaturstudie.* Bochum.

Scharpf, F. W. (2000). *Interaktionsformen. Akteurzentrierter Institutionalismus in der Politikforschung.* Opladen.

Scheele, A. (2000). *Ford EWC and Management Sign Pioneering Agreement on Visteon Employees* <http://www.eurofound.europa.eu/eiro/2000/04/inbrief/de0004254n.htm> accessed on 30 May 2010.

Schein, E. (1995). *Unternehmenskultur. Ein Handbuch für Führungskräfte.* Frankfurt am Main.

Schimank, U. (2000). *Handeln und Strukturen. Einführung in die akteurstheoretische Soziologie.* Weinheim/Munich.

Schreyögg, G. (2000). *Organisation. Grundlagen moderner Organisationsgestaltung. Mit Fallstudien.* Wiesbaden.

Schreyögg, G./Sydow, J./Koch, J. (2003). 'Organisatorische Pfade – Von der Pfadabhängigkeit zur Pfadkreation?'. In Schreyögg, G. and Sydow, J. (eds), *Managementforschung*, pp. 257–294, Wiesbaden.

Schulte, A. and Hirsch-Kreinsen, H. (2002). 'Internationalisierung von Unternehmen: Das Phänomen der Rückverlagerung', *WSI Mitteilungen*, 55(7), 389–396.

Schulten, T. (1995). 'Europäische Betriebsräte – Stand und Perspektiven einer europaweiten Regulierung der Arbeitsbeziehungen auf der Ebene transnationaler Konzerne'. In Mesch, M. (ed.). *Sozialpartnerschaft und Arbeitsbeziehungen in Europa*, pp. 335–363, Vienna.

— (1996). 'European Works Councils: Prospects for a New System of European Industrial Relations', *European Journal of Industrial Relations*, 2(3), 303–324.

— (1997). 'Europäische Modernisierungskoalitionen? Der Beitrag Europäischer Betriebsräte zur Neuordnung der Arbeitsbeziehungen in Europa'. In Flecker, J. (ed.), *Jenseits der Sachzwanglogik. Arbeitspolitik zwischen Anpassungsdruck und Gestaltungschancen*, pp. 71–102, Berlin.

— (1998). 'Tarifpolitik unter den Bedingungen der Europäischen Währungsunion. Überlegungen zum Aufbau eines tarifpolitischen Mehr-Ebenen-Systems am Beispiel der europäischen Metallindustrie', *WSI-Mitteilungen*, 51(7), 482–493.

Scott, W. R. (1987). 'The Adolescence of Institutional Theory', *Adminstrative Science Quarterly*, 32(4), 493–511.

— (2001). *Institutions and Organizations.* Thousand Oaks/London/New Delhi.

Shimitsu, K. (1998). 'A New Toyotism?'. In Freyssenet, M., Mair, A., Shimizu, K. and Volpato, G. (eds), *One Best Way? Trajectories and Industrial Models of the Worlds Automobile Producers*, pp. 63–90, Oxford/New York.

Shimokawa, K. (2003). 'Honda, an Independent Global Automobile Company, Out of the "Four Million Units Club"'. In Freyssenet, M., Shimizu, K. and Volpato, G. (eds), *Globalization or Regionalization of the American and Asian Car Industry*, pp. 163–184, New York.

Simon, H. A. (1957). *Models of Man.* New York.

Sisson, K., Freyssinet, J., Krieger, H., O'Kelly, K., Schnabel, C., Seifert, H. (1999). *Pacts for Employment and Competitiveness. Concepts and Issues.* Working Paper of the European Foundation for the Improvement of Living and Working Conditions. Luxembourg: Office of Official Publications of the European Communities.

Speidel, F. (2005). *Mitbestimmte versus managementbestimmte Globalisierung in der Automobilindustrie. Ein Vergleich der Internationalisierungsstrategien und ihrer Verarbeitungen durch die Akteure der industriellen Beziehungen am Beispiel VWs und Renaults.* Munich/Mering.

Streeck, W. (1997). 'Neither European Nor Works Councils: A Reply to Paul Knutsen', *Economic and Industrial Democracy,* 18(2), 325–337.

— (1999). 'Social Citizenship under Regime Competition: The Case of the "European Works Council"'. In Streeck, W. (ed.), pp. 124–158, *Korporatismus in Deutschland,* Frankfurt am Main.

Streeck, W. and Vitols, S. (1995). 'The European Community: Between Mandatory Consultation and Voluntary Information'. In Streeck, W. and Rogers, J. (eds), *Works Councils: Consultation, Representation and Cooperation in Industrial Relations,* pp. 243–281, Chicago/London.

Taylor, P. and Groom, A. J. R. *(eds)* (1988). *International Institutions at Work.* London.

Telljohann, V. (2005). 'The European Works Councils – a Role Beyond the EC Directive?, *Transfer. European Review of Labour and Research,* 11(1), 81–96.

— (2007). 'Interest Representation and European Identity: A Twofold Challenge or European Works Councils'. In Whittall, M., Knudsen, H. and Huigen, F. (eds), *The Case of the European Works Council,* pp. 150–168, London/New York.

— (2009). 'European Works Councils: Emergence of a European Collective Identity or Still National Bound Actors?'. In Hertwig, M., Pries, L. and Rampeltshammer, L. (eds), *European Works Councils in Complementary Perspectives,* pp. 71–97, Brussels.

Tempel, A. (2001). *The Cross-National Transfer of Human Resource Management Practices in German and British Multinational Companies.* Munich/Mering.

Tolliday, S. (2003). 'The Origins of Ford of Europe: From Multidomestic to Transnational Corporation, 1903–1976'. In Bonin, H., Lung, Y. and Tolliday, S. (eds), *Ford: The European History, 1903–2003,* pp. 153–242, Paris.

Toyota (2009a). *Toyota Motor Europe. Toyota in Europe,* Brussels <http://www.toyota.co.uk/bv/1024downloads/ToyotainEurope.pdf> accessed 31 May 2010.

— (2009b). *Toyota Motor Europe. Toyota European Sustainability Report.*

Traxler, F. (2003). 'Die Struktur der nationalen Gewerkschaftssysteme im Vergleich'. In Schroeder, W. and Wessels, B. (eds), *Die Gewerkschaften in Politik und Gesellschaft in der Bundesrepublik Deutschland,* pp. 543–564, Wiesbaden.

Traxler, F. and Huemer, G. (2007). *The Handbook of Business Interest Associations, Firm Size and Governance. A Comparative Analytical Approach.* London and New York.

Trinczek, R. (1987). *Zur Struktur innerbetrieblicher Aushandlungsprozesse.* Erlangen.

— (2004). 'Management und betriebliche Mitbestimmung. Eine interessentheoretisch fundierte Typologie kollektiver Orientierungsmuster'. In Artus, I. and Trinczek, R. (eds), Über Arbeit, Interessen und andere Dinge, pp. 181–209, Munich/Mering.

Tulder, R.J.M. van, Berghe, D.A.F. van den, and Muller, A.R. (2001). *Internationalization of the World's Largest Firms.* (Erasmus (S)coreboard of Core Companies). Rotterdam: Rotterdam School of Management/ Erasmus University Rotterdam.

Uhl, H.-J. and Brüning, M. (1999). 'Der Volkswagen Weltkonzernbetriebsrat', *Personalwirtschaft*, 10, 58–61.

Uhl, H.-J. and Lavon, E. (1997). 'Der Europäische Volkswagen-Konzernbetriebsrat. Strukturwandel und Globalisierung, Internationale Solidarität und solidarischer Beschäftigungsausgleich'. In Deppe, J., Hoffmann, R. and Wieland, S. (eds), *Europäische Betriebsräte, Wege in ein soziales Europa*, pp. 216–232, Frankfurt/New York.

UNCTAD (2002). *World Investment Report 2002.* New York: UNCTAD.

UNCTAD (2008). *World Investment Report 2008.* New York: UNCTAD.

Vitols, S. (2003). *Management Cultures in Europe: European Works Councils and Human Resource Management in Multinational Enterprises*, Final Report of a Study Commissioned by the Forum Mitbestimmung und Unternehmen, Bertelsmann-Stiftung und Hans-Böckler-Stiftung, Berlin.

— (2009), *European Works Councils: An Assessment of their Social Welfare Impact.* Working Paper 2009.04 of the European Trade Union Institute, Brussels.

VW (2007). *Driving Ideas. Annual Report.* Wolfsburg.

— (2008). *Driving Ideas. Annual Report.* Wolfsburg.

Wächter, H., Peters, R., Tempel, A. and Müller-Camen, M. (2003). *The 'Country-of-Origin Effect' in the Cross National Management of Human Resources*, Munich/ Mering.

Waddington, J. (2003). 'What Do Representatives Think of the Practices of European Works Councils? Views from Six Countries.«, in: European Journal of Industrial Relations, Jg. 9, H. 3, S. 303–325.

Waddington, J. and Kerckhofs, P. (2003). 'European Works Councils: What Is the Current State of Play?«, in: Transfer. European Review of Labour and Research, Jg. 9, H. 2, S. 322–339.

Walton, R. E. and McKersie, R. B. (1965). *A Behavioral Theory of Labor Negotiations. An Analysis of a Social Interaction System.* Ithaca.

Weber, T., Gilman, M., Vallve, C. and Casinhas, C. (1997). *The Renault Case and the Future of Social Europe* <http://www.eurofound.europa.eu/eiro/1997/03/feature/ eu9703108f.htm> accessed 30 April 2010.

Weiss, M. (1996). 'Workers' Participation in the European Union'. In Davies, P., Lyon-Caen, A., Sciarra, S. and Simitis, S. (eds), *European Community Labour Law: Principles and Perspectives*, pp. 213–236, Oxford.

— (2006). 'Arbeitnehmermitwirkung. Kernelement des Europäischen Sozialmodells', *Industrielle Beziehungen*, 13(1), 5–20.

Welge, M. K. and Holtbrügge, D. (2003). *Internationales Management. Theorien, Funktionen, Fallstudien.* Stuttgart.

Whitley, R. (1992a). 'The Comparative Study of Business Systems in Europe: Issues and Choices'. In Whitley, R. (ed.), *European Business Systems. Firms and Markets in their National Contexts*, pp. 267–284, London.

— (1992b). 'Societies, Firms and Markets: The Social Structuring of Business Systems' In Whitley, R. (ed.), *European Business Systems. Firms and Markets in their National Contexts*, pp. 5–45, London.

Whittall, M. (2000). 'The BMW European Works Council: A Cause for European Industrial Relations Optimism?', *European Journal of Industrial Relations*, 6(1), 61–83.

Whittall, M., Knudsen, H. and Huijgen, F. *(eds)* (2007). *Towards a European Labour Identity: The Case of the European Works Council.* London.

— (2009). 'European Works Councils: Identity and the Role of Information and Communication Technology', *European Journal of Industrial Relations*, 15(2), 167–185.

Widuckel-Mathias, W. (1993). 'Chancen einer sozialorientierten Bewältigung des Strukturwandels in der Automobilindustrie – am Beispiel des Europäischen Volkswagen-Konzernbetriebsrats'. In Steger, U. (ed.), *Auf dem Weg zum Euro-Betriebsrat? Ansätze zur Arbeitnehmermitbestimmung in Europa,* pp. 146–162, Frankfurt/Main, New York.

Widuckel, M. W. (2001). 'Globale Integration von Unternehmen und Interessenvertretung von Arbeitnehmern am Beispiel der Volkswagen AG', *Industrielle Beziehungen*, 8 (3), 333–340.

Widuckel, W. (2004). *Paradigmenentwicklung der Mitbestimmung bei Volkswagen. Schriften zur Unternehmensgeschichte von Volkswagen.* Wolfsburg.

Windolf, P. (1989). 'Productivity Coalitions and the Future of European Corporatism', *Industrial Relations*, 28(1), 1–20.

Womack, J. T., Jones, D. T. and Roos, D. (1990). *The Machine that Changed the World.* New York.

Zagelmeyer, S. (2001). 'Brothers in Arms in the European Car Wars: Employment Pacts in the EU Automobile Industry', *Industrielle Beziehungen*, 8(2), 149–179.

Zürn, M. and Wolf, D. (2000). 'Europarecht und internationale Regime: Zu den Merkmalen von Recht jenseits des Nationalstaates'. In Grande, E. and Jachtenfuchs, M. (eds), *Wie problemlösungsfähig ist die EU? Regieren im europäischen Mehrebenensystem*, pp. 113–140, Baden-Baden.

www.ingramcontent.com/pod-product-compliance
Ingram Content Group UK Ltd.
Pitfield, Milton Keynes, MK11 3LW, UK
UKHW041827290926
8980IPUK00002B/102

9 783631 670576